CW01498478

THE
GOLDSWORTHY TRILOGY

THE
GOLDSWORTHY TRILOGY

Graeme Goldsworthy

Paternoster:
thinking faith

MILTON KEYNES   ●   COLORADO SPRINGS   ●   HYDERABAD

Copyright © Graeme Goldsworthy
Gospel and Kingdom 1981
The Gospel in Revelation 1984
Gospel and Wisdom 1987

This trilogy was first published in 2000 by Paternoster Press
Tenth impression 2009

15 14 13 12 11 10 09   16 15 14 13 12 11 10

Paternoster is an imprint of Authentic Media
9 Holdom Avenue, Bletchley, Milton Keynes, Bucks, MK1 1QR, UK
1820 Jet Stream Drive, Colorado Springs, CO 80921, USA
Medchal Road, Jeedimetla Village, Secunderabad 500 055, A.P., India
www.loveauthentic.com

Authentic Media is a division of Biblica UK, previously IBS-STL UK. Biblica UK is
limited by guarantee, with its registered office at Kingstown Broadway, Carlisle,
Cumbria, CA3 0HA. Registered in England & Wales No. 1216232. Registered charity in
England & Wales No. 270162 and Scotland No. SCO40064

The right of Graeme Goldsworthy to be identified as the Author of this Work has been
asserted by him in accordance with the Copyright, Designs and Patents Act 1988.

All rights reserved. No part of this publication may be reproduced,
stored in a retrieval system, or transmitted in any form or
by any means, electronic, mechanical, photocopying, recording or
otherwise, without the prior permission of the publisher or a licence
permitting restricted copying. In the UK such licences are issued by the Copyright
Licensing Agency, 90 Tottenham Court Road, London, W1P 9HE

British Library Cataloguing in Publication Data

A catalogue record for this book is available from the British Library

ISBN 978-1-84227-036-3

Unless otherwise stated, Scripture quotations are taken from the
HOLY BIBLE, NEW INTERNATIONAL VERSION
Copyright © 1973, 1978, 1984 by the International Bible Society. Used by permission of
Hodder & Stoughton Limited. All rights reserved. 'NIV' is a registered trademark of the
International Bible Society, UK trademark number 1448790

Design by James Kessell for Scratch the Sky Ltd (www.scratch-the-sky.com)
Typeset by WestKey Ltd., Falmouth, Cornwall
Printed and bound in Great Britain by Cox and Wyman, Reading

Contents

Gospel and Kingdom

Contents

Preface

This book has grown out of a deep concern for the recovery of the Old Testament as part of the Christian Bible. It is indisputable that even evangelical Christians demonstrate a neglect of and an ignorance towards the first three-quarters of the Bible. We need not reflect here on the cause of this problem, but that it is a problem hardly needs to be stated. One could almost suggest that 'Bible-believing' Christians suffer a bad conscience over this serious lack of understanding of the Bible as a whole – and with good reason.

I have often been asked to give a series of studies on the Old Testament by various groups. 'We haven't done anything on the Old Testament for a long time. What about a series on the minor prophets?' (The minor prophets seem to have a peculiar fascination for study groups which are ignorant of the Old Testament!) I have usually responded with a counter-proposal that we hold a series of studies on the structure of the Old Testament theology and the unity of the Bible. Not surprisingly, the outcome has usually been an enthusiastic response to anything which helps to show how the various parts of the Bible hang together.

While teaching a course of biblical theology over a number of years at Moore Theological College I found it almost impossible to recommend a single book (of an introductory kind) on the subject. Obviously what was needed was something for the pastor and teacher, as well as for the ordinary Christian, which would give basic principles of Christian interpretation of the Old Testament. The frequent requests by students for recommended books was from time to time replaced by a pointed challenge to undertake my own work for publication based upon the course of lectures given at Moore College.

This little book is the outcome. In writing it I have tried to keep in mind the needs of all those who, with little or no formal training, undertake the task of reading the Bible for their own edification or in order to teach others also. Experience would suggest that pastors and preachers are also in need of help of a fairly uncomplicated and non-technical kind. The risks of over-simplification are very great, but the pressing nature of the task makes such risks worth taking.

I owe a debt of gratitude to my many teachers who have instructed me in biblical and theological studies. I am particularly beholden to Archbishop Donald Robinson for imparting to me some of his enthusiasm for and insights into the study of biblical theology. I am also grateful to those who willingly helped with the typing of the manuscript.

Graeme Goldsworthy
Brisbane

Introduction

Killed Any Good Giants Lately?

The Sunday school anniversary service has just begun and the hall is packed with children under the watchful eyes of teachers and parents. They all sing lustily with the help of an accordion and a couple of guitars, while the song-leader conducts energetically from the platform. The children's eagerness for the Bible story soon to be presented is not shared by the young man sitting on the platform and nervously thumbing through his assorted illustrations and flash-cards. Perhaps more thoughtful than most, he is seized by a sudden doubt about the application he intends to make from the Old Testament story he is about to tell. There is nothing wrong with his visual aids, and his story-telling technique is recognized to be of a high standard. There is something which bothers him. How is he to take those far-off events of a thousand years or more before Christ and make them say something to his youthful hearers of the twentieth century?

This uncertainty is not a sudden thing. Let us suppose our friend (call him Ken) is someone who has been brought up in a Christian home and a live, Bible-based church. Over the years he has been well taught the contents of the Bible and has learned a way of applying these to his own Christian existence, assumed to be the only 'proper' way. As a Sunday School teacher he gradually acquired a skill in this kind of application, but was never quite sure of the principles behind the method. But through an interest in biblical studies he began to be aware of the variety in the literature of the Bible as well as of the historical context of its events. Not that he shared the doubts of some of the books he read as to the inspiration of the Bible, but he did become aware of the rather haphazard approach to both the original meaning of the text and to its application to the 'here-and-now' which he previously accepted.

The invitation to speak at the anniversary service has faced Ken with a new problem. He cannot simply rehash the story in accordance with the lesson material of their Sunday School curriculum (not that he was very happy with it anyway!). His uneasiness about the method of telling a Bible story was intensified a couple of weeks previously when he listened to another speaker at a children's rally present the story of David and Goliath. It had been well done and the children loved it. There had been lots of excitement in the play-acting of that great victory by God's chosen leader, and the use of visual aids had been carried out with care and precision. But Ken was most troubled by the way the speaker had applied the story. The fellow dressed up as Goliath had progressively revealed a list of childhood sins by peeling cardboard strips off his breastplate one by one, as the speaker explained the kind of 'Goliaths' we all have to meet. Then a strapping young David had appeared on cue, and produced his arsenal – a sling labelled 'faith' and five stones listed as 'obedience', 'service', 'Bible reading', 'prayer' and 'fellowship'. The speaker had omitted to say which stone actually killed Goliath, a matter which caused a little mirth when Ken discussed the talk with some friends. But underneath the mirth was a real sense of uneasiness and confusion over the matter of how such an Old Testament story should be applied.

Ken was troubled by all this because, six months ago, he would have done exactly the same thing. But now as he prepares to take the platform he is very unsure about it all. He has come to appreciate more of the historical unity and progression of the biblical events. Somehow the ingenious jumps from Goliath to our sins, from David's weapons to our faith and Christian virtues and, more significantly, from David to ourselves seems at the one time both logical yet arbitrary. Any wonder Ken is still troubled. He is about to give a talk which leans heavily on the same kind of approach and which seems to say something valid without clear reasons for its validity.

✶ ✶ ✶ ✶ ✶

This story could be written a thousand ways to fit your situation and mine. If you are not a Sunday School teacher, you are a camp counsellor, a holiday Bible club helper, or maybe just an ordinary Christian struggling with the question of the relevance of the Old Testament to your Christian life. Or you are a Christian parent who wants to lead your children towards a sense of the meaningfulness of the Bible, and towards a maturity in the handling of the text of Scripture. Every time we read the Bible we meet this problem of the *right* application of the text to us, the meaning of the ancient text to today's world.

This book has been written to help bridge this gap. In order to build a bridge that will link this ancient world to modern man, we must know what manner of gap separates us. This is not an easy task, but we must make a start. If we believe that even children can learn to understand something of God's way of speaking to them through the Bible, then we must accept a life-long calling to increase our understanding of God's word so as to build surer bridges.

This book aims to provide a basic structure upon which to build a more confident use of the Old Testament, and thus of the Bible as a whole. It is intended to help Christians cross the deep ravine that separates them from the original meaning of the biblical text. It does not tell the whole story of biblical theology, but offers an invitation to begin the exciting task of reading the Bible as a living whole.

Chapter One

Why Read the Old Testament?

Before commencing to build our bridge, we must ask a more basic question: why bother bridging the gap in the first place? For many Christians, the problem is not how to read the Old Testament but *why* it should be read at all.

Why Some People Don't Read the Old Testament

Some people still are influenced by the intellectual climate of the nineteenth century, which did much to undermine a positive appreciation of the Old Testament. The philosophical stand-point of the time led people to conclude that the Christian religion, as found in the New Testament, was nothing more than the natural evolution of man's ideas about God. Consequently the Old Testament was regarded as a primitive, and therefore outdated, expression of religion. It was seen not only as being *pre-Christian* because it failed by several centuries to be concerned with the events of the gospel, but also as being *sub-Christian* because it failed to reach the ethical and theological heights of the New Testament. Yet many people who are quite unaffected by such ideas about the Old Testament may in practice adopt a similar attitude. For they see it as no more than a background to the teaching of the New. Perhaps they would refuse to downgrade the theological importance of the Old Testament because of their convictions about the inspiration and authority of the whole Bible. But in practice such people can be even more neglectful of the Old Testament than other Christians are, who do not hold such a high view of inspiration.

Ironically, the evangelical view of scripture itself can make the problem worse. For the 'evolutionist' is happy to dismiss as crude and primitive those parts of the Old Testament which he finds morally offensive. The 'conservative', on the other hand, has to find some way of reconciling his view of the Old Testament as the word of God with such things as . . . Israel's slaughter of the Canaanites, the cursing of enemies in some psalms, or the wide prescription of capital punishment in the law of Moses. Even if parts of the Old Testament do not appear morally reprehensible to the 'conservative' Christian, other parts appear to be completely irrelevant.

For a third group of people, the problem with the Old Testament is simply that on the whole they find it dry and uninteresting; it is wordy, cumbersome and confusing. Whatever their view of scripture, the sheer weight and complexity of this collection of ancient books (more than three times the bulk of the New Testament) leads to boredom, apathy and neglect rather than deliberately thought-out rejection.

There is a simple way to avoid these difficulties. Our consciences are less likely to prick us for the neglect of the Old Testament if we are giving ourselves to the study of the New! After a while the Old Testament drops right out of sight and that does not cause us any pain at all.

Why Other People *Do* Read the Old Testament

Happily there are people who still read the Old Testament. Their conviction that the Old Testament is part of God's written revelation is no doubt partly responsible for this. Also, if it is interpreted correctly, the Old Testament yields much to interest both young and old. Children's speakers and designers of Sunday School curricula are amongst the most consistent users of the narratives of ancient Israel for they contain a wealth of excitement and human interest to capture the imagination of children of all ages. Tell a good story about one of Israel's battles and you can have the kids on the edge of their seats! Yet pitfalls abound for the teacher who wants to draw out a Christian message from the Old Testament, though they may not be apparent until the unity of the Bible is understood.

False Trails

Failure to recognise the unity of Scripture led some of the early expositors to follow false trails. The emergence of the allegorical method of interpretation in the early church provides a good example. Because much of the Old Testament was seen as unhelpful or sub-Christian, the only way to save it for Christian use was to distinguish a hidden 'spiritual' sense, concealed behind the natural meaning.

Allegory seemed to be a legitimate method of interpretation because it was controlled by the content of the New Testament or, later on, by Church dogma. What was lacking, however, was the kind of control the New Testament itself applied when it used the Old Testament. Instead the relationship between the natural

meaning of the Old Testament and the teachings of the
New was left to the ingenuity of the expositor. One serious effect of the allegorical method was that it tended to
hinder people from taking the historical or natural
sense of the Old Testament seriously.[1] Nor did this problem exist only for the Old Testament. In the Middle
Ages the logic was taken a step further. Not only was
the 'unhelpful' natural sense of the Old Testament
given its spiritual sense from the natural sense of the
New Testament; even the natural sense of the New Testament was seen to require its own spiritual interpretation, which was found in the tradition of the church.[2]
Thus authority now lay, not in the natural meaning of
the canon of Scripture, but in the teachings of the church
as it interpreted the spiritual meaning according to its
own dogma.

---

[1] See Beryl Smalley, *The Study of the Bible in the Middle Ages* (University of Notre Dame Press, 1964), Chapter 5. Stephen Langton
(died 1228) applied the allegorical and spiritual interpretation
with vigour. For example II Kings 1:2 – Ahaziah fell through the
lattice in his upper chamber in Samaria and lay sick – signifies a
church prelate who enters hastily into the perplexities of his pastoral charge and falls into sin. Boaz in the Book of Ruth is made
to represent God. When he enquires of the reapers 'Whose maid
is this?' (Ruth 2: 5) he is enquiring of the doctors of theology concerning the status of the preacher who gathers sentences of
Scripture for his preaching. A modern example of allegorical
exposition with very great similarities to the mediaeval method
of interpretation is to be found in W. Ian Thomas, *If I Perish I Perish* (Grand Rapids: Zondervan, 1967). The author deals with the
Book of Esther and makes Ahasuerus represent the soul of man,
Haman the sinful flesh, Mordecai the Holy Spirit, and Esther the
human spirit.

[2] See J.S. Preus, *From Shadow to Promise* (Cambridge, Mass.: Harvard University Press, 1969).

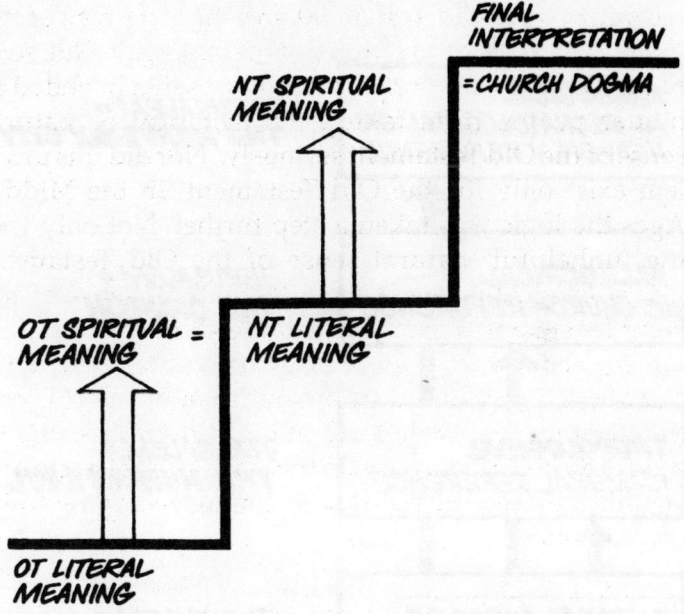

Figure 1   The Process of Spiritualizing

The Middle Ages saw the development of interpretation according to the four meanings of Scripture:

(a) the literal or natural meaning
(b) the moral reference to the human soul
(c) the allegorical reference to the church, and
(d) the eschatological reference to heavenly realities.

Not all texts were read with four meanings, and there was considerable activity in the field of biblical studies (especially from the 12th to the 15th centuries) as scholars sought to give proper place to the literal meaning.[3]

---

[3] A useful introduction to the subject of interpretation is found in R.M. Grant, *A Short History of the Interpretation of the Bible* (New York: Macmillan, 1948).

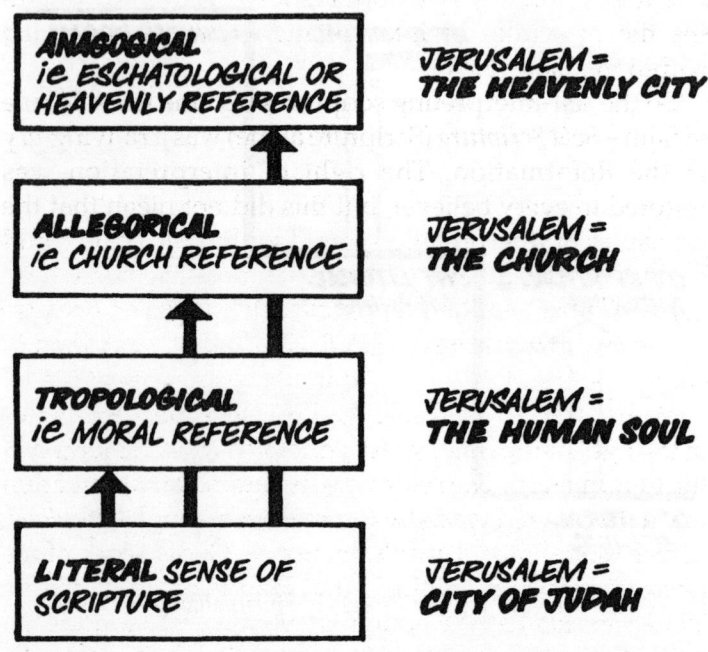

Figure 2   The Medieval Four-Fold Method of Interpretation

The Reformation Path

It was the Protestant reformers who helped the Christian church see again the importance of the historical and natural meaning of Scripture, so that the Old Testament could be regarded as having value in itself. When the reformers recovered the authority of the Bible they not only reaffirmed a biblical doctrine of the church and salvation, but also a biblical doctrine of Scripture. Protestant interpretation was based upon the concept of the *perspicuous* (clear and self-interpreting) nature of the Bible. By removing an authority for interpretation from outside of the Bible – the infallible Church – the reformers were free to accept and see the principles of interpretation that are contained within the Bible itself.

So the self-interpreting scriptures became the sole rule of faith – *Sola Scriptura* (Scripture alone) was a rallying-cry of the Reformation. The right of interpretation was restored to every believer, but this did not mean that the principles of interpretation found within the Bible could be overlooked and every Christian follow his own whim. The allegorical method became far less popular, because the historical meaning of the Old Testament was found to be significant on its own, within the unity of the Bible.

Perhaps we understand the Protestant position better in the light of the other great principles which emerged at the Reformation. The reformers maintained that salvation is a matter of *grace alone*, by *Christ alone*, through *faith alone*. 'Grace alone' meant that salvation is God's work alone unconditioned by anything that man is or does. 'Christ alone' meant that the sinner is accepted by God on the basis of what Christ alone has done. 'Faith alone' meant that the only way for the sinner to receive salvation is by faith whereby the righteousness of Christ is imputed (credited) to the believer.

What had this got to do with the Old Testament? It meant that the reformers were establishing a method of biblical interpretation in which the natural historical sense of the Old Testament has significance for Christians because of its organic relationship to Christ. God's grace seen in his dealings with Israel is part of a living process which comes to its climax in his work of grace, the gospel, that is in the historical events of the Christ who is Jesus of Nazareth. Just as it is important to assert that this Old Testament 'sacred history' or 'salvation history' must be interpreted by the Word, Jesus Christ, it is also important to recognise that the gospel is God acting in history more specifically, through the history of Jesus.

Mediaeval theology had internalized and subjectivized the gospel to such an extent that the basis of acceptance with God, of justification, was no longer what God did once for all in Christ, but what God was continuing to do in the life of the Christian. This *de-historicizing* of what God had done once and for all in the gospel went hand-in-hand with the *allegorizing* of the history of the Old Testament. The Reformation recovered the historical Christ-event (the gospel) as the basis of our salvation and, in turn, the objective importance of Old Testament history. This is, of course, a very different thing from the modern approach of seeing the Old Testament as part of the historical development of man's religious ideas, or as merely a background history to the New Testament age. Basically, the Old Testament is not the history of *man's* developing thoughts about *God*, but the whole Bible presents itself as the unfolding process of God's dealings with man and of his own self-disclosure to man.

Is the Old Testament For All Christians?

The most compelling reason for Christians to read and study the Old Testament lies in the New Testament. The New Testament witnesses to the fact that Jesus of Nazareth is the One in whom and through whom all the promises of God find their fulfilment. These promises are only to be understood from the Old Testament; the fulfilment of the promises can be understood only in the context of the promises themselves. The New Testament presupposes a knowledge of the Old Testament. Everything that is a concern to the New Testament writers is part of the one redemptive history to which the Old Testament witnesses. The New Testament writers cannot separate the person and work of Christ, nor the life of the Christian community, from this sacred history which has its beginnings in the Old Testament.

It is, of course, of great significance that the New Testament writers constantly quote or allude to the Old Testament. One estimate is that there are at least 1600 direct quotations of the Old Testament in the New, to which may be added several thousand more New Testament passages that clearly allude to or reflect Old Testament verses.[4] Of course not all these citations show direct continuity of thought with the Old Testament, and some even show a contrast between Old and New Testaments. But the over-all effect is inescapable – the message of the New Testament has its foundations in the Old Testament.

Contrary to what is sometimes suggested, the New Testament writers were not in the habit of quoting texts without reference to their context. In fact a quotation is sometimes intended to prompt the recall of an entire passage of Old Testament scripture. For example, Paul's quotation in I Corinthians 10: 7 of part of Exodus 32: 6 refers to the festivities of the Israelites. The intention is to bring to mind the whole narrative of Israel's idolatry and the golden calf.

A person may become a Christian without much knowledge of the Old Testament. Conversion does, however, require a basic understanding of Jesus Christ as Saviour and Lord. The Christian cannot be committed to Christ without being committed to his teaching. It follows that Christ's attitude to the Old Testament will begin to convey itself to the Christian who is carefully studying the New Testament. The more we study the New Testament

---

[4] Henry M. Shires, *Finding the Old Testament in the New* (Philadelphia: Westminster Press, 1974), p. 15.

the more apparent becomes the conviction shared by Jesus, the apostles and the New Testament writers in general: namely the Old Testament is Scripture and Scripture points to Christ. The manner in which the Old Testament testifies to Christ is a question that has to be resolved on the basis of the New Testament, since it is the New Testament which provides the Christian with an authoritative interpretation of the Old.

The effect of this is twofold. As Christians we will always be looking at the Old Testament from the standpoint of the New Testament – from the framework of the gospel which is the goal of the Old Testament. But since the New Testament continually presupposes the Old Testament as a unity we, who are not acquainted with the Old Testament in the way the first Christians were, will be driven back to study the Old Testament on its own terms. To understand the whole living process of redemptive history in the Old Testament we must recognize two basic truths. The first is that this salvation history is a process. The second is that this process of redemptive history finds its goal, its focus and fulfilment in the person and work of Christ. This is the principle underlying this book.

Failure to grasp this truth – largely because the proper study of the Old Testament has been neglected, has aided and abetted one of the most unfortunate reversals in evangelical theology. The core of the gospel, the historical facts of what God did in Christ, is often *down-graded* today in favour of a more mystical emphasis on the private spiritual experience of the individual. Whereas faith in the gospel is essentially acceptance of, and commitment to, the declaration that God acted in Christ some two thousand years ago on our behalf, saving faith is often portrayed nowadays more as trust in what God is doing in us now. Biblical ideas such as 'the forgiveness of sins' or 'salvation' are interpreted as primarily describing a Christian's personal experience. But when we allow the whole Bible – Old and New Testaments – to speak to us, we find that those subjective aspects of the Christian life which are undoubtedly important – the new birth, faith and sanctification – are the *fruits* of the gospel. This gospel, while still relating to individual people at their point of need, is rooted and grounded in the history of redemption. It is the good news *about* Jesus, before it can become good news for sinful men and women. Indeed, it is only as the *objective* (redemptive-historical) facts are grasped that the *subjective* experience of the individual Christian can be understood.

At this point, some readers may be thinking that we have strayed from our original aim by discussing the history of biblical interpretation. I hope that a few technical points will not deter them, for it is my solid conviction that all Christians need to develop a biblical way of understanding the Bible and of using it. It is not only possible but even necessary for all Christians, including children, to gain a total perspective on the whole Bible so that the really important relationships between its parts begin to appear.

Chapter Two

Bridging the Gap

The first gap we must bridge is the gap of time and culture. The people and events of the Bible are so far away from us. In fact, the more we become aware of the historical context of any portion of the Bible, the more we come to recognize the great gap in time, language and thought forms which separates us from that text.

But time and culture are not the only aspects of that gap. There is a more vital dimension to the Bible which has to do with how God has revealed himself as well as *what* he has revealed, a dimension which is bound up with what we call 'theology'. Perhaps it should be said right now that the word *theology* properly refers to the knowledge of God, that is, to what is to be known about God through his self-revelation. Only in a secondary way can the word be applied to the whole variety of religious study and discussion carried on both by people who accept God's self-revelation in Scripture and people who disagree with (parts of) it. We look at this in greater detail at the end of Chapter 3.

A Straightforward Example

To illustrate the problem of this gap of time, culture and theology, let us suppose that we, as contemporary

Christians, open our Bible at one of Paul's letters. We read some of his theological exposition and then move on to the exhortation to live consistently with the truths of the gospel. Granting that certain adjustments have to be made, certain allowances for the fact that Paul wrote nineteen hundred years ago to some people in Asia Minor or Italy, we nevertheless do not feel that this is a serious barrier to our understanding. More important, we do not find that this gap seriously inhibits us from accepting Paul's words to, say, the Galatians as God's word to us. The reason is obvious: Paul addressed a group of Christians on the basis of the gospel and we recognize that, despite the difference in time and culture, there is sufficient common ground theologically between the first and the twentieth centuries for us to hear the words as if addressed to us.

As we analyse what has been happening, we see that we have recognized almost intuitively that, from the point of view of God's revelation and God's dealings with men, the Christian church in all ages is one. It belongs to the same era of God's dealings. The limits of this era at one end are the birth of the New Testament church at Pentecost, and at the other the return of Christ in power and glory to judge the living and the dead. Whenever we come to a text outside these bounds, the gap is widened, and greater care and skill is required to bridge it.

The 'Gap' Widens

Let us take a short step back from our clearly defined 'gospel' era. In Acts 1 Luke describes a situation – the post-resurrection appearances and ascension of Jesus – that is dramatically different from ours in that it occurs before the giving of the Holy Spirit. There is a uniqueness about this period, also shared by the Pentecost narrative in Acts 2, which raises the question how much can such a unique period provide information which applies directly to us? After all, we do not share the situation of the people as they waited for the once-for-all beginning of a new era. An important principle of biblical interpretation is involved that we must not generalize the events of a historical narrative without some good reason for doing so. (What makes a good reason is a question we shall examine later.)

In the same way we may continue to move further into biblical history increasing our distance from the normal Christian situation to which we belong. The Gospels, for example, contain much narrative dealing with a time which is not only pre-Pentecost, but also pre-Resurrection and pre-Crucifixion. We may not simply assume that narrative about disciples and their relationship to Jesus in his earthly life provides normative instruction for us. We know that we have to make adjustments for the fact that our relationship with Jesus, who is not here in the flesh but in heaven, is by faith and through his Spirit dwelling in us. We now look back on the finished work of Christ in his life, death and resurrection, while the narratives of the Gospels only anticipate this completion. It may be, for example, that John 1: 12 does have relevance to modern evangelism – *'to all who received him, who believed in his name, he gave power to become children of God'* – but we may not assume this until we have examined the original significance of the passage. It speaks of Jesus coming physically and literally to the Jews as their Messiah, he came to his own people, but they would not receive him (verse 11). The Jews as a whole did not acknowledge him as the Christ, but those who did were made children of God.

If we find this problem faces us even in the New Testament, we find much greater difficulty in the Old

Testament. For there we are not only in a pre-Resurrection situation; we are in a pre-Incarnation and pre-Christian one. In fact the differences between the Old Testament situation and our own are much easier to discern than the similarities. Because of this we tend to grasp at the obvious similarities, so that they become our guide for interpretation and application. The God of Israel is our God and his character is unchanging. The faithful people of Israel, the 'saints' of the Old Testament, are true saints even though they do not know Christ. We tend to shelve the question of how they were saved without knowing Christ and simply ask instead how they illustrate the life of faith.

The 'Character Study' Approach

It is here that the Old Testament character studies come into their own. There are many more real-life situations to draw from in the Old Testament than in the New – many more historical narratives that reveal to us men and women who are realistically portrayed, 'warts and all', in their encounters with God. But the difficulties we met in the historical narratives of the Gospels and Acts are increased when we come to the Old Testament narratives. We cannot simply transfer the experiences of the past wholesale to today. There are two dangers to avoid in regard to historical narrative:

(a) We must not view these recorded events as if they were a mere succession of events from which we draw little moral lessons or examples for life. Much that passes for application of the Old Testament text to the Christian life is only moralizing. It consists almost exclusively in *observing* the behaviour of the godly and the godless (admittedly against a background of the activity of God) and then *exhorting* people to learn from these observations. That is why the 'character study' is a favoured approach to Bible narrative – the life of Moses, the life of David, the life of Elijah and so on. There is nothing wrong with character studies as such – we are to learn by others' examples – but such character studies all too often take the place of more fundamental aspects of biblical teaching. Paradoxically, they may even lead us away from the basic foundations of the gospel. Certainly we do not solve the problem by using the allegorical method and turning every historical detail into a prefiguring of Christ without regard to the whole structure of the Bible.

(b) We must guard against a too-ready acceptance of the example of biblical characters, whether good or bad, as the source of principles of the Christian life. If we concentrate on how David saved Israel from Goliath, on what response Elijah made to the threats of Jezebel, on where Saul showed the chinks in his moral armour, as examples to follow or to avoid, then we have reduced the significance of these people to the lowest common denominator. This approach easily obscures any other unique characteristics that may be part of revelation.

The danger in the 'character study' approach is that it so easily leads to the use of the Old Testament characters and events as mere illustrations of New Testament truths, while at the same time giving the appearance of being a correct exposition of the meaning of the Word of God. But if the real substance is drawn from the New Testament, and it alone, we may well ask what is the point of applying ourselves to the Old Testament; why we may not just as well use non-biblical material to illustrate the New

Testament. To make this criticism is not to deny the value of Old Testament narrative in illustrating New Testament principles; but we should not assume that such an approach uncovers the primary meaning of the text.

To press this point even further – it should be recognized that the 'character study' approach is frequently used in a way that implies quite wrongly that the reader today may identify with the character in question. But we must reckon with both the historical and theological uniqueness of the characters and events if we are not to misapply them. Is it in fact true that if God took care of baby Moses, God will take care of me? Such application simply assumes that what applied to the unique figure of Moses in a unique situation applies to all of us, and presumably all the time. But why should our children be privileged to identify with Moses rather than with other Hebrew children at the time who may not have escaped Pharaoh's wrath? The theological significance of Moses and of his preservation is all but ignored in this case.

With whom may the Christian identify in the narrative of David and Goliath – with the soldiers of Israel or with David? (Certainly not with Goliath!) But, someone will say, there is a lesson for us in both the soldiers and in David. The former show us the Christian who lacks faith, and the latter exemplifies the man who truly trusts God and overcomes against great odds (never mind the ingenious bit with the stones!). To a point this is true; the soldiers are afraid and David is a man who trusts God. But is that all? It certainly is not all when we read the narrative in its context, for then we find that there is something unique about David which cannot apply to us. David is the one who, immediately prior to the Goliath episode (I Samuel 17), is shown to be God's anointed king. He receives the Spirit of God to do mighty deeds for the saving of Israel, according to the pattern of saviours already established in the book of Judges. So when it comes to his slaying of Goliath it is as the unique anointed one of God that he wins the battle.

The application of this truth to the believer is somewhat different from a simple identification of the believer with David. Rather we should identify with the ordinary people of God, the soldiers, who stand and watch the battle fought on their behalf. The same point may be made about the lives of all the biblical characters who have some distinct office bestowed on them by God. If their achievement is that of any godly man the lesson is clear, but if it is the achievement of a prophet, a judge or the messianic king, then to that extent it no more applies to the people of God in general than does the unique work of Jesus as the Christ.

The Unity of the Bible

I have sought to put the problem as it is likely to confront us in the practical situations of Christian service – beach mission talks, Sunday School lessons and the like. The case of the anniversary speaker in the introduction is almost autobiographical. I'm sure such examples of misapplication still flourish. Behind it all is the problem of the unity of the Bible. This is not an academic question, but one in which even our children are involved at the simplest level of Bible instruction.

If we are to avoid flights of fancy in interpretation we need some understanding of what governs the right approach to the meaning of the Bible. Most of us assume (rightly, I believe) that there is some very basic unity to the whole Bible and to its message. It is more than a collection of holy books in that it contains a single story of salvation. If there is such a unifying theme throughout the Bible,

then the *structure* of the biblical message – the overall relationship of each part to the whole – becomes of prime
importance for interpretation.

We cannot escape the fact that every attempt to read the
Bible is an exercise in the science of interpretation or, as it
is called in technical terms, *hermeneutics*. Even a personal
letter from a friend demands that you interpret the way
your friend uses language to convey to you his intended
meaning. We all know how much harder it is to converse
by letter than by speaking face-to-face. In conversation we
use not only words but also facial expressions and
changes in the tone of voice. We can vary the speed, loud-
ness, and the emphasis of words. We can stop and clarify a
statement when a slight change in facial expression in our
hearer signals lack of understanding. But the written
word lacks many of these aids to interpretation even in a
personal communication from someone we know well.
Hermeneutics obviously cannot be ignored when we are
dealing with the ancient texts of the Bible, for they were
written in foreign languages and addressed to people of
another age.

Let us use the analogy of a map. If you open a map or
consult a tourist plan of a large city, one of the things you
take for granted is that the plan represents a real unity.
Thus we believe that the information on how to get from
one place to another is based on the actual relationships of
the parts of the city and of the streets which connect them.
If someone, for a joke, had glued half a map of Sydney
onto half a map of Melbourne, a planned journey from the
Melbourne Town Hall to the Sydney Opera House would
be impossible on the basis of that map. The two parts do
not belong together and there is no unity. Now if we wish
to move from a biblical text of the pre-Christian era to ourselves in the twentieth century of the gospel era, we must
not only assume that there is a connection between the

two, but we must understand how they connect. As with our map, so with the Bible – we must know the kind of unity that exists within it. Obviously this unity is not a static uniformity, as if the Bible were merely a large reservoir of proof texts which may be selected and applied at random with no thought for their context. Unfortunately some people tend to work with the Bible on this basis with little credit to themselves or to the message they extract.

Let us think of this question of relationships in another way. There is a well-used saying: 'A text without a context is a pretext'. This sound wisdom reminds us that the Bible is not a collection of isolated sentences or verses to be used at random in establishing doctrine. One of the unhappy results of the division of the Bible into chapters and verses (which did not take place until the late Middle Ages) is an unnatural fragmenting of the text. Paul wrote one letter to the Romans, not sixteen separate chapters containing a varying number of units called verses. Most of us recognize this fact to a point – we know that anyone can prove almost anything by lifting a few verses out of context. We recognize also that the basic literary unit for conveying thought is the sentence. But do we always understand how much the meaning of a sentence is governed by its place in a larger unit of communication?

How wide must we stretch the context in order to gain a good understanding of one sentence? We might arbitrarily set a paragraph as the limit – if we could only be sure what the equivalent of a paragraph would be in the Hebrew or Greek text, which used neither paragraphs nor punctuation. But a paragraph usually occurs in the context of a number of other paragraphs. We could go from paragraphs to chapters (also units unknown to the authors), and then to the complete books. It may not always be necessary to go this far in providing the context needed for the understanding of a given verse or sentence, but any supposition of unity in the given book means that knowledge of the whole and knowledge of the parts are inseparable. The logical conclusion to be drawn is that, if the unity of the Bible has any meaning at all, the real context of any Bible text is the whole Bible. Any given text is more meaningful when related not only to its immediate context, but also to the entire plan of redemption revealed in the whole Bible.

Summary

To summarize our problem: accepting the whole Bible as the Word of God raises the question of how it speaks to us in the twentieth century. How may we legitimately understand, as a relevant and living word from God, that which was addressed to people in situations of varying degrees of remoteness from our own?

To be aware of the nature of a problem is to be on the way to a solution. Our problem of interpretation is very closely bound up with the question of the nature of the unity of the Bible. We need to understand the relationships between the various parts of the Bible, and this means understanding not only the unity but also the disunity which is there. We have seen how the gap between us and the biblical text widens as we move farther back away from the gospel age to which we belong. The coming of Jesus in the flesh is the unique event which creates discontinuity in the Bible, and which has made its mark in human history through the distinction between B.C. and A.D.

We have seen some important differences between the post Pentecost, the pre-Pentecost and the pre-Christian ages. We must now ask what unites these ages so that the sixty-six books of the Bible form an organic unity of revelation.

Chapter Three

What is the Old Testament?

When dealing with anything as complex as the Old Testament it is as well not to assume anything, but rather to attempt to understand what makes up the complexity. (Readers who are already fairly familiar with the Old Testament will need to be patient at this point!)

The first and most obvious dimension of the Old Testament is the *literary* one. The Old Testament is a book, or rather, a collection of books. Secondly we note that a common feature of these books is their association with a *history* which embraces a single continuous time span and also a single continuous part of human history. Thirdly, the Old Testament presents a *theological* dimension in that the history, which is the subject of the literature, is represented as a single history of God's dealings with the world and with man. Let us now consider some of the implications of these three key dimensions of the Old Testament (and for that matter of the whole Bible) – the literary, the historical and the theological.

The Old Testament as Literature

The Old Testament is a collection of thirty-nine books written by a variety of authors over a period of maybe

1,000 years or more. Nearly all of the Old Testament was written in Hebrew, an ancient language of the North-West Semitic group, which was closely related to the language of the Canaanites. Some parts of the Old Testament were written in Aramaic, another Semitic language which was spoken throughout the Babylonian empire from where it was adopted by the Jews in the sixth century B.C. The earlier parts go back to the time of Moses, which was probably the thirteenth century B.C., while the latest sections were written before the Greek period of the fourth century B.C.[1]

It has been customary to divide the individual books of the Old Testament into four groups: law, history, prophecy, and poetry. This has some value, but the classifications are very broad and it is helpful to be a little more specific about the literary types of the Bible. Different literary forms or types function in different ways and some appreciation of the various forms in Hebrew literature is essential if we are to avoid a misinterpretation of the authors' intentions. We must not expect the Hebrew authors to be bound by the same rules of literary expression to which we are accustomed. The Bible is not a bound volume of twentieth century works; it is an ancient collection using an ancient language to express thought forms which frequently differ from our own.

We should not be concerned to classify entire books since within any one book many different literary types

---

[1] Scholarly opinion differs over the date of the Book of Daniel. Taken on face value, Daniel belongs to the sixth century B.C. and the book provides an account of events which occurred during the captivity in Babylon. Many modern scholars believe that Daniel is an exposition of the persecution of the Jews under the second century B.C. Hellenistic ruler Antiochus Epiphanes, and that it is cast into its sixth century mould in order to obscure to all but the initiated the true significance of the book.

may be found. Each type must be recognized for what it is before it can be properly interpreted. Thus the intention behind a section of historical narrative will be different from that which is behind a parable or a precept of the Mosaic Law. Some of the literary types will be familiar enough to us and will present few difficulties as literary expressions. Others will be strange to us, and their intention will be not so clear until we have discovered the nature and function of such types. In the Old Testament we find:

historical narratives	wisdom sayings of the
laws and statutes	proverbial kind
prophetic oracles	instructional wisdom
genealogies	hymns of praise
songs of many kinds	thanksgivings
taunts	laments
parables and fables	apocalytic visions . . .
riddles	and much else.

We do not have to become experts in ancient literary types in order to avoid the pitfalls. But we should at least try to become more familiar with them and to understand the way they function. It is really amazing how neglected the literary dimension has become when you reflect that we are talking about the medium of communication used by God. It is equally amazing that some interpreters seek to impose a single code of interpretation of literature, such as 'literal' interpretation. Literalism is, of course, perfectly valid as an approach to literature, if it is conceived of broadly enough to accommodate the different ways in which language may be used to communicate. But it is not the purpose of this book to discuss the complex questions of literary types. Let us, however, maintain an openness to the ancient conventions of the literary medium of communication by becoming sensitive to the wonderful variety of expression in the Bible.

The Old Testament as History

We cannot hope to understand the way the Old Testament functions as part of the Bible, without some grasp of the whole sweep of Old Testament history. But the answer, for most of us, is not to wade through a large volume on the history of Israel. That should come later. We ought to begin with a basic framework of biblical history, a 'birds-eye view', which will show us the main events in the progression of the history. This, contrary to supposition, is easily done for there is really a very simple historical outline to be discerned in the Bible, even if this is not the immediate impression gained by the reader who has become bogged down in the Books of Kings. The simple diagram on page 36, which I learned from one of my own teachers, provides one effective representation of the history in the Old Testament.

The simplicity of this diagram allows for further detail to be added as one becomes more familiar with the contents of the Old Testament. It cannot be over-emphasized that, without a sense of the historical progression and of the relationship between the principal events and characters, it would be very difficult to make much sense out of the Bible. The overwhelming conviction of the biblical authors is of the activity of God in history. God acts not in a fragmentary, capricious or unrelated way, but in a single purposeful span of history. The Bible is not a deposit of abstract ideas or even of formulated doctrines, but a marvellous unity of salvation-history.

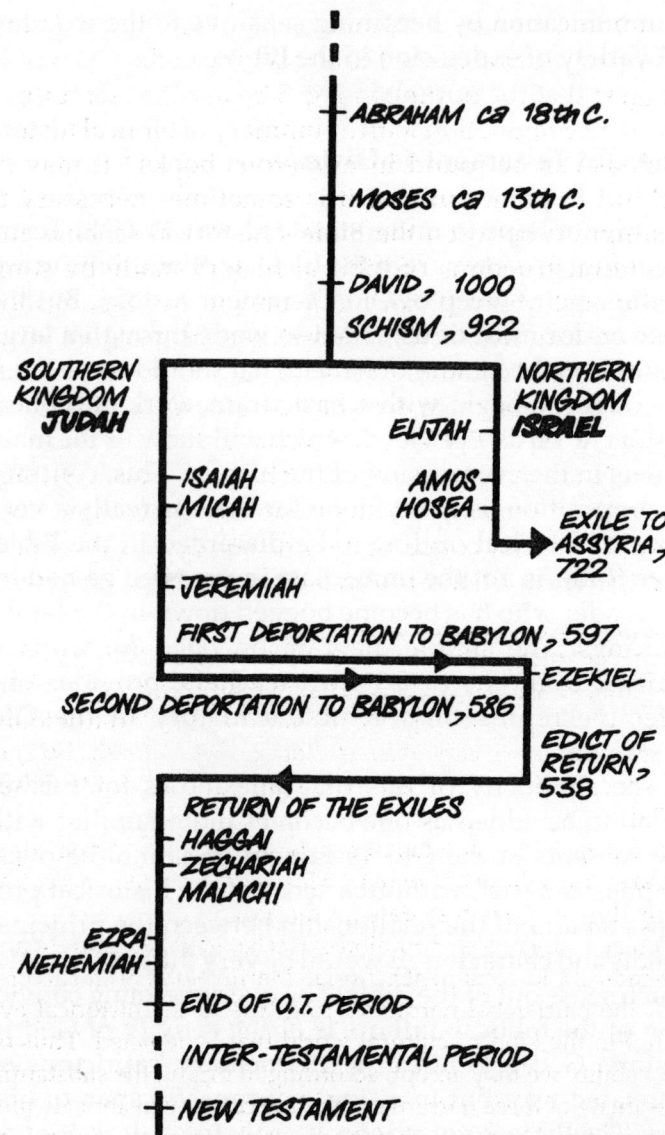

Figure 3   Outline of Old Testament History (Not to scale)

If you have never taken time to grasp the basic historic progression of the Bible it is time to do so. I would suggest that the outline in Fig. 3 be used, or something like it, in conjunction with a summary of biblical history such as can be found in numerous books.[2] It may be helpful to point out that it is sometimes necessary to distinguish between the Bible's historical schema and the reconstructions of biblical history made by some historians. Many historians work on the assumption that we can accept only what can be verified from sources and evidences outside the Bible. For some, the earliest biblical history that is verifiable is that of the period of the settlement in Canaan in the late thirteenth century B.C.[3] Others assert that we can go back with some certainty to the period of Abraham.[4] But here we are not concerned with the possibility of testing the truth of the biblical narrative, but only with

---

[2] For example see John Stott, *Understanding the Bible* (London: Scripture Union, 1972); also any good Bible dictionary will provide an outline of biblical history. Fuller treatments can be found in John Bright, *History of Israel* (London: SCM Press, 1972) or Charles Pfeiffer, *Old Testament History* (Grand Rapids: Baker, 1979).

[3] The dates of the Exodus from Egypt and of the settlement in Canaan are subjects of debate. Most scholars today accept an early thirteenth century date for the Exodus.

[4] A major difference of opinion exists between John Bright and the radical Old Testament historian Martin Noth. Bright accepts that the patriarchal narratives ring true to the historical evidence in the kind of cultural world that is depicted. Thus on probability we may accept, according to Bright, the substantial historicity of these narratives. Noth rejects any historical value in the biblical narrative before the settlement in Canaan. The controversy is explained in John Bright, *Early Israel in Recent History Writing* (London, SCM Press, 1956).

understanding the pattern of events as the Bible presents them.

Biblical History as the Bible Presents It

We are thus dealing with a history which begins with the creation of the universe, the world and man. The history then focuses on man (Adam) and on his relationship with God. After being ejected from paradise in Eden because of his rebellion against the Creator, man's history is one of increasing and widespread sinfulness. This leads to destruction through the flood and to the preservation of one family. From this family of Noah the lineage of man is shown to divide among the nations of the world although the focus is on the line of Shem leading to Abraham.

Abraham was called by God to leave Mesopotamia and to go to Canaan where he received certain promises concerning his descendants (of which there were none as yet). This promise was later passed on to his son Isaac and to Isaac's son, Jacob. Eventually the descendants of Jacob migrated to Egypt and in time became a large nation. When this people was subjected to a cruel slavery by the Egyptians, God sent Moses to lead them into the land of Canaan which he had promised to give to Abraham's descendants. This process was long and involved and included the making of a covenant at Mount Sinai in which this nation of Israel was bound to God as his people with all that that implied.

The dispossession of the inhabitants of Canaan, and the settlement in the land, led to the development of the need for some form of government or administration of the covenant. After a false start under King Saul, Israel received a great leader in the person of David. He united the tribes, established a capital city, secured the borders and set up a proper administration. Unfortunately David's successor, Solomon, became too ambitious and unwise policies led to eventual dissatisfaction. When his son came to the throne, there was a rebellion and the ten tribes of the north seceded to become the kingdom of Israel while the dynasty of David continued to rule over the southern kingdom of Judah.

The secession led to a general decline in both north and south, although the prophets continued to call the people back to faithfulness to the covenant God. The north finally suffered defeat at the hands of the Assyrians (722 B.C.) and ceased to be an independent state. More than a century later the might of Babylon was aimed at the south and, with the destruction of Jerusalem (586 B.C.) and the deportation of most of the people, Judah as a political entity ceased to be.

The exile in Babylon came to an end for the Jews when Cyrus the Persian overcame the power of Babylon and allowed captive peoples to return home (538 B.C.). Many of the Jews chose to remain in Babylon, for life had been quite kind to them. But those who returned had a real struggle to reconstruct the state of Judah. Eventually, with Persian co-operation, some stability was reached and Jerusalem and the Temple were reconstructed. But the glory of the golden age of David and Solomon never returned and the Old Testament period comes to an end with a whimper rather than a bang!

Some three-and-a-half centuries intervened between the two Testaments. During this time the most complex political developments occurred in the Jewish state. The Persian Empire crumbled when Alexander the Great pushed into Asia Minor and advanced to Egypt and beyond Babylon to the borders of India. Hellenistic culture was imposed upon Alexander's empire by his successors and the Jews did not escape the fearful results of the conflict between the pagan Greek philosophies and way of life, and the Hebrew devotion to the Law and religion of the one True God. In the middle of the first century B.C., the Romans entered the Middle East region and the Jews found themselves a province of the great Roman Empire.

What Old Testament History Is Not

At first sight the history contained in the Old Testament may seem to be that of a fairly insignificant nation, which spent most of its time in political subjection to whatever great power had the ascendancy in the Middle East. Unfortunately this is often the impression to be gained from a concentration on the details of Old Testament history. Now, the study of detail is certainly important but it is a human weakness to fail 'to see the wood for the trees'. Too much initial concentration on the details of Israel's history may obscure important relationships and the overall pattern in the events.

It is essential to remember one of the cardinal points of history writing, that no history is ever the mere record of a succession of details or events. The historian writes *selectively* according to his *purpose*. Of course he cannot completely isolate one aspect of human life from all others, but he can direct his attention to one or other aspect so that others fall more or less into the background. Thus we might have in relation to the same nation in the same period of time a political history, an economic history, a social history, a military history and so on.

What kind of history is Old Testament history? First let us see what it is not. It is not merely a history of *Israel*, for part of it deals with a period before the birth of the nation, and this material cannot be treated as only background. Genesis I–II is far too important to be dismissed so simply.

Nor is Old Testament history a *religious* history, for that would entail nothing more than the attempts of historians to deal with religious thought and activity. The Old Testament claims to be much more than that, especially since it continually passes judgement upon mankind's religious activity – even upon that of the Israelites. In fact, to treat the Bible as a history of religions was the great mistake of the rationalistic age of the nineteenth century.

What Old Testament History Is

Insofar as the Old Testament is history, it is a *theological* history. Rather than a religious history (a human record of human religion), it is God's record of God's own dealings with the world and with men. It is characteristic of the Bible that it does not record the events in the affairs of men as if they were determined by chance, by blind fate, or by a necessary chain of prior events. The history of the Bible is *purposive*; the purpose which governs the events is God's purpose. The biblical historians relate events, not as events in themselves, but as the deed of God – or as the deeds of men which are to be judged according to the character of God. It is God who calls Abraham from Ur, who brings Israel out of Egypt, who raises up Cyrus to free Israel from Babylon, and who judges human actions according to whether they are good or bad in his sight. It is this purposive element in biblical history which makes the Bible unique, giving it its distinctive dimension.

Furthermore the biblical history (history-as-the-Bible-presents-it, rather than merely the history of Bible times) is therefore a part of God's word to man. God's own interpretation of the events of biblical history makes known to us the purposes he is pursuing within this history. It is this interpretation of the events as God's events which give the Bible its character of divine revelation. This is the consistent testimony of the Bible as it records how God speaks to man *declaring* his purposes and intentions, how he acts on the basis of his word, and how he then *interprets* the events by his word. Thus we see, contrary to some modern interpretations, that God declares to Moses what he will do for Israel (free them from Egypt and give them Canaan) and on what basis he will do it (the promises to Abraham). When the Exodus has taken place, God then declares: 'I am the Lord your God who brought you out of the land of Egypt, out of the house of bondage' (Exodus 20: 2).

Now this purposive history not only reveals the mind of God; it also affects the way in which those thoughts are communicated. The selection of events and the recording of details is governed by the theological meaning rather than by any military or political significance. The theology controls the writing of the history. The fact that God acts in the history of men and interprets his acts means that these historical events will form a pattern that relates to the purposes of God. Biblical history is theological history.

What Is Theology?

Theology means the knowledge of God as God himself reveals it. We have seen that biblical theology consists of the study of the revelation of God as he acts in this world, in the history of men. The most important concern in the study of the Bible is the revelation of God: What is God saying to us in the record of his acts? What did God do in entering in a special way into the history of mankind? We have already raised the question of the unity of the Bible; we are here asserting that the aspect which above all else creates the Bible's unity is its theology. It is the one God who acts and speaks throughout the history in the Bible. Furthermore God acts and speaks with a unity of purpose. God's message to us is one unified discourse, not a series of isolated and disconnected messages.

The task which lies ahead of us is to try to discern what God is saying and how he says it. In doing this we may say that we are primarily interested in revelation – in theology. But we may not separate what God says and does from the context in which he says it and does it (the history) nor from the way he says what he does (the literary record). We shall be looking for the essential unity of the Bible, without ignoring its diversity and its complexity.

Chapter Four

Biblical Theology and the History of Redemption

Three characteristics have now been presented in our search for unity and structure in the Bible. These are the literary forms, the historical framework and the theological structures. Each must be given its due weight and be taken into account in the process of interpreting the biblical text. Since the really unique feature of the Bible is its revelation of God and of his purposes (its theology), it is unfortunate that so little emphasis is given these days to the study of biblical theology. In recent years there have appeared numbers of books, written at the non-academic level for the ordinary Christian reader, which deal with surveys of the Bible as literature, with biblical history and with Christian doctrine. But there is hardly a book to be found on the subject of biblical theology.

Christian Doctrine and Biblical Theology

We need to be aware of the distinction between Christian doctrine and biblical theology. The approach to biblical interpretation adopted in this book is based on the method of biblical theology. Christian doctrine (systematic or dogmatic theology) involves a systematic gathering of the doctrines of the Bible under various topics to form a body of definitive Christian teaching about man, sin, grace, the church, sacraments, ministry, and so on. This systematizing of theology depends for its validity on the interpretation problem being satisfactorily handled. It asserts, on the basis of the texts written *then*, what is the truth to be believed and proclaimed *now*. However, it is important to see the limitations of this approach. The structure and contents of the Bible are not systematic – there is no one section which sets out the doctrine of sin and another that of salvation. The formulation of Christian doctrine requires that we transform the material which is set within the framework of the dynamic processes of biblical history, into a form which is true to the Bible and applicable to the present time. The theologian wants to avoid the pitfalls of 'proof-texting' in which it is assumed that all biblical texts have equal value in establishing doctrine, irrespective of the context in which they occur. Thus the more static kind of propositions of Christian doctrine depend for their validity on the correct handling of the dynamic revelation which the Bible records in the very different form of an historical progression of God's dealing with man.

Biblical theology, as defined here, is dynamic not static. That is, it follows the movement and process of God's revelation in the Bible. It is closely related to systematic theology (the two are dependent upon one another), but there is a difference in emphasis. Biblical theology is not concerned to state the final doctrines which go to make up the content of Christian belief, but rather to describe the *process* by which revelation unfolds and moves toward the goal which is God's final revelation of his purposes in Jesus Christ. Biblical theology seeks to understand the relationships between the various eras in God's revealing activity recorded in the Bible. The systematic theologian is mainly interested in the finished article – the statement of Christian doctrine. The biblical theologian on the other hand is concerned rather with the progressive unfolding of truth. It is on the basis of biblical theology that the systematic theologian draws upon the pre-Pentecost texts of the Bible as part of the material from which *Christian* doctrine may be formulated.

Using the method of biblical theology we may examine how the events in the time of Moses, for example, relate theologically to the events predicted by the later prophets, and how these in turn relate to the New Testament gospel. If we can thus discern a development in the biblical revelation, we are in a better position to say what relevance the law of Moses, the narrative of the manna in the wilderness or any other event of the Old Testament, may have to us who live on the opposite side of the 'Christ event'.

The History of Redemption and the Kingdom of God

We have seen that the Old Testament is not a mere textbook of the history of Israel as we understand it today, but a theological history.

How can we characterize this history so that we are able to see the real unity within it? I suggest we look at the Old Testament as a *history of redemption*. In other words, the key to the Old Testament is not the part Israel plays – as important as that is – but the part *God* plays in redeeming a people from slavery and making them his own. The first approach would be to reduce the Old Testament to an example of ancient national history; the second interprets Israel's history as a part of God's redeeming activity to man.

Nor is redemption the only theological idea which provides structure to the Old Testament, for redemption is a process which leads to a goal. Has not the Old Testament something to say about that goal? Indeed it has – the redeemed people of God are the people of God's kingdom. I would even suggest that this goal, *the Kingdom of God*, is a more central issue in the Old Testament than is the redemptive process of bringing people into that Kingdom. Of course we cannot really separate the two so strictly. The process needs a goal; the goal has to have a process or method of attainment.

Some Features of the History of Redemption

First the history of redemption is *progressive*. That is easy to see simply by comparing the light which the patriarchs (Abraham, Isaac and Jacob) had on God's purposes, with the understanding possessed by a post-exilic Jew who could draw on Moses and all the prophets. When we look at the New Testament, we find the full light of the gospel and all its implications are expounded. Central to this gospel is the Kingdom (see for example Mark 1: 14–15).

Does this mean that truth was rather dimly understood at the start, and became brighter until the coming of Jesus? Not really. The idea of a gradual 'dawning of the light' is useful to a point, but it does not explain what appear to be important peaks or climaxes within the process. What we find is a series of stages, each self-contained, each coming to a climax leading in turn to a new stage. The emphases given to certain events and people historically and theologically, direct the reader's attention to such climaxes.

Secondly the history of redemption is *incomplete without the New Testament*. The fact that the Kingdom forecast by the prophets is never fulfilled in the Old Testament is of concern only if we ignore the New Testament. The great 'saving events' of the Old Testament (the saving of Noah, the call of Abraham, the exodus from Egypt, the establishment of the united monarchy, the destruction of Jerusalem by Babylon and the prophetic forecast of the new and perfect kingdom) are all fulfilled in Christ and the Kingdom of Christ. It is the New Testament that gives focus to the saving events of the Old.

Christianity does not differ from Judaism by asserting that the Old Testament is incomplete, for Judaism also recognizes the future hope of prophecy which remained unfulfilled in Old Testament times. Some, both Christians and Jews, have tended to lose sight of a future messianic fulfilment, and have thus reduced the Old Testament to a code of morals encased within an interesting but rather irrelevant era of ancient history. The essential difference between the two faiths lies in how the completion of the hope of Israel is brought about. According to the New Testament it is the Christ event which brings this hope to its appointed goal. Judaism, on the other hand, rejects Jesus of Nazareth as the awaited messianic fulfiller, and looks for other ways.

Thirdly the history of redemption is *to be interpreted*. Since our concern is with biblical theology first and foremost, we intend to follow the method which biblical theology requires:

(a) We begin with the New Testament because it is there that we encounter the Christ of the gospel, through whom by faith we are made God's children.

(b) The New Testament drives us back to the Old Testament because it everywhere presupposes the Old Testament as the basis of the gospel.

(c) The New Testament establishes for us that the Old Testament involves promise and hope of a goal which is fulfilled in Christ. It thus directs us to take account of 'the dynamic', the living process and movement, of the Old Testament which leads us on to the Christ of the Gospels. Because the New Testament declares the Old Testament to be incomplete without Christ we must understand the Old Testament in the light of its goal which is Christ. Jesus is indispensable to a true understanding of the Old Testament as well as the New.

Applying the Text to Today

All this is of interest because it opens the way to making the biblical text applicable to ourselves. Biblical theology shows us the kind of bridge needed to overcome the gap between the text and the modern Christian. It may be

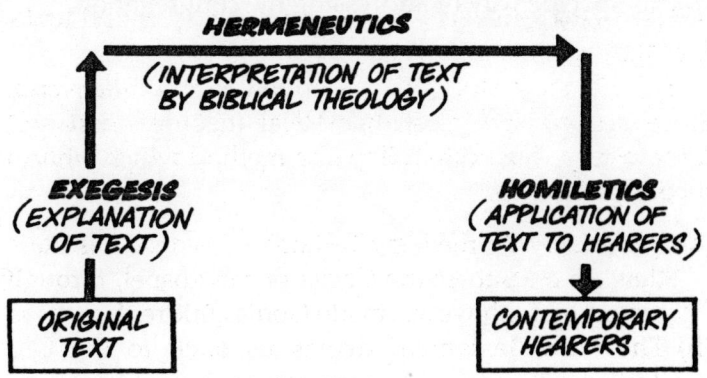

Figure 4   Bridging the Gap Between Text and Hearers

helpful at this point to outline the three stages involved in bringing the text across to ourselves.

(a) *Exegesis* This is the term used to refer to the business of finding out what the text originally meant. Before we can ever show the relevance of any part of the Bible we must know what its author intended to convey to his readers.

(b) *Hermeneutics* The hermeneutic or interpretative process is concerned with showing how the ancient biblical text has general relevance here and now. This book is mainly concerned with this stage and seeks to show how interpretation depends on the structure of the revelation of the Bible.

(c) *Application* The general application of the text is turned into specific application to the life of the reader or hearer. Homiletics (preaching) is one such method of application as the preacher brings the meaning of the text from its original meaning (exegesis) through its general Christian interpretation (hermeneutics) to its specific way of addressing the congregation.

Chapter Five

The Covenant and the Kingdom of God

The Covenant

The creation of man in the image of God distinguished man from the animals. Man is not the end of a chain of evolution for he is qualitatively distinct from the animals. Man was created in fellowship with God and with dominion over the rest of the created order. Thus there is a unique relationship between God and man. However, we cannot ignore the similarity between man and the animals – man is never more than a creature and, as such, totally dependent upon the Creator. For instance the word of God to Adam forbidding him to eat from the tree of the Knowledge of Good and Evil expresses the fact that man, the creature, is bound by the limits of his creaturehood. There are real limits set by the Creator. As such they are expressions of the sovereignty of God – of his absolute lordship. But this Lord is good and he establishes his creature-man in a relationship which brings both rule and blessing. God is king, man his subject. And the place where all this happens is the very best place of all – it is the garden paradise of Eden.

The Heart of the Problem

Man's sin is his attempt to renounce his creaturehood and to assert his independence of God, the Creator. The consequent judgement (in the 'fall' of man) establishes a break in the relationship between man and God. The world becomes a fallen world for fallen man to live in (see Romans 8: 19–20). But just as a fallen creation still reflects God's glory (Psalm 19: 1, Romans 1: 20) so man still reflects something of God's image. One aspect of the mercy of God is that he reveals a gracious attitude towards fallen man. Even in the Fall, God's grace permits the world to continue, and sustains an order in which man may live and multiply.

The measure of God's grace is not only the 'common grace' shown in the ongoing universe; it is seen in the declaration of the purpose to redeem a people to be the people of God. The relationship between God and man as it once existed in Eden provides some indication of God's intention for his new race of people.

The Covenant with Abraham

Leaving aside for the moment the question of what is revealed between the fall of man and the beginnings of the Hebrew nation (in Genesis 4–11), we now examine the call of Abraham. God's promise to Abraham, expressed in Genesis 12 and subsequent chapters, provides one of the central themes of the Bible. The form of the promise described as *covenant* is essentially an agreement between parties. But this is no ordinary human covenant involving mutual consent of equals, but a lordly covenant dispensed by the gracious act of a God greatly offended and sinned against. The covenant is an agreement in the sense that the recipient must agree to any terms that may be proposed. But before all else we must see this covenant as one of *grace* – undeserved favour. God's promises to Abraham involved:

(a) a people who are his descendants,
(b) a land in which they will live,
(c) a relationship with God in that they shall be God's people.

This covenant relationship, then, consists in being called the people of God. Every later expression of this relationship stems from the original covenant. We discover that this promise to the forefathers of Israel (Abraham, Isaac and Jacob) becomes the basis of the relationship of all the people of God in the Bible. Even in the New Testament the concept of being the children of Abraham is transferred to those who by faith embrace the gospel (Galatians 3: 29). Every Christian is a son or daughter of Abraham! Later we shall look at the different areas where the covenant is given distinct expression in the Old Testament.

The Kingdom of God

To understand the covenant we must examine its contents and its terms. The content of the covenant, like the goal of redemption, is the Kingdom of God, since the covenant is related to our redemption as children of God. What is the Kingdom of God? The New Testament has a great deal to say about 'the Kingdom' but we may best understand this concept in terms of the relationship of ruler to subjects. That is, there is a king who *rules*, a people who are *ruled*, and a sphere where this, rule is *recognized* as taking place. Put in another way, the Kingdom of God involves:

(a) God's people
(b) in God's place
(c) under God's rule.

Given this basic analysis, it is clear that the fact that the term 'Kingdom of God' does not occur in the Old Testament is unimportant. The basic idea is woven through the whole of Scripture.

We first see the Kingdom of God in the Garden of Eden. Here Adam and Eve live in willing obedience to the word of God and to God's rule. In this setting, the Kingdom is destroyed by the sin of man – and the rest of the Bible is about the restoration of a people to be the willing subjects of the perfect rule of God.

There are many more episodes in the Bible where the Kingdom of God is given expression.

The Promise to Abraham

This is recorded in Genesis 12. 1–3. God promises the patriarchs that their descendants (God's people) will possess the promised land (God's place) and be the people of God, underneath his authority (God's rule). The historical process by which the people are brought into that situation takes the form of a redemptive act of God. God redeems Israel when he rescues it out of captivity in Egypt.

The Monarchy

Israel's 'golden age' comes during the period of the Monarchy, when northern and southern kingdoms are united as one nation. The political, economic and religious achievement of the kingdom of David and Solomon fulfils in a very tangible way the promises to Abraham. This kingdom is by no means perfect but it displays all the elements of the Kingdom of God. So a pattern is emerging: the revelation of God's kingdom begins with a very basic promise to Abraham, and then moves through a process of fulfilment which includes a redemptive experience (the Exodus) and climaxes in a fulfilment (the Monarchy). This last stage contains some things not even specifically stated in the original promise (such as the city of Zion, the Temple and the Kingship of David).

The Prophetic Kingdom

Solomon's kingdom fails and this serves to underline what has been apparent all along – that the historical process from Abraham to Solomon always falls short of the glory of God's true kingdom, even though it reveals the nature of that kingdom. In the face of the judgement upon Israel's sin (climaxing in the destruction of the nation), the prophets restate the promise of the Kingdom as something that will be fulfilled in the future.

The return from the Babylonian exile fails to produce the Kingdom foretold by prophets such as Isaiah, Jeremiah and Ezekiel. The post-exilic prophets, Haggai, Zechariah and Malachi, continue to direct the eyes of Israel away from their present history to the great future day when the perfect and everlasting Kingdom of God will be revealed. The Old Testament ends on the note of promise and expectation. There is no fulfilment in sight as the Jews enter nearly four hundred years of prophetic silence between the two Testaments. During this time the Jews develop a variety of solutions to the problem. The best known is that of the Pharisees, who sought a literal return to the Israelite monarchy and the freedom of Israel from all foreign oppression.

The Gospel Kingdom

Jesus declares: 'The time is fulfilled; the Kingdom of God
is at hand' (Mark 1: 14). He thus introduces the gospel as
the bringing-near of the Kingdom. What it means for the
Kingdom to be 'at hand' rather than fulfilled emerges as
the New Testament expounds the gospel. Jesus is the fulfilment of the promises but, at this stage, the fact that
God's kingdom will triumph can only be received by
faith. The New Testament describes in various places the
future consummation of the Kingdom where the people of
God know fully and by sight that which they now only
have by faith. When Christ appears at his second coming,
the saints of God will appear with him and the eternal
Kingdom will be made plain (Colossians 3: 4).

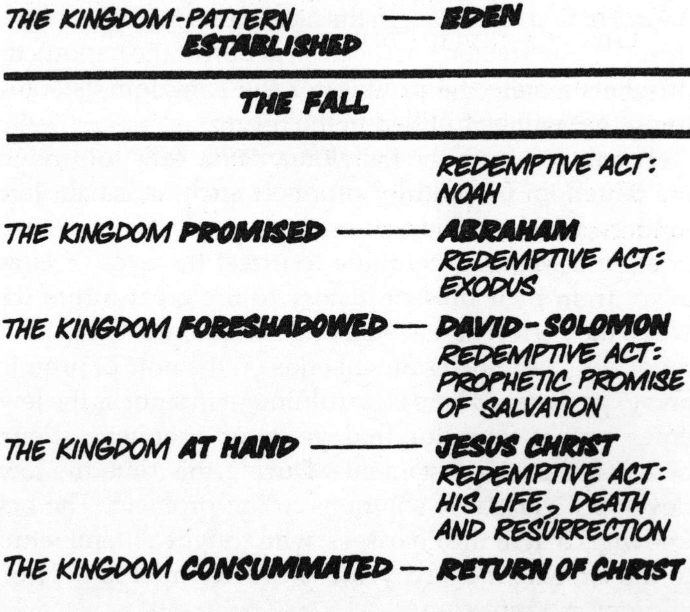

THE KINGDOM-PATTERN   —— EDEN
         ESTABLISHED
_____

                THE FALL
_____

                          REDEMPTIVE ACT:
                          NOAH

THE KINGDOM PROMISED ——— ABRAHAM
                          REDEMPTIVE ACT:
                          EXODUS

THE KINGDOM FORESHADOWED — DAVID-SOLOMON
                          REDEMPTIVE ACT:
                          PROPHETIC PROMISE
                          OF SALVATION

THE KINGDOM AT HAND ——— JESUS CHRIST
                          REDEMPTIVE ACT:
                          HIS LIFE, DEATH
                          AND RESURRECTION

THE KINGDOM CONSUMMATED — RETURN OF CHRIST

Figure 5   'Kingdom' Revelation in the Bible (see also Fig. 8)

It is now clear why the history of redemption is not simply a gradual unfolding of the truths of the Kingdom, a dawning of the light, but rather a series of stages in which the Kingdom, and the way into it, are revealed. In each stage all the essential ingredients of the Kingdom are given expression, but each successive stage builds on the former until the full revelation of the gospel is achieved. At the risk of over-simplification, we might organize our material on the Kingdom of God in several 'blocks' of revelation:

(a) The Kingdom revealed in Eden
(b) The Kingdom revealed in Israel's history (Abraham to Solomon)
(c) The Kingdom revealed in prophecy (Elijah to John the Baptist)
(d) The Kingdom revealed in Christ (New Testament times to return to Christ).

We must now consider in a more exact fashion just how these stages or blocks of revelation relate to each other. The conclusions we reach about this will control our method of interpreting Old Testament texts and our understanding of their relevance to us as Christians today.

Chapter Six

The Kingdom Revealed in Eden

The Creation

The creation story must never be regarded merely as a sort of biblical 'once-upon-a-time'. The fact that God is Creator and that man is his creature establishes at the outset the basis for understanding the Kingdom of God. When we speak of the *sovereignty* of God, we use a word which means his kingship, a kingship which is absolute and uncompromised. The creature is ruled and belongs, as a creature, within the sphere of God's perfect rule. In making all things by the power of his word (II Peter 3: 5), God shows the right he has as Creator to rule all things. The only perfect existence for the creature is that which is found within the framework of the rule of God.

The creatorship of God tells us that all reality is *God's* reality; all truth is *God's* truth. Nothing exists except by the will and word of God. One could write whole books on the implication of creation for a Christian approach to education, politics, economics, family life, moral values, or scientific research. If we believe in God as Creator, we may not divide the world into spiritual and secular. The fact that all reality depends upon the creative word of God means that the word of God must judge the ideas of men about truth and error, not the other way round. Thus the Christian doctrine of the authority of Scripture has its roots in the Creation. The famous comment about the Bible's authority made by the nineteenth century preacher C.H. Spurgeon ('Defend the Bible? I'd as soon defend a lion!') is well-known and appropriate. But we also need to be reminded of the relationship of God's word to the reasoning of man the creature about what is true – one does not take a pocket flashlight and shine it on the sun to see if the sun is real![1] The truth of God's word cannot be subject to the puny light of man's self-centred reason. God's word created what is and must interpret what is.

Man in the Image of God

What is 'our image' (Genesis 1: 26)? God created man in his image and delegated to man authority over the rest of the created order (Genesis 1: 26f). Some scholars see this dominion of man, his *ruling-function* in creation, as the 'image' of God. Others point out that man in the image of God is both male and female. The 'image' may therefore be seen in the *relationship of man and woman*, particularly that which comes to its fullest expression in the union of husband and wife and which is based upon their sexual polarity (Genesis 2: 24). If the Bible does not clearly define the image of God in man at this stage, it will later point to Jesus Christ as the true image of God.

The basic points to notice at this stage are (i) the uniqueness of man as the summit of creation and the

---

[1] This aspect of the proper function of human reason is discussed in C. van Til, *Apologetics*, (unpublished syllabus, Westminster Theological Seminary, Philadelphia (nd.) p. 67).

image of God and (ii) the creaturehood of man who is wholly dependent upon the Creator for his existence.

Eden – the Garden Kingdom

As Creation speaks to us of the King, so Eden speaks to us of the Kingdom of God. In the previous chapter we saw that the Kingdom of God (a New Testament term) is a wholly biblical idea – the concept of the Kingdom dominates the whole biblical story. The point where this pattern is established is the Garden of Eden. Here we see the people of God (Adam and Eve in their innocence), the garden paradise (the place which God prepared as the perfect environment for his people) and the rule of God expressed by his word. God, as the sovereign king, sets the limits of freedom: 'You may freely eat of every tree of the garden but of the tree of knowledge of good and evil you shall not eat' (Genesis 2: 16–17).

Because this is the Kingdom the king may not be challenged by his subjects. The perfect relationship between Creator and creature, between ruler and ruled, cannot exist if the creature seeks to usurp the role of Creator by rejecting his rule: 'For in the day that you eat of it you shall die' (Genesis 2:17).

The description of the Garden of Eden does not tell us everything about the Kingdom of God, but it does provide the essential framework for understanding the nature of the Kingdom as:

> God's people (Adam and Eve)
> in God's place (the Garden of Eden)
> under God's rule (the word of God).

We shall see this pattern emerge over and over as the goal of all God's activity. As it was in the creation, so it will be in the redemptive process which leads to the new creation. It is not accidental that the tree of life, which was denied to rebellious Adam, turns up in the description of the new Jerusalem in Revelation 22 (compare Genesis 3: 22f with Revelation 22: 2) or in John's prophecy of the victory of the saints in Revelation 2: 7: 'To him who conquers I will grant to eat of the tree of life which is in the paradise of God'.

The Fall of Man

As with the creation, so it is easy to underestimate the significance and effects of the Fall. If the creatorship of God is given its full weight, then the Fall, as the outcome of man's unilateral declaration of independence, is a very serious thing. The serpent's temptation was directed to this end: 'Has God said . . .?' This initially subtle questioning of the authoritative word of God is followed by the outright denial of the truth of that word: 'You will not die' (Genesis 3: 1–4). The result was that Adam and Eve rejected the rule of God and asserted that even in the activity of reasoning, they were quite self-sufficient and independent.

It is impossible for God to be true to himself and at the same time tolerate his own dethronement by the creature. Thus judgement is both inevitable and radical (in the sense of striking at the root of the situation). 'On the day that you eat of it you will die' said God, and die man did. The fact that the final physical sign of death in the dissolution of the body was not immediate did not lessen the fact of death which came upon man. Dead man is sinful man, man who has rejected the Kingdom of God. Dead man is man outside the Garden.

The Sovereignty of God and the Kingdom of God

We need to distinguish here between the absolute sovereignty of God and the Kingdom of God. Neither man nor devil can escape the sovereign power of God, no matter how hard either may fight against it. In the end all who rebel against the Creator will be forced to submit to the undeniable reality of God's lordship. But the Kingdom of God as the Bible reveals it is the sphere of God's rule in which his creatures submit willingly to this righteous rule. God's sovereign rule is universal; the Kingdom of God is not. There is hell as well as heaven, the world of darkness as well as the Kingdom of light.

At this stage it is not necessary to supplement the records of Genesis with the New Testament material, which enlarges upon the meaning of the sentence of death which came upon man at the Fall. The Genesis account provides the framework upon which the Scriptures elaborate. It is impossible to separate the seemingly contradictory elements in the Fall of man – the righteous judgement of God and the incredible graciousness of God.

Judgement

The judgement involves firstly the disruption of the relationship between man and God. This is most clearly seen in the ejection of man from the Garden. Secondly there is the disruption of the relationship between man and woman, as the perfect harmony of male and female gives way to rivalry and accusation (Genesis 3: 12, 16). Thirdly there is a disruption of the relationship of man to his environment as the physical creation is no longer seen to be under the dominion of man (Genesis 3: 17–19). The word 'disruption' is not intended to detract from the seriousness of the sentence of death. Man outside the Kingdom is not merely under the sentence of death, but he is dead. The real meaning of death lies in the separation of man from the willing relationship of the Kingdom. Autonomous man is God-denying and therefore life-denying as well. Fallen man is dead spiritually. Outside of Eden there is no return. Man has made his choice to be a rebel and he is bound by his decision. Nor is there any free choice for the posterity of Adam. Adam's fall from the Garden Kingdom is a fall of the whole human race. Every man is born outside the garden; every man is born an active rebel asserting autonomy and independence of the God of life. Human history and Scripture will show that man's death state means that he infallibly chooses to hate God, for that is his 'outside Eden' nature. It is no longer a question of freedom to choose right or wrong, for man is free now only to be what he is – a sinner who hates God (cf. Romans 3: 9–18, 8: 6–8). Man has become a slave to sin – a slavery that is death.

Grace

Grace refers to the attitude of God towards rebellious sinners in showing to them mercy which is not only undeserved, but the very opposite of what is deserved. This attitude of God is not an abstract thing, but is known to us only through the saving activity of God. The incredible story of Genesis 3 is one of both judgement and grace. To begin with, we note that God does not purpose to obliterate man as he might justly have done when Adam sinned. The very fact that the race is preserved and that God continues to speak to man is a mark of his grace.

Grace is seen in the judgement of the serpent. God is righteous, and the father of lies is destined for his ultimate reward. Genesis 3: 15 has long been recognized as a word of grace, a *proto-evangel* (that is, the first reference to the gospel), promising that the 'seed of woman' shall actually share in the reversal of wrong. The serpent has led man to his fall and is blameworthy. Man is also blameworthy because he was willingly led. Grace operates in the face of blameworthiness.

Grace is seen in the maintenance of some semblance of society. The image of God in man is not entirely obliterated and hence man retains some dignity over the rest of creation. Man and woman continue to relate and to propagate even though the relationship is corrupted. The universe, in order to remain under man's dominion, and despite its ongoing challenge to man's dominion, is made to fall with man. The world outside the garden is fallen, for man cannot survive in an unfallen world. 'The creation was subjected to futility, not of its own will but by the will of him who subjected it in hope' (Romans 8: 20).

The Two Lines of Man

Genesis 4–11 contains a compact story which covers a very long period of time. In keeping with the method of biblical theology, we look at the emphases of these chapters in order to discover the overall message they contain. This first history of fallen man in a fallen world is an example of history that is theologically orientated. The two lines of people, characterized by the heads of the lines Cain and Abel, the sons of Adam and Eve, are arranged schematically. The device of genealogy, or family tree, is used a number of times in the Bible and we should not be too quick to dismiss the genealogies as uninteresting or spiritually irrelevant. The diagram below demonstrates the genealogical structure of Genesis 4–11.

The narrative of Cain and Abel depicts one effect of the fall of mankind – rivalry and murder. The account then

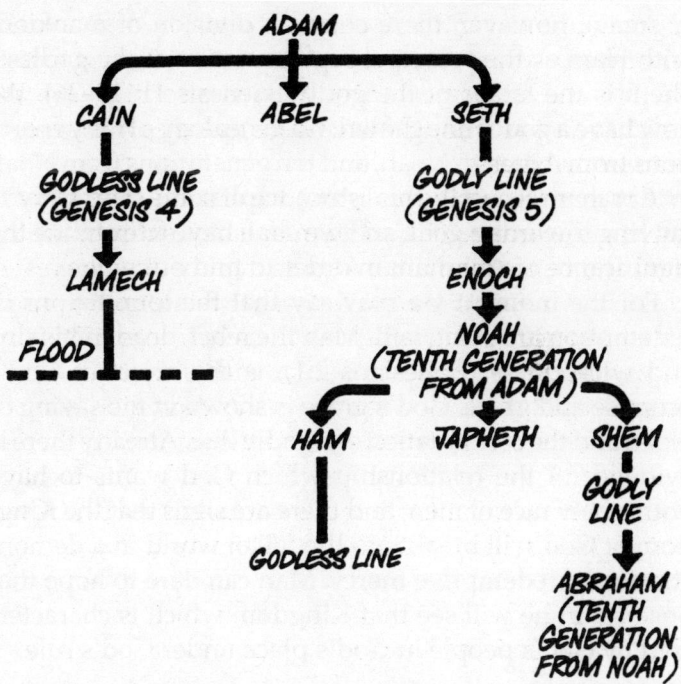

Figure 6   The Two Lines of Man

turns to the genealogy of Cain's ungodly line of descendants, characterized as developers of the city and of industry, and climaxed by the viciousness of Lamech (Genesis 4: 17–24). The godlessness of man is again stressed in Genesis 6 as God declares his intention to destroy man (v. 7). This godless line of course disappears in the flood.

Meanwhile a godly line begins with Seth who takes the place of his murdered brother (Genesis 4: 25). The exemplars of this line are Enoch, who walked with God, and Noah who found grace in the eyes of the Lord. The salvation of Noah and his family is an act of God's grace leading to a new beginning.

Again, however, there comes a division of mankind, with Ham as the principal representative of the godless. Shem is the father of the godly (Genesis 11: 10–26). We now have a godly line shown in a genealogy of ten generations from Adam to Noah, and ten generations from Noah to Abraham. Clearly this is not haphazard. The story is moving towards a goal, and we shall have to examine the significance of Abraham in order to find out where.

For the moment we may say that the foundations of redemption are being laid. Man the rebel, dead in his sins and wickedness (Ephesians 2:1), is the object of God's promise and grace. God's grace is shown in the saving of Noah and the continuation of a godly line. Already there is evidence of the relationship which God wants to have with a new race of men, and there are signs that the Kingdom of God will break into the fallen world in a demonstration of redemptive mercy. Man can dare to hope that once again he will see that Kingdom which is characterized by God's people in God's place under God's rule.

Chapter Seven

The Kingdom Revealed in Israel's History

We have seen how the pattern for the kingdom of God is set in Eden. In this chapter we outline the structure of Israel's history from Abraham to the Babylonian Exile, a period of over a thousand years. We will not be concerned to summarize the historical facts (these can be found in any handbook or Bible dictionary), but rather to uncover the structure of the whole range of history – to see a purposeful relationship in the whole sequence of events. As Christians, we recognize that Israel's history is not haphazard, nor a series of random incidents, but, as in *all* history, it is governed by the purpose of God. The unique feature of Israel's history was that its purpose involved both revelation of salvation and the way of salvation. Since God is Lord, and since salvation has reference to the bringing of sinners into the Kingdom of God, that same Kingdom will be reflected in the history which is 'salvation history'.

Abraham and the Patriarchs – The Kingdom Promised

The most important thing about the history of Abraham is God's covenant promise. The whole narrative (Genesis

12–24) is dominated by the promises, which conveyed three main elements:

(a) Abraham's descendants would become a great nation (Genesis 12: 2, 13: 16, 15: 5, 16: 10, 18: 18).
(b) These descendants would possess the promised land (Genesis 12: 7, 13: 14–15, 15: 18–21, 17: 8).
(c) These descendants would be God's own people (Genesis 17: 2 and 7–8, 18: 19).

We should also note a fourth element which points to this gracious promise of God's being extended to those who are not physically descended from Abraham (see Genesis 12: 3. 17: 4–6, compare Romans 4: 16–18).[1]

What is this covenant promise if not the promise of the Kingdom of God? Certainly it is made in terms which are localized and earthbound. God in fact promises Abraham that his descendants would be God's people in God's place under God's rule, and all the Abraham stories must be seen in this light. An important element in the story is the way that tension develops because Abraham possesses the promise but not the substance of it. He must accept God at his word in faith, while at the same time all the natural events seem to work against the fulfilment of the promise. Even for Abraham the Kingdom of God must firstly be received by faith alone (Genesis 15: 6).[2]

---

[1] The multitude of nations has a double reference, for Abraham was the father of non-Israelite nations who did not directly share in the covenant, e.g. Ishmael's descendants and those of Esau (Edom). But the reference goes beyond this to the inclusion of the Gentiles in the blessings, as Paul indicates in Romans 4: 16–18.

[2] That is why Paul uses Genesis 15:6 as the foundation for his exposition of the basic gospel truth that we are justified through faith (Romans 4).

Having been given promises of descendants and a land, Abraham watches his greedy nephew, Lot, occupy the best pasture land (Genesis 13: 8–11). But see how God then sustains Abraham with his promise (verses 14–17)![3] As for the promise of descendants, this is difficult for two very old people to accept (Genesis 15: 1–5) and the narrative of Hagar and Ishmael shows the stress Abraham and Sarah are under. Isaac, their natural-born son, is eventually designated the heir (Genesis 15,: 4, 17: 19, 21, 18: 10). When Isaac is born the relief must have been enormous; he is truly the child of promise. So why the command to sacrifice the young boy (Genesis 22: 1–2)? This event shows that Abraham is not only obedient to God in a general way but that he believes the specific promises of God, despite the apparent challenge to their fulfilment that the sacrifice would entail. Again he is reassured by the promise when his faith has stood firm (verses 15–18). When Sarah dies, Abraham is forced to haggle over the price of her burial plot which he must buy from his own inheritance (Genesis 23)!

Isaac's children; Esau and Jacob, are the objects of the sovereign choice of God, for the younger (again an unnatural choice) is selected over the elder for the covenant line (Genesis 25: 19–23). Jacob is not a good person at all – quite the opposite. His election is not grounded on his merits foreseen by God (compare Romans 9: 10–13). But Jacob is converted by the grace of God and becomes the father of the covenant people. Thus it will be through the children of Jacob that the Kingdom of God will be demonstrated.

---

[3] The difficult narrative in ch. 14 does not easily fit with the rest of this section in that it does not obviously express the same main emphases. However, the mysterious encounter with the priest king Melchizedek, and the paying of tithes to him, show that Abraham is content to forego the opportunity to enrich himself in this land until the land in his.

The rest of the patriarchal story[4] takes us with Joseph and his brothers to Egypt, where the stage will be set for the next chapter in the history of redemption. The very fact that the descendants of Abraham are forced to go to Egypt for their welfare is also to be seen in the light of the covenant promises. For even when it appears (much to the dismay of the King of Egypt) that they are becoming a mighty nation, the land of promise is far off and inaccessible.

Moses and the Exodus – the Promises Activated

The Exodus

'Now there arose a new king over Egypt, who did not know Joseph' (Exodus 1: 8). Suddenly the once favoured sons of Israel (Jacob) are no longer welcome guests in the fertile Nile delta. Sojourn becomes captivity and privilege becomes enslavement. The covenant promises are removed one stage further, for the people not only live away from the promised land, but are now prisoners of a cruel monarch. Again the experience of the recipients of the promises seems to contradict the promises. But from a more positive angle we can begin to put together some pieces of the puzzle. Why has God not fulfilled the promises? It is one thing to talk of faith, but faith is not to be confused with delusion and wishful thinking. The promises must be based on a reality which will be achieved if they are not to be a cruel hoax.

At this stage we can only observe that God must have a reason for creating this tension. To what purposes are the

---

[4] The patriarchs are the 'fathers', i.e Abraham, Isaac, Jacob and his twelve Sons.

promises channelled through this extraordinary Egyptian experience? The Book of Exodus will show us the answer to this question. Exodus begins with the story of Moses' birth, preservation and preparation for his mission. These events are not only favourite subjects in Bible teaching programmes for children but are also frequently mishandled. The story of Moses in the rushes must be related to the declared purpose of God in Exodus 2: 23–25, which shows us that Moses is to be the mediator of God's acts in fulfilling the covenant promises made to the patriarchs. Notice the stress given to the identification of the God who sends Moses to be Israel's leader. He is the God of Abraham, Isaac and Jacob (Exodus 2: 24, 3: 6, 13, 15 and 16, 4: 5, 6:2–5).

That the God of Israel is the God who is faithful to the covenant with Abraham is a fact now associated with the personal name of God.[5] In most English versions of the Bible this holy name is translated LORD. Wherever you read LORD in your English Old Testament as the name of God remember it is his special personal name, and not merely a title – it expresses the character of God which has been revealed in his acts to redeem his people. The act and the knowledge of the name are frequently related: I will take you for my people . . . and you shall know that I am Jehovah (the LORD) your God (Exodus 6: 7, compare 7: 5).

So Israel is in bondage, through no obvious fault of her own, in Egypt far from Canaan. Now God acts on the basis of the covenant to release the children of Jacob. But Pharaoh is a cruel tyrant and refuses to let the people go. God, through his servant Moses, works a series of signs and

---

[5] Exodus 6: 2–5 stresses the relationship of the name of God to his character as the covenant keeper. LORD is usually used to translate the Hebrew proper name YHVH from which the name Jehovah is derived. The Israelites at some stage ceased to pronounce this name because it was so holy and instead substituted the word *ADONAI* (=my Lord). Hence the translation LORD.

wonders to make Pharoah release Israel. Each plague inflicted is a demonstration of the superior might of Jehovah over Egypt and its gods. The final plague is associated with a redemptive picture that Israel was never to forget. As God pronounces death upon all the first-born in Egypt, a way of escape is provided for believing Israelites. The sacrifice of a lamb and the sprinkling of its blood on the doorposts would cause the angel of death to pass over each household that complied. The Passover redemption of the Israelite firstborn is coupled with the escape from Egypt, so that the redemptive picture is extended to include all Israel. The effect of this tenth plague on Pharaoh is to cause him finally to let the people go. Up to this point his heart is hardened and even now he is to have second thoughts and pursue the fugitives to the Red Sea.[6]

The way out of Egypt would naturally be by the well-trodden way from the Delta through the coastal strip to Canaan But God does not lead them that way (Exodus 13: 17) but through the wilderness to the shores of the sea. This is like running into a blind-alley with walls on all sides. But God's purpose is still to be seen; he has already overcome the barrier of Pharaoh's hard heart and now he will overcome the barrier of the sea. It will not be by following the easy trade-route, but by the strong hand of God that Israel will come out of Egypt – redemption is a miracle that only God can perform (Exodus 6: 6b, 13: 9–16) Even the magicians of Egypt have recognized the finger of God at work (Exodus 8: 19).

Now we can answer the question we posed above: why has God not fulfilled the promises? Israel was brought to Egypt and the patriarchs never possessed the land,

---

[6] The Hebrew *Yam Suph* means Reed Sea not Red Sea. There is some dispute as to where Israel actually crossed the water, but this hardly affects the miraculous significance of the crossing.

because God intended to reveal the way into his Kingdom. It is a way involving a miraculous redemption from a bondage that holds us and keeps us out of the Kingdom. Only a miracle of God can bring us back to the Kingdom. The Exodus will remain now the key model for the understanding of redemption in the life of Israel, and the people of God will be made to recall it as the basis of their response to a God who saves (see Exodus 20: 2, Deuteronomy 6: 20–25, 26: 5–10, Joshua 24: 6–13, Nehemiah 9: 6–12, Psalms 78, 105, 106, 114, 135 and 136).

The Sinai Covenant

The escaped Israelites came to Sinai where the next great aspect of Moses' ministry was to take place – the giving of the law. So much confusion has arisen at this point that we must endeavour to understand clearly the purpose of the law. Part of this confusion occurs because of a misunderstanding of the attitude to the law in the New Testament. Because Paul says of Christians, 'You are not under law but under grace' (Romans 6: 14), and because he stresses that justification means a righteousness which is 'apart from law' (Romans 3: 21), it is too easily assumed that the law is not only bypassed in the gospel, but even overthrown. It is not unfair, I think, to say that many Christians have an understanding something like this: God gave Israel the law at Sinai as a programme of works whose goal is salvation. The history of Israel shows how complete was the inability of Israel to achieve the required standard. God, therefore, in a kind of desperation, scrapped plan A (salvation through works of the law) and instituted as an emergency plan B (the gospel). The Old Testament thus becomes essentially the record of the failure of plan A. Its relationship to the New Testament is almost wholly negative.

In order to gain the right perspective on the Sinai law we must be more careful to examine the treatment of it in both Old Testament and New Testament. We must look at the positive statements about the law in the New Testament and also understand the reason for the many negative statements. If the depreciation of law in the New Testament is seen to apply not to law in itself, but to the perverted use of the law in Israel, the proper understanding and use of law will also be seen in the Old Testament.

To begin with, we acknowledge that two major events stand behind Sinai. The one is the Exodus and the other is the covenant with Abraham. If the Exodus means anything it means freedom from bondage. It is therefore clear that the law could not originate at Sinai as another form of bondage. The continuity of the declared purpose of God requires us to place Sinai in the context of the purposes of God to make a people for himself on the basis of his grace. The call and covenanting of Abraham was an act of grace. The descendants of Abraham were promised the kingdom by grace. The mighty acts of God in Egypt were performed because of the promise to Abraham (Exodus 2: 23–25). The Exodus event becomes a model of salvation by grace, its goal being the fulfilment of the promises to Abraham in the promised land. It is utterly inconceivable that God should break off his programme of salvation by grace in mid-stream (between Egypt and Canaan) and, despite his promises to Abraham, saddle his people with a frustrating programme of salvation by works! The narrative of Exodus does not allow such violence to be done to its theological continuity. The only reasonable assessment of the Sinai law in this context is that it is part of the programme of grace whereby God works to fulfil his promises to Abraham. This is no 'plan A' to be jettisoned later on, but part of a single, comprehensive plan God had from the beginning.

The heart of the law is the Ten Commandments (Exodus 20) which are prefaced by the significant phrase, 'I am the Lord your God, who brought you out of the land of Egypt, out of the house of bondage'. These words should govern our understanding of the Sinai law. Here we see that God declares that he is the God of this people, that he has already saved them. What follows then cannot be a programme aimed to achieve salvation by works since they have already received it by grace. The law is given to the people of God after they become the people of God by grace. Sinai is dependant upon the covenant with Abraham and is an exposition of it. At Sinai God spells out for his people what it means to be the people of God. They cannot know how to live consistently with their calling in life as Jehovah's people unless he tells them. What he does tell them reflects in various ways his own character. It is their faithful response to the character of God that will demonstrate that they are his children. The law explicates further the knowledge of God's character already revealed in his dealing with their forefathers and in his acts in Egypt (Exodus 6: 6–8).[7]

---

[7] This interpretation is supported by recent studies into treaty formulations in the Ancient Near East. It has been demonstrated with a fair degree of certainty that the form of the decalogue, i.e. the Ten Commandments, and possibly even the whole book of Deuteronomy, is the same as the conventional form of treaty covenants imposed by conquering kings on the conquered. These treaties set out the stipulations which governed the life of the vassal people as members of the great kingdom. If the analogy of 'form' holds, the use of this form for the decalogue would be appropriate only if the law of Sinai was intended to be a covenant which stipulated the conditions imposed upon the people made subjects of the God of the covenant.

Given this understanding of the Sinai covenant, the moral prescriptions are easy enough to understand. But what of the ritual details and the many laws concerning what is clean and what unclean (especially with regard to food)? It is helpful to know something of the range of prescriptions given in Exodus and Leviticus, but the individual precepts should not be viewed apart from the context of the whole covenant. The sum total of the covenant of Sinai equals the great covenant summary: 'I will be your God and you will be my people'.[8] It explains in detail the demands of the character of God: 'You shall be holy, for I the Lord your God am holy' (Leviticus 19: 2). The fact that many of its regulations do not touch directly the moral character of God stems from the nature of this preliminary revelation of God's kingdom. Some laws must deal with the national life of Israel, because that is where they are. Others are ritual requirements which depend on a later fulfilment for their full meaning. A group of apparently meaningless food laws become meaningful in the context of the Sinai covenant.[9] They instruct the people in one

---

[8] This particular summary statement occurs first in Leviticus 26: 12, but is also contained in the partial form given in Genesis 17: 7f, Exodus 6: 7. The significance of the declaration is highlighted by its repeated use through the Bible, e.g. Exodus 29: 45, Jeremiah 24: 7, 31: 33 and 32: 38, Ezekiel 11: 20, 34: 24 and 37: 23, Zechariah 8: 8, II Corinthians 6: 16, Revelation 21: 3. The relationship expressed is the same that is included in the idea of the Kingdom of God.

[9] I cannot accept the view that the rationale behind food laws – what is clean for eating, and what is unclean and therefore forbidden – lies only in considerations of hygiene. Even if some aspects of hygiene may be detected these cannot be the main purpose. The 'passing away' of the food laws (e.g. Colossians 2: 16f) results from the coming of Christ, not from the invention of the refrigerator!

aspect of the unique relationship they possess as a holy people, separated from all other allegiance and separated to Jehovah.

The details for the building of the Tabernacle (Exodus 25–31) must be looked at in the light of the overall purpose of the Tabernacle and not be interpreted for their own sake. A secondary aspect of all the detail is that it expresses clearly the fact that Israel cannot be left to design things without God's revelation. What we might call the 'symbolic aids to worship' must conform to a given pattern, otherwise the heart of man will create something else which reflects not the character of God but only the evil inclinations of man's heart. For this very reason Israel is forbidden all forms of visual aids to worship and of pictures or images of God. Man is incapable of portraying God without falling into idolatry. The purpose of the Tabernacle is expressed as the dwelling of God (Exodus 29: 45) which means the symbol of God's presence among his people. But on the other hand the barriers against access to the 'holy of holies' mean that a sinful people have only indirect access through the mediation of priests, and that only on the basis of substitutionary sacrifice for their sins.

Breaking the law carries heavy penalties, the most severe being death or excommunication. Israel as a nation is expected to be faithful to the law if it is also to enjoy the blessings of God. It is this fact (e.g. see Deuteronomy 28) which may be misinterpreted to imply that the blessings of salvation are the reward for the works of the law. We should note however that the New Testament carries exactly the same conditions. And no New Testament teaching destroys the principle of salvation by grace (e.g. I Corinthians 6: 9–10 and 10: 6–12, Ephesians 4: 1, Hebrews 12: 12–17, James 1: 26–27, I John 3: 14–15). In both the Old and New Testaments the principle operates that the people of God should exhibit a holiness which is consistent with their calling. The deliberate flouting of this principle is clear demonstration that we are not members of God's people.[10] In both Testaments the demand to be holy stems from the prior saving activity of God. Much more could be said about the Sinai covenant but we must be content here with these few comments about its significance and purpose.

The Entry and Settlement

The book of Numbers relates the incidents between Sinai and the entry. In so doing it presents a rather gloomy picture. Israel, which rides the crest of the wave of its salvation-experience in coming out of Egypt and in being constituted the people of God under the covenant of Sinai, is shown to be rebellious and ungrateful. The grumbling of the escaped nation becomes an immediate pattern (e.g. Exodus 16–18). After the Sinai encounter the nation asserts its independence of God by refusing the opportunity to take possession of the promised land (Numbers 13–14). The forty years wandering in the wilderness disposes of the generation of adults who came out of Egypt, leaving their children to go in and possess the land.

---

[10]   It is clear that in both Old and New Testaments we see a distinction between the root cause or basis of something, and the instrumental cause. Thus, we cannot be saved without faith, but on the other hand we are not saved because of faith. Faith is the instrument, but the basis of salvation is the righteousness of Christ. Likewise we cannot be saved without the new birth, yet the new birth is not the root cause or basis of salvation; if it were, Christ need never have died. The New Testament, as does the Old Testament, indicates that we cannot be saved *on the basis* of good works.

Prior to the entry Moses relates the covenant to this anticipated possession of the land and then hands over his leadership to Joshua. This 'second law', as the name of the book of Deuteronomy signifies, once more emphasizes the gracious provision of God for his people as he fulfils the promises made to Abraham, This grace contrasts sharply with the rebelliousness of Israel in the wilderness.

We may well wonder why God continues to show loving kindness to Israel despite the lack of response. Of course this is really no different from the question of why God shows grace to humanity at the Fall or to us today! Israel's rebelliousness is a recurring theme of the Old Testament, but so also is God's covenant love as he saves a remnant of faithful people out of the mass of the people. Indeed the remnant is an important theme which goes back to the beginning of redemptive history.[11] In the midst of all this rebellion the fact must not be overlooked that God is always saving the faithful remnant.

Deuteronomy is an important book as it emphasizes the relationship of law and grace. The first four chapters tell the story of salvation history, from the time spent at Sinai to the point of preparation to enter Canaan. The salvation history is interpreted in the light of Israel's

---

[11] The separation of the godly line from the godless in Genesis 4–11 is the beginning of this process. As the pattern develops, we see that the remnant itself becomes the subject of a separation of a new remnant and so on. Thus from fallen humanity comes the godly line. From this comes the family of Noah, from Noah the family of Shem, from Shem the family of Abraham. Then comes the family of Isaac and Jacob. It is in this family of Israel that we now see the differentiation between the faithful response to the covenant and that of rebelliousness. In other words the membership of the covenant people on the basis of *birth* never guarantees automatically the *blessings* of the covenant.

faithlessness and of God's continuing kindness. Nowhere are law and gospel more clearly related than they are in Deuteronomy 6:20–25. The child asks, 'What does the law mean, what is it all about?', and the answer is given in terms of 'gospel', that is, in terms of what God did in history to save his people.[12] Does God act like this because Israel deserves it? Deuteronomy answers with a resounding 'No'. God 'loves because he loves' is the logic of Deuteronomy 7: 7–8. Israel is allowed to dispossess Canaan, not because Israel is worthy and merits it but because Canaan deserves judgement (Deuteronomy 9:4–6). Always behind this is the promise of God to Abraham, to which God remains faithful despite Israel's rebelliousness (Deuteronomy 7: 8 and 9: 5).

The book of Joshua takes up the history narrative from Deuteronomy as Joshua, the successor to Moses, prepares to lead Israel into the land. One cannot escape the emphasis here that God is about to act for Israel. The great acts of God for Israel in the Exodus are to be continued since salvation is not complete until the people are brought into the inheritance. Once again a miracle will allow the people to pass through the waters on dry ground (Joshua 3: 7–13). They will not need to sneak over in some remote area, but will cross opposite the great fortress city of Jericho (Joshua 3: 16). God will fight for them, not only in the destruction of Jericho and Ai, but in the subjugation of the whole land. And these events, which later pass into Israel's history,

---

[12] It cannot be stressed too much that the biblical expression of the gospel is an historical event as God acts on behalf of his people to save. The gospel is the holy history worked out in the life and death of Christ. The gospel is *not* man's response to this event, nor is it the work of God in us now as he regenerates and sanctifies the believer. So in the Old Testament the 'gospel' is the declaration of what God did 'out there' and 'back there' at a fixed place and time in history.

became part of the 'gospel of the mighty acts of God' along with the crossing of the Red Sea (Joshua 4: 2 1–23).

Thus the book of Joshua describes the process of dis-possession of the various groups of Canaanites from their land by Israel. Although some pockets of resistance remain and troubles beset the Israelites from within the land and without, yet the assessment of the author may be accepted: 'The Lord gave Israel all the land which he had sworn to give to their forefathers; and having taken pos-session of it, they settled there. And the Lord gave them rest on every side just as he had sworn to their forefathers; not one of all their enemies had withstood them, for the Lord had given all their enemies into their hands. Not one of all the good promises which the Lord had made to the house of Israel had failed; all came to pass' (Joshua 21: 43–45). Again we note that this fulfilment of the gracious promises in the saving acts of God is not to be divorced from the covenant's demands upon Israel. Joshua calls upon the people to remember the serious consequences of transgressing the covenant (Joshua 23: 14–16). The book ends with a moving account of a covenant renewal cere-mony which again stresses the gospel of what God has done for his people (Joshua 24: 2–13), and which describes the demand upon the people to respond with faithful obe-dience (verses 14–27).

The Progress Towards Monarchy – Judgeship

We must be brief in describing this most detailed area of Israel's historical narrative. The period covers more than two centuries of the most important developments in the national life of Israel. The book of Judges records a certain instability which may on first sight appear to contradict the glowing terms used in Joshua 21: 43–45. However,

Judges does not deny that God gave all the land into Israel's hand, but rather stresses the fact that the tribes of Israel were slack in following through the instructions to utterly drive the inhabitants out. By tolerating little pockets of the enemy within the land, they weakened their position and the way was opened for difficult times ahead.

The theology of the book of Judges is summarized in Chapter 2. Contact with the enemy was always dangerous, not only because it could threaten national security, but principally because it threatened the integrity of Israel's faith. Both situations threatened the covenant. Again it is clear that the whole process of covenant fulfilment is being worked out at the level of national existence in a way which does not succeed in bringing the whole realm of human existence into the Kingdom. To put it another way, Israel's experiences show the way God acts and what the Kingdom is like, but as people the Israelites remain sinful and rebellious. We do not see the whole nation submitting perfectly and willingly to God's rule. This fact will shape our understanding of the extent to which the Kingdom of Israel exhibits the truth of the Kingdom of God.

So in Judges 2: 11–23 we find the theological interpretation of the events of the whole book. The stories of the heroic deeds of Ehud, Gideon, Samson and the other judges, are stories of 'mini-salvations'. The same cycle is there in each case – Israel's sin, judgement at the hand of the enemy, Israel's repentance and call for help, and the saviour judge who rescues Israel from the enemy. Every victory under the leadership of one of these judges is a saving act of God by which he establishes the people in their inheritance. From our perspective these repetitions of salvation may seem to disrupt the harmony of the overall historical events in revealing salvation and the

Kingdom. But we must recognize that God's loving kindness is at work in the generations following the Exodus from Egypt, repeatedly showing his saving mercy. This period does not become too complicated as long as we maintain a perspective on the major events and their theological significance in revealing the kingdom. The account of this period of upheaval comes to an end with the significant statement: 'In those days there was no king in Israel; every man did what was right in his own eyes' (Judges 21: 25). If this indicates that the author is looking back on these events from the time of the monarchy, it also indicates that he sees the monarchy as necessary to provide stability and order in Israel.

Samuel and Saul

From the fragmentation of national life and the localized activity of the judges there develops a movement towards a more coherent and structured situation. Samuel the prophet-judge figures prominently in this trend. He is accepted as a prophet, the first national prophetic figure since Moses, from Dan to Beersheba (I Samuel 3: 19–20).[13] The enemy now is the Philistine nation. The leadership of Samuel during this extreme threat puts him in the path of a new political development. The Israelites perceive the advantage of stable government and, following the example of the neighbouring states, demand a king to rule over them and to lead them in battle (I Samuel 8: 19–20).

That the motives of the Israelites in asking for a king are all wrong can be seen in the nature of their expectations

---

[13] These two towns represent the extreme north and the extreme south of the land respectively, and thus express the truly national, rather than local, nature of Samuel's influence.

which are political and military rather than truly religious (verse 20). The request is seen as a rejection of God's rule (I Samuel 8: 7). However, this does not indicate that kingship was not in God's purpose, nor does it mean that kingship is granted solely as a rope for the people to hang themselves. We must distinguish between the kind of kingship asked for and the kind of kingship which lay in God's purposes. If the people hang themselves, it is by means of Saul. Saul is God's answer to the wrong motives of the Israelites, but at the same time the opportunity remains for Saul to prove himself and to succeed as God's anointed.

Kingship as such was already a permitted possibility in the words of Moses. In Deuteronomy 17: 14–20 we have the pattern of true kingship which is fully consistent with the theocratic ideals of Sinai. Essentially this king exemplifies the law in his life and does not lift up his heart above his brethren (verse 20). He is contrasted with the oriental despotic monarch who uses his position for personal aggrandizement and exercises an absolute power which is inconsistent with theocracy (verses 16–17). It would appear that Samuel has this Deuteronomic prescription for kingship in mind when he warns the people of the folly of desiring to be ruled by a despot (I Samuel 8: 10–18). He understands only too well that political stability can be bought at a very heavy price; the 'law and order' ticket has been the crowd-winner for dictators all through the ages.

The pattern of Saul's behaviour may be discerned very early in his reign. He appears with all the charisma of the hero warriors that we know as judges (I Samuel 10: 23–24, 11: 5–15), but also with all the seeds of corruption and of rejection of his theocratic position as the Lord's anointed (I Samuel 13: 13–14, 15: 10–31). Samuel, as prophet, remains the Lord's spokesman and brings the word of judgement against the disobedient Saul. This relationship of prophet to king will persist throughout the monarchy in Israel, for the prophet is ever the guardian of the covenant of Sinai against which the lives of all Israelites are measured.

Positively, then, Saul is one mere link in a chain of historical figures who represent the purpose of God to administer salvation through a human mediator. Saul's significance as the 'Lord's anointed' becomes of prime importance to David so that, even when Saul is seeking to kill David, he will not retaliate. However imperfectly he does it, Saul brings a coherence to rulership in Israel that has not existed since the wilderness days. We should not let the negative elements in Saul detract from the positive significance of his reign. It is characteristic of the Old Testament persons and events that despite their imperfections, they foreshadow the perfect which is to come (I Cor. 13: 10). In fact it must be this, for if the foreshadowings were perfect they would no longer be mere shadows and would become the solid reality. Saul, along with the judges before him, and the kings after him, is part of the historical foundation laid in the Old Testament for the revelation of the perfect human king, Jesus of Nazareth, who mediates God's rule.

David

The length of Saul's reign is difficult to ascertain and the narrative does not dwell on it longer than to indicate the salient features. However, Saul's rejection by the prophet Samuel (Samuel 13: 14, 15: 26–28) serves not so much as the precursor of Saul's death as of the introduction of Saul's successor David. 'The Lord repented that he had made Saul king over Israel' (I Samuel 15: 35) is the preface to the events in chapter 16.

For the second time Samuel is called upon to designate the Lord's anointed. This time the narrative describes with great dramatic effect the choice of Jesse's youngest son as the man after God's own heart (I Samuel 13: 14). Since this takes place long before Saul's death, the story records the drawn-out rivalry between the two men that ends only with Saul's suicide in the battle of Gilboa. During this period from the anointing of David to the death of Saul the narrative focuses not on Saul but upon David as the up-and-coming ruler.

The first major event recorded in David's experience as the anointed one, is his slaying of Goliath (I Samuel 17). Here we see another part of the transition from judge-saviour to king-saviour. David, the anointed one, challenges the enemy of God's people and kills the giant with the same result as the victories of the judges. It is a saving event in which the chosen mediator wins the victory, while the ordinary people stand by until they can share in the fruits of the saviour's victory. Preparation is thus made for the gospel events in which God's Christ (Anointed One) wins the victory over sin and death on behalf of his people.

Until the death of Saul increasing tension between himself and David shows Saul's appalling jealousy of the one chosen to succeed him. David, by contrast, is completely subdued by his regard for Saul's office as the anointed king. Though persecuted by Saul and forced to roam the wilderness with a band of outlaws, David steadfastly refuses to pre-empt the sovereignty of God by killing the Lord's anointed (I Samuel 24: 4–6, 26: 8–11). The hapless Amalekite, who seeks to curry favour with David by claiming to have killed his persecutor, learns the hard way the strength of David's convictions in this matter (2 Samuel 1: 14–16). Again we can distinguish part of the pattern-making aspect of those events in the rejection and suffering of the king-designate before he is vindicated and raised to the throne to rule in glory.

David's reign continues to exhibit the mixture of theocratic ideal and human sinfulness that has characterized salvation history. Indeed if it were not for the prophetic assessments of David made after his death, in which the ideals of God's rule through human kingship are stressed, we might wonder at times if David is much of an improvement upon Saul. Certainly his rule sees a growth in prosperity and the stabilizing of the whole political, economic and military scene. But even that aspect, as we well know from the ministry of Samuel, is full of potential for evil. Furthermore, the portrayal of David as an adulterer and murderer hardly enhances the theocratic ideal!

In order to maintain the proper perspective on David we must preserve the framework of the covenant and salvation history. The stability and prosperity achieved by David in finally removing the threat of Philistine incursion into the promised land, and also in rooting out the last pockets of Canaanite influence, represent fulfilment of the covenant promises. Now some substance is given to the covenant summary, 'I will be your God, you shall be my people'.

It is at this point that a new prophetic word is heard, giving an important perspective on the significance of David. Now that the wanderings of Israel have ceased and the people possess the land as promised to Abraham, the obvious symbol of God's dwelling would be a permanent temple rather than the portable tent-tabernacle. Such a temple is eventually built by Solomon, but at this juncture an important clue is given to the way in which the tabernacle-temple symbolism will reach its true fulfilment in God's kingdom. Nathan's prophecy to David (II Samuel 7) is in a sense a word out of due time, for it anticipates a prophetic perspective which does not fully emerge until the latter prophets, beginning with Amos and Hosea.

The following key points emerge from Nathan's prophecy in II Samuel 7:

(a) David proposes to build God a dwelling, yet this has never been commanded by God (verses 5–7).
(b) God declares that he will build a house for David as he gives rest to his people (verses 8–11).
(c) This house is a dynasty of David's royal descendants and David's son will build God's dwelling (verses 12–13).[14]
(d) David's son will be the personal embodiment of the people of God and is declared to be God's son (verse 14).[15]

There is much more that could be said about David's reign, but we must be content with these few theological aspects and turn to the significance of Solomon as David's son.

Solomon

The first and obvious point to note about Solomon is that as the son of David he fulfils in an immediate sense Nathan's prediction that the house of God would be built by such a son. But Solomon must be remembered for more than his temple building activity. In fact he is an enigma,

---

[14] There is a play here on the Hebrew word *bayit*. On the one hand it signifies *house* meaning 'dwelling', and on the other it signifies *house* meaning 'household' or 'dynasty'.

[15] It is reasonable to suggest that 'I will be his father, and he shall be my son' is an individualizing of the covenant statement 'I will be your God and you shall be my people'. David's line is thus declared to be representative of God's people or, to put it another way, David's son is the true Israel.

for he was both the perfecter of Israel's glory and the architect of its destruction.

The form of the narrative of Solomon's reign in I Kings is instructive. The problem of the throne succession having been settled in Solomon's favour, the narrator deals at once with two apparently contradictory aspects of Solomon's behaviour. First we are told of the marriage alliance with the king of Egypt (I Kings 3: 1), which becomes a cause of stumbling in that it is the first stage of the apostasy described in Chapter 11: 1–13. Secondly we are told of Solomon's desire for an understanding mind – a request which receives God's commendation.

The wisdom of Solomon and the splendour of his kingdom go hand in hand, and both are seen as undergirding national prosperity and safety: 'Judah and Israel dwelt in safety, from Dan to Beersheba, every man under his vine and under his fig tree, all the days of Solomon' (I Kings 4: 25). So the writer sums up the situation in a way that suggests that the prosperity of Solomon's reign is indicative of the fulfilment of the promises to Abraham. The people are in the land, they are safe, and the land yields its fruit in Eden-like plenty.

Solomon's wisdom, at first sight, is found in strange company. 'God gave Solomon wisdom and understanding beyond measure, and largeness of mind like the sand of the seashore, so that Solomon's wisdom surpassed the wisdom of all the people of the east, and all the wisdom of Egypt' (I Kings 4: 29–30). Clearly Solomon's wisdom was of a kind that might be compared with that of pagans. The narrative describes the 'wise men' of other lands coming to hear Solomon (chapter 4: 34), as well as the adulation of the Phoenician king Hiram (chapter 5: 7), and of the Queen of Sheba who came to test Solomon's wisdom (chapter 10: 1–5).

We know from the book of Proverbs that 'wisdom' was seen as concerned with the complexities of daily life and with the real world of human experience. As such it would naturally be a concern of all men, Israelite and pagan alike. Perhaps it was this very worldliness of the wisdom of Solomon (see I Kings 4: 32–33) that made it possible for a wise man to move from a wisdom guarded by the framework of the 'fear of the Lord' (Proverbs 1: 7) into a wisdom which spoke of the same things but which forgot the revealed will of God.

So Solomon, who beautified Israel with the Temple (I Kings 7 and 8), becomes the apostate from whom the kingdom is removed with a word that recalls the rejection of Saul – 'I will surely tear the kingdom from you and give it to your servant' (I Kings 11: 11). The story which follows is a long one which leads firstly to the division of the kingdom with the revolt of the northern tribes against Rehoboam, and then to the decline and fall of both North and South.

We must be content here to point out only the salient feature of the history of the divided kingdom. Both the kingdom of Israel and the kingdom of Judah move with gathering momentum towards a cataclysmic judgement of God upon their sinful rejection of the covenant. The final outcome of Solomon's apostasy is the obliteration of the natural existence of Israel. All that the covenant to Abraham had promised was under Solomon both realized and lost. To say this is to say that the realization of the promises must be qualified by all the deficiencies due to human sinfulness. In whatever sense the Kingdom of God is fulfilled in Solomon's reign, something is yet lacking. The pattern of Kingdom existence is certainly there, but its perfection is not. If the united Kingdom fulfils the covenant promises it does so only in shadow. So if God is faithful, the solid substance of that fulfilment must be yet to come. Such is the message of the prophets.

Chapter Eight

The Kingdom Revealed in Prophecy

The 'Old Order' Prophets

For the purposes of our discussion we may divide the prophets of Israel into two main groups. The first group comprises the prophets who live in the period of the Kingdom in history (as described in Chapter 7) and whose message is mainly orientated to that epoch of revelation. The second group consists of those living in the period after the schism between Judah and Israel when the history of Israel ceases to contribute positively to the revelation of the Kingdom.

We may note that the first group contains the 'non-writing' prophets while the second group contains the 'writing' prophets.[1] It is reasonable to ask why the later prophets, from Amos on, have their oracles preserved in books while the earlier ones are known only in the context of wider historical narratives. The answer may well lie partly in the fact that the writing prophets belong to a new

---

[1] This terminology is not precise since it is not at all clear how much of the prophetic literature was actually written by the prophets themselves. Essentially the prophetic oracle was a spoken word and its committal to writing was a subsequent event.

epoch of revelation of the Kingdom of God and consequently there is a greater need for the new revelation to be
preserved in a formal way.

The 'old order' prophets belong to the Kingdom of God
as it is revealed in Israel's history. The definitive prophet
of this period is Moses (see Deuteronomy 18: 15–22, 34:
10–12 and Numbers 12: 6–8). In the Old Testament a variety of activities are described as prophetic so that we must
avoid being simplistic in the description of the prophetic
office. Nevertheless it is fair to say that a prophet was
essentially one who was called to communicate God's revelation to men. This is the aspect that we now consider.

In the epoch of Kingdom revelation in Israel's history, it
is Moses who mediates (i.e. communicates) the declared
purpose of God to save Israel out of Egypt, and who is
God's instrument in carrying out this purpose. Later, it is
Moses who receives the covenant law of Sinai by which
the people are constituted as the people of God's kingdom. The entire history of the fulfilment of God's promises to Abraham, as it is worked out from Moses to
Solomon, is regulated by the Kingdom ideal contained in
the Sinai covenant. The history of Israel in the promised
land is given its meaning within the framework of the
promise to Abraham, the release from Egypt, and the covenant of Sinai.

All the prophets after Moses stand as the watchdogs of
the society of God's people, working always within the
framework of the covenant of Sinai. The prophets hold the
law as a mirror so that individuals and the whole nation
may see how they transgress. They call people back to
faithful obedience to the covenant and, when necessary,
denounce the unbelief and disobedience of their day.

The prophetic office is closely related to the conditions
laid down for enjoyment of the Covenant blessings.
Although Israel's salvation has for its basis God's gracious

acts in saving the people out of Egypt, there is a close link between enjoyment of the final outcome of salvation and Israel's obedience. At first sight this appears to mean that Israel's salvation is achieved by obedience to the law, but this is not so. Grace comes first in the saving acts of God, then law binds the saved people to God as his people. Should these people refuse to accept their responsibility to live as God's people, then they must suffer removal from the land of blessing.[2] This conditional nature of blessing is clearly set out in many parts of the Sinai covenant, not least in the Ten Commandments (Exodus 20: 5–6,7 and 12) and in Deuteronomy (for example see Deuteronomy 11: 26–32, 28: 1–68, 30: 15–20).

Samuel, Nathan, Gad, Ahijah and Shemaiah are among the prophets of the age of prophecy stretching from Moses to Elijah and Elisha. All of these men are orientated towards the Sinai covenant and the maintenance of the Kingdom of God as it is meant to be expressed in the history of Israel. Even, when the kingdom of Israel is divided and begins on the slippery down-grade to destruction, the overlapping ministries of Elijah and Elisha combine in an effort to bring the people of God back to the covenant obedience. In keeping with this here-and-now concern of the prophets we find that their words of judgement and grace are worked out in the context of the present Kingdom epoch.

---

[2] The relationship of good works to salvation is essentially the same in both Old and New Testaments. In both salvation is by grace, but grace never stands alone without good works. To put it another way we may say that no-one (in Old or New Testaments) is saved *because* of good works, but no-one is saved *without* good works. This is one aspect of the unity of the two Testaments which makes the Old Testament so applicable to Christians. The same unity underlies Paul's use of the exodus situation in I Corinthians 10: 1–12.

Pre-Exilic Prophets

With the ministry of Amos we enter into a new period of
prophecy which both continues certain features of the old
order and also introduces some significant new characteristics. While we must be careful not to oversimplify the
prophetic message, it is possible to discern a distinct
development in emphasis particularly in the prophetic
view of eschatology[3] or the end time.

Transgression of the Law

There are three essential ingredients in the oracles of
these latter prophets. First there is the covenant of Sinai
which remains the rule of faith and behaviour. This
God-given law is never considered a temporary thing.
It stands as the expression of God's character which is
unchanging, and as such it is the point of reference
when the prophets interpret events as God's dealings
with Israel. Against this law the conduct of the covenant people is seen to be lacking and a terrible provoca-
tion towards God. Whatever specific aspect of
transgression the individual prophets concentrate on,
the underlying implications are always the same –
Israel (or Judah) has broken covenant with the merciful
God who saved this people for himself.

Amos, for example, emphasizes social injustices:
Amos 1: 6–8,4: 1–3, 5: 10–13, 8: 4–6. Isaiah's opening
chapters detail the formalism of Israel's worship as well
as outright idolatry and apostasy. Ezekiel stresses the
apostasy in Judah before the final destruction of Jerusalem in 586 B.C. The prophets do not really differentiate

---

[3] The study of the last things (*eschatos* means 'last' in Greek) or
of the end of the age.

between social and religious sins any more than the Sinai covenant does. All sin is transgression of the covenant.

Judgement

Secondly, the prophets are the dutiful mediators of the message of judgement. The particularizing of covenant-breaking in the accusations against various forms of evil-doing is the grounds for the pronouncement of impending judgement. Insofar as these prophets are still orientated to the present Kingdom epoch, there is a conditional element to the message which indicates that repentance and faithful obedience may yet avert the judgement. More and more, however, the prophets present a picture of a terrible and final judgement. This aspect partly reflects the reality of the situation in that history gave no grounds for optimism. Given the pattern of rebelliousness that can be discerned from the very moment Israel is saved from the Egyptian captivity (Exodus 15: 22–24, 16: 1–3. See also Psalm 95: 8–11), there is little basis for confidence in the outcome unless this sinful bent of human character is taken care of. Consequently we notice a growing sense of the inevitable course of history towards the self-destruction of the covenant people. Even the most concerted efforts at reform are powerless to correct the situation (see II Kings 23: 24–27).

The form of the judgement to come is described in various ways but we may discern two emphases. One is to depict *a fairly immediate and local judgement* of God, and even retrospectively to point to *past events* as warning judgments (Amos 4: 6–11). In the northern kingdom of Israel the approaching doom is pin-pointed as the Assyrian invasion which subsequently brought about the end of that nation in 722 B.C. (Hosea 9: 1–6, 10: 5–10, 11: 5). In

Judah the fate of Israel is cited as a warning and example (Isaiah 10: 10–11, Ezekiel 16: 51, 23: 1–11) and a similar fate at the hands of Babylon is predicted (Isaiah 39, Jeremiah 1: 13–16, 20: 4–6, 22: 24–27). The Other emphasis is to portray judgement as something which is *of universal or cosmic proportions* (Jeremiah 4: 23–26, Isaiah 2: 2–22, 13: 5–10, 24: 1–23, Nahum 1: 4–6, Habakkuk 3: 3–12, Zephaniah 1: 2–3, 18, 3: 8, Ezekiel 38: 19–23).

We cannot separate these emphases of the judgement oracles as if the prophets clearly distinguished the judgement upon Israel and Judah from universal judgement. From our vantage point in time we see separate historical events – the destruction of Samaria in 722 B.C. and the destruction of Jerusalem in 586 B.C. – and we may anticipate a future final judgement. But we must not think that the failure of prophecy to distinguish clearly between these two aspects is due purely to a lack of historical perspective. Theologically all these manifestations of judgement are inextricably bound together. God's judgement of sin in the covenant people is not in principle different from his judging sin in all humanity.

Salvation

The third major element in prophetic preaching is the declaration that God is faithful to the covenant and on that basis he will save a remnant of the people to be his own true possession. Like the judgement oracles, the salvation oracles depict two related aspects of saving restoration. God will restore the covenant people to their inheritance and he will also restore the whole universe to a glory which has not been known since man was ejected from Eden. We will reserve a detailed discussion of the salvation oracles until later in this chapter when we look at the kingdom pattern in prophecy.

The Nations

There is another prominent feature in prophetic preaching which demands comment, Although little evidence exists outside the Book of Jonah that prophets ever preached to the Gentiles, there are many recorded oracles directed against the nations although preached to Israel or Judah. In fact these oracles are of such significance that they have sometimes been collected and presented as a group in the formation of the prophetic books (So Amos 1–2, Isaiah 13–23, Jeremiah 46–51, Ezekiel, 25–32).

The judgement against the nations is part of the overall judgement of God against sin which is noted above. We should also note, however, the relationship of judgement to salvation. In judging the nations God is putting down all rebellion against him. This activity is integral to the establishing of the Kingdom of God. Thus the judgement of the nations is seen not only as part of general judgement but also as the accompaniment of the salvation of God's people. God is the warrior who fights for his people and rescues them from captivity and oppression (Exodus 14: 14, 15: 3–6, Deuteronomy 9: 3–5, Psalm 68). He will judge the nations for having directed their ungodliness at God's own people (Joel 3: 1–21, Habakkuk 3: 6–13, Zephaniah 2: 5–15, Haggai 2: 21–23, Jeremiah 46: 27–28, 50: 29–34, 51: 24).

The Exilic and Post-Exilic Prophets

The exilic prophets, Ezekiel and Daniel[4], are those who ministered to the exiles in Babylon. The post-exilic

---

[4] We include Daniel among the prophets although in the Hebrew Old Testament this book is not placed with the other prophetic books. (See also Chapter Three, note 1).

prophets, Haggai, Zechariah and Malachi, ministered
to the restored community after the return from Babylon. We note them here only to point out that, with the
Babylonian catastrophe either a present reality or a past
event, these prophets place a greater emphasis on the
universal and final acts of God both in salvation and
judgement. It is during this period that a new way of
expressing future expectations is developed in the form
of *apocalyptic*.

Actually most Jewish apocalyptic writings appeared
in the period between the two testaments, but some elements of it may be discerned in Daniel and Zechariah.[5]
In the visions of Daniel chapter 7 and 8 and Zechariah
chapters 1 to 6 many apocalyptic characteristics are
seen, including symbolism and bizarre imagery. More
important for this discussion is the highly developed
sense that the present age will end and a new age will be
introduced in which God's kingdom is established. The
Kingdom is seen as God's new creation which cannot
be brought in by reformation, but only by a radical
upheaval of the whole created order.

Just as the pre-exilic prophets had to interpret the
failure of Solomon's kingdom and project the hope of
the believer for the Kingdom of God into the future, the
post-exilic prophets were given the task of interpreting
the manifest failure of the return from exile to produce
the Kingdom. Once again the human cause is identified
as sin, and the remedy is to be a final and decisive intervention of God in the future.

---

[5] For a discussion of the characteristics of apocalyptic see Leon
Morris: *Apocalyptic* (London: IVP, 1972) or articles in any Bible
dictionary.

The Kingdom Pattern in Prophecy

Now we return to the pattern of future hope to which all the writing prophets contributed. It may be summed up quite simply – the form of future history will be a replay of past history but with a significant difference. All the hope for the future is expressed in terms of a return to the Kingdom structures revealed in the history of Israel from the Exodus to Solomon. The great difference is that none of the weaknesses of the past will be present. In short, sin and its effects will be eradicated.

The prophets depict a continuity from the past to the future as well as a distinction between them. All that God has revealed about his Kingdom through Israel's history remains valid. But it is modified to the extent that the new view of the Kingdom leaves no place for a further disruption and decline. The restored Kingdom will be in the context of a new heaven and a new earth, and all this new creation of God will be permanent, perfect and glorious.

The simplest way to demonstrate this characteristic of prophetic hope is to list the ingredients of Israel's history which add up to the pattern of the Kingdom of God and then show how these are repeated in the prophetic futurism. In the previous chapter we saw the following features:

i.   Captivity as a contradiction to the Kingdom.
ii. The Exodus events as God's mighty act of salvation on the basis of the Abrahamic covenant.
iii. The Sinai covenant binding Israel to God as his people.
iv. The entry and possession of Canaan.
v.   The focusing of God's rule through the Temple, the Davidic king, and the city of Jerusalem.

Why does God move at all to do a work of salvation for a rebellious nation? From the point of view of the Old Testament it is because he is faithful to his covenant made with

Abraham as an everlasting covenant (Genesis 17: 7). God wills to show steadfast love or covenant love to his chosen people (Isaiah 54: 7–8, 55: 3, Jeremiah 33: 10–11, Micah 7: 18–20).[6]

Now on the basis of this covenant love God is doing a new work, and each of the features of the historic kingdom revelation will be renewed in the last days when God acts finally for salvation.

1. *The new captivity* The predictions of the pre-exilic prophets that Judah will be devastated and the people taken to Babylon provide a very obvious analogy with the Egyptian captivity, which is not overlooked. There is one new development. The reason for this captivity is clearly stated as sin or transgression of the covenant.

2. *The new exodus* The pattern of the Egyptian exodus is recalled in many oracles of the return from Babylon (Jeremiah 16: 14–15, 23: 7–8, Isaiah 43: 15–21). A number of passages in Isaiah allude to the exodus from Egypt in describing the coming exodus from Babylon (Isaiah 40: 3–4, 41: 17–20, 42: 7, 43: 1–2, 16–20, 48: 20–21, 49: 24–26, 51: 9–11, 52: 3–4, 11–12, 61–1).

3. *The new covenant* From one point of view it is accurate to say that the prophets see a renewal of several covenants – the Noahic (Isaiah 54: 8–10), the Abrahamic (Isaiah 49: 5–9, Jeremiah 33: 25–26), the Mosaic (Jeremiah 31: 31–36) and the Davidic (Jeremiah 33: 19–26). But it is easy to see from Jeremiah 33: 19–26 that the Abrahamic and Davidic covenants are closely related.

---

[6] The Hebrew word *hesed* is commonly translated *mercy* or *steadfast love*. It is a technical term which expresses the idea of faithfulness to a covenant bond. Consequently it is a favourite word evoking praise and thanksgiving from the faithful as they contemplate God's covenant faithfulness. See, for example, Psalm 136 where each verse contains the refrain 'for his *hesed* endures for ever'.

There is in fact an essential unity to all the covenants. Jeremiah shows the unity between the Mosaic covenant and the new covenant (chapter 31: 31–34), for the new covenant is not a new thing replacing the old, but rather the old renewed and applied in such a way that it will be perfectly kept.

4. *The new nation* The prophets predict the return of a renewed people, a faithful remnant. This is a people whose heart is changed and to whom a new spirit is given so that law is fulfilled within them (Isaiah 10: 20–22,46: 3–4,51: 11, Jeremiah 23: 3, 31: 7, Ezekiel 36: 25–28). Then God will establish the nation in the land and Zion will be rebuilt (Isaiah 44: 24–28,46: 13, 49: 14–21, 51:3, 60:3–14). The new Temple in Zion will be glorious (Ezekiel 40–47) and it will be a work of the spirit of God (Zechariah 4: 6–9). In accordance with the covenant with David (II Samuel 7), the new David will reign as God's shepherd king over his people (Isaiah. 11: 1, Jeremiah 23: 5–8,33: 14–26, Ezekiel 34: 11–13, 23–25, 37: 24–28). And when all this glory of the new Zion is revealed, the nations will also receive a blessing in accordance with the promise to Abraham (Gen. 12:3, cf. Isa. 2: 2–4, Micah 4: 1–4, Zech. 8: 20–23).

5. *The new creation* We have already seen that there is a continuity between the Kingdom of God revealed in Eden and the Kingdom of God revealed in Israel's history. It is therefore not surprising that the prophets occasionally refer to the Edenic kingdom as the pattern for the new kingdom to come, and even mingle elements of Eden and Canaan. Isaiah speaks of the redemption of Israel in the framework of the new creation, new heaven and a new earth (Isaiah 65: 17–21) In the context of this cosmic re-creation the new Jerusalem is a new Eden in which the harmony of nature is restored (cf. Isaiah 11: 1–9). All the references to the

deserts becoming fertile recall the expectations that
Canaan would be a land flowing with, milk and honey
– an imagery borrowed from Eden (see Isaiah 41: 18–
20). God will make Zion's wilderness like Eden (Isaiah
51: 3, Ezekiel 36: 33–36).

Postscript

When Judah is restored after the Persian takeover in 538
B.C., the situation is to all intents and purposes set for the
great day of salvation predicted by the prophets. In fact
such fulfilment of prophecy as does take place is only a
pale shadow of the expectation. The books of Ezra and
Nehemiah, along with Haggai, Zechariah, and Malachi,
give quite a clear picture of the reconstruction. All the
ingredients of the Kingdom promises are there but, far
from exceeding the former glory, they do not come anywhere near to even matching it. Hence the need for the
post-exilic prophets to explain why this is not the hoped-
for day, and to project hope into the future yet again. This
hope is often to flicker like a candle in the wind as year
after year sees change but never true release from the
oppressive domination of foreigners.

After the close of the Old Testament era during the Persian ascendancy the Jews underwent many trials. More
than once the covenant faith was seriously threatened by
pagan philosophies and lifestyles. The Temple was dese-
crated by Hellenists and many martyrs shed their blood.[7]

---

[7] Alexander the Great brought Greek power and culture into
the biblical world towards the end of the fourth century B.C.
After his death in 323 there was continual strife and rivalry for
power until the advent of the Romans. The conflict of Hellenism
with the faith of the Jews is well illustrated in the apocryphal
books of I and II Maccabees.

Jewish faith developed different expressions through numbers of sects – Pharisees, Sadducees, Zealots, Essenes – while power in the Near East changed hands from the Persians to the Greeks and finally to the might of Imperial Rome. Through it all a faithful remnant waited for the consolation of Israel.

Chapter Nine

The Kingdom Revealed in Jesus Christ

Most Christians have some idea of a link between the Old Testament and the New Testament. For many it amounts to little more than a belief that some messianic prophecies were fulfilled by the coming of Jesus. In Chapter 2 we saw that any recognition of a unity of the whole Bible demands that we seek to know what kind of unity exists in order to be able to relate the Old to the New. In Chapter 3 we saw that being a Christian implies a certain method of approach to the unity of the Bible. To be a Christian is to recognize in Jesus Christ the goal of all things including the goal of the history of redemption. Because Jesus Christ is the perfect image of God (Colossians 1: 15–20, 2: 9–10, Hebrews 1: 3) we see him as the one towards whom all the former revelation of God is leading, and in whom it is fulfilled and given its meaning.

That the Old Testament anticipates the New and is fulfilled in the New is underlined by many general statements of the New Testament:

'In many and various ways God spoke of old to our fathers by the prophets; but in these last days he has spoken to us by a Son, whom he appointed the heir of all things' (Hebrews 1:

1–12). 'For all the promises of God find their Yes in him' (II Corinthians 1: 20).

'We bring you the good news that what God promised to the fathers, this he has fulfilled to us their children by raising Jesus' (Acts 13: 32–33).

'Beginning with Moses and all the prophets, he interpreted to them in all the scriptures the things concerning himself' (Luke 24: 27).

It is important that we understand very clearly that this fact of the Old Testament's progression towards a fulfilment in the New is not merely an invitation to understand Jesus Christ as the end of the process. It is also a demand that the whole Bible be understood in the light of the gospel. It means that Jesus Christ is the key to the interpretation of the whole Bible, and the task before us is to discern *how* he interprets the Bible. It should be realized at the outset that when we speak of Jesus Christ as the key to interpretation we must speak of Jesus Christ as he is revealed – the Christ of the gospel. It is not sufficient to stress the ethics of the man Jesus of Nazareth out of the context of the saving acts of God (as many liberals do), nor to stress the supernatural presence of the Christ with the believer out of the context of the meaning of the historical humanity of God come in the flesh (as many evangelicals do). Obviously we need to be clear about the gospel itself if we are to be clear about the significance of Christ for interpreting the Bible.

The Gospel

What is the gospel? Pick any ten Christians and ask them this question and you will probably get ten different

answers. Perhaps none of them will be wholly wrong, but
the difference will suggest a certain confusion. Take two
extremes to illustrate. The liberal Christian often stresses
the *humanity* of Jesus. Jesus was a good man, in fact the
only truly good man. The gospel of the good man must be
reduced to some kind of example to follow, a demonstration inviting us to try to do likewise. There is obviously
some truth in this view. On the other hand the evangelical
often stresses the divinity of Jesus. The Christ is the supernatural Son of God who is alive today in the hearts of
believers. The gospel of the divine Christ tends to be one
of the supernaturally changed life. And there is obviously
some truth in that.

Let us be clear on this point. To suggest that these two
views are extremes containing some of the truth is not in
any way at all to propose that we need a balance or a middle road which recognizes a little of each extreme. It is
rather an invitation to come to grips with the biblical
perspective.

Essentially the gospel is a declaration of what God has
done *for* us in Jesus Christ, rather than (as is often implied)
what God does in the believer, although we may not separate the two. It is the objective historical facts of the coming of Jesus in the flesh and the God-given interpretation
of those facts. When Peter preached the gospel at Pentecost he was quick to divert attention from what God had
done in the apostles by the giving of the Holy Spirit, and to
concentrate on the facts concerning Jesus of Nazareth
(Acts 2: 14–36).

The facts are those of the incarnation, of the perfect life
of Jesus of Nazareth, and of his dying and rising from the
grave. The interpretation of the facts is that this took place
'for us men and for our salvation'. In these two simple
statements of fact and interpretation we sum up the
breadth and depth of biblical revelation.

In referring to the birth of Jesus as *incarnation* we take seriously the biblical assertion that this was no mere man, nor even a man with some divine qualities. The baby in the manger was at one and the same time, in one and the same person, both Son of God *and* son of man – both fully divine *and* fully human; both God *and* man. Without the recognition that Jesus Christ was truly God and truly man we cannot maintain the gospel as good news nor as the power of God for salvation. This is why belief in the incarnation is not merely a theoretical matter. The gospel is saying that, what man cannot do in order to be accepted with God, this God himself has done for us in the person of Jesus Christ. To be acceptable to God we must present to God a life of perfect and unceasing obedience to his will.

The gospel declares that Jesus has done this *for us*. For God to be righteous he must deal with our sin. This also he has done *for us* in Jesus. The holy law of God was lived out perfectly *for us* by Christ, and its penalty was paid perfectly for us by Christ. This living and dying of Christ *for us*, and this alone is the basis of our acceptance with God.

Only the God-Man Jesus Christ could both live the true sinless human life and rise victorious over death after paying the penalty for man's sin. We cannot understand how the one person, Jesus Christ, contained two distinguishable yet inseparable natures. No more could the apostles understand it, yet they were driven to accept the fact as integral to the gospel. About this we shall have more to say later.

To sum up: the gospel is what God has done for us in Christ for our salvation. And as the two natures of this Christ must be distinguished, so also we must distinguish what God does *for us* and what God does *in us*. Likewise, as we must not separate the two natures of Christ, neither must we separate the gospel from the fruit of the gospel. It is by the gospel that we are born again (I Peter 1: 23–25), it is the gospel that evokes true faith (Romans 10: 17), and it is the gospel which produces the sanctified or Spirit-filled life (Colossians 1: 56).[1] Now, somehow all this is related to the Old Testament, and we must try to understand how.

The Gospel of the Kingdom

The gospel is sometimes referred to as 'the gospel of the kingdom' (Matthew 4: 23,9: 35, 24: 14). Mark informs us that Jesus preached the gospel of God by declaring that 'the kingdom of God is at hand' (Mark 1: 14–15). The theme of the gospel has to do with the Kingdom, and this idea of Kingdom is not something completely new – it is 'at hand' because the 'time is fulfilled'. What is more, the term 'kingdom of God' must have meant something to those who heard Jesus even though it is not of itself an Old Testament term.[2]

The unavoidable conclusion from the New Testament evidence is that the gospel fulfils the Old Testament hope of the coming of the Kingdom of God. But we

---

[1] It will be seen from this that the mystery of the incarnation is of the same order as the mystery of the Trinity – three persons, one God. This is to be expected if Jesus is the supreme revelation of the Triune God. Furthermore, just as we must distinguish but not separate the two natures of Christ, so also we must distinguish but not separate the three persons of the Godhead. To rightly distinguish is to express the unity of the three without confusing them. Thus we must not confuse the Son with the Spirit, not the work of the Son with the work of the Spirit. Hence the need to be clear about the distinctions between God's work for us in the Son, and God's work in us by the Spirit.

[2] The theme of the Kingdom of God as a unifying element in the Bible is discussed by John Bright in *The Kingdom of God* (New York: Abingdon Press, 1955).

must be more specific about what this means and how it is worked out in the New Testament itself. We have looked at the Kingdom idea in the Old Testament as it is expressed in three distinct yet related epochs or strata – Eden, Israel's history, and prophetic futurism. If the gospel fulfils the expectations of the Kingdom we should be able to discern how this is so by looking at the New Testament evidence. Furthermore, we are now in a position to clarify one aspect of biblical interpretation. The fact that the various strata of Kingdom revelation in the Bible define the progressive nature of revelation reminds us of the diversity of expression within the overall unity. Each kingdom expression – Eden, Israel, Prophetic Kingdom, and now the Gospel – represents the same reality, but each expresses that reality in a different (yet related) way.

Related – yet different! Each kingdom expression differs from those that preceded it. But many Christians do not understand the implications of this fact. For the New Testament says that the reality is in the gospel – in Christ himself. That is why he must interpret all Scripture. Now some Christians see the implications of their view of the inspiration and authority of Scripture as requiring what they call a literal interpretation of Scripture. But this is not so if by literal is meant that fulfilment must be in the precise terms of the promise, and that the reality is only a future repetition of the foreshadowing.

The New Testament knows nothing of this kind of literalism. It repeatedly maintains that Christ is the fulfilment of these terms, images, promises and foreshadowings in the Old Testament which were presented in a way that is different from the fulfilment. For the New Testament the interpretation of the Old Testament is not 'literal' but 'Christological'. That is to say that the coming of the Christ transforms all the Kingdom terms of the Old Testament into gospel reality.[3] Let us examine this process of transformation in more detail.

The People of the Kingdom

The first element of our Old Testament Kingdom of God was the people of God. In Eden God's people is Adam and Eve.[4] In Israel's history, the people of God is essentially the descendants of Abraham through Isaac and Jacob. In prophetic hope, the people of God is the faithful remnant of Israel. In the gospel, the people of God is Jesus Christ.

First, Jesus is depicted as *the true Adam* (or last Adam). Consider the following:

Jesus is descended from Adam (Luke 3: 23–38).
Jesus overcomes temptation where Adam failed (Mark 1: 12–13).
Jesus' baptism identifies him with Adam's race (Luke 3: 21–22).
Jesus is the last Adam (Romans 5: 18–21, I Corinthians 15: 20–22; 45–49).

---

[3] Not everything is necessarily changed and obviously literalness remains applicable to some aspects of prophetic fulfilment. Thus messianic prophecies regarding the birth of a child and the place of Bethlehem are fulfilled literally. This literalness is a function of the fact that in order to redeem sinners God enters into the fallen world of sinners. The whole point of the incarnation is that God enters into an intimate relationship with our world through Jesus Christ.

[4] This is not bad grammar! 'People' in Hebrew is a collective singular referring to the nation or race as a single entity thus signifying a solidarity. In modern English usage people often has come to be weakened to a plural of person or individual.

Jesus is the Son of Man (a term meaning human being and thus a member of Adam's race).[5]

Secondly, Jesus is the *seed of Abraham*. On first reading Paul is using unfair tactics when he argues this point in Galatians 3: 16.[6] But Paul's argument comes out of the whole Old Testament background in which the solidarity of the race with its head is to be discerned. Paul is establishing that the seed of Abraham, Israel, has its meaning only in Christ. He alone is the true Israel. The same point is seen in the Gospels. Matthew's genealogy establishes Jesus as the son of Abraham through David (Matthew 1: 1). Thirdly, Jesus is the true Israel. This is but a development on the last point, for Israel is the seed of Abraham. Matthew makes this point when he applies Hosea's backward reference to the exodus – 'out of Egypt have I called my son' – to the return of Jesus, Mary and Joseph after the death of Herod (Matthew 2: 15). Whatever else it may signify, the application of an historical reference concerning Israel to a similar event in Jesus' life must imply some kind of identity to warrant the description of 'fulfilment'. We also note the account of Jesus' temptation in the wilderness (Matthew 4: 1–11, Luke 4: 1–13). Each of the scriptures quoted by Jesus to counter the temptations comes from the early chapters of Deuteronomy which deal with Israel's temptations in the wilderness of Sinai. The implication is that where old Israel was tempted and failed, Jesus (the true Israel) overcomes.

---

[5] There are numerous references in the Gospel to Jesus as Son of Man. It is certain that many of them link Jesus to Adam via the vision of Daniel 7 where the figure is not only human but also heavenly.

[6] 'Now the promises were made to Abraham and his offspring. It does not say "And to offsprings" referring to many; but referring to one, "And to your offspring", which is Christ'.

Fourthly, Jesus is the *Son of David*. The promise God made to Abraham's descendants was frequently summarized with the great covenant formula, 'I will be their God, they shall be my people'. In II Samuel 7: 14 the son of David has this promise applied to him in a personal way, 'I will be his father, he shall be my son'. The solidarity between leader and people is again expressed. The king embodies the whole people and is their representative.

These various identities of Jesus establish one clear point. Jesus Christ is the head of the new race. All who are united to him are members of that race, but only because he *is* that race. Thus whoever is 'in Christ' is a new creation (II Corinthians 5: 17), that is, he belongs to the new order of which Christ is head.

The Location of the Kingdom

The second element of our Old Testament kingdom we called 'God's place'. This may be a less than satisfactory way of describing the New Testament idea of kingdom which is not confined to such a strict spatial concept as a garden (Eden) or a land (Israel) – though it continues to employ Old Testament terms from time to time. Nevertheless we must find some way to convey the sense of 'place' in the New Testament.

In our first stratum of revelation the place of the kingdom was *Eden*, and in the second it was the *land of Canaan*. Since both are presented as part of this created earth, there is a predictable area of continuity between them despite the fact that one belongs to the period before and the other to the period after the Fall. The third stratum, the prophetic futurist kingdom, adapts the Canaan model of kingdom location but 'glorifies' it. As we have already seen, there emerges in some prophetic predictions a clear mixing of elements which belong to both the previous strata – Eden and Israel's Canaan.

In the Old Testament salvation includes a restoration of God's people into the environment which best fits their restored relationship with God. As Eden represented the perfection of the first creation so the redemptive process entails a remaking of the Eden-paradise. This progression of imagery may thus be summarized as the garden paradise in the beginning, the land 'flowing with milk and honey' in Israel's history, and the new heavens and earth with a new paradise in the prophetic view.

The New Testament continues this progression. Jesus declares his kingdom is not of this world (John 18: 36), yet at the same time the earthly Old Testament images are repeated but with greater clarity. Peter repeats Isaiah's prediction of a new heaven and earth but says it represents such a complete break with things as they are now that this present order must pass away (II Peter 3: 10–13). The Old Testament develops the 'Israel' stratum by focusing on Jerusalem (*Zion*) as the centre of God's land. Thus the prophets often depict the restoration of Zion as the manifestation of the kingdom of God. It is to Zion that the returning faithful remnant come, and likewise it is to Zion that the Gentiles come who are being drawn into the kingdom.

Now, if Israel's hope was that the nation would return to Zion (for example Isaiah 35: 10) we must enquire of the New Testament where Zion is to be found. Hebrews 12: 22 indicates that a Jew comes to Zion by being converted to Christ. Zion is *where Jesus reigns now* at the right hand of God and this is where we come by faith in the gospel.

Another important passage is Hebrews 11: 8–16. Here the theme is the inheritance of God's people, in this case Abraham and the patriarchs. From the interpretative standpoint of the gospel the writer can describe

Abraham's hope in gospel terms – he looked forward to the city which has foundations, whose builder and maker is God (verse 10). Of the patriarchs' hope he maintains that they desired a better country, that is, a heavenly one (verse 16). It is the gospel which enables the writer to transform the Old Testament image, which is bound to this old order, into an aspect of the new order. One other important focal point in the locality of God's kingdom is the Temple. The Temple could function as such a focal point because it represented the dwelling of God among his people. It demonstrated that the promised land was not merely living space for people but was the setting for a relationship between God and man. The Temple was thus integral to the existence of the Kingdom of God and by it the Kingdom could be identified.

The use made of the Temple theme in the New Testament is vital to our understanding of the relationship of Old and New Testaments. One thing is clear: the New Testament declares that the new Temple has already come into existence, for it is none other than Jesus Christ. John describes the incarnation thus: 'The Word was made flesh and dwelt among us' (John 1: 14). The literal translation of the Greek is '. . . and *tabernacled* among us'. In other words, John saw Jesus as resembling the tabernacle in the wilderness. Why is Jesus the Temple? Because he is God dwelling among us.

But the idea is developed even further: Jesus is God and man in closest union. The very being of Jesus is the most perfect relationship of God and man. Thus when Jesus disputes with the Jews over his cleansing of the Temple (John 2: 13–22) he proposes as a sign of his authority: 'Destroy this temple and in three days I will raise it up' (verse 19). His opponents are obsessed by the old order and can think only of the bricks and mortar of Herod's temple. But John tells us that Jesus was referring to his own body as the Temple so that it was his resurrection from the dead which gave the disciples the key to what he had said (verse 22).

These images of locality – garden, land, city, temple – all reach their fulfilment in the gospel. For the New Testament the locality of the Kingdom is Jesus Christ himself. And, lest we be misled by a misplaced and unbiblical emphasis, Jesus Christ is shown as risen and seated on the right hand of God in the heavenly places.[7]

The Rule of the Kingdom

The third element in our Old Testament kingdom pattern is the rule of God over his people by his word. The different covenants of the Bible all testify to this in their own contexts. We may discern two important aspects of this covenant rule of God – the covenants themselves and the mediator of the covenant.

We have already seen how God ruled in Eden by the word which defined Adam's freedom. As for Abraham, not only did God call him, direct him, and make promises to him; the goal of it all was the relationship expressed in the great covenant summary 'I will be your God, you shall be my people'. Later, when Israel understood itself as God's people, this was expressed in the covenant of Sinai which defined the role of God's people in terms of daily living. Later still, the prophetic hope saw not a different covenant ruling the restored people, but a newly applied

---

[7] It is necessary to stress this fact because of the frequent emphasis given in popular preaching and piety to Christ as enthroned in the heart of the believer. This way of speaking has biblical support (Galatians 2: 20, Ephesians 3: 17, Colossians 1: 27), but must be understood in the light of the biblical emphasis on Christ risen above and coming to us by the Holy Spirit.

covenant – written upon men's hearts – so that there would be a perfect compliance with God's character and will (Jeremiah 31: 31–34).

References to covenant as such are fairly infrequent in the New Testament but there is plenty to show that the gospel is the fulfilment of the hope of the new covenant. The song of Mary is an example of the interpretation of the coming of Jesus as Old Testament hope come to fruition (Luke 1: 46–55). Likewise the songs of Zechariah and Simeon interpret the incarnation in Old Testament terms of covenant (Luke 1: 68–79, 2: 29–32). At the last supper Jesus declares that the cup 'is the new covenant in my blood', thus indicating that his death establishes the reality of the new covenant just as the old covenant was sealed with sacrificial blood by Moses (I Corinthians 11: 25; cf. Exodus 24: 8).

The most detailed exposition of the gospel as the new covenant of Jeremiah is given in Hebrews 8–9. In saying, as the writer does, that the new covenant is so much better than the old which has become obsolete, he in no way implies that old is unconnected with the new. In fact, he establishes the new by showing how it achieves perfectly what the old could only foreshadow. Those who see a radical discontinuity between old and new often support their position with such statements as, 'You are not under law but under grace' (Romans 6: 14). We have already dealt with the law as covenant – a fact established by Jeremiah 31: 31–34 – so New Testament references to the place of law are important. The proper context of such passages showing distinction are those which show unity. Jesus came not to destroy the law but to fulfil it (Matthew 5: 17–20). The law remains the standard of God's righteousness (Romans 2: 13), and faith does not overthrow the law but upholds it (Romans 3: 31). Thus it was to fulfil the demands and the penalty of the law that Jesus lived and died for us. The fact that we cannot do it ourselves does not remove the demand, and if we believe Christ did it for us we uphold the demand.

The other main theme relating to God's rule is the concept of kingship. The judges in Israel are forerunners to the king in some regards but it is with David that the significance of this mediation of God's rule emerges. The pattern of kingship is given in Deuteronomy 17: 14–20 in which we see the king as the mediator of the covenant. In II Samuel 7 the kingly rule is seen in relationship to the Temple so that throne and Temple become almost synonymous in their significance.

How then does the New Testament take up the hope of the restoration of the rule of David in the Kingdom of God? Firstly, by showing that Jesus is the Son of David who by implication will rule in God's Kingdom forever. Secondly, by showing that the fulfilment of the prophecies concerning David's restored rule occurred at the resurrection: 'Being therefore a prophet, and knowing that God had sworn with an oath to him that he would set one of his descendants upon his throne he foresaw and spoke of the resurrection of the Christ'. (Acts 2: 30–31, 36). 'And as for the fact that he raised him from the dead, no more to return to corruption, he spoke in this way, "I will give you the holy and sure blessings Of David" ' (Acts 13: 34).

We have already mentioned the Temple in relation to the place of God's kingdom. Now we note that the whole use of this 'temple' theme in the New Testament indicates that in the gospel the Kingdom of God comes to its fulfilment. It was as a sign that God dwelt amongst his people to rule that the holy of holies in the tabernacle contained the ark of the covenant inside which was the written law (Exodus 25: 21–22). Solomon's temple prefigured the fulfilment of the promises to David concerning the rule of David's son given in II Samuel 7. Ezekiel focused on the new temple as the sign of God's ruling and life-giving presence in the kingdom (Ezekiel 47: 1–12). Zechariah saw a new temple built by David's descendant Zerubbabel through the Spirit (Zechariah 4: 6). For John the true temple is the bodily presence of Jesus the 'Logos' or Word (John 1: 14, 2: 21). Stephen understands the need to let go of the man-built temple and to move out to the gospel fulfilment. To hang on to the old is to resist the Holy Spirit (Acts 7: 46–51). For Paul the temple is fulfilled both in the resurrection of Christ (Acts 13: 34; cf. Ephesians 2: 6), and in the presence of Christ through the Holy Spirit (Ephesians 2: 18–22, I Corinthians 3: 16, II Corinthians 6: 16). Peter also sees both the heavenly Temple (Acts 2: 30–31) and the earthly creation of the Spirit (I Peter 2: 4–8). The climax comes in Revelation 21 and 22 where we see the heavenly reality as the ultimate point of reference. Here God himself is the Temple so there is no need for symbolic structures (Revelation 21: 22). Also we see the throne of God in the place of the Temple in Ezekiel's vision (Ezekiel 47) from which flows the river of life (Revelation 22: 1–5). Temple theology is fulfilled through the gospel, the goal of which is aptly stated by the heavenly voice: 'Behold the dwelling of God is with men. He will dwell with them, and they shall be his people' (Revelation 21: 3).

The Kingdom: Now and Not Yet

Can we say that all Old Testament prophetic hope is fulfilled in the gospel, if that gospel is anchored to historical events that happened two thousand years ago? We cannot simply ignore the second coming of Christ and the promise this holds of a glorious transformation for believers. What about the promised 'end of the world' and the events before and after it? To put it another way: how do we relate the present reality of salvation for the believer to the final revealing of the Kingdom of God in all its glory? Many people in effect regard the second coming of Christ as involving a whole new work of God. This conclusion is forced upon them because they do not accept that all promise is fulfilled in the gospel. Thus, despite the scriptural evidence (cited above) to the contrary, they see the return of Israel, the rebuilding of the Temple, the restoration of Davidic kingship as unrelated to the gospel and requiring separate fulfilment on some future occasion.

If the argument of this book is valid we must conclude otherwise. The New Testament portrays the 'Christ event', which happened two thousand years ago, as the finished, perfect work of God for the salvation of all his people, both Jew and gentile. The gospel – the first coming of Christ – wins for believers all the riches of glory. The acceptance of the believer with God is perfect the moment he believes because Christ and his work are perfect. The status of the believer can never be improved upon – he possesses all the riches of Christ. There is nothing the believer will possess in glory that he does not now possess *in Christ*. All this he possesses by *faith*, but that it is by faith does not make it any less real.

The Christian thus lives in tension between the *now* of living 'by faith' and the *not yet* of knowing the full reality of the kingdom 'by sight'.[8]

One implication of what we are saying is that the Book of Revelation, for many an object of puzzlement, for

[8] 'The gospel must determine our view of eschatology. The reason is this: the gospel is the report about the "finished work of Christ". And if "the finished work of Christ" is a reality rather than an empty slogan, it means that the last things are simply an unveiling of what has already been done'. R.D. Brinsmead, 'Eschatology in the light of the Gospel', *Present Truth*, Vol. 3, number 4, Sept. 1974, p. 4.

others a stimulus to wild speculation about the future, is to be interpreted by the gospel. We must also say that the first coming of Christ interprets the second coming. For the believer the second coming of Christ will be the manifestation of his glory and of the glory of his kingdom, a glory which we already grasp by faith. For the unbeliever the second coming will be a manifestation of judgement, which judgement already rests on all sinners even though they do not acknowledge it.[9]

Christ the Kingdom

When we begin to put all the pieces together, so that we can see the way the overall pattern of Old Testament revelation is handled in the New Testament, a frequently overlooked truth emerges. To see the kingdom of God we must look at Jesus Christ. This is not an inert cliché of pious jargon but it has some important implications for the way we handle the Bible.

We have defined the Kingdom of God as God's people in God's place under God's rule. Now we discover that the

---

[9] It will be seen that this discussion implies radical disagreement with some popular teachings on prophecy. While controversy is not the aim of this book, many readers will long since have recognized that the system known as Dispensationalism (represented by the Scofield Reference Bible), and its modern derivatives (such as Hal Lindsey's *The Late Great Planet Earth*) have given a very different understanding of prophetic fulfilment. I only ask those who disagree with me to give my case a fair hearing in the light of scripture, and not to reject it simply because it puts across cherished beliefs. It is of interest to me that Hal Lindsey in *The Late Great Planet Earth* all but ignores the mass of material in the New Testament which deals with the fulfilment in the gospel of the prophecies concerning Israel.

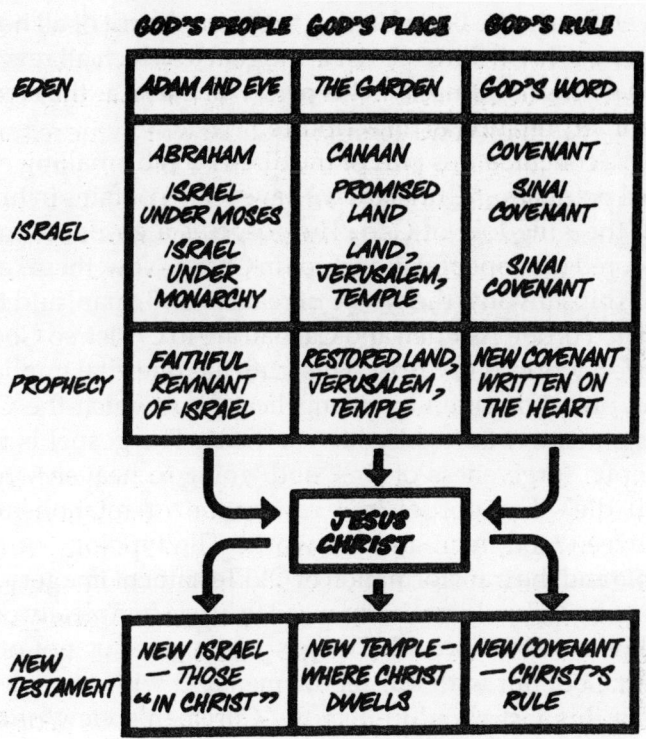

Figure 7   The Kingdom of God and the Gospel

New Testament sees the primary point of reference for each of these aspects in the Person of Jesus Christ. He is the true people of God, the true kingly sphere, and the true rule of God.

This brings us back to the starting point in biblical theology referred to in Chapter Four. As Christians we recognise Christ to be the way to God and we believe the gospel of Christ to be the power of God for salvation. Viewed in the light of the whole unity of Scripture, these well-worn phrases take on a depth of meaning that may previously have escaped us. Biblical theology shows us the process of revelation in the Bible leading to the fulfilment of all hope in Jesus Christ. Since Christ is the goal to which all revelation points he, himself, in his person and acts, is the key to the interpretation of all scripture.

We conclude this part of the discussion by making one final point. Jesus Christ (as we have seen) contains in himself the Kingdom of God. The gospel is a gospel of man restored to proper relationships in Christ. Now, these relationships involve the whole of reality: God, man, and the created order. As Eden and Canaan are in Christ, so God's perfect world is in Christ. This truth has one vital implication often forgotten by evangelicals, but which the Old Testament reinforces by its historicity. The gospel is not simply 'forgiveness of sins' and 'going to heaven when you die'. The gospel is a restoration of relationships between God, man and the world. The typology of the Bible and the transformation of Old Testament imagery by the gospel should not be misused to lift us completely outside the created world. The gospel involves us not only with God, but with our fellow men and with the world. How this fact should affect the Christian's view of the world, politics, culture, the arts, ecology and science, should be our continuing concern.

Chapter Ten

Principles of Interpretation

In chapter four, hermeneutics, or interpretation, was described as the process of determining how the ancient biblical text has general relevance here and now. We may now put this a little more exactly: hermeneutics aims at showing the significance of the text in the light of the gospel. To interpret an Old Testament text we establish its relationship to the revelation of God in Jesus Christ. In order to do this we draw upon our knowledge of the structure of revelation that biblical theology has opened out for us.

The study of the Kingdom of God concept has shown that each stratum of Kingdom revelation has the same essential ingredients relating to the saving acts of God and the goal to which they lead. Each stratum prefigures the realities of the gospel. Each step is not only a movement in the chronological sequence of revelation, but is a movement in the process of making clearer the nature of God's Kingdom until the full light of the gospel is revealed.

These relationships are shown in the figure on page 124 which represents. both the unity of the whole Bible and the distinctions between the several strata. In the diagram the boundaries between the Kingdom epochs are indicated by covenant expressions relating to the Kingdom. The Kingdom is promised to Abraham and foreshadowed

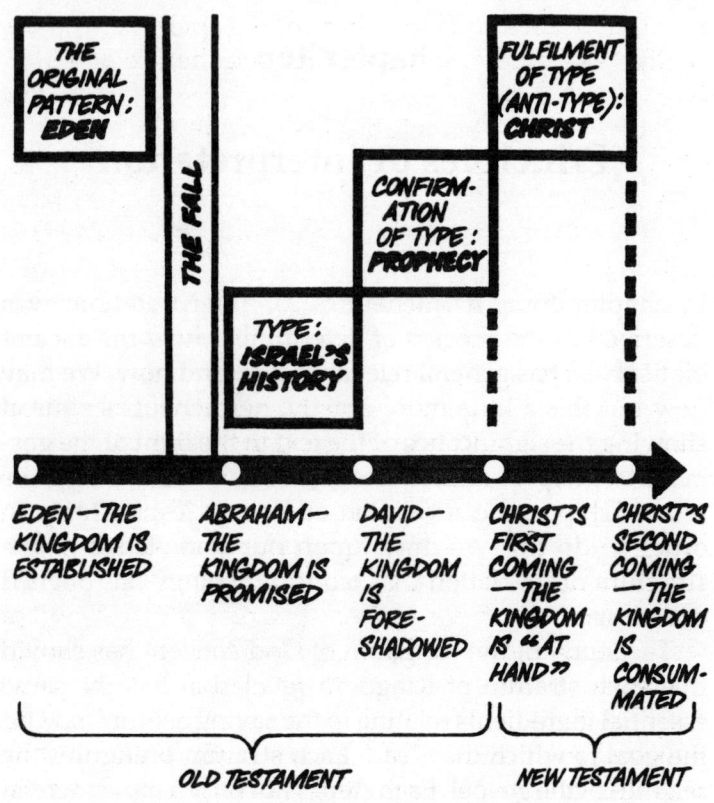

Figure 8   Revelation of the Kingdom of God

(typologically fulfilled) with David. The prophets renew the promise of the Kingdom which is declared to be 'at hand' with the coming of Christ. At the second coming of Christ the Kingdom will be fully revealed and consummated.

No diagram can tell the whole story, but this representation at least provides a basis for interpretation of any Old Testament text. Our whole study of progressive revelation goes to show that the Gospel event is the reality which determines all that goes before and after it.

We may look at it another way. From man's point of view we see the Scriptures unfold a step-by-step process until the gospel is reached as the goal. But from God's point of view we know that the coming of Christ to live and to die for sinners was the pre-determined factor even before God made the world.[1] We must not think of God as trying first one plan and then another until he came up with the perfect way of salvation. The gospel was pre-ordained so that at the exact and perfect time God sent forth his Son into the world.

In the meantime, until that perfect 'fulness of time' should be reached, God graciously provided a progressive revelation of the Christ event. These pre-figurements of the gospel had two purposes. First, this progressive revelation led man gently to the full light of truth. Secondly, it provided the means whereby the Old Testament believer embraced the gospel before it was fully revealed. The Old Testament believer who believed the promises of God concerning the shadow was thus enabled to grasp the reality. It was by Christ that the saints of Israel were saved, for such is the unity of the successive stages of revelation that, by embracing the shadow, the believer embraced the reality.

Only in this way can we account for the 'unity expressions' of the New Testament which speak of Old Testament believers as hearing the gospel, seeing

---

[1] Matthew 25: 34, Ephesians 1: 4, 1 Peter 1: 20, Revelation 13:8, 17: 8.

Christ, or hoping for a heavenly kingdom.[2] How then may we put this structure of revelation to work for us? Broadly speaking, we do this by showing with what aspect of the gospel revelation the Old Testament text has its essential unity. Already we have seen how we may express each stratum of revelation in terms of the dimensions of the kingdom of God. Every Old Testament text relates in some way to the basic structure of the kingdom revelation and is therefore capable of being related to the New Testament at the corresponding point. Thus a saving event in the Old Testament relates to the one great saving event of the gospel; a priestly mediator of the saving event in the Old relates to the one great priestly mediator of salvation in the gospel, and so on.

The Method in Practice

We may summarize the process in the following way:

1. Identify the way the text functions in the wider context of the kingdom stratum in which it occurs.
2. Proceed to the same point in each succeeding stratum until the final reality in the gospel is reached.
3. Show how the gospel reality interprets the meaning of the text, at the same time as showing how the gospel reality is illuminated by the text.

---

[2] E.g. John 8: 56 – 'Abraham rejoiced to see my day'.

1 Corinthians 10: 4 – 'They drank from the supernatural rock which followed them, and the rock was Christ'.

Galatians 3: 8 – '. . . preached the gospel beforehand to Abraham'.

Hebrews 11: 16 – 'They desire a better country, that is, a heavenly one'.

Before offering some examples a few words of warning are indicated. It should be remembered that the structural analysis given in the previous chapters is of the most basic kind. We may not overlook the Old Testament's complexity which calls for care and precision. One aspect of this complexity is the repetition of certain aspects of the structure within one given stratum. Thus, while the exodus is the definitive saving event, every deliverance effected by judge, king or any other means, is a saving event. Another aspect which our diagram does not represent is the significance of the history of Israel after the zenith of the united monarchy. Nor have we said anything yet about those of Israel's faith expressions which do not relate easily to the history of Israel or to prophecy. The wisdom literature has long been a problem to scholars at this point.

A second word of warning relates to our use of the word 'text'. It will, I hope, be evident that by 'text' is not meant simply a single verse of Scripture. It is not possible to lay down rules about how much of the text constitutes an interpretable unit. The lesson of biblical theology is that no text stands alone, and the whole of Scripture is its ultimate context. So we should beware of taking every portion of a size convenient for daily reading (whatever that might be) and forcing it to yield up some self-contained Christian truth. In our efforts to make every snippet of Scripture revelant and edifying to the Christian we may in fact destroy the very message which is present for us in the wider context.

Despite the difficulties mentioned, the gospel and the whole witness of the New Testament should inspire us with confidence that the task can be done; It requires hard work and application, but our efforts will be rewarded as we achieve a clearer understanding of the riches of the gospel.

Chapter Eleven

It's That Giant Again!

It is time now to see our principles put into practice. In this chapter we shall look at some Old Testament passages and consider the application of christological interpretation methods. Provided we do not regard these principles as a kind of magic key to every difficulty, and provided we are prepared to work hard at the business of understanding the text, we should be able to avoid the hit-and-miss of so much handling of the Old Testament and to move in the right direction.

David and Goliath: I Samuel 17

In Chapter Two we considered some points about this famous story in its context of the life of David. We could not do better than to hear Martin Luther on this text:

> When David overcame the great Goliath, there came among the Jewish people the good report and encouraging news that their terrible enemy had been struck down and that they had been rescued and given joy and peace; and they sang and danced and were glad for it (I Samuel 18: 6). Thus this gospel of God or New Testament is a good story and report, sounded forth into all the world by the apostles, telling of a

true David who strove with sin, death, and the devil, and overcame them, and thereby rescued all those who were captive in sin, afflicted with death, and overpowered by the devil.[1]

The important point to note is that Luther has made the link between the saving acts of God through David and the saving acts of God through Christ. Once we see that connection, it is impossible to use David as a mere model for Christian living since his victory was vicarious and the Israelites could only rejoice in what was won *for* them. In terms of our interpretative principles, we see David's victory as a salvation event in that the existence of the people of God in the promised land was at stake. The gospel interprets this event by showing it as pre-figuring the true saving event of Christ. But David's experience also puts the saving event into an historical situation which helps us to appreciate the New Testament terminology concerning the gospel events.

We must be careful not to make too much of incidental details which belong to the immediate life-situation described in the text. David's taking of food to his brothers in the army hardly demands interpretation any more than the dimensions of Goliath's armour. Some areas of the narrative, on the other hand, spell out what is significant in theological terms (e.g. verses 45–47). Other details form a pattern within the wider context which again emerges in the gospel events. David is declared king in God's eyes (I Samuel 16) but is despised, scorned and rejected. He wins his victory at the point where he seems to be about to suffer total defeat, and his people continue a fight against an already defeated foe.

---

[1] *Word and Sacrament* (Philadelphia, Muhlenberg Press, 1960), Luther's Works, American Edition, Vol. 35, p. 358.

All Old Testament passages which deal with the Lord's battles against Israel's foes must be evaluated in the light of the saving work of God *for* us.

Rahab's Scarlet Cord: Joshua 2: 15–21,6: 22–25

One well-worn line of interpretation focuses on the redness of Rahab's cord as a type of the blood of Christ. This is difficult to maintain while the emphasis is merely on the redness of each. But in our desire to be hermeneutically pure we should not over-react. The conquest of Jericho is part of the saving acts of God for Israel, and of his judgement on the godless Canaanites. That Rahab found safety from this judgement and was saved through obeying the instruction to display a sign of identification, has many real parallels to the passover in Egypt. In that sense the tying of an easily-seen coloured cord to the window had saving significance for Rahab, and the fact that she became incorporated in the people of God (Joshua 6:25) is a type of salvation. It may seem a small distinction, but it is not the redness which establishes the typology, but the saving significance of the event.

The Rahab passage has another important message because it, along with other passages, demonstrates the purpose of God for the gentiles as promised to Abraham in Genesis 12: 3. As examples of gentile converts we have Jethro of Midian and his daughter whom Moses married, Rahab the Canaanite, and Ruth the Moabitess.

The Polluted Spring: II Kings 2: 19–22

The healing of the polluted spring at Jericho by the last of the old-order prophets may well stimulate thoughts about the need for the human heart to be cleansed. The question of human moral pollution is of course closely related to salvation – in fact it is inseparable from it. But let us never lose sight of the fact that God does not save us by eradicating our pollution. We are not saved by our changed lives. The changed life is the result of being saved and not the basis of it. The basis of salvation is the perfection in the life and death of Christ presented in our place.

Now the spring of water in the promised land is closely related to Israel's salvation. Jericho was under a curse from the time Joshua destroyed it (see Joshua 6: 17, 26). The city site ceased to have the same significance as the inheritance of Israel which was a fruitful land flowing with milk and honey. This is not an easy passage, but it would appear that sanction is given for a re-inhabiting of Jericho by the prophet's act. The physical sustenance of the people in the promised land is part of the whole salvation process.

The ritual use of salt lies in some obscurity, but apparently indicates cleansing or a break with the past.[2] We may allow that Elisha's act involved redemption of the potentially life-giving spring from under the curse of the ban. Once again we see this as a saving act of God for his people rather than a purifying act in the believer. To drink of the purified spring was in itself to partake of the life that God provided for his people. To take of the water of life is to have life itself. The orientation of the pure spring is Christ himself, not the heart of the believer. God graciously provides the pure water of life in the place of the cursed. We should interpret this passage in the light of Christ as the fulfiller of the place where God keeps his people in eternal life. Canaan and all its fruitfulness is in Christ.

---

[2] See Leviticus 2: 13, Numbers 18: 19, Judges 9: 45, Ezekiel 43:24.

Blessing the Child-Killers: Psalm 137

This psalm contains one of those difficult imprecatory passages which call down terrible curses from heaven upon the enemy in what appears to be a wholly immoral fashion. Psalm 109: 6–20 is a more extended imprecation which some have sought to excuse by understanding it as the words of the wicked (v. 2) against the psalmist himself. But there are other clear cases which still leave the problem. (e.g. Jeremiah 15: 15, 18: 19–23 Psalm 69: 22–28).

Psalm 137 has an easily discernible context. It springs from the agony of the Babylonian exile, when the pious Jew was torn from the promised land and transported to a foreign country to be tormented with memories of the destruction of Jerusalem and the temple. The whole covenant relationship with God and the salvation of the people were called into question.

The theological context of the controversial verses 7–9 is the hope of redress against the enemies of God's people. Whatever the actual form and content of the expressions, the imprecations are cries for God's Kingdom to come. However much we may allow the culture and the times to have conditioned the prayer, it is essentially a longing for the day of vindication, when the coming Kingdom will introduce terrible judgement on all who oppose it. The psalmist was not conditioned by unrealistic notions about the innocence of children, but by a sense of solidarity of all age groups in a sinful mankind. However cruel the destruction of the next generation of Babylonian soldiers may appear to us, it was seen to be integral to the final overthrow of the enemies of God at the coming of his Kingdom.

As we move to the New Testament it is true that a clearer perspective is to be had. The real enemy is not flesh and blood but principalities and powers. On the other hand the New Testament is quite clear that the human enemy whom we must love, will also come under judgement on 'the great and terrible Day of the Lord'. To pray, 'Thy kingdom come', is a solemn thing indeed.

We have not said all that can be said about the moral problem of child-killing. However we may be disposed to interpret the biblical references in the light of the 'primitive' state of Israel's civilization (a dubious concept), the theological perspective must take precedence. It is distasteful to us that Israel slaughtered whole civilian populations during the conquest. But these historical facts as well as the psalmist's imprecations, cannot be interpreted apart from certain salient aspects of biblical revelation. Firstly that Israel's own moral failure did not disqualify her from being the agent of God's justice, in the same way that godless nations became God's agents against Israel. Secondly, such slaughter and retribution visited by Israel on another at God's command was truly deserved (see Deuteronomy 9: 4–5). Thirdly, while the judgement in the Old Testament takes the form of death, which man naturally sees as the ultimate punishment, the New Testament depicts a far more horrendous fate for the godless. Death by the sword in the Old Testament is only a pale shadow of the eternal judgement on the godless in the New Testament.

Nehemiah Rebuilds Jerusalem: Nehemiah 2: 17–4: 23

Some years ago a popular radio Bible session broadcast a sermon on this section of Nehemiah in which the speaker used a well-worn but quite inexcusable method. In order to make this piece of post-exilic history applicable to the Christian, key words were taken, in this case the names of the repaired gates of Jerusalem, and a kind of association of ideas used to lead us to some useful but largely unrelated New Testament truth. So the Horse Gate led us from horses to soldiers and thence to armour, and finally to the putting on of the whole armour of God in Ephesians 6. The Sheep Gate under repair served as a spring-board from which the speaker jumped without apology to the Good Shepherd of John 10.

Now Ephesians 6 and John 10 have important lessons for us, and these lessons may well overlap the meaning of the original Old Testament passage in question. What is at issue here is the method used. Sermons on the Old Testament should demonstrate, and even spell out in explicit terms, the legitimate relationships of the text to the New Testament.

What are the points to watch in this passage from Nehemiah? First, it belongs to the post-exilic reconstruction age which is not one of our principal strata in the structure of biblical revelation. The return from Babylon did not herald the expected fulfilment of prophecy, but it did bring about a shadow fulfilment in which all the ingredients of the kingdom existed, although very imperfectly. Thus we may treat this period as a kind of interim fulfilment in which the nature of the Kingdom of God is clearly discernible, but during which the problems of imperfection and non-fulfilment of the prophetic hope had to be dealt with.

Secondly, the rebuilding of Jerusalem must point to the prophetic hope for the future glorification of the city of Zion, the focal point of God's Kingdom. At the same time its imperfection says something of the 'not yet' as a dimension in the existence of the people of God. Thirdly, it is the whole event which interprets the details and not the other way round. We should be prepared to forego the Christianizing of details unless the theological significance of these details can be established with some certainty. If there is a way to Ephesians 6 from this passage it is not by way of the Horse Gate! Rather the resistance to Nehemiah's work which is offered by his enemies highlights the ongoing conflict with godlessness referred to by Paul in Ephesians 6: 10–20.

Conclusion

This discussion has been at risk throughout simply because of the aim of keeping it to modest proportions. The reader will inevitably – and rightly – feel that many problems have been left untouched. The aim has been only to establish basic principles of interpretation. Underlying the survey has been the conviction that twentieth century evangelical Christians have experienced a radical loss of direction in handling the Old Testament. One of the contributing causes is the severing of evangelicalism from the historical perspectives of the faith. This introduces a vicious circle, because devotion to study of the Old Testament is an important means of preserving the historicity of the gospel. Evangelicals have lost sight not only of biblical history, but of their own historical heritage in the Reformation. By reverting to either allegorical interpretation on the one hand, or to prophetic literalism on the other, some evangelicals have thrown away the hermeneutic gains of the Reformers in favour of a mediaeval approach to the Bible.

The other great contributing factor to modern misuse of the Old Testament is a generation of bad habits in Bible reading. Evangelicals have had a reputation for taking the Bible seriously. But even they have traditionally propagated the idea of the short devotional reading from which a 'blessing from the Lord' must be wrested. Failure to gain this undefined blessing is usually seen to be a function of the spiritual state of the reader rather than of the nature of the text itself. This mentality is almost paralysed by such phenomena as the genealogies of the Bible. Consequently one is unlikely to find genealogy texts included in daily devotional selections! The difficulties of dealing adequately with the Old Testament when this mentality prevails have been amply discussed in the previous pages.

The pivotal point of turning in evangelical thinking which demands close attention is the change that has taken place from the Protestant emphasis upon the objective facts of the gospel in history, to the mediaeval emphasis on the inner life. The evangelical who sees the inward transforming work of the Spirit as the key element of Christianity will soon lose contact with the historic faith and the historic gospel. At the same time he will come to neglect the historical acts of God in the Old Testament. The Christ enthroned in the human heart loses his own incarnate humanity, and the humanity of the Old Testament history will be soon discarded so that the 'inner spiritual' meanings may be applied to the inner spiritual life of the Christian.

The crisis of the Old Testament today is only another form of the crisis of the Protestant faith. Inner-directed Christianity, which reduces the gospel to the level of every other religion of the inner man, might well use a text from the Apocrypha to serve as its own epitaph for the Reformers:

There are others who are unremembered;
they are dead, and it is as though they had never existed.

(ben Sirah 44: 9)

By contrast, we should think of these fathers of the faith in the way indicated by the writer to the Hebrews (11: 4):

They, being dead, yet speak.

Appendix A

Readings

These are some suggested readings from the Old Testament which will introduce the reader to some of the salient features and themes. The passages should be read with the outline of Old Testament history in mind, and in the light of the biblical theology discussed in this book.

Basic List

Genesis 1–3, 12–24.
Exodus 19–24.
Leviticus 1–7, 16, 23, 26.
Joshua 23–24.
Judges 1–5.
I and II Samuel.
I Kings 4, 8–12.
II Kings 16–25.
Ezra 1, 7.
Nehemiah 1–6, 8.

Amos.
Jeremiah 1–9, 26–44.
Lamentations.
Ezekiel 34–48.
Haggai.
Malachi.
Psalms 68, 105, 106, 136, 137.
Proverbs 8–9.
Job 1–2.
Daniel.

Advanced List

Genesis 37–50.	Micah.
Exodus 1–15, 25–35.	Proverbs 1–7, 10–15.
Deuteronomy 1–12, 26–30.	Job 1–14, 32–33, 38–42.
Joshua 1–12.	Psalms 1–41.
Judges 6–12.	Ezekiel 1–11.
I Kings 16–22.	Ecclesiastes.
II Kings 1–12.	Zechariah.
II Chronicles 24–36.	Esther.
Hosea.	Psalms 107–150.
Isaiah 1–39.	

Appendix B

Group Study Questions

In order to facilitate the use of this book in group (or private) study, the following questions may be used as a basis for discussion. The members of the group should read carefully the respective chapters before the study hour.

Chapter One

1. What are your greatest difficulties in reading the Old Testament? Why do these difficulties exist for you?
2. Why is it important to study the Old Testament with the New Testament in mind?
3. Consider the implications for Old Testament study of Luke 24: 25–27, 44–47.

Chapter Two

1. Is the Book of Acts normative for us today? If not, why not?
2. What place is there for the character study?
3. How does the content and imagery of Revelation 21: 1–4, and 22: 1–4 help us in understanding the nature of the Bible's unity?

Chapter Three

1. How does a study of literary types assist the understanding of the Bible?
2. Does it matter if the events recorded in Old Testament historical narrative happened or not?
3. What do we mean when we say that the biblical history has a theological purpose? Can we see the outworking of this in Acts 2: 22–36?

Chapter Four

1. What do we mean by the term biblical theology? How does it differ from dogmatic or credal theology?
2. What is meant by progressive revelation?
3. How does the history of redemption figure in Acts 7: 1–53?

Chapter Five

1. What is the Kingdom of God?
2. What do you understand by salvation?
3. How does the Kingdom of God theme relate to the covenant expressions of Genesis 12 and II Samuel 7?

Chapter Six

1. How is the Kingdom of God seen in Eden?
2. What does the Eden story and its sequel tell us about the meaning of grace?
3. How does Paul relate the Adam history to Christ in Romans 5 and I Corinthians 15: 20–26?

Chapter Seven

1. How does the exodus event relate to the promises to Abraham in Genesis?
2. In what sense is the gospel pre-figured in Israel's history?
3. How does the revelation of the Kingdom of God progress from Abraham to Solomon?

Chapter Eight

1. What is the main difference between the message of the old order prophets and the message of the new order prophets?
2. How does the prophetic view of the future kingdom differ from the past historical kingdom in Israel?
3. How do the prophets use past history to describe the future?

Chapter Nine

1. What is the gospel?
2. How does the New Testament handle the relationship of the gospel to the fulfilment of prophecy?
3. What has the Second Coming of Christ to do with prophetic fulfilment?

Chapter Ten

1. What is the difference between a legitimate typology and the allegorical interpretation?
2. What do we mean when we say that prophecy must be interpreted christologically?
3. Why is the New Testament the ultimate source of the principles of interpretation of the Old Testament?

Appendix C

Some Passages for Interpretation

Prepare outlines of Bible Studies or Sunday School lessons on the following passages. Remember the three basic questions put to any text:

1. What did the text mean to the original writer?
2. What does the text mean in the light of the Gospel?
3. What is its specific meaning to me or my hearers now?

   (Do not refer to the comments on the following pages until you have attempted your own answers.)

1. Deuteronomy 6: 20–25.
2. I Samuel 26.
3. I Kings 18: 17–40.
4. Isaiah 21–4.
5. Psalm 114.
6. Amos 5: 18–20.

   Some more difficult passages for the adventurous:

7. Proverbs 3: 1–42.
8. II Samuel 23: 1–7.
9. Ezekiel 1.
10. Malachi 4.

Notes and Comments on Passages for Interpretation

1. *Deuteronomy 6: 20–25.*

Exegesis must take account of the context of the law-giving as the sequel to the exodus. Note the important relationships which are involved: that of law and grace (or gospel), or that of works and salvation. In verses 20–23 the law is related to the past saving events, while in verses 24–25 the doing of the law is related to the future saving events. Verse 25 should be dealt with in the context of v. 21. Remember that the New Testament also speaks of rewards for good works and denies a place in the Kingdom to those who do not do them (Romans 2: 6–10, I Corinthians 3: 8,11 Corinthians 5: 10, Galatians 5:21, I Corinthians 6: 9–10).

2. *I Samuel 26*

Take care to relate the principal characters to the theological structure. Do not be quick to see examples for ourselves, until the real functions of the characters and events are worked out. Notice how David is guided by theological understanding while Abishai is guided by circumstances. Consider the implications for christology of the continuing humiliation of David before his accession to the throne.

3. *I Kings 18: 17–40*

The historical background of apostasy is important. Note carefully that Elijah's part in the contest is not merely to outdo the Baal prophets' attempt at miracle, but to reinstate the prescription of the law concerning the sacrifice for sins – see v.v. 30–32, 36–37. There is good fodder here for a gospel sermon.

4. Isaiah 2: 1–4

Try putting the questions when? where? what? and why? to the text. The hermeneutics rest upon determining the New Testament counterparts to the answers. Probably the most disputed point will be whether the fulfilment takes place from the beginning of the gospel era or only at the end. We can settle this only by clearly establishing when are the latter days, and when the New Testament sees the restoration of Zion and the Temple taking place.

5. Psalm 114.

There should be little difficulty in fitting this psalm into its historical and theological contexts. After that it is a matter of determining the mood of the psalm as an expression of the faithful man who recalls the saving acts of God.

6. Amos 5: 18–20

Although this is probably the earliest reference in Scripture to the day of the Lord, the term obviously has a recognized meaning in Amos' time. It would be a good idea to research its meaning with the aid of a concordance. For Amos there is a double significance to this great future event, for it was anticipated as a day of light, but for some it would be darkness. This must be interpreted in the context of the biblical teaching of judgement.

7. *Proverbs 3: 1–72*

The main obstacle in this kind of passage is the understanding of what the wisdom literature is all about. This is a relatively straightforward 'instruction' passage which belongs to the expressions of faith in the ongoing life of the people of God. Essentially wisdom speaks of understanding the relationships of man to man, to the world, and to God. It does so with greater emphasis on the responsible freedom of man to respond to the world than on the revealed saving acts of God. Proverbs 1: 7 reminds us that this freedom is true freedom only while it is exercised within the bounds set by God's revelation. This passage deals directly with wisdom in its theological context, but this should not be allowed to obscure the wisdom stance which is behind the proverbial material such as is in Proverbs 10 and following.

8. *II Samuel 23: 1–7*

This psalm-like passage, along with Chapter 22, has obviously been placed at the end of the David narratives for a purpose. It highlights the fact that the narrative material is not only biographical or historical but shaped by theological purpose. These last words of David sum up the theological meaning of the covenant of II Samuel 7 and indeed of the whole reign of David. The covenant and reign of David are key elements in the messianic hope developing in the Old Testament. Both the man and his office are idealized here without the qualifications of the historic blemishes. As such they form an important link in the chain of christological reference in the Bible.

9. Ezekiel I

The historical context is no problem. The literary form may well be influenced by the emergence of apocalyptic. The vision of the 'heavenly locomotive' does not necessarily demand an interpretation of every detail, especially when it is seen as the background to the essential element which is the glory of the Lord. The passage does not really stand on its own, and the progressive departure of the glory of the Lord in Chapters 1 to 11 provides the real key.

10. Malachi 4

Salvation and judgement are the parallel themes in v.v. 1–3. It is verses 4–6 that will probably give most trouble. We may be partly guided by the assertion in Matthew 17: 10–13 that John Baptist is the Elijah spoken of here. Elijah did what the prophet does in v. 4 – he called the people to faithfulness to the covenant. Moses and Elijah thus became symbolic of the righteousness of God as he upholds his own law in salvation. The relationship of law and gospel again emerges as a point to be considered (see Romans 3: 21–31, especially v. 31).

The Gospel in Revelation

Gospel And Apocalypse

DEDICATED

TO ALL WHO SUFFER PERSECUTION
FOR THE SAKE OF CHRIST,
AND ESPECIALLY TO THE CHRISTIANS
IN FORMERLY SOVIET-OCCUPIED ESTONIA.

Ja nemad on tema
võitnud Talle vere tõttu
ja oma tunnistuse sõna tõttu

Ilmutuse 12: 11
(Revelation 12:11)

Contents

Preface

This book is not a commentary and it is not intended to compete with the already large amount of commentary on the text of the Book of Revelation that is readily available. It is largely the outcome of my own attempts to expound the essential, contemporary message of Revelation in three separate Bible Study groups and in a series of public lectures at a Bible College. These expositions took place within a period of some nine or ten years and each lasted about three or four months. Within that period I was prompted from time to time to reflect on the broad plan and purpose of Revelation in relation to the overall pattern of biblical revelation. Exposition in informal groups permitted much useful dialogue with other Christians about how Revelation spoke to our real life situations. Perhaps it was also inevitable that my own keen interest in the Christian significance of the Old Testament should lead me to that book which not only contains more Old Testament quotations than any other book of the New Testament, but which also preserves the Old Testament literary idioms and thought patterns in a way unparalleled in the New Testament. I am grateful to those colleagues and friends who read the manuscript at various stages, and who made helpful suggestions and encouraged me. I am especially indebted to Mrs. Ellenor Neave for typing the manuscript.

Graeme Goldsworthy
St. Stephen's Anglican Church
Coorparoo, Brisbane

Introduction: Principles of Interpretation

The Key to Understanding Revelation

The Book of Revelation seems to occupy one of two positions in most people's affections. Either it is almost totally neglected or it is elevated to a prominence shared by no other biblical book. As to the former position, the reasons are not hard to imagine. Apart from the letters to the seven churches in Chapters 2 and 3, the book is almost entirely given over to exotic and florid literary forms. The weird visions coupled with the constant use of Old Testament images and ideas, put the book in the 'too hard' category for many ordinary readers. Few Christians today are used to reflecting on their existence and its meaning in terms of seven-headed beasts and apocalyptic horsemen. Since the idioms of Revelation are so strange to us we tend rather to concentrate on those parts of the New Testament which come to us in the straight-forward forms of letters and narratives.

Neglect of Revelation is also, paradoxically, related to the fact that there are those who seem to give it undue prominence. When the modern prophets and futuristic gurus have finished their extraordinary explanation of every visionary detail, and have mapped out the most complex chain of events due to start just about any time now, the ordinary reader is frightened almost out of his wits. His fright is not so much caused by the awful events that are imminent, but by the measure of expertise required to interpret the intricacies of this unusual and unfamiliar book. Better leave it to the specialists! And, of course, it works the other way too. By vacating the interpretative arena pastors, teachers, and their flocks leave a vacuum which looks very inviting to someone who desires the prophet's mantle. To be an expert on 'things to come' is a sure way to fame (and sometimes fortune).

Certain habits of Bible reading are also risky in this matter. The commendable habit of daily reading of the Bible can easily become hardened into a set of rules on how we deal with the text. The practice of meditation on short passages is often productive but always open to danger. Short passages, by definition, are usually isolated passages cut loose from their wider context. This can cause misunderstanding as to the meaning of the passage even when it appears clear and beneficial as it stands. It can also cause perplexity. How does one meditate on the description of an apocalyptic monster? What encouraging thought for the day does the destruction of one third of the world's rivers provide? What is the message from the Lord to me in the catalogue of precious stones adorning the foundations of the heavenly city? Better leave well alone! Let the specialists deal with Revelation while we meditate on the clearer passages of the New Testament.

I once sat, very patiently I thought, while a caller to my home explained at very great length how all the events of contemporary world history gave out the unmistakable signal that the second coming of Christ was very near. The exposition was ingenious, and gave the message of Revelation a note of urgency. But there was a problem in it for me which I still cannot avoid. The urgency belonged wholly to *now*, to the last part of the twentieth century. Why, then, was John so urgent some nineteen hundred years before this? What was the *contemporary* meaning of that revelation which made the author of the book a concerned messenger of God writing to a small and persecuted minority of Christians in a hostile pagan world? If he wrote out of the agony of his own exile on Patmos, addressing specific churches in Asia Minor by name, what relevance to them was to be found in far-off events belonging, according to our modern prophets, to the nuclear-technological age?

Of course the New Testament has much to say about certain events of the future. The return of Christ, the resurrection of the dead, and the consummation of the kingdom of God are all future events. Furthermore, few commentators would dispute that the Book of Revelation speaks of these events. Insofar as John refers to these events and makes them relevant to his own day, he points to the fact that it is not *when* these will happen, but rather *what* it is that happens, which constitutes the urgency. These events, many of them future, were not given contemporary significance by John and other biblical authors by dating them in their lifetime, or in that of their readers. The New Testament writers probably had varying ideas about when the appearance of Christ in majesty would occur. But they all agreed on one thing, and that was that the first advent of Christ had brought all time and history into crisis. We can see this in the way they regard all time which follows the life, death and resurrection of Jesus as *end time*. About this I shall have more to say later on. Suffice it to say that, according to the New Testament, the gospel event of

Jesus Christ throws all succeeding history into a new light. Whether men acknowledge it or not, the coming of Christ to live, die, and rise again, is the goal of all history. God not only created all things through Christ and for Christ (Colossians 1:16), but it was his eternal plan to bring all things to their fullness in Christ (Ephesians 1:90 and that in the fullness of time (Galatians 4:4).

Principles of Interpretation

In talking about principles of interpretation, I do not want to give the impression that there is some *secret* key which unlocks all. There is a key, but it is not a secret. Nor do I want to suggest that it is a wholly technical matter which removes interpretation from the grasp of the simple minded and the theologically untrained. All disciplines and specialization of interest have some technical terms. A housewife tells me that she is a simple person and not up to any theological technicalities, and then turns without a thought to operate the latest in sewing machine gadgetry, or to interpret without a mistake a knitting pattern which makes Egyptian hieroglyphics pale into insignificance. A man tells me he is uneducated and not able to understand anything beyond the 'simple gospel', and then proceeds to tune a car engine with the aid of some very sophisticated electronics. More often than not, it is unfamiliarity which daunts us rather than inherent difficulty. If we are motivated, most of us can and do come to grips with technical terms and abstract ideas.

There are two main principles of interpretation which come from the nature of the Bible itself. These have to do with the literary characteristics of the text and with the theological structures of the whole Bible.

1. Literary Idiom[1]

The subject matter will frequently dictate the kind of literary expressions that are used in recording it. However, there is also a range of options open to any writer as to how he treats his material. An account of some significant historical event is probably best dealt with in straight historical narrative. But it is also possible to record it in the form of an epic poem or even to clothe it in symbolical language. Each idiom may convey the truth, but it will do so with distinctive shades of meaning and emphases. It is the task of the writer to strive to communicate what he sees as the truth of the matter in the idiom he believes to be best suited for his purpose. The reader's task is to penetrate to the writer's meaning. Straightforward prose description usually presents least problems because it most closely approximates to the general idiom of the day-to-day speech which we all use. In this twentieth century, poetry is usually a medium in which only a few feel at home. If a preacher were to deliver his sermon in poetic form he might well be dismissed as obscure. But the prophets of Israel, it would appear, regularly did just that, for most of their recorded sermons are in poetry. One can only presume that the average Israelite was much more accustomed to dealing with poetry as a medium of communication than we are.

Thus, when we are reading the Bible, or any other ancient literature, we are likely to find that there is a considerable gap between our modern literary methods and those of the ancient author. We cannot ignore this gap and pretend it isn't there. On the other hand let us not be

---

[1] *Idiom* means use of language in a way distinct to a particular person or group. It can also mean, as it does here, one of a number of acceptable ways in which words are used to convey the one idea.

discouraged. Much of this is a matter of being sensitive to the range of options open to any author. Sometimes we may need to dig a little into the background of some particular literary idiom in order to discover how it was used and with what intent. The Book of Revelation contains a number of different literary forms each with its own characteristics and functions. The most obvious are these: –

a. Letters
b. Prophetic Oracles
c. Hymns of Praise
d. Apocalyptic Visions[2]

The principle of interpretation which emerges from this is that we must allow the author to use the literary conventions that exist for him in his time and culture, and to use them in the way that will suit his purpose. Most of the time the distinctive biblical idioms are so familiar to us that we accommodate ourselves to them without giving the matter a second thought. Often the idioms will be familiar to us in their biblical setting, as part of biblical literature, but unfamiliar to us in their original cultural setting. For example, most Christians will not find any difficulty with Jesus' words, 'I am the good shepherd' or 'I am the door of the sheep' (John 10). We have heard them often and we appear to comprehend them. But one day we hear an exposition of John 10 in which the cultural and historical background of ancient near eastern methods of keeping sheep are described. Suddenly the details of the passage take on a depth of meaning which we had never realized was there.

---

[2] Most readers will be familiar with Revelation and the visions which are there in abundance. If, however, you are not sure what is meant by the term 'apocalyptic vision', I suggest you read a couple now, eg. Daniel 7 and Revelation 13.

The doctrine of the inspiration of the Bible is extremely important but we must not misunderstand it. When John wrote under the inspiration of the Holy Spirit he was still John. He continued to think and to express himself in the thought forms and language patterns that were characteristically his. Inspiration did not suspend the human personality but worked through it. Thus when John chose, under the Spirit's inspiration, to write using the common literary forms of his day, he wrote according to the rules and conventions of a first century Jew. Our task in interpretation is to learn to recognize the different ways in which a first century Jew would write and how the different kinds of written expression function. The fact that the Jews developed a popular style of religious writing using a fairly standard kind of reported vision does not detract from John's visions, nor does it call into question the truth of his claims to have had such visions.

One further thing needs to be said here. Some forms of literary expressions are less familiar to us than others. The twentieth century mind can cope more easily with letters and straight narrative than with apocalyptic visions. There has been a lot of attention paid to this apocalyptic material in recent times by biblical scholars.[3] But, it is still very mystifying to the ordinary person. Added to this is the fact that apocalyptic visions, while often employing symbolic features which are frequently used and easily recognizable to the person familiar with them,

---

[3] Commentaries on Revelation by H.B. Swete and R.H. Charles were published early this century. These could be regarded as monumental works in the English language. In more recent times a number of books have appeared on the subject of apocalyptic literature in general e.g. D.H. Russell, *Apocalyptic: Ancient and Modern* (Philadelphia: Fortress Press, 1978); Leon Morris, *Apocalyptic* (London: IVF, 1972).

nevertheless may contain symbolisms which are either deliberately ambiguous or else obscured by our distance from them. When we encounter such difficulties in the biblical material, particularly when some background information still fails to yield a clear meaning, there is a simple principle that applies. We must allow the clearer texts to take precedence over the more obscure. In practical terms, we cannot allow a point of doctrine to be established on an apocalyptic vision against clear statements to the contrary in the epistolary material of the New Testament (i.e. the Letters).

2. *The Centrality of the Gospel*

Our second principle of interpretation is often the most neglected, and yet it is absolutely basic to proper understanding. Simply stated this principle is that the gospel of Jesus Christ is the key to the interpretation of the whole Bible.[4] That is, Jesus Christ in his person and work, gives the meaning to the whole Bible. The New Testament states this principle in a number of different ways and, of course, applies it constantly. For example, when Paul says that the gospel is the power of God for salvation to everyone who believes (Romans 1:16), he means the whole of salvation, not just our introduction to it through initial conversion. Salvation, for Paul, is the salvation of the whole person, and it is the fullness of salvation. Part of our being saved by the gospel is the saving of our minds, our understanding. 'Be transformed by the renewing of your minds' (Romans 12:2). How does the gospel 'save' our minds? First, it does so by putting us on the same side as God so

---

[4] This matter has been dealt with in some detail in my book *Gospel and Kingdom* (Exeter: The Paternoster Press, 1981; Minneapolis: Winston Press, 1982).

that we want to think his thoughts after him. We want to know his will and understand his Word. Secondly, the actual content of the gospel event shows to us the goal of all God's revealed purposes. So the Bible presents a unity of God's action for our salvation, first in the shadows of the Old Testament history and prophetic word, and then as the solid reality in Jesus Christ. One of the main aims of this book is to examine how the gospel interprets the Book of Revelation.

As we apply this principle to the Book of Revelation it will be not only because the gospel is evident within that Book. It is vital with Revelation, as with all the books of the Bible, that we do not treat it in isolation. The visions of Revelation must be read in the light of the unified message of the Bible which reaches its goal in Jesus Christ. There is one particular line of interpretation which does not follow this principle. It sees Revelation as answering to many of the prophecies of the Old Testament, but in such a way that neither these prophecies, nor Revelation are integral to the gospel. The gospel is not totally dissociated from these parts of the Bible, but it is nevertheless regarded as an intrusion into the process of the fulfilment of the prophecies in such a way as to suspend the process. Only after the gospel has run its appointed course in the world will the process of prophetic fulfilment be resumed. Such a view seems to ignore the New Testament's own testimony that the gospel is not a digression from prophetic fulfilment but rather the very essence of it.

What About the Millennium?

From the outset I wish to state my belief that the millennium is not the central theme of Revelation. The explicit references to Christ's reign of a thousand years are confined to one passage in the whole of the Bible: Revelation 20:1–10. Unfortunately, the specific interpretation of this passage has often been made the test of orthodoxy. I have tried to handle the subject in a way which neither gives it unwarranted prominence nor dismisses it as unworthy of serious consideration.[5] I see the millennium as only one of many pieces of imagery which contribute to the overall pattern of John's revelation. My aim has been to deal with it in a manner consistent with the interpretative principles which I have just outlined.

Perhaps one significant aspect of the ongoing debate about the millennium is that it serves to highlight different approaches to interpretation. Thus, the subject can be a fruitful area for the study of hermeneutical or interpretative method. What we should not wish to see, in my opinion, is this brilliant portrayal of the end of the conflict between Christ and Satan being made a perpetual battle ground and the cause of conflict between Christians.

The uninitiated may be rather irritated by distinctions between the premillennial, postmillennial and amillennial positions.[6] If so, they will probably identify

---

[5] There is plenty of literature on the subject for those who wish to pursue it, e.g.: L. Boettner, *The Millennium* (Philadelphia: The Presbyterian and Reformed Publishing Company, 1964); R. Clouse, *The Meaning of the Millennium* (Downers Grove: Inter-Varsity Press, 1977); W.J. Grier, *The Momentous Event* (London: Banner of Truth, 1970).

[6] Premillennialism anticipates Christ's return before a literal thousand year reign on earth. Postmillennialism interprets the millennium as symbolic of a period in which the world becomes largely Christianized, after which Christ returns. Amillennialism is similar to postmillennialism in that Christ returns after the millennium. The millennium is symbolic of this whole present age in which the gospel is preached. Unlike post millennialism, amillennialism does not look for a golden age of

with a jocular comment of a friend of mine who claims to be a panmillennialist because he is sure 'it is all going to pan out in the end'! However, it is important to realise that most commentaries on Revelation come down on one or other position in the millennial debate simply because a particular view seems to the author to be in accord with his overall interpretation of the book. For example, one of the best introductory commentaries, in my view, is *I saw Heaven Opened* by Michael Wilcock.[7] There is no doubt as to Wilcock's amillennial position, but his work should not be judged purely on that basis. The reader will no doubt easily discern my general position on the millennium, but I hope that these few comments will encourage perseverance in those whose views differ from mine on this point, and in those who have little interest in the narrower confines of the debate. It is my hope that *The Gospel in Revelation* will lay the foundations for a more detailed study with the aid of a good commentary.

Footnote 6 (continued)   gospel ascendancy as a prerequisite of the return of Christ. Unlike premillennialism, it does not look for a literal reign of Christ on earth for a period of one thousand years. (Figure 1 on p.166 illustrates these three views).

[7] London: Inter-Varsity Press, 1975, an amillennial treatment. The reader will also find the following useful: Leon Morris, *Revelation*, Tyndale New Testament Commentaries (London: Tyndale Press, 1969).

Premillennialism

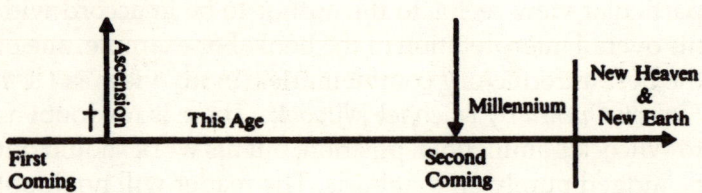

Postmillennialism

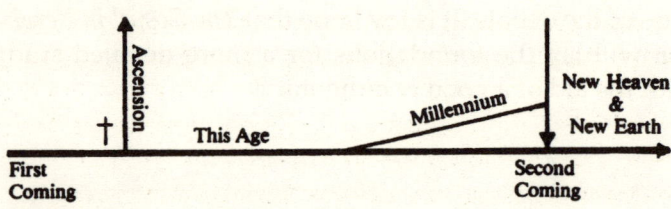

Amillennialism

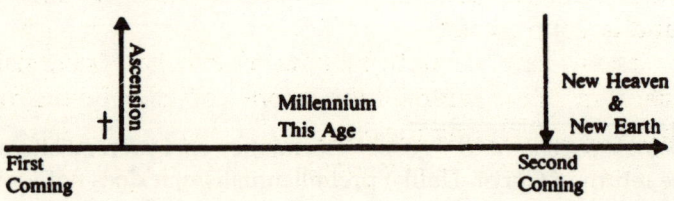

Figure 1   Three Views about the Millenium

Chapter One

'I Saw a Lamb Standing as Though it had Been Slain'

The Gospel as the Key to Revelation

Then I saw in the right hand of him who sat on the throne a scroll with writing on both sides and sealed with seven seals. And I saw a mighty angel proclaiming in a loud voice, 'Who is worthy to break the seals and open the scroll'? But no-one in heaven or on earth or under the earth could open the scroll or even look inside it. I wept and wept because no-one was found who was worthy to open the scroll or look inside. Then one of the elders said to me, 'Do not weep! See, the Lion of the tribe of Judah, the Root of David, has triumphed. He is able to open the scroll and its seven seals'.

Then I saw a Lamb, looking as if it had been slain, standing in the centre of the throne encircled by the four living creatures and the elders.

And they sang a new song:

'You are worthy to take the scroll and to open the seals, because you were slain, and with your blood you purchased men for God from every tribe and language and people and nation' (Revelation 5:1–6,9).

The Lamb and the Lion

Apocalyptic was a form of religious writing that became very popular amongst the Jews from about the second century BC. One of its characteristics was that the visionary related how he received a revelation from God (Apocalypse comes from the Greek word for revelation), and was then told to write it in a scroll and seal it until the time for revealing should come. The publication of the scroll would mean that the time had come and the secrets were out! John recalls this characteristic in Revelation 5. The scroll contains the message of God, the truth about his kingdom. But who is able to reveal it? John weeps because none is found who is worthy to reveal the truth about God and his kingdom and, so it seems, it must remain sealed in the scroll. But then he is given good news. There is one who has triumphed and is therefore able to open the scroll. He is the Lion of the tribe of Judah, the Messiah from the royal line of David. In that brief description John captures the sense of fierce majesty and irresistible strength. Here is represented the warrior-king fresh from battle with the blood of the foe upon his sword. He is invincible and glorious in his conquests. He has filled with terror all who would resist him, and has put them to flight. Because of this power and might which has brought him triumph, the Lion is able to open to all men the mysteries of the kingdom of God.

But when John turns to see the Lion he sees no such figure of glory and majestic power. Rather he sees a Lamb standing 'as though it had been slain.' Even that verbal conundrum, so typical of apocalyptic, only heightens the effect which is to shatter the visual image of the Lord of the beasts. A slain Lamb! That is the victory which overcomes and puts the truth of the kingdom of God within our reach. By a skilful use of apocalyptic images, John illuminates the central paradox of the gospel. The victory of God was the humiliation and death of his Son. The Lion assumes the meekness of the Lamb and dies in order to overcome. Now the scroll can be opened and the voice is heard in praise:

> 'You are worthy to take the scroll and to open the seals, because you were slain . . .'

Through his suffering and death the Lamb is the revealer of God. Appropriately the book is entitled 'The Revelation of Jesus Christ.' Here we see that the key to the truth, all the truth, about the kingdom of God is Jesus Christ in his life, death and resurrection. John has woven this fact into the apocalyptic idiom by depicting the slain Lamb as the one who alone is worthy to unlock the truth. In this way John reminds us of the centrality of the gospel in his book. If we would unlock the meaning of Revelation it must be by means of the fact that Jesus Christ in his earthly ministry of redemption is the true and revealing Word of God. Revelation, like every other book in the New Testament is an exposition of the gospel. It may emphasize certain implications of the gospel, but it is about the gospel just the same. As Michael Wilcock says of the author:

> And now he was again to receive the Word and the Witness, a genuine message from God, which in due course was to be read aloud in Church meetings like other inspired scripture. It would in a sense be nothing new; simply a recapitulation of the Christian faith he possessed already. But it was to be the last time that God would repeat the patterns of truth, and he was to do so with devastating power and in unforgettable splendour.[1]

---

[1] *I Saw Heaven Opened* (London: Inter-Varsity Press, 1975) p. 31.

What is the Gospel?

Let us be clear what we mean by the centrality of the gospel. First, what is the gospel? The gospel is the message about Jesus Christ; about his life, death and resurrection for us and our salvation. It is an historic thing in that Christ redeemed us by what he was and did nearly two thousand years ago in Palestine. While the effects of the gospel events stretch both backwards and forward in time, those effects are not themselves the gospel which we believe for our salvation. It is important that we distinguish the effects or fruits of the gospel from the gospel itself. Regeneration, faith and sanctification in the Christian are fruits of the gospel. But we do not lay hold of our salvation by faith in faith, or in regeneration, or in the giving of the Holy Spirit. Only by faith in Christ, in his living and dying as my substitute Man, do I receive the gift of salvation. Even the second coming of Christ is not the gospel, but a fruit of the gospel. We are not saved by believing that he *will* come, but by believing that he *has* come in the flesh for us.

So, the gospel is distinctly the work of Jesus Christ in a way that it is not distinctly the work of God the Father or the Holy Spirit. It is a perfect and a complete work which took place in the very person of Jesus of Nazareth, and therefore not in us. It, and it alone, is the basis of our acceptance with God. In the writings of Paul, this latter fact is often spoken of as justification. To justify is to declare someone to be just or righteous. Because of the merits of Christ our substitute, God is able to credit the believing sinner with those same merits. He justifies the sinner purely on the basis of the fact that there is one who stands as righteous in the sinner's place. The sinner who believes is the sinner who trusts in the historic Christ as his or her substitute before God. This historic Christ is alive now at the right-hand of God. But he is there now as our substitute only because he was that historic substitute for us in his life and death.

When we speak of the centrality of the gospel we refer to the fact that every aspect of our salvation stems from the gospel. We mean that the gospel is truly the power of God for salvation in that it is through the gospel we are called, regenerated, converted, sanctified and finally glorified. We mean that Jesus Christ, God come in the flesh, as he lived, died and rose again, gave meaning to all history and human existence. We mean that the gospel is the only means we have of beginning, continuing and persevering in the Christian life.

The error that we must emphatically repudiate is the often held notion that the gospel is the power of God only to get us converted. I once heard a missionary speaker report how a pastor in the mission field wrote to headquarters concerning his flock: 'We all know the gospel here, and now we must go on to something more solid'. The idea is that the gospel is the gateway to Christian experience, and thus to eternal life, but once we enter that gateway we move on to another more solid reality by which we progress. Sanctification, or becoming holy, or growing in the Christian faith, is frequently depicted as a new stage after conversion. The means to it is variously presented. For some it is by an act of 'total commitment', or of 'self emptying' or of 'putting to death the old nature'. For others it is a distinct crisis experience of the Holy Spirit. Christian literature and preaching is full of 'steps to the deeper life' or 'keys to the abundant and victorious life'. This is not to quibble over pious jargon and terminology. The point at issue is simply this. When we approach sanctification as attainable by any means other than the gospel of Christ – the same gospel by which we are converted – we have departed from the teaching of the New Testament.

The Centrality of the Gospel

The centrality of the gospel can be expressed with regard to any aspect of the biblical teaching of salvation. It means that what God achieved in Christ is the goal of all God's purposes as they are expressed in both Old and New Testaments. In this lies the meaning of Christ as Alpha and Omega.

1. *Christ is the Meaning of Creation*

We do not fully grasp the biblical teaching on creation until we have dealt with those passages that speak of Christ in creation. John 1:1–2 reminds us that the Word that became flesh as Jesus of Nazareth was the agent of creation. Paul takes this a step further in Colossians 1:15–20. Here Christ is spoken of as the one *in* whom, *through* whom and *for* whom all things were created. Let us be content at this stage to note that Paul is saying that the Christ who made peace by the blood of his cross (Colossians 1:20) is the agent, purpose and goal of creation. Some may think of the gospel as a kind of afterthought of God's which he devised when sin ruined the creation. But here we see that the gospel was God's forethought to creation. God created the heavens and the earth with the express plan and purpose of bringing all things to their ultimate goal through the suffering and death of Christ.

2. *Christ is the Meaning of the Old Testament Covenants and Law*

The Old Testament sets out in great detail the fact that it was God's will to relate to his people in a specific way. In the redemptive process God relates to man in covenant. The covenant is a constitution which sets out the nature of the relationship between God and Israel, his chosen people. The law of Moses is the most comprehensive expression of this covenant relationship which is established through the gracious redemptive work of God. The New Testament picks up the covenant theme and speaks of Jesus Christ as the one who fulfils it. His birth brings to fruition all the covenant promises of the Old Testament (see Luke 1:46–55, 68–79, 2:29–32). That Jesus fulfilled the law (Matthew 5:17) means that he lived as the perfect covenant partner with God. In other words, he was without sin. His baptism at the hands of John the Baptist was the perfect expression of the human choice to live for God and not against him. And it was at his baptism that Jesus was declared to be God's true and beloved Son. Luke's use of the genealogy at this point (Luke 3:22–38) shows that the statement, 'You are my Son', denotes Jesus' acceptance before God as the true Israelite, the true man (Adam is the son of God, v. 38).

3. Christ is the meaning of prophecy

Speaking of the law and the prophets Jesus said, 'I have not come to abolish them but to fulfil them' (Matthew 5:17). It is a mistake to see this reference to the prophets as meaning that Jesus fulfilled certain messianic predictions which are scattered throughout the prophetic writings. The statement is all inclusive and means that all that the prophets spoke is fulfilled in Christ. The prophetic word of judgment against sin is fulfilled in the death of Christ on the Cross. The promises of a new convenant, a new restored people of God, a new dwelling place of God amongst men, are all fulfilled in Christ. Furthermore they are fulfilled in the gospel event. About this I will have more to say in later chapters, for this is a contentious point and I want to state clearly what I mean by it. Let us, for the moment, observe Paul's conviction that the prophetic promises find their 'Yes' in Christ (2 Corinthians 1:20). Paul expressed this in his sermon at Antioch when he said, 'We tell you the good news: What God promised to our fathers he has fulfilled for us, their children, by raising up Jesus' (Acts 13: 32–33).

4. *Christ is the Meaning of Christian Existence*

'For to me, to live is Christ', said Paul (Philippians 1:21). The Christ that he refers to is the Christ described in Philippians 2, that is, the Christ that suffered in the flesh, and was exalted to the place of honour with God (Philippians 2:6–11). It is the Christ of the gospel who is Lord. For Paul, it is this Christ who gives life its only possible meaning. Christ does this by both revealing and by re-establishing, through his redemptive act, the true relationship between God and man, man and man, man and the creation. He does this in his own being, and in such a way that the sinner who believes God's word that this redemptive act is for him is given, as a free gift, the same status that Christ possesses by virtue of his sin-free obedience. We cannot say it better than to use Paul's words: 'Christ, who is our life' (Colossians 3:4). By this Paul means that, as a consequence of his perfect life and death, everything that Christ is before God, he is FOR US. He is the sinless Son FOR US. He is the true covenant partner FOR US. He is the beloved FOR US. He is the righteous and holy one, the judged sinner, the new life, the Spirit-filled man, the perfect worshipper of God – all FOR US.

From this fact of the gospel existence of Christ FOR US, and from this fact alone, comes the motive and the power for our Christian existence. All the fruits of the gospel are just that: fruits *of the gospel*. Regeneration, faith, sanctification and final perseverance are all fruits of the gospel.

They can grow on no other tree. Legalistic demands, cajolery, and browbeatings for 'deeper-commitment' and 'total surrender', when cut loose from the grace of the gospel are but wretched weeds which can produce only despondency, disillusionment and rebelliousness.

5. *Christ is the Meaning of the Second Coming*

The first coming of Christ, the gospel-event, establishes the significance of the second coming of Christ. Perhaps one of the greatest reasons for misunderstanding of the Book of Revelation is the failure to grasp the relationship of the first and second comings of Christ. Let us be very clear about this point. Christ does not return to do some new or different work. His return in glory will be to consummate the finished work of his life, death and resurrection. At his coming he will be revealed in all his glory to all principalities and powers. That which the believer now grasps by faith will be open to every eye. That which the believer now owns by faith and which is in Christ, his substitute, will be perfected as the reality in himself. The *status* that we now have in Christ will become the *state* we have in ourselves.

It is this relationship of the first and second comings which provides the structure of John's thought in the Book of Revelation. It is the relationship of the suffering Christ to the Christ who is manifested in glory. It is the relationship of the Lamb to the Lion. The Lion is the symbol of the majesty of the glorious messiah-king of Israel who is revealed in the glory of the kingdom of God. The Lamb is the symbol of the suffering Jesus of Nazareth. John shows us that he who would see the Lion must find him first in the Lamb. The messianic kingdom of Israel has its reality only through the redemptive work of the Christ who died and rose again. Although the Lamb will ever be the Lamb, for the glorified Christ is exalted on account of his sufferings, nevertheless the majesty of the Lion will shine forth from the Lamb at his second coming.

Living by Faith Means Living by the Gospel

For the present the Lion's glory is veiled. Only faith can perceive it through the gospel. The testimony of the New Testament to Jesus as the reigning Christ is one that can only be believed or rejected, for there is no objective proof of it. We can try to evaluate the records of the four Gospels with regard to the historic events of Jesus' life, death and resurrection. But, in the end, we cannot perceive that our salvation lies in those events other than by believing that it is so because God assures us that it is so. In the Gospels we read how people responded to Jesus in different ways. Some rejected him as a false prophet. Others were enthusiastic for him only so long as they thought he would free them from the Romans or supply their material needs. A few were enabled to perceive in him the answer to the true spiritual hopes of Israel. Even his closest friends misunderstood some of what he was saying to them. In fact we see that it is only when the Holy Spirit is given at Pentecost that the followers of Jesus finally understand what it was all about.

Paul describes this present existence of the believer as that of a nomadic tent-dweller:

> While we are in this tent we groan and are burdened, because we do not wish to be unclothed but to be clothed with our heavenly dwelling, so that what is mortal may be swallowed up by life. Now it is God who has made us for this very purpose and has given us the Spirit as a deposit, guaranteeing what is to come. Therefore we are always confident and

know that as long as we are at home in the body we are away
from the Lord. We live by faith, not by sight (2 Corinthians
5:4–7).

There is a real sense of our incompleteness in being away
from the Lord. So we live by faith, not by sight. Faith is
never a vaguely defined thing for Paul. It is always
defined by its object: Jesus Christ. Faith means implicit
trust in the Christ of the gospel to save and sustain us. To
live by faith means to live by the gospel. Paul is saying that
the Holy Spirit is given to us to guarantee the final participation of the believer in the kingdom where he will no longer be away from the Lord. How does the Holy Spirit act
as this guarantee? He does so by enabling us to live by
faith. The Spirit establishes our faith and trust in the living
and dying of Jesus for us. The Spirit's work is to energize
our faith; not in faith itself, nor in the Spirit himself, but in
Christ alone. While we are absent from the Lord we must
know him as the historic Jesus of Nazareth who wrought
salvation for us. By faith we know that this Saviour is now
the Lion who has conquered, the ruling Lord of all creation. But we can know him thus only because of his conquest as the suffering Lamb.

These truths of our salvation and its effect on our present Christian existence are the commonplace of the New
Testament. John has taken them once more and reclothed
them in forms and images which are the coinage of the Old
Testament. By doing this he fulfils a purpose which we
will see is of great value to us. It is, as Austin Farrer[2] has
described it, though a rebirth of images, the old images of
a passing culture and people, that John surprises us with a
fresh glimpse of the grandeur of God's plan. He thus saves

---

[2] Austin Farrer, *A Rebirth of Images* (London: A. & C. Black,
1949).

the ordinary struggling Christian from a trivial view of himself and of his meaning. He enables us to see that the tribulation of the Lamb dignifies the tribulations, small and great, of every believer with a significance that can never be swallowed up in the chaos of meaninglessness.

Summary

The Lion is the image of the glorified and reigning Christ. He alone can unlock the kingdom of God to us and make its reality known. But, like John, we can See the Lion only as he has come to us in the form of the slain Lamb. John points to the gospel-event; the living, dying and rising of Jesus Christ, as the key to the revelation of the kingdom. It is thus also the key to the Book of Revelation. By the use of this figure, he points to the meaning of all existence as that which is revealed in the gospel. For the Christian there is a tension between the coming of the kingdom through the gospel and the continuation of the present order. Living by faith means living by the gospel. What this means is the subject of John's book.

Thesis

The Lamb-Lion tension shows that the gospel is the only key to the understanding of the Book of Revelation.

Chapter Two

'The Tribulation and the Kingdom'

The Gospel and Our Present Sufferings

I, John, your brother and companion in the suffering and kingdom and patient endurance that are ours in Jesus, was on the island of Patmos because of the word of God and the testimony of Jesus. On the Lord's day I was in the Spirit, and I heard behind me a loud voice like a trumpet, which said: 'Write on a scroll what you see and send it to the seven churches' (Revelation 1:9–11).

The Occasion of the Book

One of the neglected aspects of Revelation in many modern interpretations of it is the occasion of its writing. We should never lose sight of the historic circumstances out of which this extraordinary book arose. For our purposes it is not important to determine whether or not the author is the apostle John or some other. Nor does an exact dating really matter. John describes the background circumstances sufficiently to enable us to appreciate the purpose of the book. John is in exile on the little Aegean isle of Patmos because of his active Christian witness. He writes a circular letter to a group of churches across on the mainland of Asia Minor (what is now the eastern part of Turkey). In it he expresses his solidarity with these Christians who are also undergoing hardship because of persecutions. He comforts, encourages, chides, and exhorts them in the gospel. He reminds them of the meaning of Christ's sufferings and of his glory, that they might stand firm in the knowledge that their own sufferings are utterly consistent with the reality of God's kingdom in this present age. At a time when many Christians were possibly quite literally running for their lives, he does not detain them with a closely argued theological treatise. Rather he draws from the familiar and fertile imagery of Jewish apocalyptic in order to paint vivid word-pictures of the reality of the kingdom of God. They are images that will stick in the mind and aid the recall of the basic truths of the gospel. They are images that use bold strokes and brilliant colours to represent the victory of the kingdom of God over the powers of darkness. In the extremity of suffering when the details of a Pauline exposition of justification by faith may be difficult to recall, the simple and unlettered Christian would more easily remember what had been read to him in the assembly about the slain Lamb glorious upon his throne.

As John wrote these words, he, along with so many of his fellow-Christians, was experiencing the hard reality of the words of Jesus to his disciples: 'In the world you have tribulation' (John 16:33). This tribulation included martyrdom for many Christians in the first and second centuries. But even in times of relative calm, life for the believer was full of pressures, conflicts and bewildering circumstances. When the Church came under exceptional pressure from the pagan world, and met fierce opposition, many a believer paid for his faithfulness with his life. Then the Church cried out, as did the psalmist of Old, 'How long O Lord?' (Psalm 79:5, Revelation 6:10).

John does not urge his fellow-Christians to seek a means of escape from this tribulation, for he understood only too well that discipleship means suffering. Rather he urges them to persevere to the end and so to receive the blessings prepared for them. Patience, endurance, perseverance and overcoming are not impossible ideals which John uses in a vain and desperate bid to keep a persecuted minority from ultimate disillusionment. They are the realities of the kingdom of God as it breaks into our history and gathers its members towards the great consummation. They are born of the truth which is in Jesus himself: 'In the world you have tribulation, but be of good cheer, I have overcome the world' (John 16:33 RSV).

Once we have looked at John's purpose in this way, we are in a position to express the abiding truth and application of the Book of Revelation to ourselves in the twentieth century. The paradox of the Lamb and the Lion is translated into Christian existence when John speaks of 'the suffering and kingdom and patient endurance that are ours in Jesus' (Revelation 1:9). These are the two dimensions of our present struggle. Christian existence is lived out between the two realities of suffering and the kingdom. It reflects the suffering of the Lamb and anticipates the consummation of the kingdom through the conquest of the Lion.

The Cause of all Suffering

Suffering is the abiding experience of Christians. That may sound rather trite coming from the context of the affluence of western society and of the freedom of religious expression. In the non-communist world we are becoming more aware of the persecution of Christians in the Soviet Union and other Eastern bloc countries. We hear from time to time of the modern martyrs who really do come to the ultimate test of a faithful witness to Christ. Against these sufferings the hassles we face day by day fade almost to nothing. And yet people do suffer in the midst of political freedom and economic affluence. Suicides, divorce, mental illness, race riots and neglect of children are some of the more publicized problems of western society. Christians are immune from none of them.

Biblical reference to the suffering of Christians includes all of these and much more. Suffering is the direct result of the fall of man. Suffering comes from the dislocation of the true relationships for which God created us. The seeds of all natural disasters such as earthquake, flood and famine, lie in the fact that God cursed the earth on account of man: 'Cursed is the ground because of you; through painful toil you will eat of it all the days of your life. It will produce thorns and thistles for you, and you will eat the plants of the field' (Genesis 3:17–18).

This connection between the fall of man and natural disasters may seem fanciful to some readers. It is established not only on the basis of the scripture just quoted, but also on Paul's assertion that 'the creation was subjected to frustration,' and that 'the creation itself will be liberated from its bondage to decay and brought into the glorious freedom of the children of God' (Romans 8:20,21).

Not only is man out of harmony with the creation, but also with himself. Human relationships are ruined by sin in that selfishness has replaced concern for others. While man acknowledged his true creatureliness before God he could not exalt himself above his brother. Now, other-centredness has given way to self-centredness. The chief damage of sin is to the relationship between God and man. Sin is our rejection of God as Lord, and the desire to be lord of our own lives. All other relationships depend on our relationship to God. When the one is ruined all are ruined.

All the problems of contemporary society are but reflections of the basic dislocation of the relationship between man and God. Because God has defined us at creation in relation to himself, we are less than truly human when we are out of that relation. Central to this relationship was man's 'yes' to his Creator. When Adam refused to affirm this relationship; when he said 'no' instead of 'yes', God ceased to affirm man and judged him.

Today this judgment is visible in the natural disasters, the political upheavals, the personal tragedies, and the loneliness of people in big cities. It is seen in greedy multinational corporations, dishonest business, power-hungry unionism, and drunken driving. It is seen in cancer and birth defects, in the neglect of minorities and the rejection of the aged. It is seen in family conflict and social disturbance. It is seen in the ravaging of earth's resources, in the pollution of air, water and food. It is seen in decay and death. For all of this we and the whole of mankind are collectively to blame, for all have sinned.

The Suffering of the Christian

When a child of Adam is renewed through the gospel and made a member of the new humanity of which Christ is the head, a great deal changes. The believing sinner is the repentant sinner who seeks to forsake his former 'no' to God. He believes the word of God about sin and the forgiveness which is through Christ. He hears the word of God which assures every believer of sonship freely given on the grounds of the perfect sonship of Jesus Christ. Consequently he wants to live as a son of God and begins the struggle against the world, the flesh and the devil. He longs for the return of Christ which will mean his own perfecting and entry into the final glory of the kingdom of God.

But while there are radical and immediate changes that take place for the sinner the moment he believes the gospel and trusts Christ for salvation, there are also many things that remain the same. The believer is not perfected in this life. He remains a sinner, though forgiven. He remains a sinner even though he seeks to eliminate sins. Conversion does not remove us from this world but rather puts us into conflict with it. Salvation is not instantaneous, and the reason is not hard to find. It has pleased God to bring in his kingdom through the gospel which must be preached throughout the world. We shall see later on that this is a perspective which is distinct to the New Testament and which modifies quite drastically the perspective of the Old Testament on the coming of the kingdom.

Thus the believer becomes a child of God, but remains a sinner. He becomes an inheritor of tIe new age, but remains a dweller in the old age. He receives eternal life but, unless Christ comes first, he will suffer sickness and death before he is resurrected to life. The Christian not only does not escape the woes of this sinful world, but he must also be content to lose favour with the world through non-conformity to its standards. Suffering then, is the norm of Christian experience. Far from removing suffering from us, becoming a Christian compounds it. That is why we walk by faith and not by sight. That means that we live according to what we know by faith to be true – that we are the children of God and that our salvation is sure. It means that we do not live by what we experience. Reality cannot be gauged by what we feel or by the circumstances of our lives. What we now possess by faith is in Christ in heaven: 'Your life is now hidden with Christ in God' (Colossians 3:3). That is why John says, 'Now we are the children of God, and what we will be has not yet been made known. But we know that when he appears, we shall be like him, for we shall see him as he is.' (1 John 3:2).

Paul's view of the matter is instructive. Suffering is a reality for there is a sense in which we share Christ's sufferings. Of course the church cannot suffer as Christ did in that he was the sinless one suffering for the sins of others. But the sufferings of Christ establish the nature of service or ministry in this world. While Christ's sufferings for us were unique, unrepeatable and infinite, yet there is a sense in which Christ must go on suffering in the world for the sake of the world. These sufferings he suffers in his body the church. Paul refers to his own sufferings thus: 'I fill up in my flesh what is still lacking in regard to Christ's afflictions, for the sake of his body, which is the church' (Colossians 1:24). Again he said, 'For just as the sufferings of Christ flow over into our lives, so also through Christ our comfort overflows' (2 Corinthians 1:5). Peter says: 'Rejoice that you participate in the sufferings of Christ, so that you may be overjoyed when his glory is revealed . . . If you suffer as a Christian, do not be ashamed, but praise God that you bear that name' (1 Peter 4:13,16).

Paul has much to say about the matter in his letter to the Romans also: 'We also rejoice in our sufferings, because we know that suffering produces perseverance; perseverance, character; and character, hope. And hope does not disappoint us, because God has poured out his love into our hearts by the Holy Spirit, whom he has given us' (Romans 5:3–5). Suffering is also the mark of true sonship: '. . . But you received the Spirit of sonship. And by him we cry, "Abba, Father." The Spirit himself testifies with our spirit that we are God's children. Now if we are children, then we are heirs – heirs of God and co-heirs with Christ, if indeed we share in his sufferings in order that we may also share in his glory. I consider that our present sufferings are not worth comparing with the glory that will be revealed in us' (Romans 8:15–18).

These scriptures are consistent in what they teach us. The church as the body of Christ, and therefore the individuals within it, suffers in the world. Suffering is not a sign that God has forsaken us but, on the contrary, it is one of the marks of true sonship. This suffering is the characteristic of our ministry which flows on from Christ's suffering ministry. But suffering is not without benefit, and not without end. The end of Jesus' suffering, through his resurrection and glorification, points every Christian to his destiny of glorification. In the light of this destiny which Christ both secured for us and revealed to us in his earthly ministry, our present sufferings pale. It would be wrong to say that they pale into insignificance, for they are real and often very hard to bear. Furthermore, God in his goodness uses these very sufferings to shape our character and to fill us with hope for the true glory yet to be experienced. Even when our sufferings are culpable and self-inflicted through the hardness of our hearts, God graciously uses this for our ultimate good. Thus, 'in all things God works for the good of those who love him, who have, been called according to his purpose' (Romans 8:28).

We must reject any notion that becoming a Christian' guarantees smooth sailing all the way through life. We do not minimize the resources of the Christian to cope with life. There is a very great difference between coping with life's hardships and 'copping out' of them. With godly wisdom a Christian is able under 'normal' circumstances to avoid those things which destroy the body, debase the mind, and seduce the soul. But being a Christian does not necessarily save him from shivering on a winter's night during a power blackout, or from the hazards of natural disasters and the drunken driver speeding through a redlight. Above all being a Christian means that we have taken sides in the final warfare between light and darkness. If God wills to bring in his kingdom through the preaching of the gospel, then all of us who own that gospel stand in the front line of battle. We must never underestimate the foe.

What John does for us in the Book of Revelation is to underscore not only the fact of suffering in the Christian life, but also the real source of it in the conflict between the kingdom of God and the kingdom of Satan.

Christ's Victory

The second dimension to Christian existence is established by the fact of Jesus Christ. Jesus said, 'In the world you will have trouble. But take heart! I have overcome the world.' The answer to tribulation was not to remove the believer from it, but assure him that the world has been overcome by Christ. To the sceptic who wants the acid-test of scientific proof, this seems a very pretentious statement. Look at the facts. The leader was popular for a while but was finally forsaken and done to death. His followers did indeed spread throughout the world, but at the times when they seemed most powerful they lacked most clearly the characteristics of love and servanthood that the leader spoke of. Today, the followers go on protesting that they believe in one holy universal church. In fact it is none of these things to the observer.

The error of the sceptic is not that he perceives the weakness and the sinfulness of the church, but that he tests the truth of the gospel by these marks. Those who are mesmerized by a temporary show of strength and grandeur in the church are likewise in danger of missing the truth. It was the error of some of Jesus' contemporaries that they misperceived the implications of the coming of the kingdom. The apparent contradiction between the prophetic predictions of a glorious Israel ruled by the Davidic prince before whom all nations bowed, and those of the suffering servant who was despised and rejected in order to bear the sins of many, was too much for them to accept. These Jews forgot the suffering servant and looked only for the conquering prince. The message of a crucified messiah thus became an obstacle, a stumbling block of offence. But this offensive figure is, says Paul, 'the power of God, and the wisdom of God' (1 Corinthians 1:24).

The victory of Christ is the victory of his death and resurrection. In saying this, we do not separate these climactic events from the whole of Jesus' life. What is often called the active obedience of Christ, his perfect obedience to the law of God in his life, is integral with his passive obedience, his suffering and death. In his life Jesus displayed many signs of his victory as he exercised power over Satan's temptations, over demons, over natural forces, over material objects, over people's wills, over sickness and death. The miracles of Jesus were all signs of the arrival of the kingdom which had been heralded by the prophets of Israel.

The obedience of Christ culminated in his death on the cross. This, to the world's way of thinking, was the defeat of a pathetic dream. But God has declared this to be the decisive victory over Satan, sin and death. The hostility of sin was overcome and the rebellion of mankind overcome. 'For God was pleased to have all his fullness dwell in him (Christ), and through him to reconcile to himself all things, whether things 'on earth or things in heaven, by making peace through his blood, shed on the cross' (Colossians 1:19–20). 'And having disarmed the powers and authorities, he made a public spectacle of them, triumphing over them by the cross' (Colossians 2:15).

Summary

The two dimensions of the Christian life as John draws it, are the tribulation and the kingdom. In order to understand ourselves and the nature of Christian existence we need to understand these two dimensions and how they relate. Suffering is the common lot of humanity and not too hard to describe. Christians often need to learn, however, that their membership of the kingdom of God does not make them immune to sickness and suffering in this life. There is a tendency to make this error in some circles that stress the presence of miraculous phenomena, especially healings. The error is bred from a misperception of how the kingdom comes. In a real sense, this is the question to which Revelation addresses itself. The victory of Christ is real, for he has overcome the world. Until he comes, however, the Church must suffer in the world.

Thesis

The theme of the Lamb and the Lion points to the paradox of the normal suffering of Christians and the victory of Christ.

Chapter Three

'They Have Washed Their Robes in the Blood of the Lamb'

Justification by Faith in Revelation

Then one of the elders asked me, 'These in white robes – who are they, and where did they come from?' I answered, 'Sir, you know.' And he said, 'These are they who have come out of the great tribulation; they have washed their robes and made them white in the blood of the Lamb' (Revelation 7:13–14).

The Christian's suffering is not forever. To think otherwise would make a mockery of the gospel and of the hope of glory. Tribulation belongs to this age in which there is a real sense of 'not having.' But, it is a transitory preparation for the time when the full glory is revealed. Because of our confidence in the reality of the perfect life beyond the resurrection, suffering is given a positive dimension. Paul tells us that, because of the gospel, suffering produces endurance, patience and hope (Romans 5:3–5).

The Christian view of this life and the life to come is defined by the person and work of Christ. Unfortunately, the on-going relevance of the gospel to our life-view is often forgotten by Christians. How many Christians can give a credible statement on how we gain acceptance with

God? Far too few. And even fewer seem to have any clear idea about how our acceptance with God relates to daily life and godly living. Furthermore, what has been described as 'warmbath' Christianity encourages the idea that the heart of the Christian message has to do with being able to live an unruffled existence. Such an approach leads in time to the obscuring of the real issue which the gospel forces upon us: 'How can the sinner find acceptance with a righteous God?'

In order to answer this question biblically we must accept the Bible's answer. We must be prepared to come to terms with the kind of distinctions that the Bible makes in setting forth the work of God for our salvation. In Chapter 1 we saw that the gospel is the hub of all biblical teaching. It is the heart of the Christian message and permeates all Christian truth. It bears repeating that those who are impatient with the vital distinction between the gospel as the work of God FOR US in Jesus Christ, and the fruit of the gospel (sanctification) as the work of God IN US by his Spirit, will never grasp the meaning of the fact that the gospel is the central fact upon which all else hinges.

The Sovereignty of God in Salvation

Revelation 7 records the vision of John in which he sees the angelic agents of God's wrath. Another angel commands them to withhold the tribulation of judgment until the servants of God are marked with a protective seal. Then John says that he heard the numbers of those who were sealed: twelve thousand from each of the tribes of Israel. After this he sees another vision of an innumerable multitude from every nation, tribe and language, standing before the throne of the Lamb and praising him for their salvation. An elder standing by identifies the crowd as those who have washed their robes and made them white in the blood of the Lamb.

Let us not misunderstand John. He is not suggesting that the gospel delivers us immediately from tribulation. The time will come when we will be removed from all suffering forever. This view of final deliverance is intended to comfort us in our present sufferings by showing that no tribulation can overwhelm us and sweep us away from our place in the kingdom. Furthermore, the last great judgment of God on all sin and rebellion against his kingdom, will not touch those who are his. There is one tribulation that the believer will never experience, and that is the final visitation of God's wrath, and eternal death.

We notice also in this chapter of Revelation that John uses two distinct word pictures to express his meaning. In the first he portrays the sealing of a perfect number of the people of Israel. It is not his intention to refer to the literal nation of Israel. He has too frequently followed the other writers of the New Testament in applying the old Israelite terminology to the true people of God, the new Israel in Christ, to slip back into Jewish particularism. Nor is it John's intention to state that exactly 144 000, no more and no less, will inherit the kingdom. He is at home in the apocalyptic use of symbolic numbers and would not understand such crass literalism at all. No, John is saying that the gathering clouds of judgment will overtake the created order. The present suffering of the saints is not to be misunderstood as evidence that God can or will forget those that are his. The horrendous tribulation to come cannot threaten one single member of God's kingdom. All who are Abraham's children by faith in Jesus Christ (see Galatians 3:9) are secure from the wrath to come.

It is comforting to know that the number of God's elect is a perfect number. The kingdom of God will not lack one member that belongs to its perfection. Every place that

Christ has gone to prepare (John 14:2–3) will be filled. God's purpose to establish his perfect kingdom cannot be thwarted by man or devil. God has established the number of the elect and their names have been written in the book of life from the foundation of the world (Ephesians 1:4, Revelation 13:8). This perfect number – the square of twelve by the cube of ten – speaks eloquently of the security of the believer. I hasten to add that the doctrine of the security of the believer or, as it is sometimes known, the perseverance of the saints, means the security of the *believer*. This is no 'once saved, always saved' doctrine which allows one to ignore godliness and to sin freely on the basis of some alleged conversion experience. Perseverance means perseverance in faith and well-doing. The Book of Revelation constantly urges perseverance as the continuing life of faith.

Some may object that to speak of election or predestination is to limit the kingdom of God to a few. Does it not make God a capricious tyrant? We must answer that such objections usually stem from a refusal to accept that we are faced here with a mystery that it is not given to us to solve. There is also a radical misunderstanding which maintains that God's sovereignty in election removes man's responsibility. Such is not true. How divine sovereignty and human responsibility work together we cannot know. The Bible makes it clear that they do.

Let us remember that Jesus discriminated and limited the numbers of the saved: 'Small is the gate and narrow the road that leads to life, and only a few find it' (Matthew 7:13–14). This is in line with the Old Testament teaching that only a faithful remnant of Israel would be saved. The little remnant idea must be seen in its context of the history of Israel, for it does not mean that the kingdom will be very sparsely populated. Election must not be interpreted as the activity of a capricious God who wants to bar the masses from entry into heaven. In fact, it works the other way. Such is the nature of sinful man that without God's sovereign election heaven would be empty. It is the means by which God infallibly brings into the kingdom the perfect number out of the mass of humanity. Without it none would be saved.

John has a second picture which complements the first. This time it is not the perfect number of Israel that he sees, but the innumerable saints from every nation on earth. The church of God is truly catholic (universal), for while salvation came through one Man of one tribe of one nation, the kingdom will consist of people of every nation. This does not contradict Jesus' 'few,' nor the remnant idea of the Old Testament. Both concepts point to the exclusive office of Christ so that no-one comes to the Father except through him (John 14:6). For all that, the elect remnant of God will be a staggering multitude of people.

Now note the elder's description of these people that John sees. They have washed their robes in the blood of the Lamb.

The imagery is transparent. Cleansing from the pollution of sin is a well-worn biblical idea. The law of Moses contained many prescriptions for ritual and actual washing to symbolize a cleansing from sin.[1] Blood was used also in purification rites.[2] This shows the clear link between the sacrificial provisions of the law and the idea of cleansing from pollution. This was given constant expression in the Old Testament in the Prophets and the Psalms.[3] The imagery of cleansing also underwent some variation, for

---

[1] Eg., Exodus 30:19; 40:31; Leviticus 8:6; 14:8; 15:5–10 and 19–27; 16:24; Numbers 19:19.

[2] Eg., Leviticus 8:14–30; 14:6–8.

[3] Eg., Psalms 26:6; 51:1–19; Isaiah 1:16–20; Jeremiah 2:22; 4:14; Haggai 2:10–19.

example, in the vision of Zechariah 3. Here the High Priest, representing Israel, stands clothed in filthy robes symbolizing Israel's pollution in the Babylonian exile. The High Priest is then clothed in pure garments as a sign of Israel's cleansing. Not unrelated is Jesus' parable of the wedding feast where one guest is found without a wedding garment (Matthew 22:1–14). Whatever the reason for this man's state of undress, he is judged unworthy and cast out. His own clothing is unfit for the feast. John himself has taken up this theme in Revelation 19, and we shall examine it in more detail later.

The common message in all these purification images is that the pollution of sin must be cleansed before one may enter God's holy kingdom. The New Testament applies the death of Christ to this need:

> The blood of Jesus, his Son, purifies us from every sin.
>
> (1 John 1:7)

> Since we have confidence to enter the Most Holy Place by the blood of Jesus . . . let us draw near to God with a sincere heart in full assurance of faith, having our hearts sprinkled to cleanse us from a guilty conscience and having our bodies washed with pure water.
>
> (Hebrews 10:19,22)

John shows us in his vision of the multitude of the saved that it is the blood of the atoning sacrifice of the Lamb that removes the pollution of sin (Revelation 7:14).

Pollution and guilt are closely related. The Bible does not depict the sinner as one who has accidentally picked up some filth through inadvertent contact with what is unclean. He is in fact utterly blameworthy for his defilement. He stands guilty and condemned. To be set right before God he must be purged of uncleanness and forgiven. Having said that, we must be careful to observe that the gospel way of forgiveness takes place on the basis of the perfect righteousness of Christ and his atoning death. In other words, for a sinner to be made righteous in himself, he must first of all be declared righteous by faith. The great transaction of justification on the grounds of Christ's merits is God's way of saving us. The justified sinner is the one whom God declares to be 'not guilty.' He does this on the basis of Christ's righteousness which he imputes, or credits, to the sinner who believes the gospel. The justified sinner is one who has received by faith the gift of the righteousness of Christ to clothe him before the searching eye of a holy God. He possesses by faith everything that belongs to Christ as God's true man. He is as acceptable to God as Jesus was when God called him 'beloved Son' (Matthew 3:17).

This imputation to the sinner of a righteousness which is not his own, is not a legal fiction. It is a just transaction because the sinner's debt has been fully paid and God's justice is satisfied. It is also a loving transaction because the recipient never deserves such kindness. John is telling us in Revelation 7 that God's sealing of his saints and the washing of one's robe in the blood of the Lamb, amount to the same thing. The outcome is sure and so the believer is given a basis for full assurance of salvation.

Justification in Revelation

Justification is not an occasional theme in Revelation. It is in fact the very warp and woof of the book. The structure and message of Revelation is not based on a few spectacular events immediately preceding the second coming of Christ, but rather upon the historic facts of the gospel, the person and work of Jesus Christ. This is not so apparent at first sight because so much of the book describes various judgments which point toward the consummation of the kingdom. It would be foolish to deny that Revelation deals with eschatology[4], that is, with the things relating to the end. There is much eschatology in Revelation. It is however, important that we grasp the perspective of this eschatology, and its relationship to our present existence. Above all, we must recognize that eschatology is shaped and given its significance by the historic events of the gospel.

When we speak of justification we are using a formal or technical way of referring to the gospel and its meaning. Through the life and death of Jesus the believer is accounted by God as free from the guilt of sin, and is thus accepted by God as his child. It is this message that permeates all that John is saying to us in Revelation. We note that it was the preaching of this gospel which led to the occasion for the writing of Revelation. Thus from the beginning the historic events of the gospel stand at the centre of the message. This is the revelation of Jesus Christ made known to John who bore witness to the word of God and the testimony of Jesus (Revelation 1:1–2). In his initial greeting to the recipients of his message John identifies the source of all their salvation as Jesus Christ, who is the faithful witness, the firstborn from the dead, and the ruler of the kings of the earth. Here he refers to the life, death, resurrection and present Lordship of Christ.

John then goes on to speak of the effects of Christ 's death using a familiar Old Testament idea:

> To him who loves us and has freed us from our sins by his blood, and has made us a kingdom and priests to serve his

---

[4] Greek: *eschatos* – last. Eschatology is the study of the last things.

God and Father – to him be glory and power for ever and ever! Amen (Revelation 1:5b–6).

This recalls the words of God to Moses on Mount Sinai as he spoke of the redemption of Israel from slavery in Egypt:

You yourselves have seen what I did to Egypt, and how I carried you on eagles' wings and brought you to myself. Now if you will obey me fully and keep my covenant, then out of all nations you will be my treasured possession. Although the whole earth is mine, you will be for me a kingdom of priests and a holy nation (Exodus 19:4–6).

Israel was given this privileged position through the covenant by which the God of all the universe committed himself to one small and otherwise insignificant nation.

The use of the political model of a kingdom to describe Israel foreshadowed the time when the nation would be ruled by the royal dynasty of David. But this political model also spoke in turn of the kingdom of God of which David's kingdom was itself only a shadow. This kingdom of God is the one established through the gospel of Jesus Christ. The redemption from Egypt which, in its time, did not speak clearly of a redemption from sin, nevertheless pointed towards the gospel. The pattern of redemption seen in the history of Israel's exodus from Egypt found its fulfilment in Christ. The kingdom of priests are those who are redeemed from sin by the blood of Christ. Priests were 'go-betweens.' They went to God on behalf of the nation and to the nation on behalf of God. John describes all Christians as priests because they have access to God through the blood of Christ.

Notice how John ascribes glory and dominion to the one who suffered (Revelation 1:6). Here is the basis of the theme of the whole book. Here is the Lamb and the Lion. The Christ who suffered is now the ruling Lord. It is inevitable that all things must be made subject to him, and so his second coming in glory is a certainty. Until that time he conquers and rules through the message of his suffering. The godless do not know that their present rebellion against Christ will be turned to his glory because of his suffering. The Lamb will reveal his Lion-like qualities when he comes to judge the world. Then those whose rebellion has pierced the Lamb will be confounded (Revelation 1:7).

I must stress again the relationship that John has so quickly established between the first and second comings of Christ. The second coming is the unveiling of the Lamb to reveal the Lion. The two are one, and there is a basic sense in which the two comings of Christ are one. God alone knows how many years separate these two great events but, notwithstanding the passing of a long period of time, we must hold the two in the closest conjunction. It is the separating of the significance of these two events which has led to many of the wild interpretations of Revelation by prophetic specialists.

The same perspective is to be found in the vision of the glorified Christ in Revelation 1:12–16. John is overwhelmed by the majesty of this figure, the description of whom defies any adequate visual reproduction. When he says, 'I fell at his feet as though dead' (verse 17), we can only suppose that John was filled with the realization of the enormous gulf that separated himself as a sinful being from the holy glory of the reigning Christ. He was like Isaiah brought by a vision of God's glory to cry 'woe' in despair at his own sinfulness (Isaiah 6:5). He was like Job driven to realize his unworthiness before the Lord of the universe (Job 42:1–6). He was like Peter who, through an experience of catching fish, glimpsed for a moment the power of Christ and in panic cried, 'Go away from me, Lord; I am a sinful man!' (Luke 5:1–8).

But John is comforted and restored with the message that this vision splendid is none other than the dying and rising Saviour (verse 18). John can stand before the Lion for he has been justified by the Lamb!

The letters to the churches are instructive in this regard (Revelation 2 and 3). John's view of Christian existence set out in these letters does not differ from that of Paul or Peter in their letters. All problems, heresies and deviations from the true course of Christian living which occupy the writers of the New Testament Epistles derive from the same basic problem: a failure to bring the gospel to bear on this or that aspect of life. Consequently there is only one remedy that can ever be prescribed and that is the gospel. This assertion may surprise many, for Christian living or the general question of sanctification (holiness) is so frequently dealt with in Christian teaching and preaching as if the gospel were only the means of beginning the Christian life, and not also the means of continuing it. The New Testament, however, teaches that it is the life, death and resurrection of Jesus Christ which constitute the meaning, motive and power for Christian living.[5]

---

[5] Herman Ridderbos states: That Paul's epistles give what is no longer the first announcement of this Gospel, but rather the further exposition and application of it, does not detract from the fact that this Gospel is the sole and constant subject of his epistles also; and that therefore, if one has to characterize their general content not only as kerygma [gospel proclamation], but also as doctrine [teaching] and paraenesis [exhortation], yet this doctrine, too, has no other object and this admonition no other starting point and ground than the fulfilling and redeeming activity of God in the advent Of Christ. *Paul: An outline of His Theology* (Grand Rapids: Wm. B. Eerdmans, 1975, London, S.P.C.K., 1977), 47f. (Explanatory terms in brackets mine).

Thus we find that the seven letters in Revelation contain the same perspective even though they use more of the symbolism and images of the Old Testament than either Paul or Peter. We may summarize the diagnoses thus:

1. The Ephesians have abandoned their first love. The gospel no longer grips and motivates them as it used to do (Revelation 2:4).

2. The Smyrnans are commended for their faithfulness and urged to persevere (Revelation 2:9–10).

3. The Church at Pergamum has allowed false teaching to enter. The gospel is compromised and those responsible invite retribution (Revelation 2:14–16).

4. The Thyatirans are in a similar position because of a false prophetess in their midst (Revelation 2:20).

5. In the church at Sardis love for the gospel has grown cold. The summons is to 'remember what you have received and heard.' Happily there are some who have not 'soiled their clothes.' These continue in faith in the Son of God by whose blood they are cleansed (Revelation 3:3–4).

6. The Philadelphians are commended for faithfulness in adversity (Revelation 3:8,10).

7. The Laodiceans have lost sight of the gospel and so have lost their fellowship with Christ. This same Christ waits to be readmitted: 'If anyone hears my voice and opens the door, I will go in and eat with him.' The voice of Christ is the word of the gospel and by this alone is fellowship with Christ re-established (Revelation 3:17,20).

In Revelation 4 and 5 we come to the vision of the Lion who is the Lamb slain. I have already shown how this points to the redeeming death of Christ as the key to the opening of the scrolls containing the truth about the

coming of the kingdom of God. The opening of each seal
in turn leads to revelations of judgment. But the fifth
seal (Revelation 6:9–11) results in a vision of martyrs
crying out for vindication: 'How long, Sovereign Lord,
holy and true, until you judge the inhabitants of the
earth and avenge our blood?' The purpose of this vision
is not to tell us that the martyrs themselves are waiting
for an answer, rather it is a means of comfort to the living. Those who have died for the faith (and those who
will yet die), have not suffered in vain. They are secure
because they have the robe of Christ's righteousness.

When we turn to Revelation 11:15–19 there is a grand
affirmation: 'The kingdom of the world has become the
kingdom of our Lord and of his Christ, and he shall reign
for ever and ever.' It could be argued from the exegesis of
the text that it refers primarily to the consummation at
Christ's second coming. However, it is interesting also to
look at the context of Revelation 11. The acclamation of the
kingdom comes when the seventh angel blows his trumpet. Between the sixth trumpet (Revelation 9:13–21) and
the seventh trumpet (Revelation 11:15–19) there is a passage which uses a number of Old Testament ideas and
events to describe the conflict between the world and the
agents of God's kingdom. In the face of their prophesying
and working of signs and wonders, the world still does
not repent. Rather, the beast from the pit wars against
them and kills them. But God raises them up and takes
them to heaven while a great destruction overcomes the
earth.

Then the seventh angel blows the trumpet and the reign
of Christ is announced. The elders respond with
thanksgiving that the Lord God has taken his great power
and begun to reign. The temple of God in heaven is
opened and the ark of the covenant seen. The conjunction
of these two things is not insignificant. The ark of the

covenant can be seen because the veil of the temple is removed. The kingdom of God is thus joined to the atoning death of Christ. The veilless temple in heaven recalls the tearing of the veil of the temple in Jerusalem at the moment Christ died. The way is open for all justified sinners to enter into the presence of God through the blood of Christ.

The first question then, is not 'when' the kingdom of the world becomes the kingdom of Christ, but 'how.' This passage shows the ministry of the Old Testament prophets foreshadowing both the conflict between Christ and Satan, and the conflict between the church and the powers of darkness. The resurrection and the way of access to the ark of the covenant speak of the victory of Christ through the gospel event. Once we understand this we can sort out the 'when.' Clearly, there is a sense in which the victory of Christ is retrospective. The prophetic ministry of the Old Testament was in a real sense a gospel ministry. Moses turning the Nile to blood, Elijah stopping the rain, and every prophetic sign, all point to their fulfilment in the victory of Christ. Christ's miracles are a connecting link which show that the ministry of Christ is to fulfil the prophetic ministry by bringing in the kingdom. The resurrection of the martyrs and the opened temple are eloquent of the justification of the sinner.

Revelation 12 depicts the warfare in heaven between Michael the archangel and the dragon, who is Satan. The dragon is thrown down. Then John hears a voice saying:

Now have come the salvation and the power and the kingdom of our God, and the authority of his Christ. For the accuser of our brothers, who accuses them before our God day and night, has been hurled down. They overcame him by

> the blood of the Lamb and by the word of their testimony;
> they did not love their lives so much as to shrink from death
> (Revelation 12:10–11).

At this point let us note that the casting down of Satan is seen as the event which signals two things: the coming of the authority and power of Christ and of the kingdom of God, and the salvation of God's people whereby they overcome. Satan is here designated the 'accuser' of the brethren. The name Satan is applied to the devil in the New Testament because he functions as an accusing adversary. The Hebrew word *satan* means adversary and is used in Job I to describe the one who accuses Job before God.

Once again the apocalyptic style needs to be understood. John is not concerned so much with a sequence of events as with the dimensions of salvation. The spatial and temporal sequences of this word picture are not to be pressed into a literal description of the coming of the kingdom. Thus the warfare is described first as waged by Michael against Satan. The outcome, however, is that the brethren conquer Satan by the blood of the Lamb. John is describing the gospel event. The fact that the accuser is silenced means that the sinner is declared by the judge to be 'not guilty.' He is justified.

The brethren also are said to overcome by the word of their testimony for, says John, 'they loved not their lives even unto death.' Testimony in the New Testament means a witness to the person and work of Christ, that is, to the gospel. The frequent reference to martyrs (or 'witnesses') in Revelation does not operate so as to exclude all non-martyrs. John uses martyrdom to describe those who actually die for the faith, and also those who 'love not their lives,' and thus persevere to the end in the service of the gospel. What we should recognize is that the New Testament does not use the word testimony to describe the kind of 'ego-trip' that some Christians practise by parading themselves as living miracles. Testimony is to the Christ of the gospel and to what he did for us in his life and death.

Thus far it is apparent that the historic gospel is represented in many ways and by various images within the Book of Revelation. My only reason for treating this matter by a survey of Revelation chapter by chapter, is that I find it is so often the forgotton dimension. I am not arguing for the presence of references in Revelation to the historic gospel. I doubt if any would disagree with that. Rather, I am arguing that the Book of Revelation is about the gospel. The gospel is its central theme. Above all it is speaking of the coming of the kingdom of God through the victory of Christ at Calvary. The kingdom of God means that the people of God are cleansed and accepted. They are justified by grace as a gift.

Perhaps no image is so pregnant with the theme of the justification of the sinner as that of Christ 'the Lamb.' For the Lamb is the Lamb only because he is the Lamb who was slain. This title is used in Revelation some 28 times. If only to complete our survey, we may observe the references to the Lamb in the remainder of the book. Revelation 14:1–5 shows the Lamb in Mount Zion with the 144 000 who sing a new song. They are described as chaste followers of the Lamb. In Revelation 15:2.4 John describes those who conquered the beast singing 'the song of Moses and the song of the Lamb.' The 'new song' is a song of redemption (see Psalms 96:1; 98:1; 144:9f) and the song of Moses is a song of the Lord's victory as he redeems Israel from Egypt (see Exodus 15). The two passages are very similar: the redeemed praise God for his marvellous deeds by which they are saved. The song of Moses is the song of the Lamb. The exodus from Egypt is the shadow of the gospel.

Some of the more controversial texts relating to the Lamb occur in Revelation 20. I will delay discussion of them until I have laid the foundation for understanding that chapter. Notwithstanding that omission at this juncture, I propose that enough has been said to show that the gospel is at least a major theme of Revelation. As we proceed, the gospel will emerge as the controlling theme of the book.

The Literary Structure of Revelation
(See Figure 2, page 209)

It is time now to observe something of the basic literary structure of Revelation. It is not difficult to see that Revelation is more than a collection of disconnected visions and other material. How the contents are organically related will be discussed in a later chapter. For the moment I will suggest only a broad outline of the relation of the parts. Even a cursory look at the way different commentators handle the structure of Revelation will reveal considerable differences of opinion. This analysis is put forward as one possibility. It is not crucial to the understanding of the book, but rather proposed as an aid to the perception of an overall unity in design.

The Book of Revelation consists of six groups of mainly apocalyptic visions, preceded by a group of letters and followed by a climactic vision of the consummated kingdom. Austin Farrer suggests that the structure is sabbatical.[6] That is, there are six groups of seven followed by a final sabbath. Theologically, this is appealing because the New

---

[6] Op. cit.

Jerusalem of Revelation 21–22 corresponds with the 'sabbath rest of the people of God' (Hebrews 4:9–11). Other commentators do not find some of the groups of visions so easily divisible by seven, and this should prompt caution against being too quick to arrive at a neat and tidy analysis. However, it is difficult to deny that these groups exist and that they are mostly interspersed with sections which frequently describe a hymnic response to the visionary material. These sections act as interludes to connect the consecutive groups of visions.

Another connecting feature of these groups is that the second, third, and fourth of them delay the seventh part of their action until after the interlude. The seventh vision of the group then becomes the new group of seven. Thus, for example, the series of seven seals (Revelation 6) actually goes as far as the sixth seal. Then there is an interlude (Revelation 7), after which the seventh seal is opened (Revelation 81). What follows is not another act of judgment such as those that issued from the breaking of the first six seals. Instead John sees a new seven, this time the seven angels with trumpets. After a short introductory vision the angels proceed to blow the trumpets in turn (Revelation 8–9). Again we are taken only to the sixth trumpet before there is an interlude (Revelation 10–11). When the seventh trumpet is blown a new group of visions follows (Revelation 12–14). There is a difference of scholarly opinion as to the exact significance of this structure, but it cannot be doubted that it establishes a structural unity for the Book. The overall pattern may be represented as in Figure 2. Other questions of relationship, such as whether the groups are intended to be parallel or consecutive, must remain until we have further examined the intention of the book, and the method of carrying it out.

Summary

The gospel is the historic event of the life, death and resurrection of Jesus Christ for us. Justification is the formal or doctrinal term used to refer to the principal significance of the gospel for the believing sinner. In Revelation John uses a variety of ways to present this gospel of our justification as the heart and soul of the Christian message. In the context of the sufferings of the Christians to whom he writes, John presents a message which is as relevant today as it was then: the Christian's comfort in adversity, his corrective in error, his motive for holiness, is the gospel and only the gospel.

Thesis

The doctrine of justification is basic to the message of Revelation and is woven throughout the book.

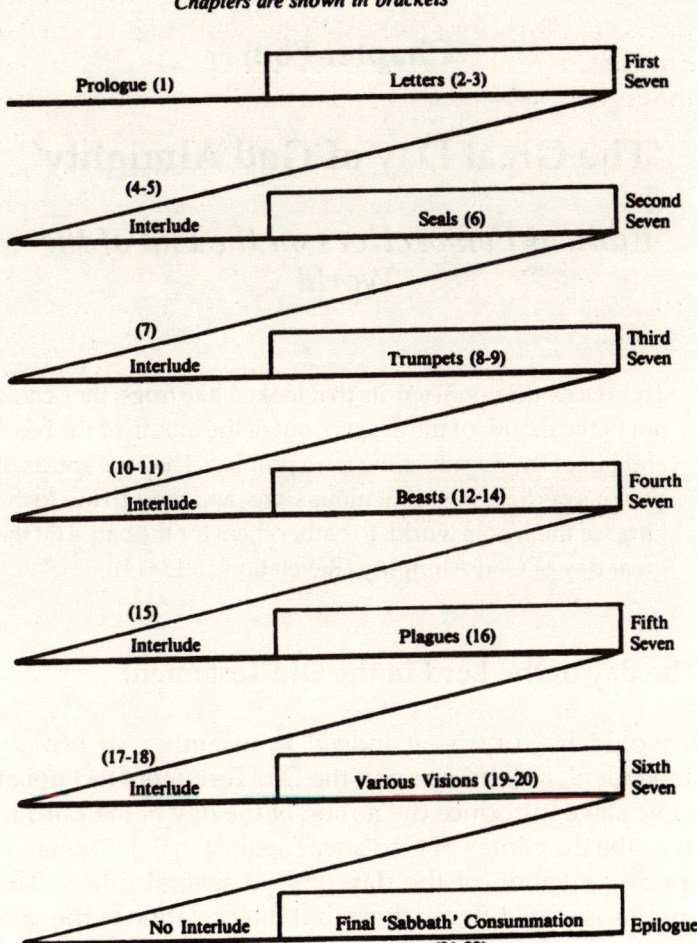

Figure 2. The Structure of the Book of Revelation

Chapter Four

'The Great Day of God Almighty'

Biblical Perspectives on the End of the World

Then I saw three evil spirits that looked like frogs; they came out of the mouth of the dragon, out of the mouth of the beast and out of the mouth of the false prophet. They are spirits of demons performing miraculous signs, and they go out to the kings of the whole world, to gather them for the battle on the great day of God Almighty (Revelation 16:13–14).

The day of the Lord in the Old Testament

It would be surprising indeed if an author so heavily dependent, as John is, upon the Old Testament did not at some stage introduce the notion of the day of the Lord to describe the climax of God's war against evil. John makes specific mention of the day of God several times.[1] The emphasis may differ in these, but their relation to the saving action of God can be confidently affirmed. The Old Testament establishes both the variety of emphasis and the ultimate significance of this use of *day*.

---

[1] eg. Revelation 1:10, the Lord's day; 6:17, the great day of their wrath; 16:14; 18:8, in one day.

The day of the Lord is the day of his victory. It is the day
on which the salvation of God is revealed and effected for
all the people of God. On the other hand it is a day of wrath
for all those who maintain their rebellious opposition to
the kingdom of God. The actual phrase, 'the day of the
Lord,' is sometimes varied or shortened to 'that day,'
'coming days,' or 'those days.' The occurrences which
give us the clearest indication of meaning are in the prophets.[2] The earliest of these references is probably that of
Amos who prophesied in the northern kingdom of Israel
during the mid-eighth century BC.

> Woe to you who long
>   for the day of the Lord!
> Why do you long for the day of the Lord?
> That day will be darkness, not light (Amos 5:18).

It seems that the phrase 'day of the Lord' was known to the
contemporaries of Amos and that it signified the expectation of a great benefit which would come by the hand of
the Lord. This oracle (Amos 5:18–27) rejects such optimism because the formal worship of God by the Israelites
was only a cloak for idolatry. They could thus anticipate
only wrath:

> Therefore I will send you into exile beyond Damascus, says
> the Lord, whose name is God Almighty (Amos 5:27).

---

[2] Isaiah 2:12; 13:6,9; 22:5; 34:8; Jeremiah 46:10; Ezekiel 7:10; 13:5;
30:3; Joel 1:15; 2:1, 11, 31; 3:14; Amos 5:18–20; Zephaniah 1:7–8,
14–18; Zechariah 14:1.
 The meaning of the day of the Lord in the prophets is
discussed in G. von Rad, *Old Testament Theology* (Edinburgh:
Oliver and Boyd, 1965) Vol H, pp 119–125.

Zephaniah, who prophesized in the seventh century B.C., used the 'day of the Lord' in the same way. It was to be a day of the wrath of God visited upon those who have broken the convenant of God (Zephaniah 1:7–18). Zephaniah resorts to the imagery of warfare and brings his oracle to a crescendo of universal destruction:

> Neither their silver nor their gold
> will be able to save them
>   on the day of the Lord's wrath.
> In the fire of his jealousy
>   the whole world will be consumed,
> for he will make a sudden end
>   of all who live in the earth (Zephaniah 1:18).

Isaiah, the eighth-century prophet, is also familiar with the wrath of the day of the Lord:

> The Lord Almighty has a day in store
> for all the proud and lofty,
> for all that is exalted
>   (and they will be humbled).
> The Lord alone will be exalted in that day,
> and the idols will totally disappear.
>
> Men will flee to caves in the rocks
> and to holes in the ground
> from the dread of the Lord
>   and the splendour of his majesty,
> when he rises to shake the earth (Isaiah 2:12, 17b–19).
>
> For the Lord has a day of vengeance,
> a year of retribution, to
>   uphold Zion's cause (Isaiah 34:8).

See, the day of the Lord is coming
 – a cruel day, with wrath
 and fierce anger –
to make the land desolate
 and to destroy the sinners within it.

The stars of the heaven and their constellations
will not show their light.
The rising sun will be darkened
 and the moon will not give
 its light (Isaiah 13:9–10).

In this latter passage one can easily see the imagery which is used also by Joel:

I will show wonders in the heavens and on the earth,
blood and fire and billows of smoke.

The sun will be turned to darkness
 and the moon to blood
before the coming of the great
 and dreadful day of the Lord (Joel 2:30–31).

The day of the Lord, then, is the day of his wrath against his enemies, the day of judgment. But it is also the day of the salvation of his people. That is why the ritual-loving but hypocritical Israelites anticipated it with optimism, and why Amos had to disabuse their minds with a warning of judgment. For those who truly wait for God there is a firm cause for optimism. Joel's prophecy, though similar to Isaiah's, is not concerned with wrath. The signs in the heavens are the accompaniments of blessing and salvation. The spirit of God will be poured out on the people (Joel 2:28) and everyone who calls on the name of the Lord will be saved (verse 32).

Gerhard von Rad has proposed that the idea of the day of the Lord emerged from the historical experience of Israel in the exodus from Egypt and the conquest of Canaan.[3] This is the day of the Lord's intervention as the divine warrior:

> The Lord is a warrior;
>   the Lord is his name.
> Pharaoh's chariots and his army
> he has hurled into the sea (Exodus 15:3–4).

The defeat of the haters of God's kingdom is the occasion of the salvation of the faithful:

> The Lord is my strength and my song;
> He has become my salvation.
> He is my God, and I will praise Him (Exodus 15:2).

This means that the kingdom of God has come, for his enemies are destroyed and his people redeemed:

> You will bring them in and plant them
> on the mountain of your inheritance –
> the place, O Lord, you made for your dwelling,
> the sanctuary, O Lord, your hands established.
> The Lord will reign for ever and ever (Exodus 15:17–18).

The day of the Lord means the coming of the kingdom of God, which brings judgment to God's enemies and salvation to his people. The exodus was certainly a pattern-making event in Israel's history which established the concept of the redemptive act of God. It spoke of the release of the Israelites from a godless captivity that

---

[3] loc. cit.

negated all that the covenant promises had made over to the chosen people. It spoke of the miraculous event by which an imprisoned people were set free to serve the living God. it marked the point at which it became possible for the descendants of Abraham to enter the land of their inheritance.

When this historical experience of Israel, which patterned salvation, reached its climax in the kingdom of David and Solomon, the rot set in. As the strength and faithfulness of Israel declined and the whole fabric which pre-figured the kingdom of God crumbled and fell apart, the truth of the kingdom was given to the prophetic word of revelation. The oracles that we have considered concerning the day of the Lord belong to this period of decline. The prophets continued the process of revelation about the kingdom of God by injecting into the actual decline of Israel's glory the word of judgment and of hope. They depicted a devastating act of God's wrath on all who broke the covenant with God, along with all the godless nations, and they depicted beyond tragedy the renewed nation of Israel resurrected in glory.

The prophets use many and varied images to describe the new age beyond the final act of God to judge and to save. However, the prophetic words of hope all build upon the past history of Israel. The model of an Israelite monarchy centring upon the Davidic prince ruling at the temple of Jerusalem becomes the essential concept which is glorified and perfected in the futuristic projection of the kingdom of God.[4] Both the history of Israel and the prophetic view of the kingdom testify to the inseparability of

---

[4] The restoration prophecies which depict the coming kingdom in terms of a glorified recapitulation of the old Israelite monarchy include: Isaiah 2:1–4; 4:2–6; 9:6–7; 52:1–12; 60:1–22; 61:1–7; 65:17–25; Jeremiah 23:1–8; 31:1–40; Ezekiel 34–48.

the elements of judgment and salvation. The salvation of the people of God cannot be achieved without judgment upon all the powers of darkness. which resist God's kingdom. But this visitation of wrath upon the spiritual powers of darkness, inevitably gathers up and includes all those human beings who have sided with darkness by their wilful opposition to God. The prophets had to make the unacceptable point that many of the people of the covenant had put themselves into that reprobate category by their evil covenant-breaking ways.

One characteristic of the prophetic expression is important for this discussion. The prophets were not bound, as we of the twentieth century so often are, by strict attention to chronology and sequence. They were quite happy to look at the same event now from this point of view, now from that. Furthermore, events which subsequently proved themselves to be distinct in time, were easily spoken of as if this distinction were unimportant. Let us be clear about this. The prophets did not sit loosely to the idea of history. They were immersed in time and history. But they did not view time and history from the same stand-point as a modern scientific historian.

Wherein lay the difference between the prophetic and the modern approach to time and history? Well, for one thing the prophets were convinced that all history was in the hand of God. Chronological sequences and cause-effect considerations were all subsumed under the sovereign will of God. Nor was this a fatalistic view of deity. Rather it was a covenantal view. Jehovah the God of Israel had revealed himself as the creator and Lord of history, but also as the redeemer of Israel Time and history took their meaning from these facts. Nothing in history had meaning apart from God and his self revealing, redemptive acts. It was the redemptive quality of the time rather than the quantity of the time which concerned them most.[5] In this the prophets laid the foundation for the New Testament view of history which likewise treated it very seriously but subjected the quantitative aspect to the qualitative. It did this by interpreting history in the light of the gospel.

In the prophets of the Old Testament we see concern concentrated upon the redemptive characteristics of the historical events (whether past or future history). So the 'day of the Lord' emerged from the past history of the Lord's warfare against his enemies in the exodus from Egypt and the conquest of Canaan. The prophets, when they speak of a future manifestation of the wrath of God, may describe it as local (e.g. a specific imminent historic catastrophe such as Israel being exiled), or as universal (a total destruction of all the enemies of God), or as cosmic (a complete dismantling of the created order). All of these manifestations can be seen as belonging to the 'day of the Lord.' In their view of salvation the prophets may describe it as an actual and predicted return of Jewish exiles to their land after a certain number of years (e.g. Jeremiah's prediction that 70 years would see a return from Babylon), or as an unspecified future event when all the true covenant people would be restored from whatever land they had been dispersed to, or as a cosmic renovation of all creation. Again all these possibilities fit the category of the 'day of the Lord.'

What we should note is this: though the prophets gave expression to these different dimensions of both judgment

---

[5] By no means may we allow these characteristics of prophetic thinking to support the thoroughly unbiblical views which dismiss historical fact as irrelevant. The prophets were not indifferent to history. However, they were not governed by twentieth century views of history.

and salvation, they really did not concern themselves with the distinctions between them as such, nor with how they were related in actual time and history. It was enough that the day of the Lord was coming. The reality of God's wrath and of his redeeming love had been seen in times past and it would be seen again in the future. As the prophets looked to the future from their standpoint in the midst of the historical failure of Israel to be the redeemed people of God, they saw the day of the Lord as the final act. Beyond that there could be no failure as in the past, but only the everlasting glory of God's kingdom. The various dimensions of the coming of the kingdom (local, world-wide and cosmic) all belonged without differentiation to the one great day of the Lord that was coming. (See Fig. 3 on p. 66.)

The apocalyptic view of the day of the Lord has one obvious difference from the prophetic view. Since it is not realistic to separate the prophetic and apocalyptic views of the future (they overlap in many respects), we should say that the distinction is one of emphasis as well as of lit-erary idiom. It is generally accepted that the apocalyptic idiom gives much sharper definition to the transition from the old age to the new age of the kingdom of God. Gone is the prophetic appeal to repentance that will avert the impending judgment. Gone also is the distinctly Israelite national emphasis. Instead the apocalyptists tend to depict the inevitable and unavoidable progress of the present evil age to the point where God says, 'No more!' Then in a catastrophic intervention of God the old is destroyed and the new age emerges. It is not so much the salvation of Israel that is presented, though that is there too, but the transformation of all creation.

When we have allowed for the differences in emphasis in prophetic and apocalyptic writing, we are still left with an important common feature which may be said to characterize the Old Testament view of history and the end of the age. Despite the fact that the prophets acknowledge the respective nature of redemptive acts and judgment (e.g. in history of Israel's exodus and conquest of the land, in the exile and return from Babylon, and in the final day of the Lord), the future day of the Lord is spoken of in a way which does not concern itself with how the local, universal and cosmic elements are related in time. The effect is an undifferentiated view of the end. The day of the Lord means the salvation of the people of God and the judgment of his enemies.

The apocalyptic emphasis, then, did not serve to displace or even drastically to qualify, the prophetic view of the day of the Lord. Rather it served only to sharpen certain aspects already present in prophetic preaching. Together the prophetic and apocalyptic views painted a picture of the linear succession of the two ages. This present age comes to an end at the point where the redemptive and judging acts of God reach their climax and final expression on the day of the Lord. At that point, and without further ado, the new age of the kingdom of God is revealed. A lot happens on the 'day.' Not only are the enemies of God finally put down, but Israel – the true believing Israel – is restored to the promised land. Jerusalem and the temple are re-built and the Davidic rule re-inaugurated. Then the gentiles, who are to be included, come running, seeking to be accepted because they have seen the glory of God revealed in the redemption of Israel (Isaiah 2:1–4; Zechariah 8:20–23). That day is the day on which the Spirit of God is poured out on people. It is a day in which salvation can still come to all who call on the name of the Lord (Joel 2:28–32). Quantitatively it is difficult to define this day, but qualitatively it is the day of salvation.

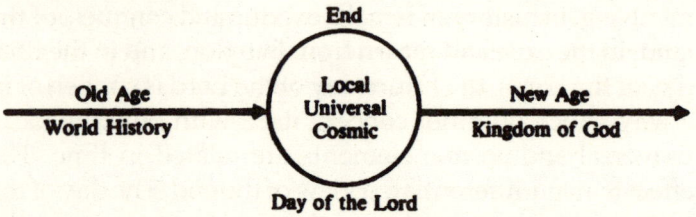

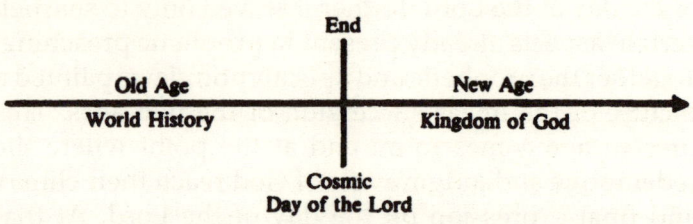

Figure 3.   The Two Ages in the Old Testament

The Day of the Lord in the New Testament

Reflect on the fact that Old Testament history ended without the predicted day of the Lord having come. Then for nearly four hundred years the Jewish people went through successive dominations of their land and threats to their religion and culture. Finally, after the Persian and Greek empires had come and gone in turn, the land of the Jews became a small oppressed province of the Roman Empire. In the midst of this unpromising experience an event of great moment took place. A child, Jesus, was born and grew up, eventually to be recognized by a small group of people as the promised Messiah who would bring in 'the kingdom of God.

By signs and wonders, by word and deed, he began to impress upon his followers that he was truly God's Messiah. But for most of them this could mean only one thing: the day of the Lord was about to break. The wrath of God would come upon covenant breakers, the godless, and in particular, on the cruel and overbearing power of Rome. Then suddenly Jesus began to tell them that *he* was going to Jerusalem to die. 'Not so!' said Peter, who must then suffer the stinging rebuke, 'Get behind me Satan.' Inexorably the events moved to their climax and the messianic prince of David, instead of ascending a golden throne, was nailed to a cross. The disciples' hopes were dashed; it was not the day of the Lord after all! The body of the leader was hurriedly put away before the sabbath began, and his followers withdrew to lick their wounds.

The following Sunday morning the incomprehensible happened: the crucified Master rose from the dead and showed himself alive to his friends. Suddenly their hopes were revived. Perhaps the kingdom of God would appear at this time after all. They begin to anticipate the glorious transition from being a tiny downtrodden nation within the vast Roman Empire, to being the shining glory of God, the centre of the earth and the envy of all nations. Gone would be the corrupt and the cruel Edomite kingship of the Herodians, and in its place would be the glory of the rule of the Davidic prince. Justice and peace would flow forth from the new Zion and the earth would become once more like the garden of Eden.

When the risen Jesus had been with the disciples for some days without the appearance of the kingdom, there was understandably some discussion amongst them about it. Finally, one day when they were together with

Jesus, the question was put: 'Lord, are you at this time going to restore the kingdom to Israel?' (Acts 1:6). What had happened to that 'day of the Lord' of which the Old Testament spoke so graphically? So they were still hard of hearing and obtuse in their minds! On the day he rose, Jesus had rebuked two of them for not believing that other less palatable message of the prophets – that the Christ had to suffer before entering his glory (Luke 24:26). But now they accepted the suffering aspect, for it had been branded on their minds by the events of Good Friday. Could they not now expect to see Jesus enthroned as the Prince of Peace on the throne of David? 'Lord, are you at this time going to restore the kingdom to Israel?'

Jesus' answer, is decisive: 'It is not for you to know the times or dates the Father has set by his own authority. But you will receive power when the Holy Spirit comes upon you; and you will be my witnesses in Jerusalem, and in all Judea and Samaria, and to the ends of the earth' (Acts 1:7–8). Some argue that because Jesus said, 'It is not for you to know the times,' he implied that the expectation of the disciples as to the nature of the kingdom and its coming was correct. Only their impatient desire to know 'when' was misplaced. On this view the promise of the Spirit is diversionary rather than integral to the answer to the question. We should then expect that the future teaching of the apostles would clearly distinguish the two things – the coming of the kingdom in exactly the terms (if that were possible) of the Old Testament prophets, and the Spirit-filled preaching of the gospel as some kind of interim activity until the kingdom comes. In fact this is *not* what happened.

First, we note that once the Spirit was given at Pentecost, the question about the kingdom ceased to have relevance, for the answer was known. The apostles preached the gospel to the Jews for what it was, the fulfilment of all the hopes of Israel, all the promises of the prophets. Christ had indeed entered his glory through his resurrection and ascension. No wonder that Christians came to refer to the day of resurrection, the first day of the week, as the day of the Lord.

Secondly, when the Spirit was given, Peter declared that this was in fulfilment of Joel's prophecy of the day of the Lord (Acts 2:15–21). It does not worry him that Joel also referred to the signs such as the darkening of the sun and reddening of the moon. He points to Joel's beautiful assurance that 'everyone who calls on the name of the Lord will be saved.' Then without further ado he preaches the gospel of Christ and calls upon his hearers to repent and be baptized. Truly this is the day of the Lord and the Davidic prince reigns gloriously in Zion:

> But he (David) was a prophet and knew that God had promised to him on oath that he would place one of his descendants on his throne. Seeing what was ahead, he spoke of the resurrection of the Christ (Acts 2:30–31).

Compare these words with Paul's in his first sermon at Antioch:

> We tell you the good news: What God promised our fathers he has fulfilled for us, their children, by raising up Jesus (Acts 13:32–33).

We find no deviation from this conviction in the rest of the New Testament. With one voice the authors proclaim the death and resurrection of Jesus as the point at which all the promises of God reach their fulfilment. This is truly the day of the Lord.

Thirdly, we note that along with the preaching of the gospel there is an assurance that Christ not only reigns now, but that he will return to manifest his kingship to all principalities and powers. It is the giving of the Spirit coupled with the ascension of Jesus that structures the fulfilment of the day of the Lord in the New Testament. The Spirit's task is to illuminate the believers with the truth of the gospel so that they can preach it down through the ages. The Spirit makes real to mankind the meaning of the gospel as the means which God uses to establish the kingdom. Since Christ ascended before manifesting the glory of his kingdom, the Holy Spirit comes to enable the church to preach the gospel. It is by this means alone that the kingdom comes in the world, but by the gospel the kingdom *does* come. Finally Christ 'will appear a second time, not to bear sin, but to bring salvation to those who are waiting for him' (Hebrews 9:28).

In this brief description we see that the Holy Spirit applied the gospel to the minds of the apostles in such a way as to demand a qualification of the Old Testament perspective. The seeds of this qualification were already there in the Old Testament, not just in the motif of the suffering servant of which Jesus reminded the two disciples (Luke 24:26), but in the very structure of revealed truth. Israel had already received a clue in the fact that salvation was something they looked back on (Passover and Exodus), salvation was an ongoing reality of daily life, and salvation was an expectation for the future (day of the Lord). It was partly their obtuseness and partly their baldly literal approach to the promises which made them reduce the day of the Lord to a purely future undifferentiated event.

What then, was the effect of the gospel as the Holy Spirit made it plain to the apostles' minds? The main adjustment was that they saw that the day of the Lord covered the past, the present and the future. In the past the day of the Lord was the decisive historic event of the life, death and resurrection of Jesus. He embodied in his person the perfection of all the covenant relationships between God and man. in that sense he was the kingdom of God come FOR US. The day of the Lord came as the wrath of God was poured out upon our substitute when he hung on the cross. The day of the Lord came as the people of God rose from the grave in the person of their substitute and ascended to sit with him at the right hand of God (Romans 6:1–10; Ephesians 2:4–6; Colossians 3:1–3). (See Fig. 4 on p. 71.)

Because of this decisive work of God in Christ for our justification the Spirit is given. The coming of the Spirit, a continuous coming since Pentecost, is the coming of the day of the Lord. The Spirit comes because of the merits of Christ on our behalf (Acts 2:33). Through the preaching of the gospel the Holy Spirit makes the kingdom real to all who believe. The once for all end of the age in the historic Jesus Christ is so applied to the believer that by faith he is made a partaker of it *in Christ*. But in so doing the Spirit brings the day of the Lord into the present. Sanctification is the end of the age being applied to our existence.

Finally the end will be openly manifest. It will no longer be something that only believers acknowledge by faith. It will be the irresistible and undeniable sense- experience of all. While Christ is known through the preaching of the gospel as the slain Lamb, only the gift of the Spirit to the elect will awaken faith in the reality that the Lamb has now, at this very moment, the glory of the Lion at the right hand of God. But, when Christ returns in glory to judge, though he will eternally be the Lamb, he will be revealed in the glory of the Lion both to judge, and to consummate our salvation.

The New Testament gospel thus restructures the coming of the kingdom in a way that it is vital for us to grasp. There is in effect an overlap of the two ages from the first

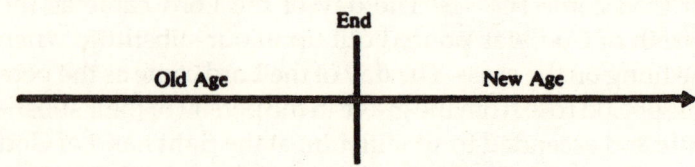

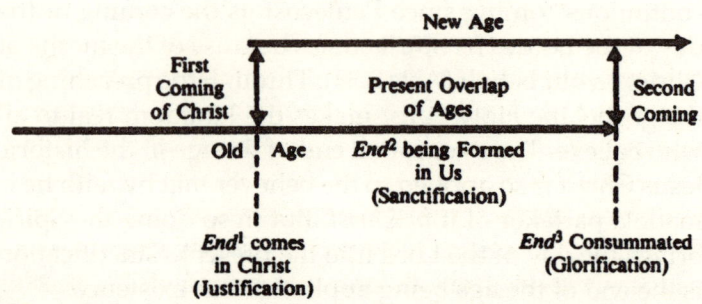

Figure 4.   Two Perspectives on the End
This diagram is based on that of Geerhardus Vos, The Pauline
Eschatology *(Grand Rapids: Wm. B. Eerdmans Publishing
Company, 1972), p.38 and is used by permission*

coming to the second coming of Christ. This creates the
Lamb-Lion tension which characterizes Christian existence in this period between the two comings. It is the tension between being in the world (as far as empirical
experience goes), but not of it. It is the tension between
being of the kingdom, but not in it (as far as empirical
experience goes). As the Lamb suffered until the glory of
his kingdom was bestowed at his resurrection and ascension, so the body of Christ must suffer until we likewise

are (actually in ourselves) raised and transformed into the glory of Christ's image.

It is a thesis of this book that John, in Revelation, has made considerable use of prophetic and apocalyptic material in which the typical and traditional Old Testament perspective of the *end* or the day of the Lord is maintained. The New Testament perspective is provided by the nature of the gospel which, as we have seen, everywhere pervades the book. Thus, unless we are aware of this necessary qualification of the Old Testament perspective by the gospel we shall be likely to misread the nature of the visions of Revelation. It is my considered opinion that this very basic error of not allowing John to use Old Testament forms – prophetic oracles and apocalyptic visions – without modification is one cause of much prophetic speculation about the Book of Revelation today. It is regrettably true that much Christian literature and preaching has lost the essential ingredient of a sound method of interpretation. It has allowed the gospel to be demoted into something less than the preeminent and central characteristic which interprets the whole meaning of the Bible. I shall endeavour to apply this gospel-centred interpretation of the Book of Revelation.

Summary

The Old Testament idea of the day of the Lord is central to the view of the end of the world that is set forth in the prophetic and apocalyptic writings. The old age passes away and the terrible day of God introduces the new age of Israel's glory. Related to this concept is the theme of God the divine warrior who fights for his people, judging his enemies and bringing salvation to his chosen. The New Testament proclaims that the day of the Lord has come with Jesus Christ who fulfils all prophetic promise. The resurrection and ascension of Jesus, coupled with Pentecost, show that the gospel modifies the Old Testament perspective in that the old and the new ages are seen to overlap for a time. John uses Old Testament literary forms, in particular the apocalyptic vision, largely without modification. Revelation thus contains many sections which speak of the day of the Lord in Old Testament terms.

Thesis

The Old Testament perspective of the day of the Lord, which is contained in John 's apocalyptic visions, is modified by the gospel. The linear succession of the ages becomes the overlap of the ages between the first and second comings of Christ.

Chapter Five

'To Him who Overcomes'

The Letters to the Seven Churches

Yet I hold this against you: You have forsaken your first love. Remember the height from which you have fallen! Repent and do the things you did at first. If you do not repent, I will come to you and remove your lampstand from its place. But you have this in your favour: You hate the practices of the Nicolaitans, which I also hate.

He who has an ear, let him hear what the Spirit says to the churches. To him who overcomes I will give the right to eat from the tree of life, which is in the paradise of God (Revelation 2:4–7).

The Function of the Seven Letters

The letters to the seven churches in Revelation 2–3 are in danger of being separated from the rest of the book. The reason is not hard to find. Of all the several parts of Revelation, these seven short letters provide fewest difficulties and stand most easily on their own. The fact that they are written as letters, and deal with pastoral problems in real congregations of Christian people, puts them in the same general category as all the other

New Testament epistles. Despite some distinct characteristics which mark them out from the other epistles,
they employ a familiar technique of exhortation. There
are a number of peripheral questions of interest which I
prefer to leave to the many commentators on Revelation because I do not think the answers will greatly
affect our understanding of the Book. For example:
what is John's source of information about these
churches and what is his relationship to them which
enabled him to write the way he does?

It is possible that John's address to seven churches in
Revelation 1:4 – 'John to the seven churches that are in
Asia . . .' – is intended as a preface only to the section
ending with the letter to Laodicea. I do not think, however, that such is the case. It would disrupt the unity of
the book and obscure the relationship between the
seven letters and the rest of the book. It is quite possible,
in view of the repeated use of seven that the seven
churches are representative of the total number of
churches in western Asia Minor. In this case Revelation
is a kind of general epistle to all the persecuted and
struggling groups of Christians with which John could
so easily identify in his own suffering and exile.

In considering the function of the seven letters, then,
we must not forget the preliminary section in Chapter
1:4–20, for it is this which is addressed to the seven
churches. In Chapter 3 above I have dealt with the gospel content of this section. It would suffice, therefore, to
remark that Revelation 1:4–20 is a beautifully constructed and vividly presented expression of the gospel
in relation to John personally and to the churches generally. The frequent references to significant passages in
the Old Testament presentation of salvation history create a richness in the theological overtones that is almost
breathtaking. In the space of five short verses (v. 4–8),

John has summed up the doctrine of God, the doctrine of the person of Christ, the doctrine of salvation and the doctrine of the end things. As daunting as that sounds, we find that it is the person of Jesus Christ which holds it all together in perfect unity. Christ is the one who brings God's grace, and he it is who bears witness to truth, who rises from the dead to rule the kings of the earth. Christ it is who loves us and has saved us to become children of the kingdom and priests to God. And Christ, this dying-rising Christ, it is who will appear again in majesty.

This summary of the gospel in action then leads into John's affirmation that Jesus is Lord. In the same way as does Peter in the Pentecost sermon of Acts 2, or Paul in Philippians 2, John describes the exaltation of Christ as a sequel to the suffering servanthood of Jesus of Nazareth (Revelation 1:9–20). John's unique reference to 'the Lord 's day' in verse 10 is usually taken to mean that it was Sunday when he received these visions. If it can be sustained that the term was used to designate the first day of the week in John's time, it still does not detract from the distinct possibility that John makes reference to the day for its theological overtones rather than to pass on the trivial piece of information about what day of the week it was. In other words John would be referring to the fact that it is Sunday because the central matter is the day of salvation and judgment which has come in Jesus Christ, and of which Sunday as the day of resurrection, is now the perpetual memorial.

When John is prostrated by the vision of Christ's glory he is gently comforted with the words, 'Fear not' (v. 17). The similarity between this passage and the 'assurance of salvation' that is sometimes pronounced by the Old Testament prophets is striking: e.g.

Fear not, for I have redeemed you;
   I have called you by name;
You are mine. (Isaiah 43:1)

The force in the assurance of salvation lay in the reminder of what God had done to save his people. This is put simply and powerfully to John with the words, 'I died, and behold I am alive forever and ever' (v. 18). The gospel is thus summed up in the death and resurrection of the now reigning Christ.

Now we should observe that the words of Christ to John beginning in verse 17, lead on to the seven letters. There is no break. The vision of Christ in glory and the assurance of salvation are the preamble to the seven messages. These messages are not given as the words of John to the churches but rather as the verbatim messages of Christ which John is told to pass on to the churches. They are the epistles of Jesus Christ who holds the churches in his hand (Revelation 1:16, 20; 2:1). Each of the seven messages begins with some reference to the Christ portrayed in the preceding vision.[1] Further more, each of these references has a counterpart in the consummation of the kingdom described in Revelation 21 and 22. That which John has by revelation is that which belongs to the whole church through what God has revealed in Jesus Christ. Christ in glory continues to be known as the suffering Christ in the gospel. But the things belonging to his present glory are the treasures in heaven which the gospel procures for us and secures for all who believe. What we now know by faith will be the experience of our senses in the consummation.

---

[1] 2:1 from 1:13,16; 2:8 from 1:17,18; 2:12 from 1:16; 2:18 from 1:14–15; 3:1 from 1:4,16; 3:7 is the converse of 1:18; 3:14 from 1:5.

The seven messages, then, serve to remind us that the drama of redemption has its ongoing effects in the world. The fact that Christ has conquered, but wills to extend his conquest into the lives of men and women through the preaching of the gospel, puts the church in the midst of the apocalyptic war. Furthermore, this warfare is not purely external, for it is also within each individual as the old nature struggles against the new, the flesh against the spirit. It would be a grossly distorted perspective if we saw the spiritual warfare as only outside of us. The seven messages translate the cosmic and spiritual warfare into the present human existence of the people of God. The struggle is hard and the suffering great. But always the vision of Christ in glory stands over every consideration of our human predicament. In the gospel event he overcame decisively. As Oscar Cullmann puts it, the decisive victory of Calvary and the resurrection has determined once and for all the outcome.[2] The sanctificational struggle of the church may be likened to the mopping up operations. Without the seven messages the Book of Revelation would lose that valuable point of contact with our present human experience. It would seem remote and detached from our struggle. Whereas Jewish apocalyptic had appeared in danger of losing the cutting edge of the prophetic demand to repentance and faithfulness to the covenant, John restores this emphasis before he moves on to the visions of heavenly reality.

As we look at the structure of these seven messages we see that there is a marked uniformity. We may summarize thus:[3]

1. Address to the angel of the church.
2. Description of the author, Christ.

---

[2] *Christ and Time* (London: S.C.M. Press, 1951).
[3] There are some slight variations, especially in the warnings and exhortations.

3. Reference to works followed by praise or criticism.
4. Warning of consequences of faithlessness.
5. Exhortation to persevere.
6. Promise to all who overcome.

What may we learn from these clear emphases in the letters?

First, the Christ who addresses the churches is their risen Lord and Saviour who holds them in his hands. He has won for all his people the prizes which are given to those who persevere. He is not therefore a 'tyrannical Lord but a loving Lord who plans to share his kingdom with those for whom he has laid down his life in his own humiliation and servanthood. The sovereignty of Christ is such that we cannot weaken it. The emphasis of apocalyptic was that none can thwart the purpose of God nor withstand his will. There are many mysteries attaching to the sovereign will of God, and in our conceited attempts to solve them we often fall into the terrible error of diluting divine sovereignty into something which is a grotesque counterfeit. The danger arises particularly when we want to appeal to human responsibility in Christian living. One hears preachers and teachers talking about God as if he were utterly dependent upon us for the success of his redemptive plan. God is said to be unable to carry out his purpose unless we first do something. God can't use us until we get rid of every known sin. God can't send us the gift of the Spirit until we totally commit ourselves to him. And so it goes on, with God being effectively reduced to the architect of a good idea, but being powerless to carry it out without our help!

Christ will have none of this in his revelation to John. The first three chapters of Revelation set forth the seeming paradox of the sovereignty of the Lord of the church and the human responsibility of his people. This has often been a problem to Christians. How can God be absolutely sovereign at the same time as man is absolutely responsible? Surely the one cancels out the other. The attempts to resolve the paradox by either diluting God's sovereignty or by curtailing man's responsibility are the attempts of the sinful mind of man to dictate the truth about God on the basis of human reason. The Christian mind is informed and renewed by the gospel, though even Christians go on bringing non-Christian ways of thinking to the problems of the Bible. The truth of the matter, as always, is in the gospel. The problem of sovereignty and responsibility is the problem of how a truly sovereign God can go on being truly sovereign while relating to truly responsible man. The gospel does not solve the problem in the sense of telling us *how* in a way that is able to be fully understood by the human mind. Rather it shows us that the mystery is characteristic of God himself. For in the gospel we see the incomprehensible has happened: true sovereign God and true responsible man have united in the one person Jesus Christ. In the history of the early church we can see how Christians grappled with this mystery. But every time they were tempted to solve the mystery either by reducing the deity of Christ to fit in logically with his humanity, or vice versa, the result was a destruction of the gospel itself. Orthodox Christianity learned to live with the mystery and indeed, to glory in it. Jesus Christ was true God in union with true man in such a way that neither nature was diminished by the other nor confused with it.[4]

---

[4] At the Council of Chalcedon in 451 the church devised a formula for speaking about this mystery. In Christ there is true God and true man. There is a union of the two natures but no fusion. There is a distinction between them, but no separation. The church also came to realise that. this 'unity-distinction' way of speaking about Christ pointed also to the nature of God himself as three persons in one God.

The gospel thus points us to and confirms us in this perspective which is everywhere in the New Testament. Here in Revelation John depicts the glories of the reigning Christ who holds the churches in his hands. His sovereignty is a reality now. But, as always, the sovereign Lord expresses his sovereignty, not by bypassing our minds and wills, but by working through them. To the mind which is uninformed by the gospel, this is a contradiction. Many Christians show that they have not brought the gospel to bear on their thinking when they reject, for example, the sovereign predestination of God as being incompatible with human responsibility. The union of God and man in Jesus Christ shows that this is not so. In fact, far from being incompatible, sovereignty and responsibility are shown to be the best of friends. Jesus Christ was the most perfect expression of humanity. He was the perfectly integrated personality, exhibiting all the virtues of humanity with none of the blemishes of sin. He may not have been conventional, and he often offended his enemies and sometimes even his friends. But he was the perfect pattern of God relating to humanity. He was the living interpretation of the doctrine of creation and of the nature of man as created in the image of God. He was and is true sovereign God and true responsible man.

Secondly, as we bring this perspective to bear on the seven messages of Revelation 2–3 we see the sovereign Lord addressing the churches which are made up of responsible people who are thus answerable for their actions. These letters clearly show that human effort and good works, and being held answerable for our works, are in no way incompatible with divine sovereignty. Furthermore, they are perfectly in harmony with the gospel doctrine of justification by faith alone on the basis of Christ's merits alone. Good works and rewards are part of New Testament teaching and they are not to be regarded as somehow contradicting justification as a free gift. The distinctive contribution of the seven messages in Revelation is to show that the good works of the people of God are part of the apocalyptic struggle between the reigning Christ and the powers of darkness. The accountability of Christians is thus highlighted. The significance of good works goes beyond mere kindness to one's neighbours and helping the missionary cause. The struggles of the local churches to live out the gospel, to resist the impact of non-Christian values and ideas, and to stay true to the revelation of God in Jesus Christ, are all part of the conquest of the world through the gospel. Behind the scenes the same conquest is being effected in the reign of Christ in heaven. In the world the church must be content to follow the example of the Lamb in his sufferings, but it is assured that the Lamb's sufferings are the key to the conquest of the Lion.

The Question of Rewards

Rewards in the New Testament, on first appearances, seem to contradict the teaching that Christians are justified by faith alone. Justification means that God accepts us for what Christ has done in our place. Since he has done the same for each and every believer, we would assume that each and every believer will receive the same inheritance in the kingdom of God. So where do rewards fit in? Are there going to be *A class* and *B class* mansions in heaven? In fact the problem is less pronounced in the seven letters than in some other parts of the New Testament as we shall see later on. But first let us consider the matter generally.[5]

---

[5] The whole subject of works and rewards in relation to Justification is dealt with superbly by John Calvin, *Institutes of the Christian Religion* Book III Chapters 14–18. Calvin is usually

To begin with, we note Calvin's argument that all good works must be regarded as God's gift and therefore cannot be the grounds of merit. It is the grace of God which produces good works in us. They are the fruit of the merits of Christ. This is not contrary to referring to them as the fruit of the Spirit since it is the merits of Christ that won for all God's people the gift of the Spirit. Now the outcome of this is the final glorification of the believer and his full inheritance of the 'reward,' the kingdom of God. The whole process of salvation, starting with God's election and call, involves our justification on the basis of Christ's merits, our sanctification through the Spirit (also on the basis of Christ's merits), and our final inheritance of glory.

The sanctification of the Christian is, therefore, in one sense automatic. We cannot take hold of Christ by faith for our justification without the Holy Spirit. It is the same Holy Spirit that both enables the sinner to believe the gospel and also works in us his fruit of sanctification. In another sense sanctification is not automatic in that the Spirit works through our minds and wills. All the admonition and exhortation in the Bible is God's way of involving us in the sanctifying work of the Spirit. To be human is to be responsible. To be Christianly human is to respond with mind and will to the gospel with good works.

Paul's magnificent description of Christ, the suffering servant, becoming the reigning Lord (Philippians 2:6–11) is immediately followed by this exhortation, in which he points up the implication of the fact that 'Jesus Christ is Lord':

Footnote 5 (continued)   considered to be suited only for the advanced reader. He is however surprisingly simple and readable. An excellent basic treatment of this subject is given by Robert Horn, *Go Free!* (Downers Grove: Inter-Varsity Press, 1976).

Therefore, my dear friends, as you have always obeyed – not only in my presence, but now much more in my absence – continue to work out your salvation with fear and trembling, for it is God who works in you to will and to act according to his good purpose (Philippians 2:12–13).

Here we see sovereignty and responsibility knit together in such a way that the outworking of salvation day by day – good works – is immediately the result of human effort, but ultimately the work of God in us.

Listen to Calvin:

Why, then, are we justified by faith? Because by faith we grasp Christ's righteousness, by which alone we are reconciled to God. Yet we could not grasp this without at the same time grasping sanctification also. For he 'is given unto us for righteousness, wisdom, sanctification, and redemption.' Therefore Christ justifies no one whom he does not at the same time sanctify. These benefits are joined together by an everlasting and indissoluble bond, so that those whom he illumines by his wisdom, he redeems; those whom he redeems, he justifies; those whom he justifies, he sanctifies.

Thus it is clear how true it is that we are justified not without works yet not through works, since in our sharing in Christ, which justifies us, sanctification is just as much included as righteousness (*Institutes*, III. 6.1).

Calvin goes on to indicate that reference to rewards does not thereby imply that works are the cause of salvation. Yet because of the intimate connection between them and the fact that good works both follow justification and also precede final glorification, the inheritance of the saints may be spoken of as reward. In the final analysis there is no distinction between, the inheritance, which is a gift of grace, and reward. But since it is God's purpose to bring us to our inheritance by way of the race of good works, the term *reward* appropriately emphasizes our human responsibility in this race. Again Calvin comments:

> The Lord rewards the works of believers with the same bene-fits as He had given them before they contemplated any works, as He does not yet have any reason to benefit them except His own mercy (*Institutes*, III. 8.2).

Overcoming by Faith

Each of the seven letters of Revelation begins with an ascription to Christ as the author and then begins, 'I know your works.' In the case of Smyrna it is 'I know your tribu-lation,' and Pergamum, 'I know where you dwell.' Each church receives a commendation, except Laodicea, but each commendation, except that of Smyrna, is qualified by a phrase like, 'I have this against you.' Each is exhorted accordingly to repentance, endurance, or perseverance. Every letter closes with a promise to 'him who over-comes.' Although the performance of these churches is mostly referred to as works, the relationship of these works to faith in Christ, or faithfulness to the word of the gospel, is everywhere apparent. Furthermore, faith which issues in good works, in the face of tribulation and attacks by false teachers and worldly prophets, is conquest when it is exercised until the end. The person who exercises this conquering faith is the one who has. an ear to hear what the Spirit says to the churches, that is, the word of the gospel.

The outcome of this conquering by faith and persever-ance is the reward, although these letters do not specifi-cally call it reward.[6] Every reward described is an aspect of the inheritance couched in terms that are appropriate to the literary style of Revelation, and which use images drawn from the Old Testament: the tree of life, deliverance from death, the hidden manna and a new name, rule over the nations, the book of life, the temple of God, the throne. To conquer is to persevere in the faith, and to persevere in the faith is to do good works in response to the love of God shown to us in the gospel.

To sum up the function of the seven messages, we see that they link the daily existence of every child of God – never in isolation, but always in the context of a local congregation – to the cosmic struggle between Christ and Satan. This struggle, in view of the decisive victory of Christ in his life, death and resurrection, can have but one outcome. Nevertheless the struggle continues until the consummation at Christ's return. Since the age of this struggle lasts from the ascension of Christ until his return, the specific problems of the seven churches serve as representative examples of the daily struggles of all Christians of all ages. We may, of course, approach these messages as warnings to seek to live more faithfully in the world. But, as noted above, the unity of the seven letters with the apocalyptic visions, and thus with the ultimate warfare and victory of the kingdom of God, brings the significance of the two distinct theatres of war together. It is impossible to regard the seven letters as simply preceding the apocalyptic visitations in time. To do this is to trivialize the struggle of each child of God. Rather we see that there is a great mystery here. Christ's 'mopping-up' campaign against Satan is actually, marvellous to relate, being worked out in the front-line trenches of local church evangelism, pastoral care, teaching and preaching. It is being worked out in the Christian home as children are instructed in their covenant privileges and taught the meaning of faith in the doing and dying of Christ. God is truly using what is foolish in the eyes of the world to shame the wise, and using what is weak in the eyes of the world to shame the strong (1 Corinthians 1:27). Those who lust for the kind of power that the world respects, who seek to establish before men a triumphal image of the church and of Christian existence, reject the victory of the Lamb at the point of daily living and declare that they are as offended by his suffering as were those Jews who could not tolerate a king-messiah who dies. The gospel pattern of daily Christian existence is one of a confident struggle. When the Spirit of God writes upon the hearts and minds of ordinary Christians the truth that the victory of God, his glory and his majesty, are all clothed in the suffering of the Lamb, he dignifies our struggle with a significance that outshines all the remarkable feats to which the world attaches fame and importance.

Summary

The seven letters to the churches serve to introduce the main themes of Revelation by dealing with them at the outset in the down-to-earth context of the daily life of the local congregations. The drama of redemption is thus shown to have on-going effects in the world of human existence. Christians are not onlookers while a cosmic conflict rages in spiritual realms, but rather they are participants. The letters prevent the apocalyptic descriptions of this spiritual struggle from being detached from our daily struggle. The risen and glorified Christ calls upon his churches to be faithful to his gospel and to persevere in well-doing. During this period of the overlap of the ages the lordship of Christ in the world is expressed through the church which is made up of responsible human beings. The good works which are demanded are part of the apocalyptic struggle with the powers of darkness.

Because the final inheritance of Christians follows on a life characterized by good works, it may be spoken of as reward, even though its basis is not those works but Christ's merits.

Thesis

The seven messages to the churches structure Christian existence during the overlap of the ages as a creative tension between the sovereignty of God and the responsibility of man.

Chapter Six

'I Saw a Beast Coming Out of the Sea'

The Apocalyptic and Prophetic Passages

And I saw a beast coming out of the sea. He had ten horns and seven heads, with ten crowns on his horns, and on each head a blasphemous name. The beast I saw resembled a leopard, but had feet like those of a bear and a mouth like that of a lion. The dragon gave the beast his power and his throne and great authority. One of the heads of the beast seemed to have had a fatal wound, but the fatal wound had been healed. The whole world was astonished and followed the beast.

All the inhabitants of the earth will worship the beast – all whose names have not been written in the book of life belonging to the Lamb that was slain from the creation of the world (Revelation 13:1–3,8).

In a book of such diverse literary forms as Revelation, it is proper at least to ask why the author switches from one style to another. Why does John start with an introduction which is heavy with Old Testament allusions and apocalyptic imagery? Why does he then change to an epistolary (letter writing) style in the messages to the churches, and then revert to heavenly visions? Why are sections of apocalyptic visions interspersed with sections that, although visionary, do not contain such a wealth of apocalyptic symbolism? Can we detect any special reason which makes apocalyptic particularly appropriate to the purpose of the book?

In Chapter 4 I discussed the way that apocalyptic depicts the day of the Lord or the day of the coming of the kingdom. We saw that apocalyptic and prophetic material shared the same general perspective. Both depict the present age coming to end and the new age immediately beginning with the full glory of God's everlasting kingdom revealed. The differences between the prophetic and apocalyptic views of the end lie in the respective emphasis on the extent of the action, and in details. They both have essentially the same perspective as far as the relationship of this present age to the new age goes. The differences in literary style are, for the most part, easy to see, although some prophetic oracles have apocalyptic features. Because prophecy and apocalyptic differ mainly in style, form and emphasis, it is possible to blend the two, or to mingle sections of each, without upsetting the general perspective. What is important for our understanding of how the apocalyptic and prophetic idioms function in Revelation, is that their perspective is that of the straight linear progression from the old age into the new. It is this perspective that I shall maintain is preserved in the apocalyptic-prophetic sections of Revelation.

What then are the apocalyptic sections and how are they connected?

The Vision of Christ (1:12–20)

John begins the book with the words, 'the revelation of Jesus Christ.' He then tells us that he testifies to everything he saw, namely the word of God and the testimony of

Jesus Christ. In his greeting to the seven churches he identifies, and gives glory to, Christ as the source of blessing. But then as he describes what he was told to write and to send to the seven churches, the idiom changes quite dramatically. The one who speaks to him is identified as Jesus Christ only by inference and because of the introductory section preceding. We are told that John sees one 'like a son of man.' Of course we are familiar with this title as it is given to Jesus in the Gospels. The origin of the title and the significance it bears must be sought in the Old Testament background to the ministry of Jesus.[1] Those references to the Son of Man 'coming with the clouds,' show the link between Jesus Christ described in Revelation 1:7 and in 1:13:

> Behold he is coming with the clouds,
>   and every eye will see him,
> even those who pierced him (Revelation 1:7).

> and among the lampstands was someone
>   'like a son of man' (Revelation 1:13).

With this we compare a typical passage from the Gospels:

> At that time men will see the Son of Man
>   coming in clouds with great power and glory (Mark 13:26).

---

[1] The debate over whether Jesus actually used the title of himself, as the Gospels claim, and if so, what he meant by it, is not really our concern. I must agree with those who accept that 'son of man' signified a central participant in the drama of salvation as worked out in the history of Israel. It is clear from Revelation 1:7 that Daniel 7:13 is in mind.

The most reasonable assumption is that these references use a concept based upon the apocalyptic vision in Daniel 7. Daniel, one of the Jewish exiles in Babylon during the sixth century BC, has a vision:[2]

> Four great beasts, each different from the others, came up out of the sea. The first was like a lion, and it had the wings of an eagle. I watched until its wings were torn off and it was lifted from the ground so that it stood on two feet like a man, and the heart of a man was given to it (Daniel 7:3–4).

Daniel then describes two more beasts, one like a bear, one like a leopard, then a fourth, more fearsome beast appears. It has ten horns and an eleventh appears with the eyes of a man and a boastful mouth. Then Daniel says:

> As I looked, thrones were set in place,
>   and the Ancient of Days took his seat.
> His clothing was as white as snow;
>   the hair on his head was white like wool.
> His throne was flaming with fire,
>   and its wheels, were all ablaze.
> A river of fire was flowing,
>   coming out from before him.
> Thousands upon thousands attended him;
>   ten thousand times ten thousand stood before him.
> The court was seated, and the books were opened.

---

[2] Many scholars do not accept that the Book of Daniel was written by or about a sixth century Daniel. It is generally taken to be a second century BC apocalyptic work which uses the figure of Daniel, quite possibly an historical person, as the basis for an anti-hellenistic work. In my opinion the arguments for this view are by no means conclusive and create as many problems as they seek to solve. However, the question is not important for this discussion since the evidence would suggest that Jewish apocalyptic began to develop during the Babylonian exile.

Then I continued to watch because of the boastful words the horn was speaking. I kept looking until the beast was slain and its body destroyed and thrown into blazing fire. (The other beasts had been stripped of their authority, but were allowed to live for a period of time.) In my vision at night I looked, and there before me was one like a son of man, coming with the clouds of heaven. He approached the Ancient of Days and was led into his presence. He was given authority, glory and sovereign power; all peoples, nations and men of every language worshipped him. His dominion is an everlasting dominion that will not pass away, and his kingdom is one that will never be destroyed (Daniel 7:9–14).

In good apocalyptic style, Daniel is given an interpretation by one standing by:

The four great beasts are four kingdoms that will rise from the earth. But the saints of the Most High will receive the kingdom and possess it forever (Daniel 7: 17–18).

The general significance of Daniel's vision is made clear by the interpretations given (Daniel 7:16–27) The beasts are the godless powers of the nations of the earth. By contrast with the beasts, a human figure comes with clouds of heaven to God and receives the dominion which has been stripped from the beasts. The interpretation either identifies the human figure with the people of God, or implies that he receives the dominion as their representative. The identification of the beasts as godless humanity is not unique to this vision. For example, Psalm 22 is obviously referring to evil men who persecute the righteous complainant:

Dogs have surrounded me;
    a band of evil men has encircled me,

they have pierced my hands and my feet.
Deliver my life from the sword,
   my precious life from the power of the dogs.
Rescue me from the mouth of the lions;
   save me from the horns of the wild oxen

(Psalm 22:16,20–21).

It is possible that this approach reflects the fall of man when, because of the sin of Adam, the dominion of man over the beasts (Genesis 1:26) came under challenge. Be that as it may, Daniel's vision speaks of the reversal of the godless power-structures of this evil age. It is significant that it is a human figure that is involved. In this regard, let us remember that 'son of man' in Hebrew and in Aramaic (the language of Daniel 7) means no more than 'human being,' and is here a contrast to the beasts.

Who, then, is the man who has dealings in heavenly places to receive the kingdom for the people of God? The New Testament claims that it is Jesus, our representative and substitute. And John's vision is of the one like a son of man who has all power and who has even assumed something of the appearance of Daniel's vision of God. Furthermore, he identifies himself as 'the first and the last,' which in Isaiah 44:6 is the self-description of the God of Israel, in order to impress the fact that 'besides me there is no god.' The son of man is the man Christ Jesus who is also true God.

So much for the background of John's opening vision. But there is also another remarkable feature. The description 'son of man' is thoroughly grounded in Old Testament apocalyptic. In fact this vision contains nothing that is not in the idiom of the Old Testament, except perhaps the references to the churches (in the plural) in verse 20. Then, when we move into the seven messages of this son of man, the author continues to be identified in these apocalyptic terms of the prefatory vision. Again the 'churches' remain the only distinctly Christian expression in the seven letters.

The Vision of Heaven (Chapters 4–5)

This prelude to the seven seals begins with a vision of the throne of God in heaven. It is very reminiscent of Ezekiel 1 where the prophet sees strange sights including something not unlike the four living creatures of Revelation 4:6–8. The message of the praise of the twenty-four elders is that God is seen to be Lord because he created all things. Then comes the drama of the seals which only the Lion, revealed as the Lamb slain, is worthy to open. John here does not depart from the apocalyptic idiom and Christ, both as Lion and Lamb, is described in Old Testament images.

The Seven Seals (Chapter 6)

In this section the opening of the seals is, with one exception, the signal for a manifestation of God's wrath. Beginning with the 'four horsemen of the apocalypse' the series moves to the description of the catastrophic day of wrath. The four horsemen (seals 1–4) recall, with some significant differences, the apocalyptic passages in the post-exilic prophet Zechariah (Chapter 1:7–17). Again it is noteworthy that this section could be removed from its New Testament context and there would be no clue to its origins in a Christian book. Only the final reference to the wrath of the Lamb might leave a pre-Christian Jew slightly bewildered.

The Sealing of the Multitudes (Chapter 7)

The first part of this vision is also without any overt relationship to the Christian message. It is the perfect number out of the twelve tribes of Israel that is sealed against the impending doom. The only mystery for our pre-Christian Jew would be the omission of the tribe of Dan and the inclusion of Joseph along with the half-tribe of Manasseh.[3] He might wonder if the writer were ignorant of the history of Israel, but he would not thereby discern the hand of a Christian.

The second part of this vision, in which John sees the great multitude gathered out of every nation, tribe and language is no more overtly Christian in its vocabulary than the first part. It contains several references to the Lamb but does not use the name of Christ or refer to his ministry in New Testament terms. The final description of the redeemed (Revelation 7:15–17) is thoroughly Old Testament, borrowing images from the prophets and the Psalms. However, the hymnic section of this vision does provide a gospel-based perspective as we shall see in the next chapter.

The Seven Trumpets (Chapters 8–9)

The blowing of the trumpets unleashes a series of fierce judgments upon the earth and upon mankind. This section is about as typically apocalyptic as it could be. In the whole two chapters there is not one phrase which identifies the material as Christian.

---

[3] The tribe of Joseph was divided into the two half-tribes of the sons of Joseph, Ephraim and Manasseh. Levi, as the priestly tribe, was given no territorial inheritance in the promised land – see Joshua 13:33,14:4.

The Angel's Message (Chapters 10–11)

Between the sixth and seventh trumpet this section intrudes as a prelude to the seventh. The angel speaks to the sound of seven thunders and announces that there is to be no more delay, 'but that in the days of the trumpet call to be sounded by the seventh angel, the mystery of God, as he announced to his servants the prophets, should be fulfilled' (Revelation 10:7 RSV). Then follows a series of allusions to events of the Old Testament. John is told to eat the scroll in a similar experience to that of Ezekiel (Ezekiel 2:8;3:3). Then he is told to measure the temple like the man of Ezekiel's vision (Ezekiel 40:3). He sees the lampstands and olive trees which are similar to those of Zechariah's vision (Zechariah 4:11–14). These are identified as God's two witnesses who have power to do the signs and wonders that Elijah and Moses did. Finally the witnesses are killed by the beast, but they are raised up and taken to heaven. Again except for the reference to the crucifixion in verse 8, this section is pure Old Testament. Only when the seventh trumpet is sounded do we hear a voice in heaven speaking of the fact that the reign of Christ has come (Revelation 11:15–18).

The Beast Visions (Chapters 12–14)

First, John sees warfare between the dragon and the woman who bears a child. The dragon, who is Satan, is thrown down and then a voice declares that the kingdom of God and the authority of Christ have come. Secondly, John sees a beast rising out of the sea. The whole description is very similar to the beast vision of Daniel 7, except that there is only one beast. This beast appears to prevail over the saints and to gain the allegiance of all whose names are not in the Lamb's book of life. A second beast appears to aid the first in his conquest of the world. All men brought under the beast's dominion are marked with his mark.

Then John sees the Lamb on Mount Zion with the 144 000 who are marked with the Father's name. Three angels emerge with stern warnings of judgment. A voice announces the blessedness of these who die in the Lord. The son of man sits crowned upon a cloud, with a sickle in his hand. The time has come for the harvest of the grapes of wrath.

Into this magnificent procession of apocalyptic pictures John injects only the one reference to the kingdom of Christ, but it is thoroughly immersed in the idiom of the Old Testament.

The Seven Bowls of Wrath (Chapter 16)

The pouring out of the seven bowls of wrath brings terrible plagues upon the earth. These are not unlike the visitations of wrath that we have already witnessed. In keeping with the apocalyptic trend of Revelation, this section contains no distinctively Christian terminology at all.

The Judgment of Babylon (Chapters 17–18)

The first part of this section maintains the apocalyptic style. John is shown the great harlot Babylon. She is drunk with the blood of the saints and of the martyrs of Jesus (Revelation 17:6). She sits on a seven-headed beast with ten horns. The angel tells John that the horns are kings that make war on the Lamb but are conquered by him. The second part of this section is marked by a shift into the cycle of prophetic oracles announcing woes upon Babylon. The fact that the historical city of Babylon figures in such Old Testament prophecy, as the evil city of the captivity of the Lord's people, makes the style of those prophets appropriate to this section. All in all only the one reference to the martyrs of Jesus interrupts the Old Testamental style and content.

The Final Visions (Chapters 19–22)

Only in the last group of visions is there a prominence of New Testament themes. But even here they are couched in apocalyptic terms and thus do little to add a gospel perspective to this Old Testament landscape. The first vision of the group (Revelation 19:11–16) presents us with yet another apocalyptic horseman. This time his identity is made clear from the description and, above all, from the name by which he is called: The Word of God. He leads a heavenly army as he rides forth to execute a wrathful judgment on the world.

Next John sees an angel summoning the birds to a feast of the flesh of the mighty men of war. Then the beast and the armies of men make ready to fight against the horseman. But the beast is captured along with the false prophet and they are thrown into the lake of fire. The armies of men are destroyed. The scene shifts (Revelation 20:1–3). An angel seizes the dragon, Satan, and binds him, then throws him into a pit for a thousand years. Then the martyrs of Christ are restored to life and reign with him for the thousand years. When this period comes to an end Satan is loosed from the pit. He gathers his armies for battle against the saints but there is no conflict. Instead fire from heaven consumes them and the devil is thrown into the lake of fire forever. Again the scene shifts to a great white throne of judgment (Revelation 20:11–15). The dead stand before the throne to be judged and those whose names are not in the book of life suffer the same fate as the beast, the false prophet and the dragon.

Finally, John sees a vision of the new heaven and new earth. He describes the holy city, new Jerusalem, as the dwelling place for God in the midst of his people in the new earth which they have inherited. It is a place that brings together all the blessings that have previously been described as belonging to Eden and the promised land. Now the conflict is ended and the people of God experience only the eternal presence of God and the Lamb.

The Function of the Apocalyptic Sections

What, then, have we learned from this summary of the apocalyptic sections of Revelation? First, we have seen that the apocalyptic has been inserted into a New Testament framework of eschatology. Although some occasional references to Christ and his kingdom occur, they do little more than identify the subject of what is otherwise entirely Old Testamental in both its form and context. The kingdom of Christ is portrayed as coming with the day of the Lord's wrath. The present evil age is terminated on that day. From first this angle and then from that, John paints vivid word pictures of the terrible doom of the day of the Lord. It is a horrendous series of images, each of which defies mere visual reproduction. There is no question of chronological sequences being strictly observed either within or between the several series of visions. No one description or apocalyptic vision can do justice to the all encompassing activity of God as he puts down the cosmic rebellion and saves his people. Every aspect of the created order, from the spiritual powers to the dust of the earth and the uninhabited planets, is caught up in the upheaval of that day.

Secondly, we have learned that the threat of undoing under the weight of God's wrathful judgment has no terrors for the redeemed. They are sealed and kept against that day, which does not spell destruction for them, but resurrection and glorification. No power in heaven or on earth can touch the people of God. They constitute in God's sight a perfect number which he will not suffer to be diminished through misfortune, chance, or onslaught of the devil. What is more significant is that the wrath of God has already been visited upon them in the person of their substitute, the Lamb who was slain. They, united to the Lamb by faith, now live in him and receive the same unqualified approval from the Father as he does.

The overall effect is to depict the tribulation of the day of the Lord which became such a prominent theme in Old Testament prophecy and apocalyptic. Apocalyptic horsemen, trumpets heralding unprecedented destruction, bowls of wrathful judgment, beasts and false prophets overthrown, the saints sealed and secure though tormented for a while by persecutions and martyrdom; all this makes up the scenario of the day of the Lord. On the one hand the battle goes on in the church, on the other it is presented in apocalyptic terms of a struggle that transcends the earthly order and yet goes on being waged on earth. The beast and the dragon, in a foul alliance of spiritual wickedness, manifest their frenzy of hatred of the kingdom of God in the history of the world. The false prophet, and all the accusers and troublers of the suffering church of Christ, gather together all godless humanity for the struggle in what is called Armageddon. Such frightening pictures could easily overwhelm the timid and faint-hearted Christian fighting for survival. But it is not left like that. Wrath is put into perspective by the sealing of the saints. Armageddon is put into perspective by the millennium.

Finally, let us suppose that some of John's readers, then and now, should ask, 'When will all these things be?' There is no doubt that for many people the burning questions about the Book of Revelation relate to when the tribulation occurs, when and where Armageddon is fought, when the millennium takes place. These questions on the lips of modern readers are often expressions of a failure to understand apocalyptic and how it operates. By his very use of apocalyptic John has answered all these questions: 'These things will be at the *end*, they are the events of the day of the Lord.' Only the gospel, which John has carefully built into the book and with which he surrounds the apocalyptic sections, will save us from exasperation at this reply to our question!

Summary

The apocalyptic sections of Revelation maintain the perspectives of the day of the Lord which belong to Old Testament apocalyptic and prophetic writing. As we follow through the visions of Revelation we find that John has found no reason to deviate in any marked way from the portrayal of the linear succession of the two ages. Furthermore, a minimum of distinctively Christian terminology finds its way into the visions. Enough is said to show that Jesus Christ is the central figure in the great conflict between God's kingdom and the powers of darkness which takes place on the day of the Lord. The New Testament perspective of the overlap of the ages is not evident in the apocalyptic visions. Yet the victory is still Christ's. The visions do not present a chronological sequence of events relating to the end of the world. Rather they show a variety of aspects of the final event in such a way as to indicate the different dimensions ranging from the personal struggles of the individual Christian to the cosmic battle in which Satan and all his allies are destroyed. Apocalyptic also provides a strong sense of the sovereignty of God in our salvation so that every believer may stand confidently in the knowledge that he is sealed against the day of wrath.

Thesis
The Old Testament perspective of the day of the Lord is maintained in the apocalyptic sections. All the events of the end, which in the New Testament are structured by the overlap of the ages, are depicted as occurring during the one undifferentiated day.

Chapter Seven

'Worthy is the Lamb who was Slain'

The Hymnic Passages

Worthy is the Lamb, who was slain,
to receive power and wealth and wisdom and strength,
and honour and glory and praise!

Hallelujah!

For our Lord God Almighty reigns.
Let us rejoice and be glad and give
him glory!
For the wedding of the Lamb has come,
and his bride has made herself ready

(Revelation 5:12; 19:6–7).

The Coming of the End

In the last chapter I attempted, without going into a lot
of the detail, to show the emphasis of the apocalyptic
visions, and the perspective they have of the end. To the
question, 'When will these things be?' I proposed that
John's answer is, 'At the end.' We must now attempt to
clarify that answer. Our difficulty lies partly in the fact

that the Old Testament idioms employed by John portray the end as a single undifferentiated point in time marking the conclusion of the old age and the beginning of the new. Many Christians still struggle with the disciples' question in Acts 1:6: 'Are you at this time going to restore the kingdom to Israel?' They struggle with it because they fail to see that Jesus' answer, by pointing to the giving of the Spirit at Pentecost, was thus pointing to the preaching of the gospel as the way the kingdom would come in the period between the ascension of Jesus and his second coming.

The main thing that I have been arguing for in this book, is that the gospel was the fulfilment of the promises concerning the kingdom of God. It is the gospel which thus restructures the Old Testament perspective as we have seen in Chapter 4 above. It is, I believe, the loss of the gospel perspective which has led to so much confusion over the Book of Revelation. When the gospel is separated from the question of the fulfilment of the promises to Israel, it leaves a void. Jesus Christ forces upon us the need to interpret the Old Testament, and all its literary idioms and forms, in the light of the New Testament. But when the gospel and this present 'church' age are interpreted as intrusions between the promises to Israel and their literal and future fulfilment, then we are in fact interpreting the New Testament by the Old. The gospel is made subservient to the Old Testament. This ought not to be.

The disciples' question about the restoration of the kingdom showed two things, one correct and the other that needed correction. The correct perception of these men was that the resurrection of Jesus, which restored their confidence in him as the promised redeemer, signalled that the day of the Lord had come. They were now at the *end*. Their incorrect perception was due to their persistence in the Old Testament frame of mind which saw the single undivided moment of the transition from one age to the next. We should not be too critical of this misperception since it would require the events of the ascension of Christ and the giving of the Holy Spirit to make clear to the disciples how the gospel, as fulfilment, has modified or qualified the form of the promises.

The nature of this gospel qualification of the Old Testament perspective has been discussed in Chapter 4; all we need here is to remind ourselves that the new understanding of the end provided by the event of Christ is extremely important. It is vital to our perception of the realities of Christian existence, particularly as this is characterized by a tension within us between the new age, already come in Christ, and the old age which still exists within us and around us.

The subject of this chapter is the way John overcomes the disadvantages which attach to his use of apocalyptic and other Old Testament forms which preserve the simple linear perspective of the two ages. I want to suggest that the Book of Revelation is provided with a framework of explicitly gospel-oriented material which prevents it from being a piece of purely Judaistic apocalyptic as far as its perception of the end is concerned. This framework consists mainly of the hymnic sections or interludes to the visions of the day of the Lord. We may also add to this the introduction and the last of the visions with their distinctly final nature.

All that I have argued for in the first three chapters relates to this dimension of Revelation. Although in actual quantity the apocalyptic visions far outweigh the rest of the material, John has left us in no doubt that the gospel is the heart of all he wants to say. Thus the *end*, as John sees it, is primarily the end come in the historic events of Jesus of Nazareth. The *end* came for us in the person of our substitute who was content to become the suffering and slain

Lamb. His was the great tribulation, his was the victory of Armageddon on Calvary, his was the binding of Satan. This was *the* event which secured for all the saints their inheritance in the kingdom of God. On this basis the pattern of our present existence is shaped. The character of the church is modelled on its Lord. What came in him and was achieved by him for us, patterns the process of reaching the end in us as the Holy Spirit creates and sanctifies the church.

But it is not simply that the church, as the gathering of the saints, is the venue in which each individual Christian is sustained in the personal struggle towards the goal of being like Christ in his present glory. It is also, as we have seen, that until the Lamb is revealed as the Lion, the body of Christ must identify with its head in his character as the Lamb. Thus the church suffers. And yet the Lamb is victorious. So the church, in the midst of its sufferings, can know what it is to conquer.

Not until Christ is revealed in the glory of the Lion shall we be glorified. The day of the Lord remains veiled from sight under the suffering of the Lamb until that time. Being veiled, it is perceived only by the faith that the gospel creates in the people of God. But it is real nevertheless, as everyone who truly believes in the gospel will affirm. The problem of Christian existence is that we easily allow the tribulation which we experience within the suffering church to obscure the glory that is already ours by faith in Christ. This is the problem that the Book of Revelation sets out to rectify. If only that object and aim of the book were kept in mind we could be spared a lot of speculative interpretation. John's first concern is not to minister to armchair prophets in some far-off age, but to the battlers of his own day who struggle to reconcile the fact of their suffering with the fact of Christ's victory over sin, Satan and death. In that concern he is our contemporary also.

The Gospel Framework

The introduction has already been discussed at some length so we need only, at this stage, remind ourselves of the prominence which John gives to the historic gospel in Revelation 1 (see Chapter 3 above). We ought never to lose sight of John's first chapter, especially when we get to the succession of apocalyptic visions. The time element in what John says at the beginning is important. Note the following –

The past:

Jesus Christ freed us from our sins by his death, and rose from the dead (v. 5). He has made us a kingdom of priests to his God (v. 6).

The present:

Jesus Christ is now the ruler of the kings on earth (v. 5). He is now also the ruler and guardian shepherd of the churches (v. 16,20). He is now alive and will live for evermore (v. 18). He holds the keys of Death and Hades (v. 18).

The future:

Jesus Christ is yet to come with the clouds so that every eye will see him (v. 7). His coming will bring consternation among the peoples of the whole earth (v. 7).

It is no light thing that John describes in greatest detail at the outset that which is the present reality. The vision of Revelation 1:12-20 is the vision of the now ruling Christ. Christian existence is a matter of the present. Of course we do not live in the present without regard for the past or the future. But live in the present we must. John writes for the present in the light of the past victory of Christ, the present reigning of Christ, and the future consummation of Christ's rule. And if Christ rules now, then he has overcome his enemies decisively in the past events of his life, death and resurrection.

It is central to the gospel as the key to biblical interpretation that the past event of the finished work of Christ determines absolutely the nature of the present and the future. This is why I have said that we may not interpret the New Testament, and in particular the Book of Revelation, on the basis of the Old Testament perspective. It stands to reason that since the gospel fulfils and reveals the final significance of the Old Testament, we must allow the gospel to determine the meaning of the Old Testament.

In terms of the structure of the Book of Revelation we observe that the gospel framework is established by the interludes to the apocalyptic sections. The introductory section is the prelude to the seven letters. The heavenly vision of chapters 4 and 5 is the prelude to the seven seals. In the first chapter we looked at the vision of Revelation 5. The Lamb slain is the only one worthy to reveal the truth of the kingdom. The song of the elders echoes this truth and attributes this worthiness to the saving acts of Christ:

> You are worthy to take the scroll and to open the seals,
> because you were slain, and with your blood you
>   purchased men for God
> from every tribe and language and people and nation.
> You have made them to be a kingdom and priests to
>   serve our God,
> and they will reign on the earth (Revelation 5:9–10).

Then the angels, the creatures and the elders sing:

> Worthy is the Lamb who was slain,
> to receive power and wealth and wisdom and strength
> and honour and glory and praise (Revelation 5:12).

Notice the emphasis on the past event of the death of Christ as that which creates the present reality of the kingdom of priests which is the church. It is said that the redeemed 'will reign on the earth,' but this future tense does not imply only a remote future but rather an ongoing reign from the time of redemption. They are *already* a kingdom (Revelation 1:6, 5:10). Neither does it exclude the remote future, for the perspective of the New Testament on what we call heaven or eternal life is of an earthly existence. It will of course be the renewed earth, but earth all the same. Some popular notions of heaven tend to be more pagan than Christian in that they remove the earthly environment and also the bodily existence of the redeemed.

The next interlude occurs in the account of the sealing of the multitude before the visions of the seven trumpets. These are the ones who are guarded against the judgment which is visited upon the earth. They are the justified saints who cry out with a loud voice:

> Salvation belongs to our God
>   who sits on the throne,
> and to the Lamb! (Revelation 7:10)

This is followed by another short hymn ascribing glory to God (v. 12). The elder who interprets for John tells him that the multitude consists of those who are coming out of the tribulation (John uses the present tense here). The psalm-like description which follows makes it clear that these redeemed saints did not escape tribulation but rather came through it. The Lamb – who is always for John the Lamb who was slain – has wrought salvation. Tribulation comes but does not overrun the saints who have washed their robes in the Lamb's blood. The relationship of this vision in time to John's day is not the important thing. What is being depicted here is the three stages of salvation: justification, sanctification (including suffering) and final glorification. This view of the security of the redeemed is not unlike Paul's overview of the unbreakable chain in the process of salvation:

And those he predestined, he also called;
those he called, he also justified;
those he justified, he also glorified (Romans 8:30).

In the passage under review, John describes the glorification of the saints as final deliverance from suffering:

Therefore they are before the throne of God
and serve him day and night in his temple;
and he who sits on the throne will spread his tent over
them.
Never again will they hunger; never again will they
thirst.
The sun will not beat upon them, nor any scorching
heat.
For the Lamb at the centre of the throne will be their
shepherd;
He will lead them to springs of living water.
And God will wipe away every tear from their eyes
(Revelation 7:15–17).

The question whether this glorification is intended to be understood as happening now or only after the general resurrection is not the concern of this passage. It is the purpose of this vision to reassure the suffering saints that the past event which brought the Lamb through his suffering death and resurrection to the throne, has fixed once and for all their destiny to be forever with the Lamb in his glory.

The next interlude, between the seven trumpets and the series of beast visions (Revelation 10–11) includes the description of the two witnesses of God whose testimony evokes a fearful attack by the beast. The sounding of the seventh trumpet (Revelation 11:15) brings us to another hymnic section as a prelude to the next series of visions. Loud voices are heard in heaven saying:

> The kingdom of the world has become
> the kingdom of our Lord, and of his Christ,
> and he will reign forever and ever (Revelation 11:15).

Then the twenty-four elders worship God saying:

> We give thanks to you, Lord God Almighty,
> who is and who was,
> because you have taken your great power
> and have begun to reign.
> The nations were angry and your wrath has come.
> The time has come for judging the dead
> and for rewarding your servants the prophets
> and your saints and those who reverence
> your name,
> both small and great –
> and for destroying those who destroy the earth
> (Revelation 11:17–18).

The most logical understanding of these hymns is that they refer to the final glory of Christ's kingdom and to the last judgment. Certainly, if we link them with the preceding description of the two witnesses, this appears to be the case. Thus once again John describes the mission of the church, under attack, but victorious.

The 'two witnesses' vision is, as we saw in the previous chapter, almost entirely lacking in specifically Christian terminology. The witnesses are described as Old Testament prophets. Only the reference to the place 'where their Lord was crucified' (verse 8) shows them to be witnesses to the gospel. Like their Lord they are killed, and like their Lord they are raised and taken to heaven. Then the kingdom of Christ is announced. The two witnesses are a description of the present church age which is characterized by conflict and persecution. John's interest in martyrs is born out of the reality of his day. The death of the witnesses does not thereby mean the obliteration of the church at some point in this world's history. John reassures his readers that even martyrdom cannot overcome the power that raised Jesus. The description is too reminiscent of the suffering, death, resurrection and ascension of Christ to be accidental. Once again the church is reminded that its character and experience must reflect the character and experience of her Lord. The singling out of martyrdom does not remove this passage from the sphere of every Christian's experience. Again there is an affinity with the message of Romans 8:

As it is written:
  'For your sake we face death all day long;
We are considered as sheep to be slaughtered.'
No, in all these things we are more
    than conquerors
through him who loved us.

(Romans 8:36–37[1])

---

[1] William Hendriksen has caught the spirit of John's message in the title of his exposition of Revelation – *More than Conquerors* (Grand Rapids: Baker Book House, 1939).

The prelude to the seven bowls of wrath includes the song of the saints who have conquered the beast (Revelation 15). Before the last plagues are announced these saints are seen by the sea of glass mingled with fire. The next reference to their song as the song of Moses and the Lamb perhaps suggests that the sea represents the trial that they have passed through, just as Moses led Israel through the Red Sea. There Israel witnessed the saving acts of God in wrathful judgment on their enemies. Moses sang a song praising the triumph of Jehovah the divine warrior. Now, in John's vision, the saints sing the song of Moses and the song of the Lamb:

> Great and marvellous are your deeds,
>> Lord God Almighty.
> Just and true are your ways,
>> King of the ages.
> Who will not fear you, O Lord,
>> and bring glory to your name?
> For you alone are holy.
> All nations will come and worship before you,
>> for your righteous acts have been revealed.
>
> (Revelation 15:3–4)

Although it is called the song of Moses, this hymn has little verbal similarity to the song of Moses in Exodus 15, except perhaps in the phrase:

> Who is like you –
>> majestic in holiness,
> awesome in glory,
>> working wonders? (Exodus 15:11)

The main similarities lie in the perspective of salvation. The song of Moses recalls the objective acts of God in history whereby he saved Israel. That event foreshadowed the true and spiritual exodus achieved by the Lamb, the mediator of the new covenant. The great and marvellous deeds, of which the saints of John's vision sing, are the objective historical events of the gospel. The day of the Lord came in the person and work of Jesus Christ.

Then we were told that those who sing this song are those who have been victorious over the beast. According to the seven messages to the churches this is the victory of the life of faith and perseverance, but made possible only because of the victory of Christ. Thus the day of the Lord comes also in and through the life of the church in the world as it makes the gospel known. The saints of this vision have finished their struggle and have entered into their reward. The fact that this is portrayed before the last plagues should not concern us. The pattern of apocalyptic in general, and of Revelation in particular, does not require a strict chronological sequence. It is quite appropriate for John to depict the saints in consummate glory before describing the final tribulation of wrath. For one thing, Revelation is clearly not, in strict chronological order; there is repetition. For another, the nature of the end as the gospel defines it makes it difficult to define from the apocalyptic passages, any reference to one, and only one, aspect of the coming of the end. For John to refer to the seven last plagues does not mean that they occur only at the point of Christ's return.

After the pouring out of the seven bowls of wrath the interlude includes the apocalyptic description of Babylon the harlot city (Revelation 17), and the prophetic oracle on the downfall of Babylon (Revelation 18). Then comes the hymn of the great multitude in heaven:

Hallelujah!
Salvation and glory and power belong to our God,
for true and just are his judgments.
He has condemned the great prostitute
who corrupted the earth by her adulteries.
He has avenged on her the blood of his servants

(Revelation 19.1–3).

Later John hears the voice of the great multitude again:

Hallelujah!
For our Lord God Almighty reigns.
Let us rejoice and be glad
    and give him the glory!
For the wedding of the Lamb has come,
and his bride has made herself ready.
Fine linen, bright and clean,
    was given to her to wear

(Revelation 19:6–8).

Having emphasized many times that the tribulation of
the last days cannot overcome the saints, John also
speaks of the fact that the enemies of the kingdom of
God, the godless powers of the world, are doomed to
suffer utter destruction. Once again the overall perspective is included. Babylon has been the persecutor of
God's people. The apocalyptic struggle has ever characterized this day and age of grace. The history of the true
church is sprinkled liberally with the blood of martyrs.
The justice of God may seem to be a pipe dream to the
down-trodden and the persecuted. But it is real. 'Vengeance is mine, I will repay, says the Lord' (Romans
12:19, RSV). When this vengeance is finally visited
upon the godless, the marriage feast of the Lamb will
have begun. The gospel age will inevitably give way to

the final destruction of Babylon which heralds the consummation of the kingdom.

Before we come to the epilogue (Revelation 22:6–21), we should note some of the distinctives of the last group of visions. In many respects this group (Revelation 19:11–22:5) shares the same characteristics as all the other apocalyptic visions. As we saw in Chapter 6, the form and style continue to be predominantly Old Testamental. Christ, rather than the Lamb, is specifically mentioned with regard to the millennial reign (Revelation 20:4–6), but the perspective is unchanged. However, when we come to the vision of the great white throne (Revelation 20:11–15) and the vision of the New Jerusalem (Revelation 21:1–22:5), there is an increasing sense of the finality of the end. The lake of fire is described as the second death, and Death and Hades are consigned to it. This finality has been anticipated in the casting of Satan into the lake of fire forever (Revelation 20:10). From this point on, the description is not of an undifferentiated end but of the consummation. In many respects this finality must be inferred from the fact that John allows no more place for suffering or for the onslaughts of the devil. The promises and purposes of God are fulfilled:

> Now the dwelling of God is with men, and he will live with them. They will be his people, and God himself will be with them and be their God. He will wipe every tear from their eyes. There will be no more death or mourning or crying or pain, for the old order of things has passed away (Revelation 21:3–4).

This final version will be considered in more detail in Chapter 9. Here let us note that even if John continues the apocalyptic style, as he clearly does, we may expect some indication that the consummation is a reality to which all things eventually come.

Finally, the epilogue brings us back to the present. No more apocalyptic visions here, only the reality of Christian experience in the here and now. There is an urgent call to face the reality that *now* is the end. In the older apocalyptic style the writer was told to seal up in a book that which was revealed to him. There it would remain until the appointed time of the APOCALYPSIS, the *revelation*. The seals would be broken and the secrets of the visions revealed. This would be the time of the end. But the angel says to John, 'Do not seal up the words of the prophecy of this book, because the time is near' (Revelation 22:10). There is no time to seal it and lay it aside for the future. As John writes down the visions it has been granted to him to see, at that very moment, the end is upon the world. Furthermore, while the tribulation of the end may last for years, everyman's consummation lurks around the corner of his life. For in the moment that he thinks not, the evil man is caught in the midst of his evil-doing, the righteous man taken in the midst of his right-doing (v. 11). Then, irrespective of the centuries, even millennia, that will pass before the universe is caught up in the consummation, each will find that there is no more time. Christ's coming is for each of us as close as the moment of our own death. Blessed indeed are those 'who have washed their robes, that they may have the right to the tree of life' (Revelation 22:14).

Summary

While the apocalyptic sections speak of the end of this age in the manner of the Old Testament, John fits them into a framework of passages which impress the gospel perspective upon us. The end is the end as it came for us in the person of Jesus Christ. The end is the end as it goes on coming in the church. And the end is the end as it will come in consummation at the return of Jesus Christ. This perspective is provided principally by the hymnic interludes between the apocalyptic visions. Only in the last section of apocalyptic visions is the gospel perspective of the interludes reinforced. Here John explicitly resolves the ambiguities that exist in the other apocalyptic sections. That is, he makes it quite clear that the overlap of the ages is no more. The devil is finally removed forever and the new age emerges alone as that to which the saints are finally conformed.

Thesis

The Old Testament perspective, which remains unmodified in most of the apocalyptic sections, is modified by the gospel framework in the introduction, interludes (hymnic sections), and in the epilogue.

Chapter Eight

'And there was War in Heaven'

Conflict and Armageddon

And there was war in heaven. Michael and his angels fought against the dragon, and the dragon and his angels fought back. But he was not strong enough, and they lost their place in heaven. The great dragon was hurled down – that ancient serpent called the devil or Satan, who leads the whole world astray. He was hurled to the earth and his angels with him (Revelation 12:7–9).

Conflict is Inescapable

In Chapter 2 we considered the reality of suffering as the normal experience of Christians in the world. We saw that what Jesus said about the matter was very relevant to the theme of Revelation: 'In the world you have tribulation, but be of good cheer, I have overcome the world' (John 16:33). Now I want to take an overview of John's use of the conflict theme in Revelation. Conflict and tribulation are related very closely in the biblical picture of the coming of the kingdom of God. In the Old Testament direct causes of suffering and disruption are often stated without analysing the total picture of the origin of evil in the world. But if we are prepared to allow the essential unity of the Bible we may arrange the evidence into an overview of the situation. Revelation follows the kind of dualism which develops in Old Testament apocalyptic. That is, we observe a conflict between light and darkness, good and evil, God and Satan which may be thought of as taking place in the spiritual sphere or heavenly places, but which also has its outworking in the affairs of men on earth. One immediate and exciting implication of this is the fact that the affairs of the church in the world have cosmic effects. We tend to think of our personal struggle and the struggles of the church as nothing more than the residue of the blight of sin. Yet Paul, for example, reminds us that the struggle is with spiritual powers (Ephesians 6:12).

It would not be true to say that conflict occurs only because God has refused to allow Satan's challenge. The deists believed in a god who withdraws from the world and is no longer interested in it. Such a withdrawal could not prevent conflict, for creation can be in harmony only when related to God. Some conflict then is the direct effect of sin which destroys proper and harmonious relationships within creation. The God of the Bible is not the god of the deists. He has not left the world to its own devices. Nor has he allowed Satan to steal his world. Rather he has challenged Satan's claim, and invaded his usurped domain in the person of Jesus Christ. Every saving act of God is a direct rebuke to the devil. *The* saving act of God was the living and dying of Jesus Christ. This experience of the slain Lamb was the definitive conflict by which redemption comes to all the people of God.

By entering into the human realm, into our human existence, through the incarnation, Christ entered into the realm of our slavery to Satan. He must either conquer or submit. In his very being he constituted the kingdom of God for he was both God and man relating in perfect harmony. For Christ to have submitted to Satan is as unthinkable as God abdicating the throne of heaven and allowing Satan to take his place as ruler of the universe. The incarnation of Christ was the necessary pre-condition to salvation. It was the focusing of the area of God's action into human existence. This is where it had begun. Since man had been created as the pinnacle of all creation, Satan attacked the kingdom of God at that point. He had decided to get at God through man. The temptation of Eve and the subsequent sin of our first parents was, to all appearances, Satan's victory over God's kingdom. Sin and death came by man, and likewise righteousness and life must come by man:

> As one man's trespass led to condemnation for all
> men, so one man's act of righteousness leads to
> acquittal and life for all men (Romans 5:18, RSV).

> For as by man came death, by a man has come also the resur-
> rection of the dead (1 Corinthians 15:21, RSV).

What we often forget is that, just as the sin of Adam had cosmic consequences, so also the salvation of Christ has cosmic consequences. The whole of creation is involved in both situations. In other words, just as the sin of man led to the disruption of the whole universe so the righteousness of Christ leads to the restoration of the whole universe. And this does not happen apart from us. The redemptive suffering of Christ occurs in the field of conflict between God and Satan. Christ's death on the cross was, in fact, his victory over Satan. it was his victory over every demonic power which enslaves us. The miracles of Jesus in which he casts out demons are indications that the messianic mission must include victory over that dimension of reality.

The conflict between God and Satan has various dimensions to it which belong to the nature of things as the Bible reveals it. Paul's use of the analogy between Christ and Adam is very important. Romans 5 is the main passage which expounds this relationship. Most people can grasp the idea that Adam was the man who brought sin into human existence, and Christ was the man who dealt with the problem. Adam was tempted and sinned, thus bringing mankind out of the garden paradise into the wilderness. Christ came into that wilderness, was tempted and withstood the devil, thus making open the way back into paradise. Paul's argument, however, is a little more involved than that. He is saying that Adam represented all humanity so that his sin was our sin. In like fashion Christ represents the whole of the new humanity so that his righteousness is our righteousness.

Let us take this argument a step further. Because we all, by virtue of our unity with Adam, share his guilt, we then express this original sin by living sinfully. So also, because by virtue of our faith unity with Christ we are accounted as righteous as he is, we then go on to express this righteousness in our lives. Of course we do not express it perfectly because of the sin that will remain until we are fully redeemed. The point is that the life of man is a reflection of what he is in his representative head. If we are Adam's then we express Adam's nature. If we are Christ's then we express Christ's nature. It has been emphasized constantly in this study that the Lamb stamps his character upon the body of those united to him by faith. That is, the church assumes the character of its head. The Lamb's conflict with Satan is also a suffering and redemptive act. That is why the church will go on suffering until the Lamb is revealed in all the glory of the Lion.

A further implication of this is that the representative and substitutionary suffering of the Lamb, which is *the* conflict with Satan, goes on being reflected in his people. The church's suffering and conflict with Satan reflect that great battle which climaxed in Calvary. What happened in the person of our representative head for us, is reflected in our lives until the consummation when the final cleavage comes and evil is put away forever.

The Conflict for our Justification

The conflict motif, like every other aspect of God's saving acts, belongs to all three dimensions of salvation: justification, sanctification and glorification. In this regard the New Testament shows the onslaught on demonic powers and their overthrow depending upon the first of these dimensions which is the gospel. Jesus' victory over the demons, as recorded in the Gospels, is central to the motif of conflict. For example, in Luke 11:14-23 we have the record of the casting out of a demon, which caused the opponents of Jesus to offer the illogical argument that Jesus was in league with the devil: 'By Beelzebub, the prince of demons, he is driving out demons.' Obviously Satan does not set out to wreck his own domain. 'But,' says Jesus, 'if I drive out demons by the finger of God, then the kingdom of God has come to you.' It is probable that Jesus uses this unusual metaphor for the power of God (*hand* and *arm* are more frequently used to denote power) to recall the event when the magicians of Pharaoh were forced to admit defeat before the superior power of Israel's God (see Exodus 8:19).

The conflict motif in the Gospels presents us also with the discomforting fact that all mankind is caught up in the war between Christ and Satan. In the exorcism just referred to Jesus goes on to say, 'He who is not with me is against me, and he who does not gather with me, scatters' (Luke 11:23). This is pointedly directed at those bystanders who accused him of using demonic powers to cast out demons. In Mark's account the accusation is linked with the blasphemy against the Holy Spirit (Mark 3:29–30). In another place Jesus says to his opponents, 'You belong to your father, the devil, and you want to carry out your father's desire' (John 8:44). The demonic hold over mankind is nowhere more sensationally revealed than in the confession of Peter at Caesarea Philippi (Matthew 16:13–23). Peter confesses, 'You are the Christ, the Son of the living God.' Jesus replies, 'Blessed are you, Simon son of Jonah, for this was not revealed to you by man but by my Father in heaven.' Only God could give a sinful man the eyes to recognize his Christ. But this same man is still capable of thinking like a sinful human. The Christ of God must die to redeem us. 'Never, Lord!' says Peter. The rebuke from Jesus must have cut him to the quick: 'Out of my sight, Satan! You are a stumbling block to me; you do not have in mind the things of God, but the things of men.' The unpalatable truth is there: when a man recognizes the Christ it is by the grace of God. When he thinks like a man he is the emissary of Satan.

So the pattern develops. Jesus brings redemption and the kingdom of God. He does this only by paying the price of his own suffering and death. He casts out demons only because he has deflected the arrows of Satan's temptations in the wilderness, and is set to run the course of total obedience to his Father's will. The mystery of iniquity is such that we cannot understand why Satan both seeks to divert Jesus from his redemptive suffering and also remains the agent of that suffering (see Acts 2:23). We do know that the conflict was decided by that redemptive act of Christ: 'Having disarmed the powers and authorities, he made a public spectacle of them, triumphing over them by the cross' (Colossians 2:15). Of his coming death Jesus said: 'Now is the time for judgment on this world; now the prince of this world will be driven out. But I, when I am lifted up from the earth, will draw all men to myself' (John 12:30–33). The gospel is the power of God to overcome the powers of evil. The disciples received a foretaste of this as the seventy were sent to preach the good news that 'The kingdom of God is near you' (Luke 10:8–18). When they returned rejoicing that even the demons submitted to them, Jesus said, 'I saw Satan fall like lightning from heaven.'

The Conflict in our Sanctification

We have established that Satan gained his hold over the universe through his entry into the arena of human existence. The redemptive act of God, like a surgeon's knife attacking a deadly cancer, must take place in the same arena. Christ's justifying work in his living and dying included his victory over Satan's power in the world. The structure of salvation has been adequately discussed in previous chapters, and this structure is now applied to the area of Christ's victory over Satan. What Christ did for us has its outworking in all believers as sanctification. What we already are in Christ (victorious over Satan) begins to take shape in our experience as the Holy Spirit conforms us more and more to the reality which is in Christ. The Christian struggle is against the world, the flesh and the devil.

When Paul concludes the Ephesian letter by turning from the practical issues of life (Ephesians 5:1–6:9) to the matter of spiritual warfare (Ephesians 6:10–18), he does not take up a new subject. The practical matters of daily life in a hostile world *are* the spiritual warfare against principalities and powers. In urging us to put on the full armour of God, Paul is not departing from the perspective that is consistently his, namely that, by standing firm and clinging to the truth of our justification, we live the life of sanctification. The gospel at work in the believer, in the congregation of believers, is the demonstration to all the spiritual powers that Christ has triumphed (Ephesians 3:10–13).

The Conflict of Glorification

The question as to why the decisive defeat of Satan at the cross was not also his final destruction is the same as the question in Acts 1:6 about Christ restoring the kingdom (see Chapter 7). It has pleased God in his wisdom to bring many Sons and daughters to glory through the preaching of the gospel in this present age. Peter describes it as the forbearance of God giving opportunity to people to repent. 'But,' he says, 'the day of the Lord will come like a thief' (2 Peter 3:8–13). The day of the Lord is, in this context, the consummation of the kingdom. The consummation of Christ's victory will be the final and complete abolition and destruction of Satan. But this can be only because Christ has already won the victory over Satan on the cross. The final overthrow is not some new redemptive work of God. It is the outworking of the victory of the cross in the whole universe as God makes all things new. When Satan is thrown into the lake of fire (Revelation 20:10), all conflict, suffering and death cease forever and ever.

The Conflict in Revelation

With this general overview of the spiritual warfare, what shall we make of the motif of conflict in the Book of Revelation? Let us first summarize the conflict as it occurs throughout Revelation.

The church in the world described in the seven messages (Revelation 2–3)

Each of the messages describes some aspect of the struggle. It is not a passive suffering, but one born out of the conflict that comes from declaring oneself for Christ. Persecution is the work of the devil:

> You did not deny my faith even in the days of Antipas
> my witness, my faithful one, who was killed among you,
> where Satan dwells (Revelation 2:13, RSV).

> To the rest of you in Thyatira,
> to you who do not hold
> to her teaching and have not learned Satan's so-called
> deep secrets . . . Only hold on to what you have until
> I come (Revelation 2:24–25).

> I will make those who are of the synagogue of Satan,
> who claim to be Jews though they are not, but are liars –
> I will make them come and fall down at your feet and
> acknowledge that I have loved you (Revelation 3:9).

Others struggle against the enemy within, against immorality, false doctrine and against lethargy and complacency in the church. But to all is given the promise that the final blessing is for him who overcomes, who conquers in this unremitting warfare against the world, the flesh and the devil.

God in Conflict With a Sinful World (Revelation 6–7)

The opening of the seals leads to terrible judgments on the created order. This is the ultimate manifestation of the curse of Genesis 3. But the saints are sealed against this judgment by the redemptive work of Christ. Otherwise they would be caught up in the destruction.

The same kind of conflict is found in the visions of the trumpets (Revelation 8–9). The horror that is released here is that to which mankind has submitted in its rebellion against the creator. The devil has no designs to be a beneficent ruler but only to destroy. There is divine irony in the fact that the powers of darkness actually serve the purpose of God to bring about their own undoing.

The Beast Emerges as the Adversary of the Church (Revelation 11)

The preaching of the gospel by the two witnesses is strenuously opposed by the beast from the bottomless pit. The witnesses suffer a fatal blow and there is rejoicing in the earth at the apparent defeat of God's people. But the resurrection of the witnesses is accompanied by a terrible retribution upon their foes. The heavenly choirs sing praises to God, for his kingdom has overcome the powers of the world.

War in Heaven and Earth (Revelation 12–14)

The apocalyptic description of the dragon persecuting the woman with child (Revelation 12:1–6) shows the interrelationship of the spiritual powers in heavenly places and the earthly conflicts involving the people of God. What happens in heaven is inextricably bound up with what happens on the earth. Then there is war in heaven between Michael and the dragon. Satan, the dragon, is defeated and thrown down to the earth. That his downfall is due to Christ's redemptive work, rather than some primaeval fall of Satan from being a servant of God, is clear from the interpretation given by the heavenly voice:

Now have come the salvation
and the power and the kingdom of our God,
and the authority of his Christ.
For the accuser of our brothers,
who accuses them before our God
day and night,
has been hurled down.
They overcame him by the blood of the Lamb and by the
word of their testimony.

(Revelation 12:10–11)

Thus the heavenly and angelic battle corresponds to the defeat of Satan by the conquering saints who overcome by the conquest of their saviour and substitute, Christ.

Then John sees a vision of two beasts who represent the dragon and exercises his authority to deceive people and to cause them to worship the beasts. People who do not worship it are slain. All the followers of the beast are marked with a human number – 666. But then there is the glorious vision of the Lamb on Mount Zion with all that belong to him, who are marked with the Father's name. Two angels flying in midheaven call upon the dwellers of the earth with the message of grace and the message of judgment. A third angel utters a warning of the fearful consequences of worshipping the beast. 'This,' says John, 'calls for patient endurance on the part of the saints who obey God's commandments and remain faithful to Jesus' (Revelation 14:12). Then the scene changes and it is not the Lamb, but the visionary son of man from Daniel 7, who begins the harvest of the grapes of wrath.

The Bowls of Wrath (Revelation 16)

Again we see God in conflict with his rebellious creation. The earth has become the domain of the beast, the arch enemy of God. As in the previous visions of the seals and the trumpets, the curse of God on creation is extended to these terrible acts of judgment that overtake the children of Adam who have chosen to become the children of the devil. The connection between the devil and the sinful world is clear from the fifth bowl poured out on the throne of the beast so that men gnawed their tongues in agony and cursed the God of heaven (Revelation 16:10).

Once more we see the powers of darkness rushing to bring about their own downfall. The sixth bowl of wrath stirs demonic spirits to assemble the godless powers of the world for the battle of the great day of God the Almighty. This is Armageddon. The final bowl of wrath is poured on Babylon, the symbol of all Satan's strongholds among men.

The Death of Babylon (Revelation 17–18)

The seventh bowl is a prelude to a more detailed description of Babylon's overthrow. Babylon is 'the great harlot' – the biblical image for idolatry and apostasy. She is drunk with the blood of the saints. World powers make war on the Lamb but are overthrown by the Lamb. Then the logic of evil emerges again as the beast wars against the harlot (Revelation 17:16–17). Evil cannot preserve order but only consume it. It is the judgment of God which condemns evil to self-destruction.

The Divine Warrior of the Lord's Day (Revelation 19–20)

John's vision of the rider on the white horse is magnificent and terrible. He comes to smite the nations with the sword of his mouth and rule them with a rod of iron. This universal lordship is revealed in his name: King of kings and Lord of lords. Again the spiritual conflict is one that has its outworking on earth. The beast gathers the forces of the kings of the earth to war against the divine warrior. There is a terrible slaughter and the beast and the false prophet are thrown into the lake of fire. Now we come to that controversial passage about the millennium (Revelation 20). John sees an angel take Satan and bind him in the pit for a thousand years. The martyred saints come to life again and reign with Christ for the thousand years. Then Satan is loosed from the pit to gather his forces for battle against the saints. But there is no contest, for fire from heaven consumes the enemy. Then the devil is thrown, finally and forever, into the lake of fire. The conflict is ended. There remains only the judgment at the great white throne which separates the redeemed from the lost. Heaven and earth pass away and eternal day dawns on the new heaven and new earth, the dwelling place of God, the Lamb and the multitude of the redeemed.

Conflict in Apocalypse and Gospel

We must now try to bring some order out of this series of expressions of the spiritual conflict. The gospel must be allowed to be the key to our understanding. There is no reason to suppose that John has a very different perspective on the conflict from that of other New Testament writers. Indeed we have observed how he treads the same

paths of gospel-centered thinking. Allowing for the apocalyptic perspective in the Book of Revelation is crucial at
this point. In other words the great apocalyptic struggles
involving the dragon, the beast, the false prophet and the
kings of the earth against Christ and his saints, depict the
coming of the day of the Lord. The groups of visions
repeat the same theme over and over again, looking now
at one aspect, now at another. I must repeat that the question about when all this comes to pass can be answered
only by reference to the end. We should always try to put
ourselves into the shoes of the Jew nurtured on the Old
Testament when we read the apocalyptic visions. For him
the end was a single event. All the various facets of the terrible conflict and the spectacular victory of the divine warrior belong to that day.

Furthermore, we do an injustice to the apocalyptic way
of thinking when we treat its method of reckoning time in
a modern scientific way. In our discussion of the Day of
the Lord we noted that the Bible deals with time in terms
of both its quantity and its quality.[1] We are used to the former with our exact reckoning of years and months. But
with our scientific bias towards exactitude we can easily
grow impatient with the Bible's apparent slackness over
details. The constant repetition of rounded numbers –
forty years in the wilderness, forty days being tempted,
seventy years of exile, and so on – suggests a rather different approach to the quantity of time. More significant,
however, is the qualitative use of time. Here it is not the
exact amount of time that elapses that really matters, but
the quality of events which characterize the time: So
Christ's coming can be pegged to a series of identifiable
historical events and people (Luke 3:1–2) and thus be

---

1 See p. 63. See also Simon J. De Vries, *Yesterday, Today and
Tomorrow* (Grand Rapids: William B. Eerdmans, 1975).

related to quantitative time, or it can be described as the event which gives time its meaning (Galatians 4:4). The qualitative aspect can be seen also in Peter's rejection of the relevance of quantitative time with regard to the period between the first and second comings (2 Peter 3:8–10): 'With the Lord one day is as a thousand years.'

Apocalyptic takes the concept of qualitative time to its high point by the symbolic use of numbers to express, not literal quantities of time in days, months, and years, but the quality of the time. The quality of the time is determined by the significance of God's action within it either to save or to judge. It was a failure to allow for this that gave strength to the scoffers who taunted the early Christians over their expectation of the imminent return of Christ (2 Peter 3:3–4). 'Where is the promise of his coming?' they asked. If God promised a 'day of God' on which all the prophetic words about the coming of the kingdom will come to pass, how is it that he still has not appeared in his reigning glory? (And if this was the problem in the *first* generation of the church, how much more now in the twentieth century?) Peter shows us in that context that the *day* of the Lord is not confined to a quantity that we can discern as so many days or years or even millennia. But, it is still the day of God's action to bring in the kingdom. Of this new age which has intruded into the old through the coming of Christ, Paul says, 'This is the appointed time, this is the day of salvation' (2 Corinthians 6:2).

That the new age has invaded the realms of the old age is the cause of the apocalyptic conflict. But let us be clear about the perspective the gospel gives to this. As we have seen, the Old Testament views the two ages consecutively:

Old age $\longrightarrow$ Day of the Lord $\longrightarrow$ New age

The New Testament modifies this by showing that all the ingredients of the end are there in the gospel. Man's sin is judged in the person of Christ on the cross. The new humanity is resurrected in Christ and ascends to the right hand of God. Satan is confounded and cast out. His power is removed by the finger of God. The decisive conflict has taken place and the kingdom of Christ is victorious. The old age goes on but it can never be the same again. All history subsequent to the death and resurrection of Christ is history at the end.

All 'AD' history is in crisis because the Holy Spirit constantly reapplies the decisive victory of Calvary and the empty tomb through the preached word of the gospel. Goliath is vanquished and now the people of God, armed with the victory of their king, great David's greater Son, storm the cities of the Philistines with the invincible weapon of the preaching of the gospel. And it is not only evangelism that pillages the strongholds of Satan, but the ongoing battle to bring every thought captive to obey Christ (2 Corinthians 10:3–6). The conflict is in the sanctification struggle precisely because this struggle is the new age taking hold of us who were formerly children of the old.

The consummation will mean the removal of the last vestiges of the old age. If there is to be some last great conflict it will be the prelude to the universal unveiling of the new age in all its glory. The consummation will mean that what we actually are in ourselves will finally coincide with what we are in the person of our representative and substitute at the right hand of God.

Thus, what the Old Testament apocalyptic portrayed as the single event of the day of the Lord is described in the apocalyptic visions of Revelation from various angles. No one word-picture could suffice to convey the totality of the brilliance and the gloom, the glory and the horror, the joy and the dismay of the day of the Lord. Each series of visions is built upon by the next until the desired effect is achieved. Let me emphasize again that Revelation was written, not for the arm-chair prophets with their charts of historical events in the twentieth century and their intricate diagrams of the end of the age, but for the harassed subsistence-level first-century Christians of the Asia Minor province. It was written to bring them both warning and reassurance, to encourage them in their struggle and to liberate them from fear of the enemy within and without. With a genius for composition that is nowhere surpassed in the biblical literature, John's inspired mind leaves no stone unturned, and yet avoids the unnecessary and obscuring details that so many modern readers wish to read into him. The message comes to us in unfamiliar dress, but that should not be taken to mean that it is impossibly complex.

For these first-century Christians the conflict was real to the point of threatening their very lives. Nor is this to imply that persecution and martyrdom belonged only to the first century. The curious view that most of Revelation is really relevant only to those who live immediately prior to the second coming of Christ makes nonsense of John's concern for his contemporaries, and of the undying relevance of the message throughout the whole of this AD age in which the people of God struggle against the foe and eagerly await the Lord's coming.

So when is Armageddon? When are the great conflicts and judgments of John's visions? Again we answer, 'At the end.' They are the events of the day of the Lord. The day of the Lord is past, for Christ has died and Christ has risen. The day of the Lord is present, for Christ makes himself to reign on this earth through the preaching of the gospel. The day of the Lord is future, for Christ will come again. Armageddon is Calvary.

Armageddon is every conquest of the gospel as it shines into this darkened world. Armageddon will be the final putting down of this evil age and its deceitful master. And insofar as we contemplate the possibility of the horror of World War III, we should recognise that its potential for the self-annihilation of our civilization is only a more drastic form of the confusion of evil by which it consumes itself. That confusion has already been given its definitive form at the Cross where evil men were the instruments of Satan's downfall.

The Millennium

The so-called millennium of Revelation 20 is part and parcel of John's dealing with the conflict theme. At the outset I must express my doubts about the attempt to take this symbolic passage and to make a literal description of a future event. In this I am far more in accord with the view known as 'amillennialism.'[2] It is highly unlikely, to say the least, that something so dramatically significant as a thousand year reign of a reappeared Christ on earth before this age ends should nowhere else be mentioned in the New Testament. The arguments in favour of it depend almost entirely on literalistic applications of Old Testament prophecies in a way that suffers the gospel to be reinterpreted by the Old Testament rather than to have the Old Testament interpreted by the gospel.

---

[2] See Introduction p. 19 – amillennialism. This view is expounded in the commentaries on Revelation by Leon Morris, William Hendriksen (*More than Conquerors*), and Michael Wilcock (*I Saw Heaven Opened*). A symposium setting out the different views of the millennium is found in (Ed.) Robert Clouse, *The Meaning of the Millennium* (Downers Grove: Inter-Varsity Press, 1977).

That the millennium passage (Revelation 20:1–10) is one of a series of apocalyptic visions cannot be overlooked. That it contains some symbolic material is admitted by exponents of even the most literalistic interpretations. The passage is one which cries out for interpretation. In interpreting such a passage we must allow apocalyptic symbolism to be what it is. Furthermore, we cannot establish a gigantic doctrinal system on one symbolic passage. That is, we must interpret the more obscure passages of Scripture in the light of the clearer ones. Above all the gospel must be our interpretative key: the life, death and resurrection of Christ and all that it achieves for us. The 'literalist' position of the premillennial view is, in fact, largely governed by the Old Testament perspective of the linear succession of the two ages. I must point out that there is much Old Testament perspective that premillennialism does not perceive and as a result it maintains its adherence to the impossible principle of literalism. For instance, the pattern of promise and fulfilment in the Old Testament is never strictly literal. The fulfilment of promises always goes beyond the terms of the original promise. We should not think that the New Testament perspective was totally unprepared for in the Old Testament.

Whatever else we say of the thousand year reign of Christ in Revelation 20, it must be maintained that it is part of the scenario of the day of the Lord. Only by. removing this from the victory of Christ in his cross and resurrection is it possible to establish the earthly programme which the premillennialists posit for the future. The idea that resurrected saints and a glorified Christ should return to this earth, as yet not glorified, to rule among people who are bound by non-resurrection bodies, has no support anywhere else in Scripture. This earthly millennium is an attempt to come to terms with a self-inflicted problem;

that of two different future hopes. The first is the literal fulfilment of Old Testament prophecy in all its Israelite terms, and the second is the consummation of the gospel. The attempt to combine the two destroys the very principle which made this unlikely marriage necessary. That is, literalism cannot survive because the prophets did not promise a future involving both the literal restoration of Israel *and* the gospel.

The literalist-millennial solution is neither literal nor fulfilment. It is not literal in that it must adjust the Israelite expressions of Old Testament prophecy to include the gospel. The restoration involves Christians as well as Jews, Christ as well as David. The literalism is preserved only at the level of the externals – the land, temple etc. It is not literal in that the climax comes in an age of modern technology and not the primitive world of the Bible prophecy. To say that the prophets wrote in the light of their own age is to give the game away. That is precisely the point! For if modern technology is allowed to qualify the literalism of Bible prophecy, why should not an even more significant development in world history also qualify it? How strange that human technology can be accommodated in the literalist's interpretation of prophecy but not *the* event of all history: the gospel.

The literalist millennial view is not fulfilment because its exponents rightly perceive that it does not go far enough. The earthly restoration does not satisfy the millennialist's Christian instincts. So he must have a literal (so-called) fulfilment which is only temporary and which will give way to a permanent gospel consummation. The prophets foresaw an earthly restoration lasting forever. The premillennialist must curtail it in order to allow an even more perfect kingdom to come. The one thousand years of Revelation 20 is thus eagerly grasped as a description of the earthly fulfilment. This ignores the fact that the prophets said 'forever' not a thousand years. It also ignores the fact that Revelation 20 says 'a thousand years' but says nothing about a bodily presence of Christ on earth during this period.

I conclude that the premillennial solution to Revelation 20 overrides almost all the principles of sound interpretation. The whole structuring of the end-time by the gospel which is the warp and woof of Revelation – not to mention the rest of the New Testament – must be suddenly suspended at this point if the premillennial system is accepted. When we allow the clearer meaning of the gospel to govern our interpretation we are reminded that the life, death and resurrection of Christ establish the pattern of all the saving events. What will happen finally and perfectly at Christ's coming has already begun with the preaching of the gospel. More importantly, the second coming will mean the universal manifestation of what has already taken place for us in the gospel event.

According to this passage, the millennium is the day of the Lord, the day on which Satan is bound. It is the day of Christ's victory and his reign. In one sense, this is where we came in, for John began this book with his vision of the reigning Christ in glory. It is a reminder that the present conflict is not fatal, but an expression of the reigning with Christ of all who are made a kingdom of priests (Revelation 1:6 cf. Revelation 20:6). The thousand years is, as to quantity, an unknown but perfect period of time. As to quality, it is the exaltation of Christ in his glorious rule. It is the privilege of the struggling Christian to know that his very participation in the struggle and the conflict is a share in the rule of Christ. Once more John encourages the saints by removing their existence from the realm of the purely routine, the hum drum, and the meaningless. He removes it also from the realm of senseless suffering and defeat. He points to the fact that in the here-and-now every Christian can know that he, as an individual, has meaning; that his personal identity is defined by the gospel. Even world history cannot overwhelm us, for the gospel has transferred the now into the day of Satan's overthrow. The binding of Satan does not imply that there is no evil, no conflict. Rather it is an affirmation that the kingdom of God has come in Jesus Christ and now permeates the world through the church as it preaches the gospel and lives by it.

Summary

Revelation shows the members of the church in all ages that their struggle against the world, the flesh and the devil, is not a trivial nor a private thing. The theme of conflict, which John weaves throughout, draws all the saints into the arena in which the victory of Christ is achieved. As the gospel has structured the theme of the day of the Lord, so it shows that there is but one conflict in which we are all caught up. Initially the conflict was completely worked out in the life, death and resurrection of Jesus. Satan was decisively defeated at the cross. Christ's victory was for us, so that all believers are accounted victorious in him. Then the same conflict is manifested in the life of the church as Christ, through his gospel applied by the Spirit, works to conform the members of his body to his likeness. Finally the conflict is resolved in the consummation. The millennium, as an expression of the victory of Christ, cannot be confined to the consummation or to a period just prior to it.

Thesis

The conflict of the day of the Lord is structured by the gospel so that it characterizes the three dimensions of salvation – justification, sanctification and glorification. All of the conflict relates to all three dimensions.

Chapter Nine

'I Saw a New Heaven and a New Earth'

The Final Separation

Then I saw a new heaven and a new earth, for the first heaven and the first earth had passed away, and there was no longer any sea. I saw the Holy City, the new Jerusalem, coming down out of heaven from God, prepared as a bride beautifully dressed for her husband. And I heard a loud voice from the throne saying, 'Now the dwelling of God is with men, and he will live with them. They will be his people, and God himself will be with them and be their God'

(Revelation 21:1–3).

Satan's End

Up till now we have been describing the situation during the period of the overlap of the ages. It is a period of tension, suffering and conflict, it is the time of both having and not having. It is the time of walking by faith, in which the believer knows by faith that he possesses all the riches of Christ and that, in the person of his substitute Man, he has already arrived at the goal at the right hand of God. On the other hand it is the time of pressing on towards the mark, of living in hope of the blessed day when we shall actually experience the goal with all the clarity of perception of which our resurrected beings will be capable.

But a hope without a time of fulfilment is a delusion. The Christian hope is no delusion for its first fruits were revealed in history two thousand years ago in the resurrection of Christ. One day the overlap of the ages will be no more, for the old age will perish by fire. All that belongs to the old age will perish in a death more terrible than death and the great deceiver will be cast into the lake of fire. How can this final transition of the ages be presented in apocalyptic imagery which has not normally been accommodated to the overlap perspective? If the general apocalyptic perspective of the linear succession of the ages has prevailed up to now in John's use of this particular literary form, can it now signify unambiguously the consummation of the kingdom of God? We have to say that it can: John has done it in Revelation 20–22. He has done it simply by removing the ambiguity of the picture of the end. His series of conflicts and judgments that go before have all been ambiguous enough to be applied to the three-dimensional end demanded by the gospel. Now the ambiguity is pointedly removed and the 'end of the end,' the consummation, is described.

We look first at how John describes the sequel to the millennium. Satan is loosed from the pit and comes out to deceive the nations and to gather them for battle (Revelation 20:7–10). Their object is to attack the people of God, but before this can happen they are destroyed by fire from heaven. No new or extraordinary suffering of the saints is described. Nor are the saints involved in the final removal of the forces of evil. Some interpretations suffer from the need to project a new order of tribulation for the saints immediately before the return of Christ. This is not demanded by the text, nor, we must add, would it be much comfort for the already tribulated saints that John writes to encourage! This 'little while' of Satan's loosing must serve another purpose. First, it expresses the paradox that Satan, though defeated and cast out, remains the adversary who prowls around like a roaring lion, seeking someone to devour (1 Peter 5:8). Secondly, it sets the stage for the final denouement. If we may develop Oscar Cullmann's illustration of the decisive battle and victory day, this is the battle for Berlin.[1] Or again, to change the analogy, it is a kind of 'High Noon' showdown when the defeat of the enemy is made both public and ultimately effective. The overlap of the ages is past.

With a final flourish John describes the indescribable. For one last time the apocalyptic genius comes into its own. Weaving together the evocative images of the Old Testament with the distinctive elements of the gospel, John creates a tapestry of incredible brilliance. The garden of Eden, Canaan, Jerusalem, and Jesus Christ as the new temple, are portrayed with a skill that does not allow mere words to exhaust the meaning. It was never given to any either New Testament writer to re-create for us so vividly the riches we possess in Christ.

---

[1] O. Cullmann, *Christ and Time* (London: SCM Press, 1951). Cullmann uses the rather confusing notion that the death and resurrection of Jesus became, for the New Testament, the midpoint of time rather than the end. However, he does avoid the need to talk about the end in three ways as I have done in this study. He uses the analogy of war. The gospel event is the decisive victory, but the war continues until all hostilities are resolved at the end which is then celebrated as victory day. I am suggesting that, if the victory is truly *the* decisive victory, it is in the New Testament perspective the end of the war, not its midpoint. This is so even though the war goes on for some time after the decisive victory.

The Meaning of Heaven

It is significant that John draws upon Isaiah's understanding of regeneration. Too often heaven is looked on as a vague, though happy, realm of formless spirit existence. We may laugh at the commonplace cartoon representation showing people with haloes, wings on their backs, harps in hand, and standing up to their knees in cloud. Unfortunately this is uncomfortably close to many Christians' conception of heaven. It is seen as a kind of un-creation in which we are at last divested of material things and especially the clods we call our bodies. We might be tempted to think that John is using the earthly imagery of the Old Testament on the assumption that we will know how to spiritualize it. But such a pagan approach is truly unthinkable. The New Testament simply will not allow us to abolish so completely what we may call – controversially perhaps – the Old Testament view of heaven, and the reason is Jesus Christ who took upon himself our humanity, including its physical side, forever.

The incarnation of God in Jesus Christ, and his bodily resurrection and ascension, establish an important aspect of the Old Testament view of the kingdom of God. I refer to the physical creation. In the beginning God created the heavens and the earth. The earth with the sky above is what this means. This creation of all that exists is looked upon by God as good. It is destined for corruption through sin and, finally, for the destruction of fire But as the saving acts of God in time and history within this physical universe project the reality of the kingdom of God, so the universe itself is destined, through renewal, to be a part of that kingdom. This is the framework for the biblical doctrine of regeneration.

Let us look at it another way. When God created the heavens and the earth and set man in Eden, man's nature was to relate to God, to his fellow man, and to animal and physical creation. Sin disrupted these relationships so that what God had generated (created) now degenerated. Death settled over the creation. The gospel, however, was in God's mind from before even the creation of the universe, as the means by which all things would be regenerated or re-created. All the Old Testament images of the salvation of God's people involved the re-establishment of the intended relationship between God, mankind and the rest of creation. Man was created a physical being in a physical environment. This in no way detracts from the truth that he was also created a spiritual being in a spiritual environment, that is, in relation to God.

Thus every Old Testament image of salvation included the regeneration of the physical as well as the spiritual. For Noah there was the stark reality of a totally enclosed mini-world in the ark. For Abraham and his Israelite descendants it was the fruitful land of Canaan as the new garden of Eden for the people of God. In the prophets the same Israelitish environment is projected as a future attainment in which the full glory of God's kingdom will exist and yet in a physical environment. Salvation means *all* relationship restored and this includes not only moral regeneration but physical and mental. Sickness will be no more, grief and suffering will be banished. Righteousness will rule the people. The wolf will lie down with the lamb. The desert will blossom as the rose.[2]

Not only is the fruitful Eden image perpetuated, but also the religio-political structures of Israel are established as the model of the future kingdom of God. As David was anointed as the king and his son promised the throne forever (2 Samuel 7:11–14), so it is a new David who will rule

---

[2] See e.g. Isaiah 11:1–9, 35:1–10, 65:17–25. Ezekiel 36:33–36. This is discussed in greater detail in *Gospel and Kingdom*.

in God's kingdom. The temple becomes the focal point of this rule, for it, like the tabernacle before it, represents the dwelling of God amongst his people. The kingdom of God will centre upon the restored and glorified temple on Mount Zion. It is Ezekiel's beautiful image that John recreates in Revelation 22. Here (Ezekiel 47) we see the temple as the source of all life. From God's dwelling flows the river of life which supernaturally increases as it goes. It turns the desolate Arabah region – the valley of the Dead Sea – into a new garden of Eden.

No consideration of heaven is complete without this total regeneration of heavens and earth. We see that the actual word *heaven* has a dual significance. It is first the word for the sky above and, perhaps, the universe beyond. As such it is simply the indispensable canopy for the physical world in which we live, it is used in this sense in Genesis 1:1, Isaiah 65:17 and Revelation 21:1. But Old Testament man also came to recognize that since God is greater than the earth which he made, he must dwell beyond the sky. Thus heaven comes to mean the place 'out there' where God dwells. 'Heaven is my throne and the earth is my footstool' says the Lord' (Isaiah 66:1).

This transcendent 'out there and wholly other' view of God is not allowed to remain unqualified. For from the beginning, in the relationship between God and man there is intimacy as well as awe of the transcendent. Adam and Eve 'heard the sound of the Lord God as he was walking in the garden in the cool of the day' (Genesis 3:8).[3] God never ceases to be the God who dwells in heaven 'out there' (Psalm 20:6, Deuteronomy 4:39, Job 22:12, Psalm 14:2,

---

[3] This translation of the NIV correctly brings out the fact that the verb is singular and refers to God 'walking,' not Adam and Eve. This example of anthropomorphism – that is, speaking of God as if he were human – enhances the 'down here' emphasis concerning God.

33:13, 57:3, 80:14, 102:19). But he is also the God who is 'down here.' This is not the immanent God of pantheism which removes the distinction between God and creation. It is a saving act of God by which he reaches into our sin-laden existence to establish once again the true relationship between God and man. This is indicated in the placing of the tabernacle in the midst of Israel as the tent-dwelling of God (Exodus 25:8, 29:45–46). In the later history of Israel the moveable tabernacle gives way to the temple in Jerusalem. Because of the relationship between God and man that the temple represents, it is not surprising that it is elevated to great prominence in the prophetic view of the coming of the kingdom of God.

The temple as the sign of 'God with us' becomes closely related to the human agent of God's rule. David's son will build the temple, says the prophet Nathan (2 Samuel 7:12–13). This same Davidic prince is called the son of God (v. 14) – a title which identifies him principally as the true representative of Israel (cf. Exodus 4:22–23, Hosea 11:1). But the royal prince is also Immanuel – God with us (Isaiah 7:14, 9:6–7). It is not surprising then, that the New Testament combines all these images in the one person Jesus Christ. He is the true temple (John 1: 14[4], 2:19–22). He is the son of David who is also the son of God (Luke 3:22–38).

To return now to the question of the meaning of heaven. The fact that Jesus Christ is now at the right hand of the Father in heaven, and that he has gone to prepare a place for us in the Father's house, does not mean that our final destiny is to be separated from the physical universe. Jesus has taken his own body to heaven. In that is bound up the redemption and

---

[4] John 1:14. The word became flesh and dwelt among us. The Greek word translated 'dwelt' is a word derived from the word tabernacle or tent.

renewal of the physical universe. It is in keeping with the scriptural perspective that John sees the new heaven and the new earth, and that the new Jerusalem comes down out of heaven from God. We need not suppose that this is meant to convey a literal descent of the city out of the sky. It is the final touch to the regenerating work of God. It establishes the kingdom which is not from this world. The heavenly country which Abraham longed for (Hebrews 11:16) is not a land in the sky, but a tangible dwelling for redeemed mankind and one in which the people of God will relate truly to God, mankind and the world. It is a dwelling from God, a city from heaven. But when it is set up in the centre of the regenerated earth, it will mean that the dwelling place of God is with men. This is how the story began in the paradise of Eden, and this is how it will end in the regained paradise of God's kingdom.

One last point needs to be made in this regard. I have been personally amazed at just how radical a thought the resurrection can be to some Christians. Even many of those who belong to my own (Anglican) denomination, and who say week by week the words of either the Apostles' or Nicene creeds which state explicitly our belief in the resurrection of the body, seem not to have grasped the implication. On the one hand they confess a bodily resurrection, yet on the other hand they so often seem to operate with a Greek pagan notion of immortality of the soul; of a destiny of timeless and matterless eternity in an ethereal spirit state. The fact, which is often overlooked, is that the bodily resurrection of Christ points to our own, and carries with it also the guarantee of the redemption of the whole physical universe.

God and the Lamb

Throughout this study I have referred from time to time to the motif of the Lamb and the Lion in Revelation 5. It provides us with a symbolic representation of the message of the whole book of Revelation. The paradox of the majesty of the Lion revealed in the suffering of the Lamb is the paradox of the conquest of God through our Saviour Christ. It is the paradox of the church through which Christ conquers the world, a church which can be the agent of this conquest only by reflecting the nature of its head – the suffering Lamb. It is the paradox of individual and corporate Christian existence as every believer engages in the life-and-death struggle against the world, the flesh and the devil, while at the same time rejoicing in the fact that we have already overcome in Christ. It is the paradox of the overlap of the ages in which the kingdom of God, having already broken into this age in Christ, is being formed in us, and yet remains a future event. It is the paradox of the millennial rule of Christ and the 'little while' of Satan's loosing.

Is this paradox ever resolved? The answer must be 'yes' and 'no' – a further paradox! Yes indeed, as we have seen, the old age eventually perishes along with Satan and all things that belong to him. The overlap of the ages will disappear, the tension of Christian existence will be resolved. The church will cease to be the suffering-servant church and be the church triumphant. But there are some paradoxes which will never be resolved. Particularly we note that the triune being of God is a paradox. Three in one is not expressible in human logic. It is the sameness (unity) and difference (distinction) that characterizes God and which will ever characterize him and our relationship to him.

John can express this paradox only in human language.

That which he says of God he can say also of Christ. 'I am Alpha and Omega, the beginning and the end' (Revelation 1:8, 21:6, cf. 22:13, 1:17–18). The apocalyptic imagery which has so easily portrayed Jesus Christ, or the Lamb, as having separate identity, is not allowed to destroy the central paradox of the Christian faith: God is one and three. The Lamb is one with the Father and the Spirit. Yet the Lamb is not the Father, nor the Spirit. When we, as the people of God, are brought finally to this glorious consummation we shall be perfect but still human. And because we shall be still human there is no reason to suppose that we shall know God as he knows himself. The paradox of God's being is a true and eternal mystery, not merely a reflection of our fallenness. In the kingdom we shall not penetrate the mystery of the Trinity. Our perfected humanity will be precisely that – humanity and not deity. Perfect humanity will show itself in the way we shall worship at the throne of God and the Lamb. The mystery shall remain an endless source of praise.

One further paradox remains. The constant theme of this study has been the tension between the glory of the Lion and the suffering of the Lamb. In fact, I have suggested that this tension characterizes the Book of Revelation. We might therefore be pardoned for supposing that the consummation would indeed reveal Christ – at last – as the Lion. Yet, when we come to this final scene of the visions of John, to the fullness of the heavenly kingdom, it is the Lamb we find on the throne. Why should this. be? And, furthermore, does this fact not rather undermine the thesis of this study?

Let us remind ourselves from whence we have come. John was told that the Lion of the tribe of Judah has conquered and can unlock the mysteries of the kingdom (Revelation 5:5). This Lion is none other than the glorious and exalted Christ the vision of whom caused John to swoon clean away (Revelation 1:17). And yet, when John turns to see this Lion, he is confronted by the Lamb standing as though it had been slain. Now when we arrive at the point at which we might expect to see the Lion, we still see the Lamb. Obviously we have to remember that we are dealing with images. John has provided us with a series of images or word pictures by which he conveys the truth of Christian existence. It is the truly amazing thing about the gospel that the rule of God's kingdom, which the Lion represents, comes through the suffering of the Christ, which the Lamb represents. No one picture can adequately represent these truths. Thus John has given us a series of pictures which show us the reality of the coming of the kingdom from a variety of standpoints.

There can be no doubt, from John's visions of judgment and the overthrow of Satan, that the Lamb indeed rules with all the power of the Lion. From time to time we see this exalted and judging Christ. But John will never let us lose sight of the true source of this mighty rule in the Lamb's suffering. Thus, in the consummation, the kingdom itself and the glory of God will reveal the majesty of Christ, the Lion of Judah. But the people of God will go through eternity worshipping him as the Lamb that was slain. Since the kingdom came by his suffering, it is not possible that the Lamb slain from the foundation of the world should be set aside and, as it were, forgotten. Christ indeed has authority and power and majesty to reign by virtue of his being true God from all eternity. But, in the hidden wisdom of God, he has determined that Christ's rule in his kingdom shall be by virtue of his redeeming love. It is our destiny to be the subjects of Christ, not only because we are his creatures fashioned by the word of his power at the beginning, but particularly because we are his children, redeemed by his life, death and resurrection as the God-man who was and is for us.

Justification to the Very End!

One further comment needs to be made about John's way of expounding the justification of the sinner. In Revelation 14:6–12 John describes the messages of the three angels. The first has an eternal gospel for all people in the face of the inevitable judgment. The second tells us that the judgment has already fallen on Babylon. The third warns that those whose allegiance belongs to the beast will suffer his fate. Commentators differ as to the exact nature of the first angel's gospel. The significant thing is that its context is the final judgment. This is closely related to John's continued use of the figure of the Lamb to the very end. Justification which is not with respect to the final day of judgment is a hollow thing indeed. On the one hand the believer is accounted righteous and freed from the judgment on *all* his sins whether past, present or future. On the other hand the believer is constantly exhorted to endurance and perseverance to the end.

The Lamb's presence in the consummation of the kingdom is a timely reminder of this important fact of our justification. How sad it is when the biblical teaching on justification becomes twisted, as it so often does, into a partial justification. Many have taught and accepted a justification that was nothing more than a forgiveness of past sins. They have misunderstood the nature of sanctification. Because of the New Testament exhortations to godly living, and warnings against falling away, they have supposed that our final justification is based upon our own righteousness in Christian living. Having the slate wiped clean when we are converted is really small gain if it then depends on us to provide a satisfactory degree of righteousness to pass on the day of judgment. It further matters little that this righteousness is usually seen to be the result of God's grace at work in us. For unless we can come at last to the day of judgment with the perfection that God's holy righteousness demands, our sanctified lives count for nothing so far as justification is concerned. The results of this truncated view of justification for past sins only are serious indeed. Amongst protestants it leads to either perfectionism (a delusion), or to a legalism which diminishes the righteousness of God to the level of our ability to achieve. In the Church of Rome it is linked with a rejection of assurance and the doctrine of purgatory.

Let us then behold, through John's vision, the Lamb eternally enthroned. Let us glory in the fact that our justification through the merits of Christ will stand firm before the great white throne on the last day. Let us continually praise and thank our God that Christ saves to the uttermost! The saddest sight to behold within the Christian Church is that of people, young and old, whose true conversion can hardly be doubted, and yet who are plagued by uncertainty and lack of assurance. These have lost sight of, if indeed they ever knew about, justification past, present and future. How easily pastors can rob their people of a rich portion of their inheritance, namely confidence towards God during every day of their life, by failing to instruct them carefully on the distinction between justification and sanctification. Satan has worked great mischief among God's people by obscuring this distinction so that many who believe the gospel for their initial salvation begin to trust in their own sanctification for their final salvation. Let the Lamb in heaven remind us that we will live each day and enter finally into the kingdom clothed in his perfect righteousness – or not at all.

The Marriage Feast of the Lamb

The Bible contains a number of marriage metaphors which relate to the kingdom of God. It seems reasonable to suggest that those which occur in the New Testament are based upon the Old Testament idea that Jehovah, the God of Israel, has taken Israel to be his bride. The marriage relationship is descriptive of the covenant bond that God established with Israel (Ezekiel 16:8–14).[5] The most sustained treatment of this theme is given in Hosea 1–3 (see especially Hosea 2:19–20). We may not treat the marriage of Jehovah to Israel as mere metaphor, for according to Paul the relation of Christ to his church is signified by the marriage of husband and wife (Ephesians 5:31–32). That is, human marriage points to, and receives its meaning from, Christ's relation to the church. The idea of the marriage feast is indicative of the celebration of the kingdom of God is used several times by Jesus, though here the emphasis is upon the joy of being an invited guest at the banquet (Matthew 22:1–14, 25:1–13, see also Matthew 9:14–15). There is also the parable of the great feast which Jesus prefaced by the words, 'Blessed is he who shall eat bread in the kingdom of God.' The emphasis here is upon the feasting as the celebration of the kingdom; it is not a marriage feast (Luke 14:15–24).

---

5 See also Isaiah 54:6. The marriage of God and Israel is often implied by the judgment that Israel, by breaking the covenant and seeking other Gods, has played the harlot: see Isaiah 1:21, Jeremiah 2:20; 3:1–10. In Isaiah 61:10, the marriage garments are images of the righteousness of God which clothes the redeemed. Isaiah 62:1–5 depicts the marriage of Israel as her vindication. Israel is named Hephzibah ('my delight is in her') and Beulah ('married'). Here, vindication and righteousness are the same, and foreshadow justification.

So we have two metaphors which point to the reality of the kingdom. First, the marriage of God and his people Israel bespeaks the covenant relationship which, though Israel shows constant unfaithfulness, will one day be established perfectly through the redemption and renewal of the people. Secondly, the fellowship of the meal expresses the unity of God and his people in the kingdom as it also celebrates the joy of the kingdom. Although the Last Supper re-echoed the Jewish passover meal and pointed to its fulfilment in the death of Christ, it had also an important reference to the final blessedness of the kingdom of God: ' "I tell you", said Jesus, "I shall not drink again of this fruit of the vine until that day when I drink it new with you in my Father's kingdom" ' (Matthew 26:29, RSV). We have to allow that these images are fluid, that is, they are capable of being adapted and changed in order to suit the required emphasis. The parable of the wedding feast (Matthew. 22:1–14) and the parable of the ten maidens (Matthew 25:1–13) make no mention of the bride. The people of God are here represented by the guests. Indeed this is the emphasis in John's reference in Revelation 19:9: 'Blessed are those who are invited to the wedding supper of the Lamb.' But here the guests are surely not different from the bride mentioned two verses earlier: 'The wedding of the Lamb has come, and his bride has made herself ready.'

So the people of God are both bride and guests! All this means is that either image alone does not suffice to describe the relationship of the Christian to his Lord. He is at one and the same time beloved covenant partner and honoured guest at the celebration. Both emphases have their part to play in our understanding of what it means to be God's people. To these we must add one more image, that of Revelation 21. Here John sees the new heaven and the new earth and the new Jerusalem 'coming down out of heaven from God, prepared as a bride beautifully dressed for her husband' (Revelation 21:2). Again, an angel says to John:

> Come, I will show you the bride,
> the wife of the Lamb. (Revelation 21:9)

John is shown the new Jerusalem, and describes its beauty and magnitude – a cube on a base of some 1500 miles! Jerusalem the city of God, is people. To put it round the other way: the people of God is where God dwells. This fulfils most perfectly all that the covenant with Israel was meant to convey. It is a relationship which can exist because Jesus Christ himself was the new temple, the dwelling of God with us. As both God and man he was both God and true Israel.

Thus, as John sees the new Jerusalem descend, the voice declares:

> Behold, the dwelling of God is with men. He will dwell with them, and they shall be his people, and God himself will be with them (Revelation 21:3, RSV).

This one verse could be said to sum up and to contain the entire message of the Bible. The whole of the history of the covenant and of redemption lies behind this glorious affirmation. Every aspect of the hope of Israel – covenant, redemption, promised land, temple, Zion, Davidic prince, new Eden, – is woven into this one simple and yet profound statement: the *dwelling of God is with men*. In an indirect way John used the marriage theme to express this relationship. Jerusalem, not a city of bricks and mortar, but a city of people redeemed by the blood of Christ, is the dwelling place of God. Every one who overcomes is a son of God in this city and

inherits all the riches of the kingdom (Revelation 21:7).
The symbolic use of the number 12, signifying the
twelve tribes of Israel and the twelve apostles, and its
multiples in the cubed city, point to the same perfection
and completeness that we saw in the 144 000 of the
redeemed in Revelation 7.

This personifying of Jerusalem as the bride of the Lamb
is totally consistent with the movement of personification
of other images of the Old Testament hope and notably
that of the temple. The temple, above all, was to signify the
dwelling of God. But, as we have already seen, the temple
is fulfilled in the new temple which is Christ himself. Jesus
of Nazareth was God-man and, as such, he was the taber-
nacling of God in man (John 1:14). He declared his body to
be the new temple (John 2:19–21). He now creates the temple by his Spirit as he indwells the redeemed (Ephesians
2:19–22, 1 Peter 2:4–10).[6] It is the people who belong to
Christ who can be called the temple since Christ dwells in
their midst by his Spirit. So, for John's new Jerusalem no
symbolic structure can displace the actual visible glory of
God dwelling there (Revelation 21:22). God himself, and
the Lamb are there and they are the temple. That is why
the river of life must flow from the throne of God and of
the Lamb instead of from the threshold of the temple as
Ezekiel originally depicted it (Revelation 22:1–2 cf Ezekiel
47). Even Ezekiel's detailed description carries overtones
of Eden, watered by the four rivers and containing the

---

[6] Note Peter's use of Hosea's marriage passage in this context of
the temple: 1 Peter 2:10 is a reference to Hosea 2:23 in which the
significance of Hosea's marriage is interpreted in terms of God
marrying his redeemed people – see Hosea 2:16,19. Peter thus
draws together the various Old Testament concepts – temple,
chosen race, royal priesthood, holy nation, God's own people –
with this reference to Hosea.

tree of life. It was in Eden that God originally established his relationship with mankind.

Summary

The new heaven and the new earth described by John in Revelation 21:1–22:5 is the resolution of all conflict, suffering and meaninglessness in life. There can be no longer any deficiencies in the relationship between God, man, and the created order. The overlap of the ages ceases as this present world order in which we live is removed with all the evil that characterizes it. Through resurrection and glorification the believer is brought fully into the regeneration of all things. The new age alone becomes the reality of his existence. This is the realm in which the effects of Christ's life and death are perceived and experienced in all their fulness. Because we at present perceive it only by faith and live in it through our representative man Jesus Christ, it is not possible for our thought forms and language to comprehend it. Thus John, with the genius of divine inspiration, composes a mosaic of Old Testament images in order to convey the ultimate reality.[7] How much of this section is truly apocalyptic and how much prophetic is a somewhat academic question. For appropriately, at this juncture, we have a synthesis of both kinds of writing along with John's over-arching grasp of the gospel. That it carries on the tradition of apocalyptic symbolism is obvious, but in this case John has created a unique blending of the forms and images of biblical literature.

---

[7] R.H. Charles, *The Revelation of St. John*, I.C.C. (Edinburgh: T. & T. Clark, 1920) Vol. 1, pp lxxv–lxxxii lists some 20 Old Testament passages directly referred to in Revelation 21:1 to 22:5. He lists a further 7 which probably have influenced John in this section.

Each image conjures up entire scenarios of Old Testament prophetic hope and expectation. But the new message is that reality has now replaced hope or expectation. That which the gospel defines as reality will come to pass for every believer. Such hope inscribed on the heart and mind by the Spirit of God has through the ages steeled the resolve of countless little people, ordinary and unremarkable men and women (as the world counts them), to go on looking to Jesus, the Alpha and Omega, the author and finisher of our faith.

Thesis

John finally resolves the tension of the overlap of the ages by unambiguously describing the consummation of the end as that which occurs after the destruction of Satan and all that belongs to the old age.

Chapter Ten

'Come, Lord Jesus'

Living in hope for the future

Behold, I am coming soon! My reward is with me, and I will give to everyone according to what he has done. I am the Alpha and Omega, the First and the Last, the Beginning and the End.

He who testifies to these things says, 'Yes, I am coming soon.'

Amen. Come Lord Jesus (Revelation 22:12–13,20).

John's adventure into the heavenly reality of the consummated kingdom could easily stand as a fitting conclusion to this remarkable work. What could be more encouraging for the saints of all ages and of all conditions of life than to read of their coming perfection and bliss? He would be a dull and insensitive Christian indeed who did not feel some fire in his soul when contemplating these concluding words of this vision:

There will be no more night. They will not need the light of a lamp or the light of the sun, for the Lord God will give them light. And they will reign for ever and ever (Revelation 22:5).

But in the wisdom of the Spirit of God, John's readers are to be returned to earth! Breathing the unpolluted air of the new Jerusalem can easily throw us off balance, for the harsh reality of the ever present corruption of our age could jolt us out of our reverie with a shock that might easily disorientate us for a time, After all, this glimpse of heaven has been given to assure, comfort, and motivate us in the midst of this evil age. In the first chapters of the book, John has relayed the messages of Christ to the struggling churches. The reigning Christ praised, encouraged and warned the churches so that they would persevere to the end. Now once again there is warning and encouragement, but this time it is given with specific reference to the meaning of the Book of Revelation as a whole.

First, there is a reassurance concerning the testimony of this book, that it is in fact the testimony of Jesus himself (Revelation 22:6,16,20). In this John recapitulates the opening sections of the Book. There the risen and glorified Christ, ruling in the midst of his churches by his word and Spirit, is shown to be the author of this revelation. We notice that there is no room for apologetics in this situation. The Bible does not argue for the acceptability of its assertions. It states them as the truth. The reason for this is that primary assertions of the Bible relating to truth include the inability of sinful man to perceive truth because he has rejected the source of that truth, and also the gracious revelation of truth in the person of Jesus Christ. As to the mystery of how or why the godless and rebellious mind, incapable of perceiving the truth, will then respond to the truth as it is in Christ, the Bible resolves it in terms of the power of the gospel and the regenerating work of the Holy Spirit. As to the mystery of why some who hear the gospel respond and believe while others reject the truth, the Bible gives the ultimate choice to God according to his sovereign purpose of election. The cynic may regard the assertion of Revelation 22:6, 'These words are trustworthy and true,' with as much acceptance as he would regard the smooth assurances of a confidence trickster,– 'Lady, would I lie to you?' But the believer knows them to be the words of the Lord himself and receives them with well-founded confidence. They are the words of Jesus Christ the faithful witness (Revelation 1:5). Everyone must face eventually the question of absolute and ultimate truth. Since it is ultimate truth there is no greater or more basic truth by which it can be tested. If it is to communicate itself to us as the truth it must authenticate itself in terms of itself. There is no apologetic for ultimate truth. It simply takes hold of us and brings us into submission. To submit to the ultimate truth is to be blessed (Revelation 22:7).

Secondly, John recapitulates the stern warnings of Revelation: 'Do not seal up the words' (Revelation 22:10). The apocalyptists of the past used the literary technique of describing a sealed book written in a bygone age but opened at the appointed time that all may be revealed. This is what lies behind the breaking of the seven seals[1] (Revelation 5:1–8:1). But now the day of revelation has come. Jesus Christ has come in the flesh and we have entered the last days. 'The time is near' thus signifies that

[1] In the popular Jewish apocalyptic not found in the Bible, the writers claimed that a great figure of the past, such as Moses or one of the twelve patriarchs, was the author. The work was sealed up and is only now, in the writer's time, opened to reveal the truth. Hence the revealing angel is characteristically seen to command that it be 'sealed up' (see also Daniel 12:4). It is significant that in the Book of Revelation John is not the author of the truth under the seven seals, but in good apocalyptic style, the seals are broken and the truth revealed. John is not allowed to seal anything up since the day of revelation has come with Jesus Christ.

the consummation of all things is the last remaining move for God to complete the work of salvation. Since the gospel, has brought us to the last days there is no room for complacency about the final manifestation of God's glory. It can come at any time and therefore we can only exhort people to make ready for it by responding to the gracious offer of the gospel. We can be sure of this, that at a time which we do not know, the final event will overtake us. Whether it is by our own death or by the return of Christ in glory, the end result is the same – all opportunity to change our minds and to receive salvation will have passed. 'Let him who does wrong continue to do wrong' (Revelation 22:11), points to the time when opportunity for repentance is gone. John is not saying that the time has already come, for the word of invitation is still given – 'Whoever is thirsty let him come' (Revelation 22:17).

But let those who wish to live godless lives be warned. The gospel is the great divider as well as the great unifier. The conflict between Christ and Satan which has characterized the whole of Revelation still has its outworking in the daily existence of men and women. The relationship of good works and salvation that we discussed in Chapter 5 is recalled in the words of Jesus in Revelation 22:12. 'I will give to everyone according to what he has done,' does not refer to good works as earning salvation, but to good works as the fruit of salvation through faith.

The final warning is at the end of the chapter and concerns the 'prophecy of this book' (Revelation 22:18–19). Again the reason for the strong warning is that these are the words of Jesus Christ, the Lord of the church and ruler of the kings of the earth. The essence of the warning does not concern the actual details of the Book of Revelation as such. To add to, or to subtract from this prophecy means to reject the testimony of Jesus Christ to himself and to his gospel. It means, therefore, to reject Jesus Christ and his claims over us as the ruling Lord. Contrary to some popular distortions of the gospel which see accepting Christ as Saviour and accepting him as Lord to be two quite separate things, we see that to believe in Christ for salvation means, among other things, that we acknowledge him as Lord.

Thirdly, John recapitulates the blessings of the kingdom of God. 'Blessed are those who wash their robes, that they may have the right to the tree of life and may go through the gates into the city' (verse 14). The theme of justification fittingly moves the book to its close. Remember that John writes to the persecuted minority, the Christians of Asia Minor. What encouragement can be given them for the moment? The stirring message of Revelation needs to be distilled into a form that will sustain them in the moment as well as in the long term. They need to be reminded again that the power of God for salvation is the gospel of our free justification in Christ. They need to be undergirded by the truth that their transitory existence is but a part of the whole range of human history, and that Christ is Lord over all of it. 'I am the Alpha, and the Omega, the First and the Last, the Beginning and the End' (verse 13).

So John brings his readers back to the point where faith simply acknowledges, 'God rules and I am his child through the merits of Jesus Christ.' The children of the kingdom eagerly await its appearing. Meantime they seek to live as true subjects of that kingdom. Such a life of faith is one lived out between the time of the Lamb slain, and the time of his coming in the majesty of the Lion. Nor is it only, or even primarily, the suffering of the Christian that makes him long for the return of his Lord in glory. For, as Saul of Tarsus learned, the persecution of Christians is the persecution and rejection of the Lord: 'Why do you persecute me?' We long to see our Lord known no more as the humiliated Jesus of the gospel, but as the Lord of glory. We shall be restless until the holy name of our God and Saviour is vindicated, every tongue stopped, and every knee made to bow in acknowledgement of him.

The world looks on the slaughtered Lamb with pity, disdain and even abhorrence. Through the tinted glass of self-importance it views his sacrifice as a joke, or as the natural end of an outmoded ethic based in superstition. But the world itself gives the lie to its own interpretation. For had the Lamb provided such a senseless life and death, the remedy would be to leave it alone to fester and wither away. But the Lamb would not go away. Instead of a few bleached bones and the smell of putrefaction he left an empty tomb and his Spirit who so seared the truth of the gospel into the hearts and minds of his little band of followers that they began to turn the world upside down. For this the world will not forgive him. It rises up and lashes out at the Lamb while pretending that he isn't real. It does this because the one whose spirit pervades the world knows full well that the slain Lamb is his downfall.

The Christian looks at the Lamb and sees the judgment of God on his sin borne by his substitute. But he sees far more than that. He sees the unending glory of the Lion. He can never see the Lion without seeing the Lamb, and he can see the Lion only by beholding the Lamb. So it will be through all eternity. In this life it is faith alone which perceives these realities, and there is a deep longing within every child of God for faith to be turned into sight. When we are captivated by the gospel, we become more and more impatient with our lack of conformity to the reality of the kingdom. We are offended by the world's rejection of our Lord. We long to be rid of the daily struggle in a world that has the smell of death hanging over even the most sublime beauty of creation.

We cannot but yearn to see all things new. To that end we cry: 'Come, Lord Jesus.'

Appendix: What is the Mark of the Beast?

Many readers will be familiar with a popular interpretation of Revelation 13 which, I believe, has received far more attention than it deserves. The critical nature of our times, with their uncertainties, global crises, and threats of the imminent collapse of our social structure and economic systems, has created a thirst for anything that can remove the unpredictability of the immediate future. This thirst has encouraged the spread of certain views among Christians which I firmly believe to be a diversion from the central message of the New Testament.

These views are sometimes grouped under the label 'futurism' because their common assumption is that Revelation in particular, as well as the Old Testament prophecies of the coming new age of the kingdom, refer almost exclusively to the future end of this present era. It is also generally assumed that modern history, especially since the return of the Jews and the formation of the State of Israel in 1948, points infallibly to the fact that this age is rapidly drawing to a close. The literalist approach to prophecy and Revelation is usually applied in such a way that exponents claim to see all around us the evidences that the second coming of Christ is very close. Despite the fact that Jesus warned against trying to predict the time of his return, many interpreters are making predictions. These predictions are often rather cagily put ('by 1984' or 'within this decade') in a way that suggests a sore conscience for trying to do what Jesus said could not be done. Other predictions are more confident, and the passage of time has revealed many for what they are.

Recently there has been renewed interest in a part of Revelation which has always been a point of some controversy. From earliest times the mark of the beast in Revelation 13:16–18 has received attention from many interpreters proposing solutions to the enigma of 666. Because the Hebrews and Greeks both used certain letters of their alphabets to represent numerical values, it has been commonly assumed that 666 must be the total of the numerical values of the letters in a man's name. The possibilities are legion, and if the Greek version of a favoured name, for example 'Emperor Nero' does not add up to 666 then conversion into the Hebrew form has often produced the desired result. In more recent times a similar method has been used to identify the beast as Muhammed, Martin Luther, Napoleon or Hitler. Many Christians, by contrast, have preferred a more symbolic approach to that of numerical equivalence. If we allow that the Bible frequently uses the number 7 to signify perfection, then 666 can be seen as representing a repeated falling short of perfection or 'failure upon failure upon failure'.

Now a new kind of interpretation is receiving a great deal of publicity. This approach, unlike the other interpretations, takes the number 666 quite literally and, like the Nero-Hitler interpretations, relates them very precisely to the present day. It is claimed that the mark of the beast – the number 666 – is emerging in modern society in a way that shows that we are on the verge of a global economy controlled by Satan. Computerised credit is seen as gradually replacing the use of money so that in time – probably a relatively short time – we will become citizens of a world-wide cashless society. The power behind this will be the antichrist who will demand the submission of all people. Already we are gearing up for all this with the use of plastic cards and electronics. Rows of parallel black lines imprinted on supermarket commodities enable prices to be read and recorded electronically, and are a further proof of the approaching time of total control over buying and selling. When that time comes only those who submit to the mark of the beast, a personal, computerized identification number, being imprinted on the right hand or forehead, will be permitted to buy or sell. Thus Christians who refuse to worship the beast and to receive his mark will undergo a very severe persecution.

The general thrust of books which take this line is to impress upon the reader that the time is near and there is consequently a great urgency for response to the gospel. Such response will not, on some interpretations, remove the threat of this persecution for Christians are said to live through some three-and-a-half years of it before Christ takes them up out of this world. Other interpretations see this 'rapture' occurring before the final tribulation in which case there is an added incentive to respond to the gospel and so to escape the tribulation.

How seriously this matter is taken by some people is indicated by a question I was asked at a church-sponsored seminar on this subject. The questioner asked, 'What will happen if, when the cashless society comes as fulfilment of prophecy, some Christians accept the mark of the beast without realising what they are doing?' There was an obvious sense of foreboding that many Christians will be ignorant of the meaning of Revelation 13 and will walk into the trap of being marked with the beast's mark. In answer to the question I first pointed out that there was a gratuitous assumption in the assertion that the cashless society alone fulfilled this prophecy. There was, furthermore, a complete' failure to relate this apocalyptic picture to the clear teaching of the gospel. The result was an unnecessary fear that some Christians would forfeit their salvation because they lacked the right kind of prophetic instruction with regard to Revelation 13.

In the light of the principles set out in this book, there is a much more satisfactory interpretation which does not clash with the teaching of the New Testament epistles. The vision of the beast in Revelation 13:11–18 is one of a series of pictures of the conflict between light and darkness. The beast is an emissary of Satan in the conflict. He deceives many people so that they give allegiance to him, and he actively persecutes the people of God. The nature of apocalyptic does not demand that a literal economic and commercial persecution (verse 17) be posited. On the other hand it is not an impossible fulfilment since political oppression by totalitarian regimes easily carries over into the market place. It is wrong, however, to make that the only fulfilment on the grounds of an apparent correspondence to contemporary events. Such interpretation is aided by a literalistic approach to the beast's mark (verses 16–17), which supposes that we will one day be required to have our identifying number actually imprinted upon us. Of course, as with so much literalistic interpretation, it tends to break down under its own weight. For, if we follow verse 18 strictly, then every single individual will be stamped with exactly the same mark, six hundred and sixty-six, which has value only to identify the members of the group but not to distinguish one from another.

Again the two principles put forward in the introduction are relevant. First, we must reject any attempt to turn a symbolic piece of apocalyptic imagery into a literal description of an event utterly remote from John and his contemporaries. The fact that John refers to the mark of God in the adjacent vision should assist us. I suggest there is a deliberate contrasting of the two situations which is not unlike that of Revelation 7 (see chapter 3 above). Both Revelation 7 and Revelation 14 refer to the 144 000 redeemed saints in contrast to the reprobate who come under judgment. The mark of God in Revelation 14:1 signifies that these are securely sealed as the Father's own possession. No one supposes that to be a child of God we must have a literal mark on our foreheads. It symbolizes the redemption which is received by faith, and sealed by the Spirit of God. Similarly, the mark of the beast must symbolize unbelief, rejection of Christ and his gospel. It is sad that many Christians are being led to think of their eternal security as depending not upon the finished work of Christ for them but upon their prophetic astuteness in discerning the supposed relationship of the beast to the development of a new global fiscal system. Truly, the gospel and the glorious truths of our justification are becoming clouded by this modern fad.

A further implication of the thesis of this book needs mentioning here. The futurist approach which gives a literalistic interpretation and builds on it a prediction about the return of Christ this year, next year or whenever, will of course one day be right! But it will be for the wrong reasons. In the same way it is possible that many of these contemporary events which are seen to be fulfilment of a prophetic word are just that. If the cashless society comes in the way suggested it may well fit the meaning of Revelation 13. That is not really the point at issue. My argument with this line of thinking is that it uses a rather forced approach to demonstrate that the prophecies are being literally fulfilled by these contemporary events for the first and only time.

The misunderstanding here is twofold. First, the concept of signs of the times is often employed in relation to fulfilled prophecy, or in relation to prophecy that is supposedly in the process of being fulfilled. It is assumed on this view that the signs are discernible, once-for-all fulfilments which indicate that the end is near. On this basis approximate predictions of the time of Christ's return are often made. The second misunderstanding relates to the concept of the end which is exclusively applied to the second coming. I have been at pains in this book to point up the three-fold way that the New Testament speaks about the end. On the basis of this biblical perspective I believe we must come to the following conclusion: the signs belong to the whole period of the last days from the first advent of Christ until his return. Their purpose is not to help us predict, contrary to Jesus' warning, the time of his return, but to characterize this whole period as the end time from the perspective of which the return of Christ was as imminent for the apostles as it is for us. John's apocalyptic vision of the beast and his mark belongs to the whole period also, and may have many individual or continuing manifestations. Above all we must not remove this prophecy from the framework of the teaching of the New Testament in general, or from the rest of the Book of Revelation (for example, in its teaching on perseverance to the end). To do otherwise is to add to the gospel and to imply that 'faith alone' and 'Christ alone' are principles which will not operate at the very last days of this age. It seems, we are being told, that we must add to them a course of action based on a narrow prophetic interpretation. The only consistent way to deal with Revelation 13 and 14 is to see the mark of the beast as characterizing godlessness and faithlessness, while the mark of God characterizes the sealing of those who through faith in Christ, are saved eternally.

Gospel and Wisdom

Contents

Preface

At the layman's level it is still popular to classify the books of the Old Testament under the headings of Law, History, Prophecy and Poetry. This is a curious arrangement and not a little misleading. The law books are full of history, the history books contain much prophecy, the prophecy books are largely poetry, and the so-called poetry books are so diverse that their poetic content is one of the least useful marks of description. Moreover, there are large slabs of prose to be found in them. It is a matter of real concern that the category of poetry books obscures one of the important areas of literature found within it: the wisdom books. Wisdom is a significant concept in both the Old and New Testaments. It is a key dimension of the Christian life, and finds its centre in the person of Christ. Those books which tell us most about the wisdom of the Hebrews should not be confined to the limbo of a box labelled Poetry.

There are some very readable books available today which investigate the subject of Old Testament wisdom literature. A number of these are acknowledged in my footnotes. However, it must be said that there is a singular dearth of such books which go on to raise the question of the relationship of Old Testament wisdom to the New Testament in general, to Christ in particular, and to the

Christian life. My aim in this book is to apply the method of biblical theology in order to place the wisdom literature in its Christian context, that is, to try to understand it as Christian Scripture.

Since it is also my aim to present this material with as few technicalities as possible, the discussion may at times appear to the theologically trained reader to be simplistic or even patronizing in style. I hope this will not be taken as denoting an imprecise analysis of the evidence. To the reader who is not theologically trained I would say that some technicalities are inevitable in any kind of serious study. The reader's lack of familiarity with certain ideas should not be taken as a sign that the material is difficult in itself. A little patience and perseverance is all that is needed in such cases.

I have restricted footnotes to the minimum necessary to fulfil my obligations to clarify concepts, to acknowledge my sources and to make it possible for anyone to verify my references. Where such references are to works of a specialized and technical nature, I have attempted to incorporate the insights of these and other studies into a simple and basic discussion. Overall, I have endeavoured to keep in mind the practical value of wisdom for the Christian life, to remove it from the domain of an élite group, and to return it to its rightful place among all the people of God.

I wish to acknowledge my indebtedness to my teachers at Union Theological Seminary, Richmond, Virginia: Professor John Bright and Professor Patrick D. Miller Jr. who supervised my doctoral studies in the wisdom literature of the Old Testament.

Graeme Goldsworthy
St. Stephen's Anglican Church
Coorparoo, Queensland

Chapter One

The House on the Rock

Summary

Practical questions such as guidance and decision making are closely related to what the Bible teaches about wisdom. Our starting point is Jesus Christ because he links us through his gospel to God and thus to reality. Wisdom is concerned with the nature of reality. The four Gospels portray Jesus as the wise man above all others. In so doing they build upon the Old Testament's teaching about the nature and place of wisdom in the lives of God's people.

Decisions! Decisions! Decisions!

We all have those days when we are faced with a seemingly endless stream of situations demanding decisions. They can be exhausting times, especially when the decisions are important ones that will affect the course of our lives. We cannot escape decision making. It is a part of being human. Because we are concerned about the results of our decisions, we want to make the right ones. But all too often we find ourselves saying, 'If only I had done this and not that'. The 'if only' disease is a crippling one because it destroys our confidence in future decisions. It breeds an indecision which stifles our ability not only to face life, but also to go out and enjoy it. Indecision is an aspect of our sinfulness because it expresses a problem not only in our knowledge or understanding of the world, but in our whole relationship to the world and to God. It is not surprising, then, that the Bible says a great deal about decisions and how we make them.

The four Gospels depict Jesus as one who by his very presence demanded a decision from people. In his teaching the summons was to faith and commitment, not merely to receive interesting information. As then, so now; the response that we make to his entry into our world has results for eternity. Consider the conclusion to his Sermon on the Mount:

> Therefore everyone who hears these words of mine and puts them into practice is like a wise man who built his house on the rock. The rain came down, the streams rose, and the winds blew and beat against that house; yet it did not fall, because it had its foundation on the rock. But everyone who hears these words of mine and does not put them into practice is like a foolish man who built his house on sand. The rain came down, the streams rose, and the winds blew and beat against that house, and it fell with a great crash.
>
> (Matthew 7:24–27)

The message of this vivid word picture is clear. Those who take notice of what Jesus says build their lives on a firm foundation, and those who do not heed it have chosen a foundation of shifting sand for their lives. It is not comforting to be compared to a house crashing into a swirling flood under the buffeting of the wind and the rain.

The point is that Jesus' words demand decision and no one can remain neutral before them. According to the New Testament, life's decisions can be made in a way that leads to either life or destruction. This is the thrust of the evangelist's challenge to 'decide for Christ', that is, to believe the gospel. Before Christ, no decision is a 'No!' decision. The decision we make about Jesus Christ will affect every other decision that we will subsequently make. And here lies the difficulty, for it is here that we start to ask questions about the will of God for our lives. The house on the rock must, in a sense, be built up from the foundations. But how do we discern the plan, and what if we should make a wrong decision? Some decisions are easy in theory because there is clear scriptural teaching about them. Certain ethical questions and matters of Christian behaviour involve the uncomplicated application of Scripture. Of course, there are also complicated moral questions which we find more difficult, but it helps to know where to search for an answer.

There is another area of decision-making in life which is not nearly so clear-cut. Every day you and I make up our minds on all kinds of matters, some of which are important to us, others of which are trifling. Many have no obvious relationship to moral principles derived from the Bible, and are not clearly connected with questions of godliness or righteousness. A decision one way or the other would seem in no way to involve us in immorality or in a compromise of the gospel. What we have for dinner tomorrow is largely a neutral decision, provided that the overall pattern of our diet is one of reasonable care for our bodies. But what career we choose, what church we decide to join, what prospective spouse we choose, are all matters of great importance. Some options are already ruled out by Scripture. We do not choose an immoral career, an apostate church, or an unbelieving spouse. But that may still leave us with a number of live options in each case.

One of the things we link with wisdom is the ability to make the right decision. James tell us that if we lack wisdom we should ask God and wisdom will be given to us (James 1:5). So, we ask, and we expect that God will in some way guide us and prevent us from making the kind of decisions that will backfire on us. James reminds us that we should ask God in faith. What exactly does that mean for the way we go about our decision-making? From time to time I have spoken to Christians who are convinced that the gift of wisdom means nothing less than God handing down to believers ready-cut solutions to all their problems. On first sight that may be an attractive prospect. No more worries! No more weighing up all the *pros* and *cons*. No more agonizing over the possible outcomes of our choice of action. All we need do is wait on God for his leading to the right decision. The question is, of course, does God promise any such thing? Is wisdom really a hot-line to heaven, and is God in the business of steering our lives like that? Unfortunately when Christians come to this way of thinking they often become impatient of careful study of the Bible. Their decisions are not made consciously on the basis of what the Scriptures say and the principles they contain, but rather on the basis of some vague and subjective feeling about the Lord's will in the matter. The Bible does say a great deal about guidance and decision-making, but I suspect that some popular notions about these important matters are not really based on the scriptural evidence.

The Beginning of Wisdom

This book is not primarily about guidance but about the biblical idea of wisdom. The relationship between wisdom and guidance will, I trust, become very clear from the evidence we are to examine. When I wrote *Gospel and Kingdom*[1] to provide a Christian understanding of the Old Testament, there was one quite deliberate omission because of the need to be brief. Questions of Israel's piety (especially as found in the Psalms) and of her quest for knowledge and understanding (as found in the wisdom literature) were not dealt with. It may therefore have seemed to the observant readers of that work that I had conveniently ignored an important area of the Old Testament which did not fit neatly into the proposed scheme of the revelation of the kingdom of God. I intend to show in this book that such was not the case. I hope to demonstrate that, despite the difficulties, the wisdom literature of Israel can be related to her covenant faith, and that it, along with the prophetic promises, points to the coming of Christ.

So my first concern is to look at the whole question of how a Christian may read and apply to himself as Christian Scripture the books of Proverbs, Job and Ecclesiastes, and other parts of the Old Testament that we classify as wisdom literature. Over the last fifty years or so there has been a tremendous renewal of interest in Old Testament wisdom on the part of biblical scholars. Unfortunately not a lot has been done to translate the results of this scholarship into the language of the ordinary Christian untrained in the technical side of biblical studies. This book is intended as a contribution in that direction.

The word *wisdom* suggests a concern for the way we think, the way we use our minds or intellects. If that is what wisdom in the Bible is all about then we have established an important point: God gave us minds and he expects us to use them. We have only to look at the

---

[1] Exeter: Paternoster Press, 1981.

way that the New Testament speaks of the mind to be convinced of this. Paul, for example, links the renewal of the mind with the transformed life of the Christian (Romans 12:2). He reminds us that conversion includes the conversion of the mind. The Greek word for repentance (*metanoia*) literally means a change of mind. Furthermore, when the Bible speaks of the heart it refers to the whole willing and thinking side of our being. It is what goes on in the head. The fruit of the gospel in our lives includes the conforming of our minds more and more to the mind of Christ. This process of becoming holy, or sanctification, is worked by the Holy Spirit dwelling within the believer. The Spirit works in and through us. Thus we are consciously involved in the struggle to become more Christ-like and to do good works.

If you are one of those people who had a well-defined conversion experience when you became a Christian, you will easily recognize that your conversion included a turn-about in the way you thought about reality. You would not have worked out many of the implications of this at the beginning. But at least you will have recognized that God is somehow involved in all aspects of your experience in a way that you never recognized as an unbeliever. From this point on you can never look at reality in exactly the same way you did before your conversion. The process has begun of conforming both thinking and doing to the will and character of Christ. Thinking and doing can never be separated.

When we speak of a sanctified mind, many Christians will think exclusively of a morally pure mind. Conversely, a sinful mind will be thought of in terms of moral impurity. We need to broaden our understanding beyond the moral dimensions. To think Christianly with a sanctified mind is to think of reality in terms of the truth that is revealed in Christ. A sinful mind-set is one which views reality apart from what God has revealed. It may think high and noble thoughts of humanitarian kindness, but to the extent that the truth of God is left out of reckoning that mind-set is sinful.

The Christian mind-set comes about through the gospel, and so we must come to think of Christian wisdom as a conforming of the mind to the gospel. If, then, we understand the gospel only in its basic terms of Jesus dying for us, we will probably wonder how this can affect the way we think totally. We need to remind ourselves that the simple gospel is also profound. The truth, 'Jesus died for me', actually implies everything that God has revealed in the Bible about his relationship to humanity and to the created order. Growing as a Christian really means learning to apply the fact of the gospel to every aspect of our thinking and doing.

I have indicated two basic areas in which the Bible deals with the subject of wisdom. They are the wisdom books of the Old Testament and certain parts of the New Testament. Specifically it is Jesus Christ who is God's wisdom and who reveals it to us. The fact that the Old Testament points to Christ suggests that the wisdom which centres on the gospel is related to the wisdom which exercised the authors of the Old Testament wisdom books. The biblical concern for wisdom should be the concern of every Christian and not merely of those we might class as intellectuals. A primary purpose of Israel's wisdom was 'for giving prudence to the simple, knowledge and discretion to the young' (Proverbs 1:4). There is never any suggestion in the Bible that wisdom means having an above average IQ. In the Old Testament wisdom is not the property of some élite class, as it seems to have been in some other ancient peoples. In the New Testament it is asserted that wisdom belongs to all who believe the gospel.

In the Book of Proverbs the wise man is seen urging his pupils in the task of acquiring wisdom or understanding of life. 'Get wisdom', he says (Proverbs 4:7), but what is it and how do we get it? It seems to wear many faces, yet behind them all, even the worldly ones, we sense a common factor which is hard to pin down. To one person wisdom is a property owner making a shrewd investment, or a statesman whose political activity seems to pay off for the community in renewed prosperity. To another it is the successful handling of the tricky business of the generation gap in families, or the cool and effective management of a sudden crisis. To yet another it is a monk or a mystic meditating on life and its meaning. Perhaps we can begin to understand wisdom as the reflective thinking which places human beings above the animals. As Christians we will need to approach all definitions with caution and be prepared to adjust them in the light of the Bible. In the Bible the range of wisdom is no less perplexing. In one place it is a proverb about an ant, in another it is a sublime poem about the Creator and his creation. It is a way of thinking and a way of doing. It is a way of teaching and a way of expressing ideas in writing. On the one hand it is to know man and the world, and on the other it is both the way to know God and the reward for knowing him. Then, in the New Testament, there is a worldy wisdom which is really foolishness, and there is God's true wisdom revealed in Jesus Christ.

Since Jesus Christ is the fulfiller of the Old Testament, he alone can bring us to an understanding of the full meaning of the Old Testament wisdom books. On the other hand, the New Testament presupposes what the Old Testament teaches, in order to present the message of Christ. Since the two Testaments depend upon each other, it may appear difficult to decide where to begin. But upon reflection we see that we must begin with Christ because it is through him that we become Christians and are motivated to study the Old Testament as Christian Scripture. We really have two tasks when we approach the Old Testament. First, we want to see how the Old Testament increases our grasp of the New Testament message about Christ. Secondly, we apply our knowledge of Christ as the fulfiller in order to understand the real significance of the Old Testament. When we start with Christ in the gospel and go back from there into the Old Testament, we find that the Old Testament eventually leads us back again to Christ. He is, after all, the author and perfecter of our faith (Hebrews 12:2), he is the Alpha and the Omega, the First and the Last (Revelation 22:13).

When Jesus concluded the Sermon on the Mount with the illustration of the wise and the foolish builders, he spoke with an authority that the sage and the scribe never had; he spoke as the source of all true wisdom. Nothing Jesus ever said or did would support the idea that the gift of wisdom means that God makes our decisions for us. What he did say was that receiving his words and doing them is wisdom. The person and work of Jesus provide us with the only reliable basis for understanding ourselves, our experience and the world. Within that framework of understanding we must seek to make our decisions as responsible human beings. In our concern to build aright the house of our life, we should remember that the foundation rock is the word of Christ. It is not a mysterious thing that is revealed to us in some secret experience of our hearts. It is there for us in the Bible. We may be tempted to think at times that our decisions have resulted in a rather strange looking house being built on the rock. But Jesus' words should reassure us. If it is built on the right foundation the house will endure.

Questions for Study

1. What kinds of problems do Christians have in making decisions and knowing God's will?
2. In what way does coming to know God through Jesus Christ alter our understanding of ourselves and of the world?
3. What does Genesis 1:26–28 tell us about relationships between God, mankind and the created order?

Chapter Two

Christ Our Wisdom

Summary

All problems concern relationships of some kind. Our relationship to God is perhaps the greatest of all problems. The answer to this, and to all other problems, lies in Jesus who is the perfectly wise man in his relationship to God. Jesus' teaching about wisdom and his constant use of wisdom sayings prepare the way for Paul's statements about Christ as our wisdom. Wisdom is a characteristic of the person who is rightly related to God. Jesus came to be the truly God-related man for us, and therefore he is wisdom for us. One outworking of this in our lives is that our way of thinking about all things is changed through the gospel. True wisdom is a result of being related to God through the person and work of Christ.

Identifying the Problem

The Christian life is lived in an enormously complex world. In some ways the complexity is increased by our Christian faith because we find ourselves at loggerheads with the mindset of the unbelieving world. Those who long for the relative simplicity of the 'good old days' would have to admit that they probably did not have fewer problems in the past, only different ones. Our lives are made up of discoveries, decisions and relationships which give to us a sense of the meaningfulness of our existence. People who have no sense of being related to other people or to the world find life without meaning. The problem we all face is that of knowing what is in life and knowing how to get it all together. Failure to achieve any kind of integrated view of reality can lead to severe mental illness and even death.

There has never been a lack of preachers ready to tell us that Christ is the answer. But it has been well remarked: 'If Christ is the answer, what is the question?' This reminds us of the need to be precise in how we think of Christ as the answer to our problems. It is the gospel which shows us both the problem and the answer. In doing this it speaks mainly in terms of relationships. For example, the biblical definition of man is primarily a statement of how he relates to God, to himself and others, and to the world. The whole creation and fall narrative in Genesis 1–3 is written from that point of view. The idea of man created in the *image of God* is an idea about relationships; it defines man, not as what he is made up of, but by whom he relates to and how. The first effect of Adam's sin is a dislocation of the perfect relationship between him and God.

God made all things to relate to each other and to himself in ways that he determined. That means that the universe is orderly. We cannot see the full extent of this orderliness now because of the confusion introduced by sin. The disorder that sin worked is referred to in the Bible as death. Jesus Christ restores life by restoring relationships. Through the gospel we are able to see the real nature of the problem by looking at how God dealt with it. The gospel shows us that all broken relationships in the universe are a result of our broken relationship with God.

Jesus and Wisdom

We can make direct contact with the wisdom traditions of Israel in the Gospel narratives about Jesus. We will defer close consideration of the matter until we have examined the Old Testament background to it. I have already referred to the closing words of the Sermon on the Mount.[1] It is clear from the consternation which followed that Jesus was making a very exalted claim. He was saying that obedient commitment to him and to his words is the only way to secure a life which has ultimate meaning. The Scribes, who had become the guardians of the wisdom traditions of Israel, would have pointed to the fathers and to the collected wisdom of the nation as the means by which one learned to act wisely, and so find life. But Jesus did not merely point them to the whole range of the wisdom of the past. He confronted them with himself and demanded total allegiance to himself and his words. That is why the crowds were amazed 'for he taught them as one who had authority, and not as their scribes' (Matthew 7:29. RSV).

In a number of places we find broad hints to the wisdom role that Jesus was to assume in his ministry. Luke concludes his account of the events surrounding the circumcision of the infant Jesus by saying, 'And the child grew and became strong; he was filled with wisdom, and the grace of God was upon him'. This may seem to be a curious phrase if we think of grace solely as God's way of dealing with sin, for Jesus was without sin. But the emphasis is on the humanity of the Christ, and as such he

---

[1] The Greek word for wise used in this passage is *phronimos*; the most common word used in the New Testament is *sophos*. As in the Hebrew of the Old Testament, so in the Greek there are several words which cluster around the same general meaning. In English we use words like *prudence*, *discernment* and *understanding* with meanings that approximate to that of wisdom.

received from God all the endowments of true humanness. Luke then recounts an example of this wisdom and
grace at work in the life of the boy. As a twelve-year-old he
amazed the teachers of the law with his understanding.
When his parents rebuked him for staying behind in the
temple, he replied, 'Why were you searching for me? Did-
n't you know that I had to be in my Father's house?'[2] In
speaking of God as his father he claimed to be the Son of
God, which we see in Luke 3 refers to the humanity of
Jesus.[3] The temple is the appropriate place for Jesus to be
since the house of God was the place ordained by God for
meeting with his people. Jesus was thus perfectly fulfilling the role of Israel and of redeemed mankind to be the
Son of God in perfect relationship with the Father. After
this incident Luke again pointedly comments that Jesus
grew in wisdom (Luke 2:52). Wisdom, then, is a characteristic of man in relation to God. He who is restored to
friendship with God is, in one important sense of the
word, the wise man.

If Luke is somewhat neutral in his references to the
teachers who heard the boy Jesus in the temple, we find
that he does not remain so. In fact the growing conflict
between Jesus and the Jewish religious teachers is one of
the themes of Luke's Gospel. These men become

---

[2] 'In my Father's house' is found in RV, RSV, NEB and NIV. There is
no noun in the Greek, which translates literally as, 'in the
(things) of my father'. RV margin has, 'about my father's business'. It is clear that he was in the temple, but the emphasis is
rather on what he was doing at the time when his parents mis-
laid him.

[3] The genealogy, or family tree of Jesus (Luke 3:23–38), follows
immediately on the account of Jesus' baptism and the Father's
word: 'You are my beloved son'. The family tree is traced back to
Adam who is the first son of God. Between Adam and Christ,
Israel is designated as son of God (Exodus 4:22, Hosea 11:1).

increasingly unwilling to accept the ministry of Jesus. In Luke 11:29–32 Jesus rebukes the Jews because they look for signs but are too blind to see the signs that are right before them (see also Matthew 12:38–42). By contrast with the pagan queen of Sheba, they do not seem to be very perceptive. The queen of Sheba was able to recognize the greatness and wisdom of Solomon and came to learn from him. But now a greater than Solomon is here and the Jews, who have all the privileges of the covenant and the revelation of God, do not recognize him. Solomon was always regarded as the big name in Hebrew wisdom, but Jesus outshines him by far.

In Luke 11:49[4] the conflict is with the lawyers and the Pharisees. The Pharisees are concerned to fulfil all the ritual requirements of the law, to tithe even the herbs of their gardens, but care nothing for justice and the love of God (verse 42). The teachers likewise weigh people down with the details of the law but refuse to submit to it themselves. So, says Jesus, they connive with their forebears who murdered the prophets: 'Therefore also the Wisdom of God said, "I will send them prophets and apostles, some of whom they will kill and persecute" ' (Luke 11:49, RSV). 'Woe to you lawyers! for you have taken away the key of knowledge; you did not enter yourself, and you hindered those who were entering' (Luke 11:52, RSV). The point of this conflict is that these Jewish religious leaders so distort the truth of God's word to Israel that they cannot perceive the truth even when it is there in the flesh before them in the person of Jesus Christ. As they have persecuted those who in the past taught them the truth, so now they invite the pronouncement of this terrible woe upon them.

---

[4] See also Matthew 23:34, 'I will send you prophets and wise men'.

Since the traditional wise men, the Scribes, the Pharisees, and the Jews in general have shown themselves unworthy, the true wisdom of God is being withheld from them. In Matthew 11:20–30 Jesus pronounces a woe on the unrepentant and unbelieving cities of Israel. Even the degraded city of Sodom would have repented if it had had the privileges of God's revelation enjoyed by Israel. Jesus thanks God that the truth is hidden from the wise and revealed to children. He continues: 'All things have been committed to me by my Father. No-one knows the Son except the Father, and no-one knows the Father except the Son and those to whom the Son chooses to reveal him'. Here is a great mystery. Somehow the wisdom of Israel has gone astray and those who should understand it are blinded. In the wisdom of God the truth is revealed to others, to children, to the humble, even to those whom the Jews despised. And the revelation of this wisdom is in the Son. Luke 10:21 records this statement of Jesus in another context to which it obviously also applies. The seventy-two disciples are amazed at the effects of their preaching of the coming kingdom of God, for even the demons are overcome (verse 17). Jesus replies by referring to the overthrow of Satan, and to the authority given to the disciples to deal with Satan's power. These are the signs of the coming of the kingdom. Once again Jesus remarks that what is hidden from the wise (the traditional teachers of Israel) is revealed to children (his disciples).

There are many other passages in the Gospels which either refer to wisdom in relation to Jesus, or in which Jesus himself uses the traditional forms of wisdom sayings in his teachings. We will return to some aspects of these in Chapter 11. So far we have seen that the Gospels portray Jesus as the greatest of all the wise men, as the source of all true wisdom. The Gospels also highlight the fact that the Jews often failed to perceive the connection between their own wisdom traditions in the Old Testament and the ministry of Jesus. This, of course, was a failure which extended to their perceptions of Jesus as the fulfiller of prophecy.

Christ our Wisdom

By far the most concentrated exposition of wisdom in the New Testament is found in 1 Corinthians 1 and 2. There is a strong attack on *sophia*, the pagan wisdom of the Greeks, in Paul's argument. The city of Corinth provided a challenge to the gospel through its paganism and hellenistic culture. Paul meets the challenge head-on by showing that the wisdom of God which is revealed in the gospel, is completely opposed to the wisdom of the world. The idea that the son of God should suffer in the flesh and die as a way of salvation was stupidity in the eyes of the Greeks. Greek wisdom saw salvation as a way to escape from the material world of the flesh; it discarded the body for a salvation of the spirit.

The gospel, the message of the cross, is the wisdom of God for it is his way of restoring all relationships. But it is also the power of God (1 Corinthians 1:18) because it really does save and and because it confounds the wisdom of the world. Worldly wisdom is condemned to destruction because it declares God's wisdom to be foolishness (vv. 18–21). The climax of Paul's argument is to point to Jesus Christ as the wisdom and power of God (v. 24), and to describe him as our wisdom (v. 30). The gospel is not a new philosophy that rivals that of the Greeks. Rather the message is about Jesus the God-man who is the wisdom of God. To understand that, we need to know what Paul means by the gospel and what he perceives true wisdom to be.

The first Corinthian epistle does not contain an orderly exposition of the gospel such as we find in the Roman epistle. From time to time, however, Paul refers to some salient aspects of the gospel. It is the message of the cross (1 Corinthians 1:18). Its effects can be described as washing, sanctification, and justification (6:11). It is above all the message that Christ died for our sins according to the Scriptures and rose on the third day according to the Scriptures (15:3–4). Probably nothing is so distinctively Pauline as his description of the believer as being *in Christ*. This is a union with Christ in his life, death and resurrection. Although we were not around at the time, we, as believers, are accounted by God as having been crucified with Christ (Galatians 2:20), as having died and been buried with Christ (Colossians 3:3, Romans 6:3–6), and as having been raised up with Christ (Ephesians 2:5–6). In his life and death Jesus was our substitute and representative. We deserve to die for our sins and, when Jesus died for us, as far as God is concerned, we were there on Calvary dying for our sins in the person of our substitute and representative. When he rises to new life at the right hand of the Father he represents us believers. So, we are *in Christ* and *with Christ* in heavenly places (Ephesians 2:5–6). Everything Christ is as the perfect human son of God, he is for us. He now dwells in perfect fellowship with the Father, not only as the eternal second person of the Trinity, but as the well-beloved son fulfilling the role God always intended for his human sons. So Paul says, 'It is because of him (God) that you are in Christ Jesus, who has become for us wisdom from God – that is, our righteousness, holiness and redemption'. (1 Corinthians I:30)[5] The NIV translation

---

[5] RSV translates: 'He is the source of your life in Christ Jesus, whom God made our wisdom, our righteousness and sanctification and redemption'.

makes it clearer than some other versions that wisdom is equated with righteousness, holiness and redemption. It would be easy at this point to miss the meaning of the equation, especially if our ideas of righteousness and holiness are confined to purely moral concepts. This is another area we will need to consider further.

There is one aspect of all this that can be dealt with from the New Testament without examining the Old Testament wisdom material. Paul's view of justification, which is expounded in detail in Romans, is closely linked to the idea of the believer being in Christ. Our being in Christ is not some kind of mystical merging of our beings with the being of Christ. It is a declaratory thing, for God declares it to be so. It refers not to our state of being, as when we say that we are in some place or other, but to our status in God's eyes. It is Paul's way of describing the nature of our union with Christ. On the grounds of Christ's merits, God is pleased to regard the believer as possessing everything that belongs to Jesus. It is in this sense that 'Christ is our life' (Colossians 3:4). God actually treats us as if we possessed the very life of Christ as our own. In ourselves we are yet sinful, but in Christ we are righteous, sanctified, perfect. In ourselves we still suffer from the foolishness of worldly wisdom, but in Christ we are perfectly wise, for he is our wisdom before God.

The other aspect of our union with Christ is that it is a real union through the Spirit of Christ in us. Sanctification means that what we are in Christ we have begun to be in ourselves. So, if by faith we have died in Christ, we must also put to death what is earthly in us (Colossians 3:3–5). Clearly the moral dimension of sanctification is important. But we are moral beings as thinking beings. Morality implies responsibility, which in turn implies reasoning and willing. Moral transformation in the Christian is not separate from intellectual transformation or the renewing of our minds (Romans 12:2). Whatever wisdom is, we possess it perfectly in Christ. Part of our growth in holiness will be to grow in wisdom in ourselves.

Again, to anticipate the point to which we must return later, we see in other New Testament texts that wisdom is linked in very significant ways to the person and work of Christ. Look at the emphasis on the enlightenment of the believer in Ephesians 1:9–10: 'For he has made known to us in all wisdom and insight the mystery of his will, according to his purpose which he set forth in Christ as a plan for the fulness of time, to unite all things in him, things in heaven and things on earth' (RSV). Paul thus points to the intellectual content of the gospel as it reveals the ultimate plan of God. It shows us that this plan is much bigger than we may be used to thinking of it. Often we speak of salvation as something that happens to you or me or to each believer individually. Sometimes we get it together as the collective experience of all who are saved. But here Paul puts forward what we might refer to as the cosmic dimension in salvation. That is to say, God's plan, which he revealed in Christ, is to bring the whole universe or *cosmos* to its proper goal in Christ. The Greek verb here carries the idea of summing up or bringing to a head.[6] And notice how Paul stresses *all* things – things in heaven and things on earth. What may we learn from this passage about wisdom? Paul's purpose is not to define wisdom but to describe God's ultimate purpose. Yet wisdom is closely related to the knowledge of this purpose. Through the gospel we receive an understanding of the ultimate purpose of God for everything and everybody in the universe.

One specific side to this ultimate purpose is referred to later on in the same passage (Ephesians 1:17–23). Wisdom

---

[6] *anakephalaiōsasthai.*

here is knowing our destiny which God's power will effect in the same way that if effected the resurrection of Jesus. But wisdom is not only God getting it all together at the very end. It includes also how the gospel enables us to engage in the task of getting things back together in our lives now. Paul prays that the believers may have wisdom so that their lives might be lived in a way that is pleasing to God (Colossians 1:9–14). Such wisdom is not first and foremost a knowledge of how to perform good works, but of what God has really accomplished for us in Christ. Likewise in Colossians 1:28, Paul links 'teaching everyone with all wisdom' with the proclamation about Christ. The goal is to present everyone perfect, or mature, in Christ. The same emphasis is found in Colossians 3:16 where to 'let the word of Christ dwell in you richly' goes hand in hand with the mutual teaching and exhortation with all wisdom of the Christian congregation. Wisdom and the revelation of Christ are the same thing.

One last reference in this regard is Paul's statement in Colossians 2:2–3. This passage demolishes any idea that wisdom is a purely intellectual exercise. Paul refers to his striving on behalf of his readers. He says: 'My purpose is that they may be encouraged in heart and united in love, so that they may have the full riches of complete understanding, in order that they may know the mystery of God, namely, Christ, in whom are hidden all the treasures of wisdom and knowledge'. Notice how wisdom is linked with mutual encouragement and love. Growth in understanding is to be found in the mutual life of the congregation. We should understand also the force of the word mystery. It is something which is beyond human ability to find out, not open to human reason. It must be made known to us by revelation from God. Paul could not imply that knowing the mystery of God means that we can plumb the depths of God's mind and being for he exclaims: 'Oh! the depth of the riches of the wisdom and knowledge of God! How unsearchable his judgments and his paths beyond tracing out!' (Romans 11:33). No, we cannot know God as he knows himself. But we can know God truly as he has revealed himself in Jesus Christ. All the treasures of wisdom and knowledge are hidden in Christ! Do we really believe that? They are hidden in the sense that we must search them out and know them. We can never know them all for Christ is true God as well as true man. But again, what we can know we can know truly. And if all the treasures of wisdom and knowledge are in Christ, think what that means for the whole intellectual pilgrimage of mankind. If it means nothing else, it means that all of man's search for knowledge is defective in some critical way when it is not pursued in the light of Jesus Christ. The gospel has a controlling interest in all true knowledge. What I mean by that will, I trust, become clearer as we continue this study.

I will conclude this chapter by suggesting a tentative definition of what it means to be the mature Christian that Paul speaks of in Colossians 1:28. A mature Christian is one who is able to look at the whole of reality through Christian eyes. He is in the process of achieving an integrated overview of reality in those areas that belong to his experience as well as in those areas that he knows only theoretically. He is learning to understand all things in terms of what they are in this corrupted realm and of what God intends them to be by virtue of his redeeming work. Thus, he is an integrated person who is learning daily through the gospel how to relate, not only to himself, but to all things according to the creative purpose of God.

Questions for Study

1. Look up 1 Corinthians 1:26–30. How does v. 30, a statement about Christ, relate to vv. 26–27, a statement about us?
2. What does it mean in v. 30 that Christ has become for us wisdom from God?
3. In Ephesians 1:7–10 how does the gospel figure as the wisdom of God, and what does it say about restored relationships?

Chapter Three

The Wisdom of the World

Summary

There are two kinds of wisdom that need to be clearly distinguished. The first is worldly wisdom which looks at the world as if God were not real, and thus has not revealed himself in the person and work of Christ. The other is the true wisdom which comes from God, who alone can tell us what the universe really means. Yet in daily life we draw constantly on worldly wisdom because it works. It is based on human experience and involves the recognition that there is order in the universe. But when it addresses the ultimate or eternal significance of things worldly wisdom is opposed to the wisdom of God. Within the limited view of practical living, worldly and godly wisdom may coincide so that there is a meeting of the minds of Christian and non-Christian, of Israelite and pagan. But there is no agreement about the basis upon which we ultimately interpret things and events. The Christian's distinctive claim is that God the Creator alone can interpret all things in the universe.

The Foolishness of Worldly Wisdom

'Has not God made foolish the wisdom of the world?' (1 Corinthians 1:20). It is easy to agree that indeed he has. But then we are faced with a problem for, when we think about it, we are absorbing, using and approving worldly wisdom every day of our lives. Consequently, we find ourselves asking in what sense the vast storehouse of knowledge gained by a sinful and unbelieving community is foolishness, and in what sense it is wisdom.

Let us summarize Paul's assertions about the two kinds of wisdom which he makes in 1 Corinthians 1 and 2. First, Paul says that the gospel would be emptied of its power if he were to preach it with eloquent worldly wisdom (1:17). This is because the wisdom of the world judges this gospel, the message of the cross, to be foolishness (1:18). Such wisdom is therefore doomed to perish (1:19). Worldly wisdom is actually foolishness because it cannot put man in touch with reality by bringing him to God (1:20–21a). God's way of salvation through the preaching of Christ crucified is an offence to the Jews and stupidity to the Greeks, yet it is both the power and wisdom of God (1:18–24). So, that which the unbelieving world calls foolishness is in fact wiser than the wisdom of the world (1:25). Paul avoids the wisdom which the world sees as superior and persuasive, and centres his whole message on Christ crucified (2:1–4). He does this in order that faith might rest, not in man's wisdom, but in God's power (2:5). Paul's wisdom is wisdom from God which is taught by the Spirit of God (2:6–13). He who does not have the Spirit of God will never see this true wisdom for what it is (2:14–16).

Paul shows us that we must distinguish between the meaning of things in a limited sense, and ultimate meaning. Things may be meaningful to us in the immediate situation of life in which we find ourselves. Elementary arithmetic is meaningful in the context of our society which is oriented to statistics, accounting and the use of money. But how do we relate it to ultimate questions of the meaning of our existence and of eternity? Paul speaks of wisdom as it seeks to embrace such ultimate questions as the way to find our rightful place in relation to the whole of reality. He is not saying that there is no validity in the knowledge of unbelieving people, or that sinners are as depraved morally and intellectually as it is possible to be. Rather he is pointing to the inability of human wisdom to bring us to ultimate reality and meaning, and also its inability to assess rightly what God says about ultimate truth. This failure of human wisdom is not merely an incompleteness or an inadvertent loss of direction. It is in fact a deliberate refusal of the truth. It is a dimension of human sin and rejection of God. The intellectual side of repentance is to be prepared to become a fool in the eyes of the world so that we might actually become wise (1 Corinthians 3:18–20). In other words, the gospel demands of us that we forsake the non-Christian views of reality and that we begin the task of interpreting our world in the light of the gospel. That is wisdom!

The Wisdom of Worldly Wisdom

A moment's reflection will enable us to realize that, no matter how much we agree with what Paul says about worldly wisdom, we nevertheless constantly accept and act upon knowledge which does not have any distinctively Christian source or context. In everyday life it would never occur to us in most situations to enquire if some information we wanted came from a Christian or a non-Christian. If we want to know how to lay bricks or repair a lawn mower or even programme a computer, we consider it important that we get reliable information, but not that our informant be a Christian. We may seek out a Christian mechanic or electrician on the grounds that he can be expected to do an honest job, but his level of competence is not necessarily the same as his level of Christian commitment.

One of the more difficult sayings of Jesus is the story of the dishonest steward (Luke 16:1–9). In order to cushion the disastrous effects of his imminent dismissal, the steward alters the accounts of his master's creditors, hoping thereby to have some friends when in need of them. There is no question of Jesus condoning the man's fraudulent approach to his master's goods. However, he does commend the prudence of the steward in the way he pursues his own ends. We might suggest that, within the limited framework of this event, the man acted with some wisdom. He perceived the nature of his problem and he set out with cunning to solve it. When faced with possible disaster he did not bury his head in the sand but faced the problem squarely and worked out a solution. So, the children of this world often show greater wisdom than children of the kingdom of God in this sense, that they apply themselves to the problems facing them with far greater tenacity. Ronald Wallace comments, 'The average Christian of today is not willing to put into the matter of his religion even a fraction of the perseverance, patience and intelligent concentration that the man who knows only this present world gives towards perfecting his technical knowledge for his business, or even towards his hobbies'.[1] If Christians showed as much talent and shrewdness in the pursuit of the world for Christ as unbelievers show in the pursuit of riches, who could gauge what effect that would have? In ultimate terms the steward's wisdom is folly for he would be overthrown in the judgment of God. But in limited terms there is a valid aspect of wisdom in what he does. His shrewdness would need to be

---

1 Ronald Wallace, *Many Things in Parables* (Edinburgh: Oliver and Boyd, 1955), p. 76.

transformed by the gospel, but it is commendable wisdom for all that.

The General Ethos of Wisdom

So far we have seen that there is a distinction to be made between the limited validity of the wisdom of the world, and the validity, or lack of it, which belongs to worldly wisdom in its application to ultimate reality. The problem of the commendation of the unjust steward has similarities to the question of wisdom at large in the worldly sense. Most of us are aware of traditional wisdom sayings which belong to our culture. They take many forms, but the popular proverb is one of the most easily recognized:

> A burnt child dreads the fire.
> A stitch in time saves nine.
> Still waters run deep.

We know that these can apply to a variety of real life situations, and we do not discard them because they have no recognizable Christian origins. Every culture collects the wisdom of its people, much of which will be found in the form of concise proverbial sayings. In this study we will be mainly concerned with the collected wisdom of the Hebrews as we find it in the Old Testament.

Because the Bible contains a significant collection of Israelite wisdom works we are motivated to try to understand how such books as Proverbs, Job and Ecclesiastes came to be written and with what understanding of wisdom. Students of this literature have readily recognized that culturally the Israelites belonged to the wider world of the ancient Middle East. The discovery of large amounts of wisdom literature coming out of ancient

Babylon and Egypt has generated much interest, particularly during the past fifty years. What is of special significance was the discovery of the close similarities between certain non-Israelite works and parts of the biblical literature.

Unfortunately there are always those who seem bent on proving that Israel's religion and literature are entirely dependent upon borrowings from her pagan neighbours. But in reaction to this pan-oriental approach to religion and culture we should not ignore the obvious contacts that were there. For example, scholars have long concluded that Proverbs 22:17–23:11 has close verbal similarities to parts of the Egyptian work, the Wisdom of Amen-em-ope. Did Proverbs borrow from Amen-em-ope or vice versa, or did they both borrow from a third source? Some have rejected the idea that Proverbs borrows from the Egyptian work because of what seem to be the implications of that for the doctrine of the inspiration of Scripture. But the last two chapters of Proverbs are attributed to authors that do not appear to be Israelites. Clearly, we must deal with the inspiration question in another way than by pretending that the problems aren't there. At this point we can at least recognize that there is common ground shared by the wisdom of pagans and that of God's people.

Our interest in Egypt's wisdom should be aroused if for no other reason than Stephen's reference to Moses as having been educated in all the wisdom of Egypt (Acts 7:22). Stephen does not suggest that Moses needed to repent of this or to unlearn it. On the contrary he seems to be saying that it was an important part of the preparation of Moses for his ministry. But we must remember the other side of the evidence as found in Hebrews 11:24–26. Moses refused to be called the son of Pharaoh's daughter and regarded disgrace for the sake of Christ as of greater value than the treasures of Egypt. So there is a good and a bad side to his Egyptian experience.

Egypt's wisdom literature is very old. We now have material which goes back to the middle of the third millennium BC, long before the emergence of Israel. By the time Moses went to school in the court of Pharaoh there was already a long tradition of wisdom literature. A lot of it is bound up with the training of young noblemen for effective statesmanship.[2] Usually the form of this would be what is now referred to as the *instruction*. Unlike the one- or two-line proverbs the instructions are longer compositions which address a pupil with directions, conditional statements (if . . . then) and motives for certain kinds of action. The Israelite equivalent is found in such passages as Proverbs 1:8–8:36.

An interesting feature of Egyptian wisdom is the place given to Ma'at. Ma'at was personified as the daughter of the god Re, but was never elevated to the status of a god itself. It was not a part of the official pantheon of gods and does not appear in mythology. Scholars have pointed to the difficulty in translating the word Ma'at into a satisfactory English equivalent, but suggest that it approximates to *order*, *truth*, or *justice*. It seems that Ma'at represented the order that was to be seen particularly in the stability of the Egyptian state. It was not merely a political or social order, for it involved the relationship of the state to the whole of nature. There is no real parallel in Hebrew wisdom to the Ma'at concept other than some similarities to the idea of order. These similarities between Hebrew and Egyptian wisdom suggest that the common factor is the quest for the understanding of order in the universe.

---

[2] An excellent introduction to the wisdom of the ancient near eastern cultures is found in William McKane, *Proverbs*, Old Testament Library (London: SCM Press, 1970).

Hebrew wisdom was distinct in that it was shaped by the Israelite experience of covenant and redemption.

Have we any real evidence that Hebrew wisdom was seen to have features in common with wisdom of other nations in the ancient Middle East? I have already mentioned the possible non-Israelite inclusions in the Book of Proverbs, and the contact between Solomon and the queen of Sheba. Other evidence also relates to Solomon. In 1 Kings 3–4 we have the account of his being granted wisdom. On the one hand this wisdom is clearly a gift from God, and on the other it involves Solomon's experience or empirical knowledge of nature. He speaks of plants and animals, composes songs and proverbs, and makes wise judgments in his capacity as king. Initially his request was for understanding so that he could govern well. In this there is some parallel with Egyptian wisdom. Furthermore, the narrator deliberately compares Solomon's wisdom with that of certain wise men of the East (1 Kings 4:29–31). Certainly his wisdom surpasses that of his foreign contemporaries, but there is no suggestion that theirs does not have the status of wisdom.

It seems, then, that we can propose the existence of a general concept or ethos of wisdom, not only in biblical times, but also throughout history. In theological terms, this general wisdom would be an outworking of the so-called cultural mandate. By this we mean that in Eden God gave to Adam care and cultivation of the created order, and dominion over it (Genesis 1:26–28). The fall has confused this clearly defined relationship of mankind to the world, but it has not obliterated it. Man no longer recognizes that God is Lord and Creator, but he goes on making greater and greater strides in his quest for knowledge and technical know-how. To achieve the goal of continual progress, as it is usually thought of as being, he devises more and more sophisticated ways of observing, classifying and reasoning. But what modern technological man does in a highly complex fashion is at its heart no different from what man has always done. He has observed his world and tried to classify his experience as a way of getting to the underlying order of things.

Atheistic humanity is thus capable of using the faculties given by an unacknowledged Creator, and of continuing to exercise the cultural mandate, albeit in a corrupted way. Society establishes ethical frameworks in order to limit threats to social well-being that come from within. But in doing so it also rejects the prospect of a Creator who alone has the right to decree what is right and what is wrong. Conservation movements attack the doctrine of economic growth at any cost, and point to the threat of ecological disaster. The nuclear protest gains momentum because this generation not only has the capacity to destroy this planet but is in increasing danger of doing so. What was once seen as a political subterfuge by a small group of fanatics bent on control of the world, is now taken up as the genuine concern of millions of ordinary people. All these situations force Christians to face critical moral issues and to speak to them from a truly Christian perspective.

The point of these examples of common concerns is that they are *common* concerns, and there are many aspects of them upon which Christians and non-Christians will agree. This is because faith and regeneration do not remove Christians from the world. They will go on sharing the same humanity and the same universe until the end of this age. So what is the difference between a Christian and a non-Christian view of things? [3] The real

---

[3] See James W. Sire, *The Universe Next Door* (Downers Grove: InterVarsity Press, 1976), and C. Van Til, *The Doctrine of Scripture* (Ripon: Den Dulk Christian Foundation, 1967).

distinctions lie in the way they look at ultimate meaning. By refusing God's revelation of himself in Jesus Christ, the non-Christian thinks of the universe as self-contained. Its meaning is open to our investigation. There can be no question of a God who is distinct from the universe and who gives it meaning. Unbelieving man often disguises his rejection of God's revelation of himself by constructing alternative beliefs about God or gods. But whether he calls himself religious or atheist, the assumption is that he can know things truly on the evidence of his senses alone.

World-Views in Conflict

The Christian rejects this assumption of a universe which is shut up against the God of the Bible. He accepts rather that God is self-sufficient, personal, and in complete control. While the atheist view of reality is a closed system of cause and effect, the Christian view is a universe in which cause and effect are established by God and open to his sovereign intervention. We need the revelation of God in order to know that the universe is in fact like this. We do not know all the answers yet. We never will know *all* the answers because some can be known by God alone. Because God has revealed that the ultimate meaning of reality lies beyond the ability of man to discover for himself, we know that empirical knowledge is always in that sense defective. What man discovers by himself, and what he reasons from it, will never bring him to understand God and to know him. Thus, we have returned to Paul's assertion that worldly wisdom cannot know God (1 Corinthians 1:21, compare 2:12). The Bible characteristically looks at reality in terms of relationships. Because God is the creator of all things, these relationships must begin with God. To understand what it means to be human we must know man as image of God. The non-Christian can describe many things about man in a way that is useful within a restricted framework. But while we can look at man purely in terms of structure, chemistry, anatomy and so on, none of these approaches can show us the real nature of man. They do not provide a satisfactory explanation of the uniqueness of man in the purposes of God. They can never discover and pin-point the exclusive trait of humanity created in the image of God.

From the biblical point of view, then, the definition of man is primarily a definition of his relationship to God. Such relationship includes dependence upon God who is sovereign and self-sufficient. By putting man at the centre, the humanist claims to give him his proper dignity. But this assumption of the pre-eminence of man is a radically dehumanizing one since he is not perceived as imaging God. The humanist sees man's leadership in the world as the result of evolutionary accident. The Bible describes it as God-given dominion over the rest of creation. It is reasonable to infer that one aspect of the image of God in man is this dominion. This ruling function was intended to reflect the absolute rule of God over all things. It was Adam's sinful desire to substitute his own absolute rule for a reflective rule; he wanted to be God. From that point on sin confused and dislocated all the relationships which God had established. But just as the image of God in man was not totally obliterated by sin, so also the orderliness of the creation, though confused, was not completely destroyed. The planets continue in their courses, the earth moves in a mathematically predictable pattern, life is sustained on our planet, and human society maintains enough order to survive and even at times to flourish.

Because the Christian view of reality begins with the Creator who has revealed himself to us, it is in opposition to those views which establish the nature of things on the basis of experience alone. While the Christian accepts his responsibility to search for knowledge, he knows that human effort, discovery and reasoning cannot provide a comprehensive understanding of the universe. Empirical knowledge, that which is gained by investigating the world with our senses, cannot include God or the meaning which he gives to the created order. But this limitation of empirical knowledge is not a hindrance to the Christian's knowledge of ultimate reality because the one Person who has exhaustive knowledge of all things has told us by revelation what we need to know. Through the revelation in the Bible we are able to know what God wants us to know of ultimate truth.

The non-Christian is in a very different position. He has rejected God's revelation of himself, and has filled the gap either with man-made gods or with himself as independent and self-sufficient man. He sees himself as autonomous, that is, as ruling his own destiny. Even when he is being religious he is simply disguising this autonomy as he worships himself in the gods he creates. Such is the position which we broadly describe as humanist. Having rejected the Creator who established all things in determined relationships and gave reality its meaning, the humanist is incapable of understanding the real essence of anything. No matter how accurately he describes man anatomically, psychologically, or sociologically, by leaving God out of his understanding the humanist actually dehumanizes man. Furthermore, the empiricist or humanist will claim to know things truly while not knowing exhaustively. In this he is inconsistent.[4] No humanist would say that things

---

[4] This is discussed in detail by C. Van Til, *The Reformed Pastor and Modern Thought* (Presbyterian and Reformed Publishing Company, 1974).

exist in total isolation from each other. For a start he couldn't investigate them if they did, for they would also be isolated from him. And there could be no such thing as natural laws, or complexities of matter, for there would be only random particles. There would be no organisms, no people to become humanists! Once we recognize this, we will see that what things really are includes their relationship to everything else. When the humanist claims to know something truly, he is saying that he knows how it relates to everything else in existence. In other words, to know even one thing truly he must know *all things exhaustively*.

We can summarize this discussion by a contrast of three positions. First, the atheistic humanist claims to know enough to say that God does not exist. This is a claim to know everything, for if he admits that he does not know everything, how does he know that God is not included in what he does not know? Secondly, the agnostic humanist thinks to avoid the problem of the atheist by saying that we cannot know if God exists or not; he may or he may not. But this is also to claim exhaustive knowledge, for how can he know that God's existence cannot be known other than by knowing everything there is to be known? The last thing left for him to discover may be the evidence that God either exists or does not exist. Finally, the Christian knows that he does not have exhaustive knowledge. But he knows also through revelation that God does have exhaustive knowledge and can therefore define for us what reality is. By the same revelation this God has told us all that we need to know in order to know truly. The Christian can know God truly. He can know man truly, and the created order truly. He knows none of them exhaustively, but he does know them truly.

The Christian in the World

It begins to look as if distinguishing worldly wisdom from godly wisdom can sometimes be quite a difficult matter. I suspect that one important factor in biblical wisdom is learning how to master the distinction. The New Testament shows us why there is such difficulty. There is a real tension in the fact that we are citizens of a world which does not yet appear, and at the same time we must go on living in a world to which we have become aliens. The tension will show itself in many ways, but it is central to our Christian concern to live consistently with the gospel. Neither total withdrawal from this world nor total conformity to it is an option for the Christian. Unfortunately it seems that we often solve the problem by a rigid division of our lives into the Christian and the secular. It is not that we have no concern to witness in the world or to abstain from sin. But when we are involved in pursuits that seem to be morally neutral we easily think in a worldly way. Rather than muddle along like this, we need to see that the gospel of Jesus Christ gives us the only true basis for understanding all things in an ultimate sense: 'Heaven and earth will pass away, but my words will never pass away' (Matthew 24:35).

One of the lessons that this word of Jesus has to teach us is that God tells us by revelation what we need to know in order to understand as much as he intends us to understand about the nature of reality, but he does not tell us what we can find out for ourselves. We will see from our study of the wisdom literature that wisdom is both a gift of God and a human achievement. It is our task to relate our experience of the world, and our observations on life, to the things that God reveals in his word. In taking up this theme the biblical wisdom literature provides us with many pointers to what it means to be the people of God living in God's world which has become alienated from him by sin.

Hopefully as a result of our study we will be able to ask some of the right questions about the meaning of the gospel for the whole of our being and life. In a hostile world we are to be 'as shrewd as snakes and as innocent as doves' (Matthew 10:16). Perhaps one reason why unbelievers have scorned Christianity as a crutch is that Christian have made little effort to communicate a comprehensive Christian interpretation of the world. We have tended to carve existence up into unrelated parts, often under the influence of a pagan view of humanity that has infected much Christian thinking. This is no new thing, for the early church was troubled by it. A Greek concept of the opposition of spirit and matter challenged the Christian understanding of the world. Gnosticism, as it was called, said that only the spirit is good and all matter is evil. Salvation is irrelevant to the body since only the soul survives. The name Gnosticism comes from the Greek *gnōsis*, meaning knowledge, and it was by knowledge that the real person, that is the soul, was saved. Gnostics could handle neither the goodness of creation nor the incarnation. A new Jesus had to be constructed; one who was pure spirit and whose body was an illusion. The seriousness of this error is seen in 1 John 4:2–3 where John makes the coming of Jesus *in the flesh* the test of truth.

The paganizing of the gospel in this manner, so that the true humanity of Jesus is played down for the sake of his deity, is a subtle error because it can appear to be so 'spiritual'. In this materialistic age it may seem to be a healthy corrective to the rejection of the supernatural. But we soon learn from the nature of the gospel that we cannot save the spiritual by playing down the human dimension. This *docetic*[5] view of Christ, once it is entertained in Christian thinking, gives birth to some very unhealthy offspring. If Christ's humanity is not treated seriously (it does not have to be denied, just played down or largely ignored) then our own humanity will begin to seem unimportant. Salvation will be, as it is often described, a matter of having Jesus (a spirit) in your heart (soul), which means that you are born again (in your soul) and will go to heaven when you die (as immortal soul). The Christian who thinks like this has little to say to the unbeliever about the relevance of the gospel for the whole person and for the physical world.

Docetism also produces distorted thinking about the subject of holiness or sanctification. The human element in our Christian life is played down in favour of the life of Christ (his purely divine life) being lived in and through us. In popular jargon 'Let go and let God' sometimes means that human effort has no place in holy living. The believer in effect is not only being divinized, but is actually being absorbed into the being of God. The real distinction between God and rnan which was established in creation is blurred. So, to quote another popular cliché, the believer is only a suit of clothes that Jesus wears!

This distortion of the God-man relationship also affects the way we approach the Bible. A docetic Bible has no human dimension, no historical and cultural context conditioning the meaning of the words. The docetic Christian thinks it is very pious to treat the words of the Bible as conveying immediate spiritual meaning without regard to what the original writer intended to convey. Sometimes a decision is made on the basis of the assertion that 'the Lord

---

[5] Docetism was the name given to the view that Jesus was purely divine spirit, and that he only seemed (Greek, *dokein*) to have a physical body.

gave me a verse of Scripture', when in fact what the text actually says has no relationship whatsoever to the decision being made. This approach is not far removed from the belief that no human word of the Bible is needed at all since the Spirit tells me directly what to do.

The biblical wisdom literature is one of the most potent antidotes to the destructive errors of docetism. It reinforces the general biblical perspective on the relationship of God and the believer. On the one hand it is the answer to the worldly wisdom which leaves God out of its reckoning. On the other hand it rejects the false spirituality which has the appearance of being godly wisdom, but which, because it leaves our humanity out of its reckoning, is not wisdom at all but rather the resurgence of an ancient error that troubled early Christianity.

Questions for Study

1. Look up 1 Corinthians 1:18–30. What does Paul see as the problem with the wisdom of the world?
2. How does the world-view of the Christian conflict with that of the non-Christian?
3. In what sense can Christians learn truth from non-Christians?

Chapter Four

The Refining of Wisdom

Summary

When God created human beings he gave them the task of exercising rule over the created order. God's word was the means by which Adam interpreted the knowledge which he gained through nature. Sin confused the process of gaining knowledge because rebellious Adam refused to interpret reality by God's word. God chose Israel as the people through whom he would restore true wisdom to mankind. Within the history of God's covenant with Israel, wisdom began to emerge as a self-conscious human activity. It related to the way the people of God learned to act and think, and to teach their children. Wisdom began in the earliest times but flourished under David and Solomon. Israel's wisdom matured at the end of the historical period of God's revelation of his kingdom. Once the full picture of the meaning of redemption was given in Israel's history, a greater emphasis was placed upon the task of responsible living within the framework of the fear of the Lord.

Man Under God

No higher dignity can be given to mankind than that which is expressed in Scripture. Of all creation mankind alone was created in the image of God. Modern godless thinking regards man as the most highly evolved animal, a result of chance plus time. His rule over the other species is the consequence of the survival of the fittest. By contrast, the Bible sees man as the greatest of all God's creatures with the God-given task of ruling all others. The human scientific task began when Adam named the animals, and ever since then the quest for knowledge and for control of the universe has expressed man's urge to exercise dominion over all things.

The Genesis account informs us that the scientific task of humanity is regulated by God's word. Adam was not left to discover the universe unaided. The reason is simple. God had to reveal himself by his word so that Adam would know God and know the universe as it really is: the creation of God. There is no doubt that the whole creation is stamped with the character of its Creator, but that is not enough for man to know God in a personal way. When Adam sinned he turned his back on the revelation of God in his word and in his creation. So Paul in Romans 1:18–25 tells us that our sin makes fools of us all. By suppressing the truth about God which is there in the creation for us all to see, we render ourselves without excuse for the rebellion against God that is in our hearts. But even before Adam sinned, God's word was necessary for him to be able to understand the meaning of himself and his world. God spoke to Adam and told him of his relationship to God and to the whole of creation.[1]

---

1 Van Til comments, 'Originally man's very self-awareness required that organically revelational environment that comes from the interaction of word and fact revelation. After the fall, supernatural redemptive revelation must supply what the original word-revelation supplied to Adam'. *The Doctrine of Scripture*, p. 66.

Man's knowledge of the world and himself was indirect. It was always interpreted through the revelation which God gave of himself by his word.

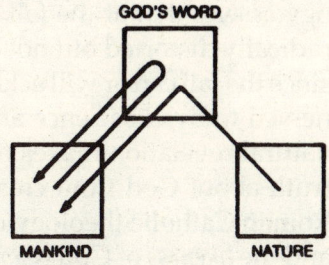

Figure 1. Wisdom at Creation

Thus, before the fall, Adam's wisdom came from a perfect combination of supernatural revelation (word from God) and the discoveries of his senses. A basic principle of this wisdom would have been to accept the bounds of freedom decreed by the spoken word of God. Only thus could the proper relationship between God and man be maintained. Adam's sin was to refuse this relationship of

Natural man leaves God out of his thinking. He sees nature, including himself, as all there is and as having self-evident meaning. If he has religious ideas they are his own attempts to avoid the revealed truth about God.

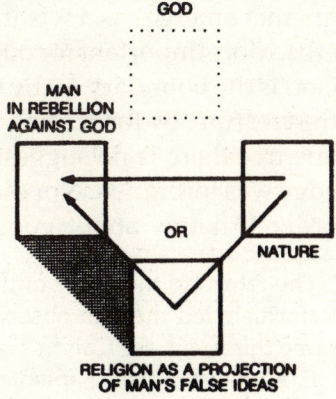

Figure 2. The Wisdom of the World

creature to Creator, and the result was the dislocation of this and all other relationships. Historic Protestant theology asserts that at the fall the image of God in man was radically distorted but not obliterated. As a result, no one since the fall can or will acknowledge the truth of God witnessed to by conscience and nature. This suppression of natural revelation makes natural theology – establishing truth about God from creation – impossible. Traditional Roman Catholic theology distinguishes the *image* of God and the *likeness* of God (Genesis 1:26) and says that the fall affected the latter much more than it did the former.[2] Thus, with the image of God virtually intact, the sinner is able to discern truth about God from nature without the aid of the Holy Spirit or supernatural revelation. Natural theology thus plays a big part in Roman Catholic thinking and, indeed, it is a key point at which Catholicism and historic Protestantism differ. It is important that we understand how these two quite different ways of understanding the effects of the fall lead to different concepts of wisdom in the Christian life.

It is true that the tree of the knowledge of good and evil has overtones of wisdom,[3] although it is rather the tree of life that emerges as a wisdom theme in the book of Proverbs. More important for our understanding of man under God is the boundary set by God for the experience of man the creature. By forbidding Adam to eat of the fruit of that one tree there is no suggestion that the quest for knowledge was forbidden. Nor did Adam need to eat the fruit in order to know about good and evil. Obedience to the

---

[2] The return to the study of the Hebrew text by the Protestant Reformers led them to observe that *image* and *likeness* are the same thing, e.g. see Calvin's commentary on Genesis 1:26.

[3] L. Alonso-Schökel, 'Sapiental and Covenant Themes in Genesis 2–3', in (ed.) D.J. McCarthy and W.B. Callan, *Modern Biblical Studies* (Milwaukee: Bruce Publishing Company, 1967).

demand would have established in Adam's understanding all that he needed to know of the matter. The prohibition thus in no way negates the cultural mandate but rather, along with every other revealing word of God, establishes the only possible basis upon which the mandate can be carried out properly.

After the fall, man under God is man under the judgement of God. Sin has dehumanized humanity so that if there is any hope at all it will be in complete dependence upon God's mercy. This mercy of God is revealed along with the judgment of God on Adam's sin. Although death comes upon mankind, the grace of God is freely given in allowing human society to continue. The end result of sin is death and destruction but the finality of this is postponed. The world, though fallen and often dangerous, remains a beautiful place in which human life is sustained, at least for a while. This common grace shown to the whole world allows sinful man to continue to perform his task although he does it imperfectly and corruptly. It also allows special or saving grace to be shown to sinners for as long as God determines. Those who receive God's word are thereby given the means to interpret reality both as it now is – distorted through sin – and as it once was and again will be.

Israel Under God

The evidence available to us of the intellectual achievements of the people in the old civilizations of the Middle East shows us that wisdom was sought after and written down very early in recorded history. There is little doubt that wisdom sayings of some kind would have been part of the emerging culture of Israel's ancestors. Indeed, the pre-history of civilized man referred to in Genesis 4–5 includes the cultural elements of music and craftsmanship. If this seems to be a rather non-intellectual wisdom, let us remember that wisdom is a term also applied to the ability of craftsmen (Exodus 26:1). It is not difficult to see how practical know-how can be embraced with the more intellectual concepts under the one term 'wisdom'.

Since the Bible is concerned with the subject of God's saving grace, it is important for us to try to relate wisdom to grace. The word grace first appears in Genesis 6:8 and relates to the salvation of Noah and his family from the deluge. The concept of grace is especially bound up with the covenant and with the election of Abraham as the father of Israel. The biblical picture is that God both revealed himself and acted for the salvation of Israel in his dealings with that nation from its birth. It would be a great mistake to allow the lack of reference to covenant and to salvation history in the wisdom literature to obscure the fact that the wise men were men of the covenant. How wisdom and covenant relate in Israel is a matter we will review later on. The covenant is a specific expression of supernatural revelation. By this we mean that it could not be observed in nature but had to be communicated by a special word from God. On the basis of the foregoing discussion it has to be said that wisdom, without special revelation to supply the valid view of reality, would be worldly wisdom and therefore incapable of knowing ultimate truth or of leading us to God.

Israel under grace is also Israel under the law. The biblical evidence leads us to say that grace precedes and governs law even in the Old Testament. Israel was elected and called by grace. Grace made Israel the people of God and saved her from Egypt before the law was given at Sinai. Grace operated within the sacrificial provisions of the law so that all who acknowledged that they failed to keep the law and threw themselves on the mercy of God, were forgiven. Grace operated in the promises that were constantly reaffirmed in the face of Israel's disobedience. And what was the purpose of grace? It would make Israel to be the centre of God's activity to redeem mankind and to restore all the relationships between God, man and the world; the relationships that belonged to a perfect creation. In the midst of Israel's history and experience of God's redeeming activity, an experience which included the giving of the prophetic words of revelation, Israel's wisdom grew, flourished, developed, languished and took some disastrous wrong turns, but never died.

Wisdom in Israel

In order to speak about wisdom in Israel we have to make some assumptions about what wisdom is. Those books of the Bible that we refer to as wisdom books have certain characteristics which are more or less distinct. The evidence from Israel, Egypt and Mesopotamia is that there was a developed form of wisdom which involved more than knowledge as such. There are characteristic ways of

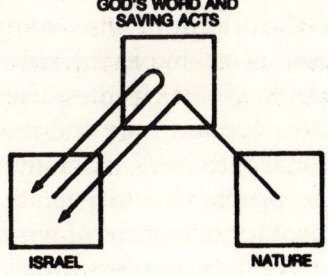

Israel's true wisdom interpreted reality in the light of the revelation of God in his word and saving acts.

Figure 3.   Wisdom in Israel

pursuing knowledge, of putting it in writing and of passing it on. Set literary forms, such as the proverb, developed as suitable to the peculiar aims of wisdom. Certain distinctive words recur again and again, and these are not only words which refer to the intellectual activity of man. But for all this, wisdom remains an elusive concept because it can describe several things. In the broadest sense it describes the thinking and acting which makes for a truly human existence with mastery of life. In the narrower sense it is a technical term for a way of thinking peculiar, it would seem, to a particular group but still available in some measure to the wider community. It is a way of writing, or rather several ways of writing. In Egypt, and possibly in Israel, it is a way of educating.

We should be prepared for the possibility that to seek a definition of wisdom in terms of distinct origins, forms or concepts, is to pave the way for an artificial idea of wisdom as a single thing with a totally independent identity. But even if we decide that we must think of it as an emphasis or series of emphases, it is proclaimed in the Bible as something worth striving after. I have already noted that wisdom's apparent lack of concern for Israel's history, covenant and law is one of its distinctive features. Perhaps we can work back from the wisdom books to look for clues to the origins of wisdom in Israel. The wisdom literature itself is lacking in the kind of historical references which would give such clues. The books of Proverbs and Ecclesiastes contain only the briefest indications of the traditional patronage of Solomon. Beyond this we must look to the prophetic and narrative literature in the Old Testament for evidences of wisdom in the life of Israel.

We may suggest four kinds of evidence which contribute to our understanding of the history of wisdom in Israel. First, there are the scattered wisdom sayings found in various parts of the narrative literature of the

Old Testament. Some of these are clues to a pre-literary stage which probably existed before there were any movements towards either schools of wisdom or written wisdom. For example, there are some instances of a popular, 'they say', type of wisdom. We all know how a statement like, 'they say it is very good for you', carries the weight of irrefutable wisdom for many, although who 'they' are and what their credentials are is never stated. The biblical examples are not always clear as to their meaning, but they indicate the existence of popular sayings introduced by such a formula as, 'therefore it is said':

> He was a mighty hunter before the Lord; that is why it is said, 'Like Nimrod, a mighty hunter before the Lord'.
>
> (Genesis 10:9)

> So it became a saying: 'Is Saul also among the prophets?'
>
> (1 Samuel 10:12)

> This is why people say, 'Is Saul also among the prophets?'
>
> (1 Samuel 19:24)

> That is why they say, 'The blind and lame will not enter the place'.
>
> (2 Samuel 5:8)

In the case of 1 Samuel 10:12 the word 'saying' translates the Hebrew word *mashal*, which is the word for proverb in the wisdom books. How these sayings functioned is not really explained, but the obscurity of some of them should not discourage us. We can at least see that out of some specific situation there emerged a noteworthy point which commended itself as of value to the understanding of human existence. We need not suppose that the sayings were used merely to recall the original event, but rather that that event invited some kind of comparison with other events.[4]

Other examples of the *mashal* found outside the wisdom books include:

From evildoers come evil deeds. (1 Samuel 24:13)

The days go by and every vision comes to nothing.
(Ezekiel 12:22)[5]

Another wisdom type is the *hidah* or riddle, but there is no uniformity in the way this term is used. In Numbers 12:8 it is the opposite of speaking 'mouth to mouth' (face to face) and may mean an obscure saying. The most elaborate example is Samson's riddle in Judges 14:12–18 which, to say the least, is presented in a rather curious form. Some commentators have even suggested that the text has got mixed up so that Samson gives the answer to which the question must be supplied! In 1 Kings 10 the queen of Sheba comes to test Solomon with 'hard questions'. The word here is again *hidah* but it is not identified with any particular kind or form of saying. There are other texts in which *hidah* is used with the same lack of definition.[6]

The second kind of evidence is in the so-called wisdom books themselves. Because of the absence of historical references in these books which would help us place them within a history of the development of wisdom in Israel, we have to look for other clues. Even the ascriptions to

---

[4] See also Jeremiah 31:29 and Ezekiel 18:2.
[5] See also I Kings 20:11. The word *mashal* is not used here, but it seems to be a known saying which is applied to this situation.
[6] Proverbs 1:6; Psalms 49:4; 78:2; Ezekiel 17:2 (used together with *mashal* followed by a kind of visionary allegory); Daniel 8:23.

Solomon in Proverbs are sufficiently vague for them to have more than one possible meaning.

The third kind of evidence is the relatively recently acquired knowledge of the wisdom literature of Egypt and Babylon. The forms and functions of this wisdom suggest parallels to Israelite wisdom, but often the differences between them are more obvious.

The fourth kind of evidence is the wisdom influences on the non-wisdom books of the Bible, although this description begs the question somewhat. There has been a rash of studies done in recent times in which it is claimed that this or that part of the Old Testament was either written by a wise man or at least greatly influenced by wisdom talk and thought. If we could be sure of the identification of wisdom influences, they would provide some valuable evidence of the place of wisdom in the main stream of Israelite thought. We would see how the wisdom ideas, which in the main wisdom books appear in almost complete isolation from expressions of the covenant faith, have been brought into organic relationship with that covenant faith.

What can we say thus far about an identifiable wisdom movement in Israel? Taking into account what we know of Israelite society, the evidences of early wisdom, the literary forms and content of Israel's wisdom, the wisdom literature of Israel's neighbours and the possible contacts that occurred, we can propose the following situation.[7] Popular folk wisdom would have emerged at various levels of society as the expression of what people learned through their life's experiences. It is not certain what form the earliest wisdom sayings took, but the evidence does not support the idea that the longer sayings developed from the one-line *mashal*. In the patriarchal society during

---

[7] See R.B.Y. Scott, 'The study of the wisdom literature', *Interpretation*, XXIV, 1970, 20–45.

the period before Israel went into Egypt, education in family groups would most likely have led to the formation of sayings used in the training of children. With the development of the organized state of Israel came the recognition of men who could give wise counsel in the matter of running the country. Somewhere along the way the sages or wise men emerged as a recognizable group. It is not clear whether these were recognized as officials of government, religion or education. It has been suggested that the scribes later came to be the guardians of wisdom.

It becomes apparent that although we may be able to identify the distinctive features of wisdom, it is not so clear that it is a single phenomenon. Man is an intellectual being whose search for knowledge and understanding is pursued in various ways. We can use the word wisdom to refer to a type of literature that contains a wide diversity within the group. We can use it to refer to certain kinds of educational activity in home and school. And we can use it for a broadly intellectual activity urged upon all people.[8]

David and the Growth of Wisdom

There is nothing improbable about the role attributed to Solomon as the patron of Israel's wisdom during its heyday. We know the wisdom of Israel's neighbours predates Solomon, and that international contacts were a continuing factor of Israel's history from the beginning. How much Egypt and Babylon may have influenced the formal development of Israel's wisdom is a point of discussion

---

[8] J.L. Crenshaw, 'Method in determining wisdom influences upon "historical" literature', *Journal of Biblical Literature*, 88, 1969, 129–142.

we will have to forego. There is some evidence that David also played a significant part in the wisdom of Israel.

David and Solomon together mark a climax in the development of Israel both from the historical and the theological point of view. It was David who really united the tribes after the abortive rule of Saul. Following the Exodus, Israel had moved through a period of semi-nomadic existence until the conquest of Canaan by Joshua. The conquest and the division of the new territories into tribal lots led to the period of the judges when the tribes were held together in a loose federation. A principal factor binding them together was the covenant and law of Sinai. The judges were 'law men' who, sometimes in spectacular fashion, led a wayward people back to loyalty to Jehovah and his covenant. The desire to change this covenant-based theocracy into a monarchy was at first a sinful expression of a desire to be like the pagan nations. It was a failure of nerve when political stability and national security were seen to be dependent, not upon trust in the God of the covenant, but upon a monarchy with a strong military basis. Eventually it was shown that a monarchy, when it was allowed to express the covenant, was not only permitted by God, but was in fact a divine gift to foreshadow the messianic rule of God's kingdom.

The evidence for David's involvement with wisdom is mainly indirect. In the first instance (2 Samuel 14) a wise woman intervened in a knotty problem involving David's family relationships and their political effects. The wise woman urged David to make a prudent decision with regard to his son Absalom who had committed murder. She flattered David as one who had the wisdom of an angel (v. 20), which is the same as the ability to discern good and evil (v. 17). In 2 Samuel 20 another wise woman was successful in bringing to an end the rebellion of Sheba, son of Bichri, against David. A disastrous schism in

the nation was thus prevented. The wisdom here is not
David's, but it appears that the reign of David was one
during which the 'wise' were emerging as a recognizable
group in Israel.

In the time of Joseph and Moses, the royal court of
Egypt had wise men with specific functions.[9] A preliminary form of statesmanship was exercised by Moses when
he appointed wise men to exercise authority over the
tribes of Israel.[10] In Deuteronomy 4:6 there is an important
connection made between wisdom and obedience to the
law:

> Observe them carefully, for this will show your wisdom and
> understanding to the nations, who will hear about all these
> decrees and say, 'Surely this great nation is a wise and under-
> standing people!'

Joshua is said to have been full of the spirit of wisdom
because Moses laid his hands upon him.[11] This is the most
significant thing that is said at this point about the leadership qualifications of Joshua. This wisdom of Joshua
would include the loyalty to the law that Deuteronomy 4:6
refers to, but it would also involve skills of leadership and
decision making about matters not directly referred to in
the law.

Thus, while wisdom went beyond the specific content of the covenant between God and Israel, it certainly
was seen to include it. Here is the character of God
shown in the way he ordered the existence of his
redeemed people. The wisdom of God sets out the

---

[9] Genesis 41:8,33,39; Exodus 7:11.
[10] Numbers 11:16–17. Here the elders are spoken of as receiving
some of Moses' spirit. In Deuteronomy 1:9–15 they are remembered as wise men.
[11] Deuteronomy 34:9.

response of the people to his redeeming love. Reconciliation to God by grace, and striving to live consistently with this grace are both aspects of wisdom. But the law did not say everything about this response. Within its framework the redeemed Israelite had to express his human responsibility before God by making a multitude of decisions about situations that were not detailed in the law. The laws and statutes could not cover every possible contingency in life. Indeed, had they done so, they would have expressed a radically different view of man from the one they in fact do express.

Having said that, we must try to gain a historical perspective on the way wisdom and law work together. To keep the law was wisdom but the law was not exhaustive. Israel was given guidelines in the law by which to understand and maintain relationships with God, man and the world. But the law was never a substitute for the God-given task of the quest for knowledge. The humanness of God's people meant much more than doing those things that were specifically stated in the law. The law did not tell Israel how to develop the arts, but it did put a significant limit to artistic endeavour:

> You shall not make yourself an idol in the form of anything in heaven above or on the earth beneath or in the waters below.
>
> (Exodus 20:4)

The law did not tell Israel how to pursue the science of animal husbandry for the provision of food, but it did clearly prescribe what animals could be used for food and what ones could not:

> You may eat any animal that has a split hoof completely divided and that chews the cud.　　　(Leviticus 11:3)

The law thus gave specific directions and established certain bounds, but it never interfered with the pursuit of knowledge or the task of establishing man's dominion over the world.

Another aspect of the relationship of law to wisdom is that during the period from Abraham to David, God revealed the meaning of the covenant primarily through redemption and law. First there was the promise to Abraham that God would be the God of his descendants and give them the land of Canaan. Then came the redemption event of the Exodus from Egypt and from domination by a foreign king. The law or covenant of Sinai was given to bind Israel to the God who had saved her. What was begun in the Exodus was continued in the conquest of Canaan by Joshua, and in the establishment of an Israelite state. But this saving history was not really finished until Israel was established as a unified nation, free from foreign threats, and constituted as a people under the covenant with God's rule represented by the monarchy. This took place for the first time under David's rule.

One of the chief lessons of the Exodus is that salvation means freedom from alien restraints; freedom to be what God intends us to be. This is the freedom to be truly human. The meaning of this freedom is revealed to us in the nature of the kingdom into which God's grace brings us through redemption. For Israel the pattern of this process of full salvation leading to the kingdom was not completed until the reigns of David and Solomon.

There are some important New Testament principles foreshadowed here. Not only is Christ the summit of wisdom, as we have seen, but he is also our freedom. Only the Son can set us free (John 8:36). Freedom and wisdom are complementary sides to being truly human as God created us. We cannot attain to either freedom or wisdom until we are united to Christ, for to be outside of Christ is to be in bondage to death and to futility of mind. Further-more, the law was given to tutor Israel until Christ came. Once Christ came, the people of God were freed from the law (Galatians 3:23–29).

The rule of Christ in his kingdom is especially prefig-ured in Israel's history by the reign of David. This is the cli-max of saving history as it is foreshadowed in Israel. The law could not pass from Israel when David ruled because Christ was yet to be revealed. But at least the freedom of Christ's kingdom was for a while foreshadowed with David and Solomon, and in like manner the wisdom of Christ's kingdom was foreshadowed. It is to be expected that once the process of salvation history in Israel reaches this critical point, the stage would be set for a flowering wisdom. The tutelage of the law loses its absolute status because the kingdom means the freedom to live wisely and responsibly.[12]

Thus wisdom grew from Israel's beginnings, but dur-ing the formative period of salvation history it was not prominent in the life of Israel. The structures of covenant and law governed the actions of the people of God much more clearly that wisdom. There are two stages by which the law lost its tutor or 'baby-sitter' status. The first took place when there was a complete model of the kingdom set up in the historical experience of Israel. This occurred with David and Solomon.[13] God wants his people to live, not by a lot of rules and regulations, but responsibly and in a manner which harmonizes with his kingly rule. The

---

[12] This concept of Israel coming of age is argued by Walter Brueggemann, *In Man We Trust* (Atlanta: John Knox Press, 1972), Ch. 2.

[13] I have discussed this revelation of the kingdom of God in the Old Testament in *Gospel and Kingdom* (Exeter: Paternoster Press, 1981).

revelation of the kingdom is not finalized with David, and so the law retains its 'baby-sitter' status for Israel, while wisdom emerges as a new dimension stressing the importance of living responsibly. Thus, with the coming of Christ we have revealed the solid reality of which David's kingdom was only the shadow. The role of the law is now taken over by Christ in the gospel. But in the Old Testament the structures of covenant and law govern the actions of the people of God much more clearly than wisdom. According to the historical narratives, direct words from the Lord guide Israel on the path of redemption, and this is the preoccupation of the narrators.

Even in the period of the judges, the first faltering years of Israel's life as a settled people, direct words from God and endowments of his Spirit guide the judges in the special task of nurturing the infant state. Gideon shows us an example of anti-wisdom or folly in his refusal to act on a direct word of God (Judges 6). His request for a sign and the putting out of the fleece show a perilous lack of faith in the prophetic word about the saving acts of God (vv. 7–10). That God granted Gideon his sign is evidence only of grace and not of the rightness of Gideon's request. Curiously this passage is frequently taken as a pattern for Christians seeking guidance, but this can be done only by ignoring its real meaning in the context of Israel's saving history.

So we come to David. The changes he effected in the structures of the nation's life, no matter how imperfectly they were made, reflect a profound theological shift in the significance of Israel's history. From a wandering people under the promise made to Abraham, Israel moved to become a settled people enjoying a measure of the fulfilment of the promise. David centralized the government in the city that he himself had captured from its Canaanite owners. He established a royal court and standing army.

Most significantly, he made Jerusalem the focal point for Israel's religious life by bringing the ark of the covenant to a permanent resting place there. For the first time in her history Israel actually came to possess, through David's military conquests, territory which corresponded to that which God has promised to Abraham.

If David is not portrayed as the wise man that Solomon is, he is shown to be the one who made Solomon's leadership of the wisdom movement possible. David set the stage for the flowering of wisdom just as he set the stage for the building of the temple. And David's son becomes the firstborn of a new era. He is the master of the new freedom of God's kingdom, he is the builder of God's house and the pioneer of a new age of wisdom. He is God's son, a prefigurement of the Son who is to come (2 Samuel 7:14).

It is with David that we find a lessening of emphasis on direct divine guidance. The counsellor emerges as someone with experience and astute judgment in matters of state.[14] Such was Ahitophel to David. There is no doubt as to Ahitophel's ability as a counsellor, for his advice was 'like that of one who enquires of God' (2 Samuel 16:23). But when Ahitophel sided with Absalom's rebellion, David prayed that God would turn his counsel into foolishness (2 Samuel 15:31). This prayer was answered indirectly, for Ahitophel gave Absalom the right advice. Absalom was the fool for heeding the false advice of David's friend Hushai who pretended to give better counsel than Ahitophel had done (2 Samuel 17:1–14).

There has been much scholarly discussion about the wisdom characteristics of the narrative in 2 Samuel 9–20 and 1 Kings 1–2.[15] This so-called 'succession narrative'

---

[14] William McKane, *Prophets and Wise Men* (London: SCM Press, 1965).

[15] E.g. R.N. Whybray, *The Succession Narrative* (London: SCM Press, 1968) and Walter Brueggemann, *op. cit.*, pp. 29–33.

may not be the work of a wisdom writer as many claim it is, but it does betray a new emphasis on statesmanship, counsel, sagacity and astuteness.[16] As Adam was entrusted with the world, so Israel 'come of age' is entrusted with the kingdom. Time would tell how well true wisdom was being learned.

Questions for Study

1. Read Genesis 1:26–28. What does this tell us about the ground-rules for Adam's search for knowledge?
2. What did God do for Israel in order to re-establish these ground-rules?
3. What are the main sources of information on the growth of wisdom in Israel?
4. What characteristics of Israel under David's reign fostered the development of the wisdom movement?

---

[16] Psalm 78 may be added to the evidence of David's involvement in the wisdom tradition. This is discussed in chapter 9.

Chapter Five

Solomon in All His Glory

Summary

The biblical evidence supports the view that Solomon, despite his failings, was a key figure in the development of wisdom in Israel. God's gift of wisdom resulted in many expressions of human wisdom: 1. Solomon's wisdom had, within a restricted framework, common ground with foreign wisdom but at the same time was superior to it. 2. Solomon was capable of making shrewd judgments in difficult situations. 3. He had a concern to understand the natural world. 4. The material glory of Solomon's kingdom was related to wisdom. 5. The temple was the means by which the Israelite could make sense of the universe because it represented the activity of God in restoring all things to right relationships with himself. 6. The focal point of wisdom was the fear of the Lord, which meant faith in the redeeming acts of God. The temple and the fear of the Lord are closely related, and they give Israelite wisdom its distinctive trait. This is how the human pursuit of wisdom is tied to the saving work of God.

The Dark Side of Glory

Solomon 'in all his glory' became a byword for the splendour that once had been in Israel. Jesus' comparison of this glory with the lilies of the field reminds us that it was quite literally a visual and material splendour (Matthew 6:29). There is nothing unspiritual about a beauty that is outward and physical. In Solomon's case it was closely related to his wisdom. But Solomon is a puzzle, a contradiction. It seems as if there were two sides to this complex man which the narrative writer neither reconciles, nor appears concerned to reconcile. No sooner was Solomon established as king than he made a marriage alliance with Egypt. In I Kings 3:1–2 the matter is noted almost neutrally even though it was a serious breach of the law. It is also mentioned without comment that, because there was as yet no temple built, sacrifices were made at high places. The connection of these high places with former Canaanite places of worship is quite probable, but the narrator does not refer to the danger of mixing pagan elements with the worship of God.

It is not until I Kings 11 that a negative assessment is placed upon Solomon's foreign alliances. The law against marrying foreigners is quite clear (Exodus 34:11–16 and Deuteronomy 7:1–4), but our narrator chose not to mention the fact until after he had told us all about Solomon's good points. The only excuse offered is that the king was led astray in his old age by pagan wives (v. 4). This passage presents a very dark side to Solomon's glory. His wives 'turned his heart after other gods, and his heart was not fully devoted to the Lord' (v. 4). He did not follow the Lord as David had done (v. 6). He built places of worship for pagan gods (vv. 7–8). God became very angry with Solomon (v. 9) because he had broken the covenant (v.11). In this way the narrator prepares us for the hitherto unthinkable: the division and final destruction of the kingdom.

If Solomon was the exemplary wise man that I Kings 3–10 seems to make him out to have been, then there is a warning in all this for us. Even a great wise man can fall, and the seeds of his destruction may be very close to those regions where wisdom means responsibility and risk. The signs of Solomon's deterioration were there not only in foreign alliances, but also in the raising of forced labour levies (I Kings 5:13), and in the warnings against turning from the Lord lest Israel become a 'proverb and a byword' among the nations (I Kings 9:7 RSV). This would be a reversal of God's intention that the nations should recognize wisdom in Israel because of the covenant (Deuteronomy 4:6). Even pagans will have the wisdom to see that it is the height of folly to forsake a God who has proved his greatness in the way he has led and saved his people.(v. 9)

Solomon's Wisdom

Solomon's prayer showed genuine humility for he knew that he was not equal to the task of ruling Israel: 'I am only a little child and do not know how to carry out my duties. So give your servant a discerning heart to govern your people and to distinguish between right and wrong' (I Kings 3;7,9). This unselfish request was rewarded with the addition of riches and honour to the list of God's gifts. Very soon the gift of a discerning mind was put to the test (I Kings 3:16–28). Two harlots both claimed to be the mother of one little baby. How does one discern the good from the evil, the truthful mother from the lying, would-be baby snatcher? Solomon, by suggesting a 'just' decision – dividing the baby in half – forced the truth into the open. Mother-love was prepared to sacrifice all claims so that the child may live. A simple, direct and uncomplicated piece of applied psychology illustrates the wisdom of a true statesman. All Israel stood in awe of this decision because they perceived that God had indeed given Solomon wisdom to administer justice (v. 28).

The narrative moves on to tell of Solomon's court, his administration and the beneficial effects of these for the people (I Kings 4:1–28). This section is sandwiched between two important statements about Solomon's wisdom, and is clearly intended to indicate some of the benefits of wisdom. There is also an obvious reference to the promises made to Abraham (I Kings 4:20–21, compare Genesis 15:18–21; 22:17) so that their fulfilment is identified with Solomon's reign. Another remarkable passage (I Kings 4:22–28) describes the food provisions for the court and the size of the horse-guards regiment. In the midst of this is the statement that during Solomon's life the nation lived in safety, 'each man under his vine and fig tree' (v. 25). This phrase so adequately sums up life in the kingdom of God that we find it used later by a prophet to describe the future bliss of the kingdom (Micah 4:4).

The connection between the riches of Solomon's kingdom and the gift of wisdom is seen also in the visit of the queen of Sheba (I Kings 10). Notice the curious mixture in the description in verses 1–5. The queen had heard of Solomon's fame concerning the name of the Lord, and she came to test him with hard questions or riddles (Hebrew: *hidot*). Solomon was obviously an expert in the kind of wisdom known to this pagan queen and he answered all her questions. His wisdom and his material wealth together left the queen quite overwhelmed (v. 5). Again in verse 7 wisdom and prosperity are linked. The queen once more expressed admiration for Solomon's God who had so blessed him. Then the two monarchs exchanged expensive gifts. The narrative proceeds to describe further the opulent riches in Solomon's possession. 'Thus Solomon excelled all the kings of the earth in riches and in wisdom' (v. 23). And when the great ones from all over the world came to hear Solomon's God-given wisdom, they brought more expensive gifts to him.

How may we assess this materialistic side of wisdom? First, the material side of life is never down-graded in the Bible. God made matter good, and he has redeemed the material world through the incarnation, death and bodily resurrection of Christ. Secondly, the promises of the covenant were material as well as spiritual, so that the growing expectation of the kingdom included material prosperity. Thirdly, wisdom maintains this perspective of the goodness of creation so that prosperity is often a sign of wisdom. None of this means that prosperity always indicates wisdom or virtue, nor that poverty is necessarily blameworthy or the sign of a lack of wisdom. It may be that in the light of this evidence we need to redefine what we mean by the word 'spiritual'. It is not the opposite of 'material' as if matter were inherently unspiritual or evil. Rather it has to do with being rightly related to God.

There are some other aspects of Solomon's wisdom yet to be considered. In I Kings 4:29–34 it is compared with that of all the wise men of the nations surrounding Israel, including Egypt. This passage, along with I Kings 10, suggests that the comparison is not of the same order as Paul's contrast in I Corinthians 1–2. Solomon's wisdom is not opposed to the wisdom of these sages, but it is greater than their's. They recognized Solomon's wisdom and they flocked to hear him. Paul's discussion is at a different level. He speaks of the antithesis between the understandings of ultimate reality which are held by the Christian and the unbeliever. He would not argue with our narrator in I Kings who is discussing wisdom at the practical level of life's experiences. But, of course, Solomon outdid these men because his wisdom came as a gift of the one true God who is the source of wisdom.

What, then, could a covenanted Israelite and a pagan discuss that could be called wisdom and about which they could have some agreement? Perhaps there is a clue in I Kings 4:32–33. As well as the prolific literary activity of Solomon, there is noted his intense interest in nature, in trees, animals and fish. This seems somewhat removed from the matters of state and the discernment of good and evil that Solomon was concerned about in his request for wisdom. However, this is not the case, for we discover that human society and nature are not separable into unrelated worlds. Man and beast were created to inhabit the world, and to live according to relationships established by God. In a sinful world these relationships between humans, animals and the natural world are clouded and confused, but they are not completely obliterated. Wisdom discerns many things about the world of nature which can instruct us for life. Western man with his concrete forests, his mani-cured lawns and clinical gardens, tends to forget how dependent he is upon the natural environment. Solo-mon has much to say to modern man about the meaning of dominion over nature.

The Temple and the Fear of the Lord

The narrative in I Kings leaves us in little doubt that Sol-omon's building of the temple was a very significant demonstration of wisdom. It is seen also as the high point of the historical expression of the covenant prom-ises to Israel. God willed to be God to Abraham and to his descendants (Genesis 17:7), not as a remote, imper-sonal deity, but as the Lord of heaven and earth dwell-ing in the midst of his people (Exodus 25:8). The tabernacle, and after it the temple, would become for Israel the centre of the universe. The Israelite knew that God could not be contained in this box, as the Lord said:

Heaven is my throne
and the earth is my footstool;
what is the house which you would build for me,
     and what is the place of my rest? (Isaiah 66:1 RSV)[1]

But the temple was the place which was to symbolize for
Israel reconciliation, meeting and fellowship with God. In
that significant way the temple was the means by which
the Israelite made sense of the universe. If Israel's God is
truly the Creator, the Lord of heaven and earth, then the
way he reveals truth to be is the way it really is. Of course,
the revelation of God was incomplete until Jesus Christ,
but incompleteness does not mean that it is not true. What
God revealed to Israel was the only truth by which sinful
man could interpret reality, not fully, but certainly truly.

When Solomon had built the temple he held a great
dedication service which is recorded in I Kings 8 and 2
Chronicles 6. The ark of the covenant was installed in
the inner sanctuary of the temple, the holy of holies.
Then Solomon stood before the altar and prayed. As he
did so, he recounted the promises made to David his
father that his descendants would reign and God dwell
among his people forever. These promises were conditional upon faithful obedience of the king and his
people. Sin would have to be repented of and acknowledged before God. What Solomon describes in his
prayer are the processes of mercy and forgiveness that
were already well established in Israel under the covenant of Sinai. What is new here is the sense of having
arrived at a high point. No longer are they pressing on
towards the promised land or towards a stable theocratic state. They have concrete evidence that the
promises of the covenant are in a real sense fulfilled.

---

[1] See also I Kings 8:27–29,39, 42–43.

Now the benefits of grace will overflow. When Israel recognizes the significance of the temple as the place where reconciliation and restoration to God can occur, it will be a people that fears God and enjoys the blessings of the covenant (I Kings 8:38–40). This great benefit will become known among the nations. Strangers will come to the temple and acknowledge God. Solomon prays that God will hear them from heaven and answer graciously so that all the nations of the earth may know his name and fear him (I Kings 8:41–43). The coming of the queen of Sheba was the first sign of this prayer being answered.

A couple of centuries later the prophets Isaiah and Micah were to repeat this hope that the temple of God would bring people from all the nations to acknowledge God. But for them it lay away in the future when God would act again to restore Israel from its troubled history of rebellion and covenant breaking. In these end-time days God would reestablish Zion, the mountain of the house of the Lord, and all the nations would come to the temple and learn God's ways (Isaiah 2:2–4, Micah 4:1–4). It is in this temple passage that Micah recalls Solomon's days when he looks towards the bliss of every man under his vine and under his fig tree.

But what is this 'fear of the Lord' that Solomon refers to in his prayer of dedication? It is clear from the biblical passages that fear in these contexts does not mean terror.[2] Rather there is a note of reverent awe. The biblical writers saw no contradiction between the fear of the Lord and the comfortable word 'fear not' which reassures the faithful that God forgives and protects his people.[3] There is some evidence that slightly different forms of the phrase 'fear of

---

[2] There is a consistent use of the Hebrew word for the fear of the Lord (*yr'*) which is different from the word for terror (*phd*).

[3] E.g. Isaiah 43:1,5; 44:2,8.

the Lord' indicate different origins and emphases.[4] In the period of the Exodus to Solomon it is faithfulness to the covenant that is in view. But we must never lose the sense of awe at the greatness of God who reveals himself in his marvellous works:

> And when the Israelites saw the great power the Lord displayed against the Egyptians, the people feared the Lord and put their trust in him and in Moses his servant.
>
> (Exodus 14:31)

God showed his love for Israel in a demonstration of terrible power as he saved his people from Egypt. Fear and trust are the response to this saving act. On the one hand there was the recognition of grace, love and covenant faithfulness, and on the other hand there was a clear perception of God's holy anger against godless resistance to his will.

After forty years in the wilderness Moses recalled for Israel what God had spoken to him at Sinai:

> Gather the people to me, that I may let them hear my words, so that they may learn to fear me all the days that they live upon the earth. (Deuteronomy 4:10 RSV)

This fear of the Lord was to be expressed in their diligence to observe the laws of God in faithful response to his saving acts:

> So that you, your children and their children after them may fear the Lord your God as long as you live by keeping all his decrees and commandments that I give you.
>
> (Deuteronomy 6:2)

---

[4] Joachim Becker, *Gottesfurcht im Alten Testament* (Rome: Pontifical Biblical Institute, 1965).

> And now, O Israel, what does the Lord your God ask of you
> but to fear the Lord your God, to walk in all his ways, to love
> him, to serve the Lord your God with all your heart and with
> all your soul?   (Deuteronomy 10:12)

> Fear the Lord your God and serve him. He is your praise; he
> is your God, who performed for you those great and awe-
> some wonders you saw with your own eyes.
>   (Deuteronomy 10:20a, 21)[5]

This concept of fear as reverence for God and his covenant
means trust and obedience towards the one who has
shown his faithfulness to his chosen people. It is inseparable from the revelation of God in his word and saving acts.
And therein, too, lies the significance of the name of God
as the Lord (Hebrew: *YHVH*, from which is derived the
name Jehovah).[6] The Lord (YHVH) is the name of the God
who has revealed his character in the covenant and in the
saving acts of the Exodus.[7] As God deals with his people
and speaks to them his name YHVH takes on deeper
meaning.

   The phrase 'the fear of the Lord' is frequently found in
the wisdom literature:[8]

---

[5] See also Deuteronomy 6:13,24; 8:6; 31:12–13.

[6] English translations of *LORD* for the Hebrew *YHVH* follow
the Jewish tradition of substituting the Hebrew word for 'my
Lord' whenever the holy and unpronounceable name YHVH
occurred.

[7] Alan Cole, *Exodus*, Tyndale Old Testament Commentaries
(London: Tyndale Press, 1973), pp. 20–22.

[8] The phrase 'the fear of the Lord', in which 'fear' is a noun in
construct, is predominantly found in the wisdom literature and
the Psalms. The use of verbal forms is found mainly in the non-
wisdom literature. See Becker, op. cit.

The fear of the Lord is the beginning of knowledge.

(Proverbs 1:7)

The fear of the Lord is the beginning of wisdom.

(Proverbs 9:10, Psalm 111:10)

The fear of the Lord is instruction in wisdom.

(Proverbs 15:33 RSV)

The fear of the Lord – that is wisdom.   (Job 28:28)

In Proverbs 2:4–6 the wise man says of wisdom and understanding:

And if you look for it as for silver and search for it as for hidden treasure, then you will understand the fear of the Lord and find the knowledge of God. For the Lord gives wisdom, and from his mouth come knowledge and understanding.

There are many more 'fear of the Lord' sayings in the wisdom books, especially Proverbs.[9] The fear of the Lord is said to be hatred of evil, a foundation of life and a refuge. The question is whether the wisdom writers understood the idea in covenantal terms. I suggest that it cannot be other wise. These were Israelites and, although salvation history is not a theme of their writings, they were not unbelieving philosophers professing a humanistic alternative to the covenant faith. They were men of God who reached out beyond the specific content of God's revelation and engaged in the search for knowledge and understanding of the world in the light of revelation.

---

[9] Proverbs 1:29; 8:13; 10:27; 14:26–27; 15:16; 16:6; 19:23; 22:4; 23:17. The verbal form is found in Proverbs 3:7, 24:21.

How then did they understand the 'fear of the Lord' and its relation to their quest for wisdom? It seems reasonable to suggest that the fear of the Lord in Proverbs 1:7 is the climax to the prologue which introduces the complete collection that some editor has put together. Even if this were not so, there are enough reminders of the fear of the Lord scattered throughout the book to indicate the importance of the idea. The evidence, in my opinion, is that the absolute necessity of God's revelation for right understanding of the world was constantly recognized.

You will notice that the relationship seems to be double-ended. The fear of the Lord as the beginning of wisdom indicates that it is the point of departure. One must begin with the new mind-set given to us by God's revelation of himself in word and saving acts. Only this perspective will enable us to know the world as it really is. But then we see that the search for wisdom is to understand the fear of the Lord (Proverbs 2:5). In this case wisdom has the fear of the Lord as its goal or point of arrival. Perhaps this double-ended relationship can be seen in a comparison of Proverbs 9:10 and Psalm 111:10. Both are usually translated as 'the fear of the Lord is the beginning of wisdom', but different Hebrew words for 'beginning' are used. In the former the word is *tehilah* which properly means the starting point. In the latter the word is *reshit* which derives from the word for head. This word is certainly used for beginning in Genesis 1:1, but it can also mean goal or chief principle.[10] If this suggestion carries any weight it means that the fear of the

---

[10] E.A. Leslie, *The Psalms* (New York: Abingdon Press, 1949), p. 52, translates Psalm 111:10 as: 'The goal of wisdom is the fear of the Lord'. Artur Weiser, *The Psalms* (London: SCM Press, 1962) disagrees, as does H.-J. Kraus, *Psalmen* (Neukirchen: Neukirchener Verlag des Erziehungsvereins, 1966).

Lord is both the presupposition or foundation, and the goal of wisdom.

We conclude that both the wisdom use of the 'fear of the Lord' phrases, and the traditions concerning Solomon as temple builder and sage, point to an important connection between the Israelite concept of wisdom and the covenant faith. This accounts for the truly distinct features of Israel's wisdom which, while it shared many of the characteristics of the wisdom of the ancient middle eastern world, never lost sight of the revelation of the one true God, Creator of heaven and earth.

That the saving acts of God should be related to human endeavour in the realm of the natural sciences, human behaviour, ethics, environmental care and social relationships ought to be no surprise. It comes as a salutary warning to modern Christians who frequently repeat the error of some early Christians in succumbing to a pagan view of the world. How little we have cared about the meaning of the gospel for our bodies, our physical world, our social relationships and political concerns. Perhaps we have been alarmed by the case of Solomon's apostasy. Was it that his relationship to the world became one in which all his past gains in wisdom were eroded as he lost sight of the fear of the Lord?

Whether we like it or not, wisdom tells us that there is a sense of risk to life. We should not be as the Israelites who grumbled about their new-found freedom, preferring instead to return to the safety of slavery in Egypt. Israel's liberation was not completed when the waters closed over the armies of Pharaoh. Not until David and Solomon did the drama of salvation history come to describe the whole process of redemption into freedom to serve the living God. But freedom entails risk in the sense that we face the uncertainty of all the unchartered areas waiting to be explored.

The fear of the Lord tells us that the risk of freedom in this sinful world is not fatal for the child of God. If Solomon lost sight of his covenantal bearings and began to conform to the standards of the world in statesmanship, religion and wisdom, there is no hint that he fell totally from grace. God does not ask us to go out into the world and risk losing our way. Indeed, he has provided the means whereby we know that we will without fail arrive at the goal. But he does not allow us to opt out of being responsibly human; of using the brains he has given us to interpret the world in the light of the gospel. The fear of the Lord is both starting point and the goal of wisdom, and in Christian terms this means living by trust in Jesus Christ, the author and perfector of our faith, the Alpha and Omega.

Questions for Study

1. Read 1 Kings 3:5–14 and 4:1–34 and list all the aspects of Solomon's life and reign that reflect the gift of wisdom.
2. How could Solomon discuss matters of wisdom with pagans or have his wisdom compared with theirs? What dangers were there in this interaction with worldly wisdom?
3. What did the fear of the Lord mean for Israelites, and how did it tie wisdom to the covenant?
4. How does a Christian fear the Lord, and how does this constitute the beginning of wisdom for us?

Chapter Six

Proverbs and the Perception of Order

Summary

The appeal of Proverbs lies in its practical concerns and its apparently direct applicability to our lives. But there is a problem of how to apply it, and with what authority. The parallel forms in Egyptian wisdom, with their concern for Ma'at or order, suggest that order may be the universal concern of wisdom. The content of Israel's wisdom supports this. Of course, Israel's wisdom differs, to a significant degree, from the pagan concept. The concern for practical life and nature, and the absence of references to salvation in history, suggest that a theology of creation underlies Proverbs and wisdom in general. Two inseparable but distinct characteristics of wisdom are to be seen: it is both the gift of God and a responsible task for us. The gift comes not merely as an implanted ability present in some people, but objectively as the self-revelation of God's wisdom, to which the Israelite responded with 'the fear of the Lord'. Our task involves a response to this gracious revelation, and our use of the gift in order to pursue the knowledge of order in the universe. Proverbial wisdom is an expression of this affirmation of humanity.

The Appeal of Proverbs

The book of Proverbs has a distinct appeal to Christians which many other books of the Old Testament do not have. This is partly due to its total lack of reference to Israel's history which would tend to tie it to events of Israel's experience. It is also lacking in any specific reference to the seemingly irrelevant, if not boring, legal material of the law of Moses. Christians have little problem with relating to the moral content of the law, but rules of cultic practice and of Israel's social structures seem remote and unrelated to our lives. For this reason Proverbs has the immediate appeal of dealing with life in terms that are often apparently unaffected by the gap in time and culture that separates us from ancient Israel. Because it looks at life without reference to the organized religion of Israel, and with a minimum of historical detail, Proverbs allows the modern Christian to feel that he can penetrate more directly to the essential meaning.

It is the thoroughly practical nature of Proverbs that appeals. Because we can identify with the more ethical tone of the material in an immediate way we do not feel the burden of translating the unique experiences of Israel, or its now defunct laws, into something which applies to us. The practical appeal is enhanced by the very form of the various parts of the book. Popular wisdom is characteristically framed in an eye-catching, attention-getting, even foot-tapping way to make it memorable. It avoids long and involved theoretical or philosophical discussions. Few of the literary units in Proverbs are more than several verses in length. Most are pithy two-liners, and some of these are possibly expansions of original one-line proverbs.

Proverbs appeals because it almost seems to invite us to

use it as a lucky-dip. Each of the literary units, whether of the longer instructions (Proverbs 1–9), or of the shorter proverbial sentences (Proverbs 10–22), can stand independently of the others. We do not need to consider some specific Israelite context or some overall development within the book in order to understand any particular saying. Of course the whole book helps us to understand individual parts, but not because they are arranged in any given order.

A word of warning! The appeal of the simple, practical nature of Proverbs may be deceptive. We may in fact find that we have been looking at it in a manner that ignores the characteristics of wisdom thought and writing. Let me illustrate. In my childhood I used to enjoy reading a weekly magazine which contained a certain comic strip. This concerned an unfortunate academic named Bookworm Basil who walked around reading books of great learning. He would read some jewel of wisdom and then test it out. But it always seemed to backfire on him. In the one example that I can still recall, Basil reads 'Still waters run deep', just as he comes upon a swiftly running stream. Reasoning that if still waters are deep then swift waters must be shallow, he steps into the stream to cross it and disappears from sight beneath the water. The author of this comic strip may or may not have perceived it, but in fact he was pointing to a characteristic of proverbial wisdom which is deceptive. The proverb contains wisdom distilled from one or a number of actual experiences, but the way it is constructed may give it the appearance of being a general law of nature or rule of life. Ironically it is this apparent generality which appeals to us, and yet the proverbial form was never intended to function in this way.

The Problem of Proverbs

The book of Proverbs is a collection of Israelite wisdom sayings of various kinds put together with little obvious order. Such collections, particularly when many of the individual parts are no more than single sentences, present special problems of how to read and understand them. If it is true that proverbial sayings are based largely on human experience, what kind of authority do they have for us? Wisdom does not come to us as revealed legal statutes or with the prophetic 'thus says the Lord'. Some wisdom sayings are overtly theological and even claim to be wisdom from God (e.g., Proverbs 8), but other wisdom sayings are simply human observations or experience.[1] Add to this the evidence for the non-Israelite origins of some biblical wisdom and we have what seems to be a real difficulty. It may be that a rigid view of inspiration applied to Scripture creates the problem for us. We need to remember that how inspiration takes place is not the most important thing. What we mean by the doctrine is that any part of Scripture says what God wants it to say. We are concerned to understand how the literature in question functions as the word of God to us. Once we realize that apart from certain reported dreams and trances, there is no indication whatsoever that the biblical authors underwent a suspension of their human faculties while producing holy Scripture, the problem is lessened somewhat. The empirical wisdom of recorded human experience is not

---

[1] R.E. Murphy, 'The kerygma of the Book of Proverbs', *Interpretation*, XX, 1966, 3–14, examines the kerygmatic or 'gospel-proclaiming' aspect of wisdom as it offers life to those who will receive it. J.W. Montgomery, 'Wisdom as gift', *Interpretation*, XVI, 1962, 43–57, proposes that certain parts of the wisdom literature express a view of grace that contributes to the biblical idea of the messiah.

really so different from a prophetic oracle, except that it lacked the prophet's consciousness that God was speaking through the author.

How are the various kinds of wisdom material meant to function; how do they instruct us? One single answer cannot be given because there is a variety of wisdom forms. The one-sentence proverbs present their own peculiar problem because they are not laws given by direct revelation from God but rather are human observations from life's experiences. Furthermore, the original context is not contained in the proverb and it has the deceptive appearance of a general rule. Therefore we must be careful not to use the proverbs as ready-made rules for living. I suspect, however, that many Christians approach them as if they were a detailing of the ethical content of the ten commandments. This is an understandable situation because alternative ways of looking at wisdom do not lie close to the manner in which twentieth-century westerners think. Perhaps we can begin to modify our thinking by considering the possibility that proverbs function not so much to give us a multitude of individual directions for right living, as to show us the way we go about learning wisdom. Wisdom is presented as both a human task and a divine gift, a combination which always causes a few hiccups in our thinking.[2]

The Forms of Proverbs

It is easy to see from the book itself that some nine distinct collections go to make up Proverbs. There is no logical or

---

[2] L.E. Toombs, 'Old Testament theology and the wisdom literature', *Journal of Bible and Religion*, XXIII, 1955, 193–6, suggests that the theological meaning of wisdom is found in the process by which wisdom comes to man.

historical order to the way they are put together, and there is little evidence of editorial activity to produce the finished work. Some attempt has been made to gather together units of a similar kind, but this is not sustained. Within the two main sections of proverbial sentences there are indications of organization according to content, but this also is not sustained. The main sections of the book are:

1. Prologue (1:1–7).
2. Instructional sayings (1:8–9:18).
3. The proverbs of Solomon (10:1–22:16).
4. Instructional sayings (22:17–24:22).
5. The sayings of the wise (24:23–34).
6. The proverbs of Solomon copied by Hezekiah's men (25:1–29:27).
7. The words of Agur (30:1–33).
8. The words of Lemuel (31:1–9).
9. The virtues of the good wife (31:10–31).

The prologue is almost certainly an editorial note covering the whole of the book and setting out its purpose and basic presupposition. It highlights the distinctive concern of wisdom in the area of our pursuit of knowledge and understanding. Reference is made to some of the popular forms of wisdom such as the proverb, the figure and the riddle.[3] Lest wisdom be reduced to a purely intellectual concern the prologue points out two vital factors. First, wisdom concerns the young and the simple as much as it does any others, and thus is not to be confused with a high I.Q. Secondly, it is synonymous with knowledge, and begins with the fear of the Lord.

---

[3] Respectively in Hebrew *mashal*, *melitzah*, and *hidah*. Unfortunately none of these words is used with enough consistency for us to be able to identify them with any fixed form.

In Christians terms that means that wisdom begins with repentance and faith.[4]

When we speak of the forms of the various literary units we are referring to how they are put together as well as to the kind of content that is typical to each. The forms are not of purely academic interest because a form will be chosen for its appropriateness in the performance of a special function. Without involving ourselves too deeply we can easily see the principles at work in the two main forms in the Book of Proverbs. These are the instruction and the proverbial sentence. The former is well represented in Proverbs 1–9 and 22:17–24:22. It was at one time suggested that the longer instructions represent a development of the early folk wisdom form of proverbial sentence. But this has been shown to be lacking in evidence.[5] Studies in Egyptian wisdom have shown close parallels to the Israelite instruction which are early and quite independent of the sentence wisdom.

The Instruction

The instruction has all the appearance of coming from a school situation, although it may have had its place in the home also. The teacher addresses his pupil, or perhaps a father his son, and guides him in specific areas of life or in general concepts of wisdom. There is a typical form of the instruction involving the use of a command (imperative)

---

[4] See Acts 9:31; 2 Corinthians 7:1; Philippians 2:12; Colossians 3:22; 1 Peter 3:15; Revelation 19:5.

[5] R.N. Whybray, *Wisdom in Proverbs* (London: SCM Press 1965), has proposed that the instructions originated in Egypt and were extended to their present form in order to adapt the originals to an Israelite way of thinking, particularly about God. A detailed discussion is given in William McKane *Proverbs*. McKane rejects the theory of development from oneliners.

supported by motive and consequence clauses, and frequently introduced by an address:

address	My son,
imperative	do not forget my teaching, but keep my commands in your heart,
motive	for they will prolong your life many years and bring you prosperity
imperative	Let love and faithfulness never leave you; bind them around your neck, write them on the tablet of your heart.
consequence	Then you will win favour and a good name in the sight of God and man.

(Proverbs 3:1–4)[6]

Sometimes the wise man praises wisdom, using the phrase 'happy is the man . . .'[7] This phrase is not confined to wisdom books as we see from Psalm 32, but it does come into the wisdom vocabulary in a way that suggests a hymn of praise to wisdom. In Proverbs 8:32–36 a combination of instruction and the 'happy is' pronouncement is appropriately placed as the conclusion of a long poem in which wisdom is personified as a wisdom teacher.

This speaking of wisdom as if it were a person in Proverbs 8 is a departure from the more standard instructions, but some features are retained. Wisdom herself summons

---

[6] The instruction form is seen also in: 1:8–19; 2:1–22; 3:1–12, 21–35; 4:1–9, 10–27; 5:1–23; 6:1–5, 20–35; 7:1–27.

[7] Hebrew: *'ashre*. Perhaps 'blessed' is a better translation since it refers to the ultimate good of man and not to a mere emotion. There is a similarity here to certain psalms also using the word *'ashre*, e.g. Psalm 1 which is generally numbered among the wisdom psalms.

men to be instructed. There is no evidence that the Israelites ever thought of wisdom as the Egyptians thought of their semi divine *Ma'at*. Personification in Proverbs 8 is almost certainly a poetic way of highlighting the important characteristics of wisdom as being both a gift of God and an activity of man. This passage has affinities with the poems in Job 28 and ben Sirach 24;[8] all are concerned with the place of wisdom in creation.[9] These are important passages for showing us how some wisdom writers came to think of the theological meaning of wisdom. They saw the universe as a wonderful creation in which each part was made to be in harmony with the whole. This orderliness of creation is the expression of God's wisdom.

While we must be careful not to remove Israel's wisdom from the covenant framework, its real emphasis was on the orderliness of creation. The wise men no doubt understood that sin was a breaking of the law (Proverbs 2:17), a repudiation of the word of the Lord, yet they concentrated on a different perspective. Sin was foolishness, the negation of wisdom. It was that which disrupted the order and the harmonious relationships between God, man and the created universe. Wisdom was the principle on which the good life was to be built. The relationship of wisdom to law was thus an indirect one. Both come from God and relate to his character as it is stamped upon the creation. Wisdom sees the order primarily in the context of creation. Law sees it primarily in the context of the saving acts of God.

---

[8] See G. von Rad, *Wisdom in Israel* (London: SCM Press, 1972) Chapter IX.

[9] Ben Sirach 24 depicts wisdom at the creation, but concentrates on Israel as the people among whom wisdom came to dwell. This joining of wisdom and Israelite salvation history is a characteristic of this apocryphal book not found in the canonical wisdom literature.

The instructions and the related-poem in Proverbs 8 thus function to teach wisdom as both gift and task. They could be said to supplement the priest's instruction in the law. Thus, while the law says: 'You shall not commit murder', wisdom means learning from experience and wise counsel how to avoid the multitude of situations that could conceivably lead to murder. Likewise, the emphasis in some instructions on the danger of sexual immorality contrasts with the law's curt prohibition: 'You shall not commit adultery'. Experience teaches us that what is forbidden in the law can be observed as the disruption of good order, and as destructive of the good life. Wisdom learns from the experience of the multiplicity of life's situations so that we are better able to cope with their subtleties. But wisdom is not to be confused with the 'wise man of the world' approach to life which must experience everything for itself. The whole concept of the instruction is that we learn from the experience of others, both good and bad. We follow the footsteps of the wise and avoid the way of fools.

The overall emphasis of wisdom is that we do not become passively dependent when we trust the Lord. Wisdom is telling us that not all of our knowledge comes from direct revelation. The fear of the Lord is the beginning of knowledge. That is, God has revealed to us what we need to know in order to be restored to a right relationship with God, our fellow man and the world. He has thus revealed to us what we need to know in order to interpret our own life's experience and the universe around us. Within the framework of revealed truth we actively go out in pursuit of the understanding of life, learning from our experiences and from those of generations before us.

The Proverbial Sentences

Among the sentence proverbs we find a variety of ways the basic form is used. In the first collection, Proverbs 10:1–22:16, many of the sentences place two statements side by side in what is called parallelism. The easiest way to explain this is with a couple of examples. The most common form in chapters 10–15 is where the statements make a contrast although not necessarily of absolute opposites.[10] By this means several key ideas are put forward in the context of real human experiences. Wisdom is set over against folly, righteousness against wickedness and so on:

A wise son brings joy to his father,
but a foolish son grief to his mother.

(Proverbs 10:1)

Another kind of parallelism builds on the first line by heightening its meaning in the second:

Grey hair is a crown of splendour;
it is attained by a righteous life.

(Proverbs 16:31)

Perhaps the most frequently achieved effect of the simple proverb is that of grouping. We often find different things placed together in a way that does not tell us why they are so grouped. No specific relationship is indicated in the way they were written in the original Hebrew text. For some reason the English translations almost always reconstruct such sentences into comparisons or into subject-predicate sentences.[11] Thus the NIV translates Proverbs 12:1a as:

---

[10] G. von Rad, *Wisdom in Israel*, p. 28.
[11] A subject-predicate sentence makes a statement about the subject.

Whoever loves discipline, loves knowledge.

The Hebrew actually puts it in the ambiguous form:

Loving knowledge, loving discipline.[12]

The effect is to establish a group of things belonging together, rather than to predicate something, that is make a statement, about one of them in the terms of the other. There is no indication of cause or effect or any other relationship between them. Thus there is room for interpretation which would not be allowed otherwise. The possibilities of this arrangement in a more complex form can be seen in those sentences which double the grouping so that A goes with B, C goes with D, and also AB goes with CD. For example, the Hebrew of Proverbs 17:19 has this form:

Loving sin (A), loving strife (B),
making high his gate (C), seeking destruction (D).

The NIV assumes a particular relationship between the two halves of each line. This reduces the possible range of interpretations:

He who loves a quarrel, loves sin;
he who builds a high gate invites destruction.

Other sentences of a similar kind have also undergone transformation in the process of translation into the English versions. For example, Proverbs 25:3, 20, 25; 26:3,

---

[12] See also 13:3a; 14:2a. These characteristics are discussed in detail in H.-J. Hermission, *Studien zur israelitischen Spruchweisheit* (Neukirchen Vluyn: Neukirchener Verlag, 1968).

7, 9, 10, 14 all simply place things side by side with a conjunctive 'and' between them:

Cold water to a thirsty soul,
and good news from a far country.

But the English versions supply 'as ... so' or 'like ... so is':

Like cold water to a weary soul
is good news from a distant land.

(Proverbs 25:25)

Then there are sentences such as Proverbs. 25:11,12,13,14,18,19,26 which place the things together without even 'and' to link them. Again the English versions supply the words necessary to build a subject-predicate sentence. This is not useless information, for the forms of these proverbs in the Hebrew help us to understand how they function in teaching wisdom. The English versions are tending to obscure that function. The wise men were not giving us general rules for ethical conduct. Nor were they defining unknowns in terms of known things. Rather they were saying that experience shows us that A and B have something in common, as do C and D. This is a form of perception of reality to which the simple proverb is admirably suited and our English versions have not, on the whole, helped us to see it. By removing the experience from its specific, concrete event the sages were not wanting to construct timeless rules, but rather to express a view of reality which demands a measure of our intellectual engagement. Thus two quite opposite (or apparently so) observations can be offered without the suggestion of inconsistency or even stupidity:

> Do not answer a fool according to his folly,
> or you will be like him yourself.
>
> Answer a fool according to his folly,
> or he will be wise in his own eyes.
>
> (Proverbs 26:4–5)

The editor of this section may or may not have placed these two contrary words together out of a sense of the humour of the situation. It is clear that no contradiction is implied, but contradiction would have been unavoidable if these had been legal precepts or timeless rules. We must suppose that the interpretation is open-ended in that we are invited to supply the concrete possibilities for each. Some situations call for silence in the company of a fool, others for his rebuke. I found similar illustrations of this principle in a collection of Yiddish proverbs which produced the following 'contradictions':

> A friend you get for nothing, an enemy has to be bought.
> A friend you have to buy, enemies you get for nothing.
>
> Sleep is a thief.
> Sleep is the best doctor.[13]

Although they are different in form, the so-called numerical sayings seem to have the same function as these grouping proverbs. The numerical sayings use a formula of numbers n-1, followed by n, thus:

---

[13] F. Kogos, *One Thousand and One Yiddish Proverbs* (New York: Citadel Press, 1970).

> Under three things, the earth trembles,
> under four it cannot bear up.
>
> (Proverbs 30:21)[14]

Other numerical sayings occur in Proverbs 6:16–19; 30:15–16, 18–19, 21–23, 24–28 (which does not use n-1), 29–31. These sayings contain the element of surprise in the listings which come almost as if they were the answer to a riddle: 'What are three things under which the earth trembles? . . .'[15] It is possible that the n-1, n formula is a way of pointing to the open-ended nature of the list, thus inviting the perceptive person to supply further items n + 1, n + 2 and so on.

Miscellaneous Sayings

The book of Proverbs contains a few sayings which do not fit into the two main categories. Two of these (6:6–11 and 24:30–34) could be described as object lessons. In the former, nature provides a lesson from the industry of the ant, which leads to a popular saying about laziness and poverty:

> A little sleep, a little slumber,
> a little folding of the hands to rest –
> and poverty will come on you like a bandit,
> and scarcity like an armed man.

The same popular saying is evoked in the second passage by the observation of the run-down property of a lazy

---

[14] Compare the use in Amos 1:3–2:8. In Proverbs the higher number is actually filled out with a list of items corresponding to it. There is no such relationship of the sins which Amos ennumerates and the 3, 4 formula.

[15] So von Rad, *Wisdom in Israel*, p. 35f.

farmer. I suggest that here we have an illustration of the way the principle of open-ended interpretation operates. The proverb would normally stand on its own waiting to be applied to a suitable concrete situation. Here we are given two such situations which show how the same proverb is employed to assess the meaning of different but meaningfully related situations.

Learning Wisdom from Proverbs

Despite its many cautions, Proverbs is an optimistic book. Wisdom and life are within our grasp because both are the gifts of God. Yet the gift is never without the task. The fear of the Lord is the beginning of knowledge and wisdom, and it speaks eloquently of God's saving grace shown to his covenant people. The young men and the simple, unsophisticated person can learn wisdom, but only if they would know the fear of the Lord. Proverbs is optimistic because God is the God of the covenant of grace. He gives good things to his children, and the greatest of his gifts is life.

Proverbs defines goodness in terms that are wider than morality and ethics. It is the order that underlies the creation. When God made the heavens and the earth and everything in them he made them in relation to one another, and all was good (Genesis 1:31). All was harmony according to the wisdom of God. Proverbs does not speak of the fall of man into sin, but the fall is everywhere implied. Wisdom, righteousness and life are in conflict with folly, wickedness and death. But despite this intrusion into the good order of God's universe, the order is not destroyed. The fool is the unredeemed sinner who says there is no God (Psalms 14:1; 53:1), who sees the universe as the result of blind chance. Yet, although he refuses to acknowledge a personal, all-wise Creator, he cannot ignore the order that is perceptible in the universe. He has no explanation for it, nor for the disruption of the order of which he himself is a living example along with all other sinners. The wise man fears the Lord and, unlike the fool, is in touch with reality.

Thus, in their distinctive way the wise men of Israel looked at what it meant to be in a disrupted order while not conforming to the disruption. The wise man had to learn to relate to God, to his fellow man, and the whole created order. But in so doing he had to learn that order was complicated by the intrusion of sinful chaos. The optimism of Proverbs is that chaos has not conquered, and that order can still be perceived.

Proverbs affirms the humanity of the wise. He who fears the Lord is not one who retreats into some fake spirituality. Wisdom saw that life is for living to the full. The man of God recognizes that his true humanity lies in his relation to God. But because God made us to relate to one another and to the universe, the restoration of a right relation to God implies a restoration of all relationships. We are encouraged to accept the tasks given to Adam in Eden which, though now confused by sin, are still open to us. In the course of our exercising of dominion in the earth a huge number of impressions are made on our senses which go to make up our experience. Dominion is not a matter of obeying legal precepts in every area of human decision. If we read Proverbs as a miscellany of legal precepts we might find that now and then a saying will occur to us as relevant to our present situation. Indeed we can see some broad principles of morality and behaviour in wisdom writings, but more to the point, we find that we are invited by the wise men to join them in developing a view of reality as a whole. Proverbial wisdom calls us to a decision to stand either with the wise man or the fool; to see all of life in the light of God's revelation of himself or to persist in the folly of making ourselves the centre of the universe.

How then is our humanness affirmed? Wisdom tells us that God has spoken and acted with sufficient clarity for us to perceive the nature of reality when we humble ourselves before a gracious God. God will not enter into our lives to do our thinking for us. He shows trust in us by giving us the equipment and then leaving us to learn about life. All of the collections, lists and comparisons in Proverbs are saying to us that it is certainly complex out there in the world, but it is not chaos. God has not withdrawn all his creative cohesion from the universe. Everywhere in the world around us are the evidences of God's maintenance of order if we would only see them. The wise men did not reduce all this to abstract statements as a modern philosopher might or as we are inclined to do. Rather they were content to observe life and to note that even the most unlikely things and events are related in some way.

For the Israelite whose history was one dominated by the consciousness of election, of the redeeming acts of God, of the law of Moses, and of the radical distinction between Israel and the nations, wisdom had an important function. The exclusivism of Israel's law which forbade what we would regard as normal relationships with other nations, had to be qualified both for practical and theological reasons. In the first instance Israel reached the zenith of its consciousness of election under David's rule. From then on it had to learn to live in such a way that acknowledged that it was in the wider world without compromising the sense of being the elect nation. Theologically Israel would have to come to terms with its role in the world as the agent of God's blessing to the gentiles. History and prophetic word showed that this role would not be truly activated until the Lord's great day of salvation, but, in the meantime, the world was still there and could not be ignored. It was not always the religiously inclined in Israel who perceived the wise relationships with sinners and gentiles. Jesus, as the very wisdom of God incarnate, fulfilled Israel's role to gentiles, but his contact with those who needed salvation caused the religious to scorn him for mixing with publicans and sinners. Being religious and fearing the Lord are clearly not necessarily the same thing.

Questions for Study

1. Read one of the instructions, for example Proverbs 3:1–10, and a sentence such as Proverbs 10:1. Do you see any points of contact between them? What are the main differences in the content of each, and in the way it is conveyed?
2. Read Proverbs 10–11 and list some of the practical issues or topics that are dealt with. Note how many proverbs (or how few) specifically mention God.
3. What are the main types of wisdom saying found in Proverbs, and how do they function?
4. What assumptions about the orderliness of the universe are evident in Proverbs?

Chapter Seven

Job and the Hiddenness of Order

Summary

The subject of the book of Job has been described in various ways. These include the problem of suffering, theodicy or justification of the mysterious ways of God, the meaning of faith, and the nature of fellowship between man and God. All of these suggestions have something to contribute to our understanding of Job. But, above all, the book is asking the question about the nature of wisdom and where it can be found. It achieves this by portraying the crisis which occurs when two concepts of wisdom come into conflict. The book expresses rebellion against a rigid understanding of the relationship between actions and their consequences. Specific observations of relationships are thus turned into general rules which then clash with further experience. Job recognizes that the order of the universe is not fully open to observation. Thus the book urges trust in God because he is above the order perceived by human beings and is not bound by it. It is this hiddenness of order which leads Job to perceive dimly our need for a mediator between us and God, whose word we must hear if we are to live.

The Purpose of Job

Reading the book of Job for the first time can leave one somewhat overawed. Ours is the age of snappy communications, of the one-word bill-board advertisement, of the twenty-second TV commercial. Job belongs to an entirely different world, But it is there in the Bible, and its forty-two chapters have a message for us today. Because of the danger of becoming bogged down in the seemingly endless verbiage of Job, it helps to be acquainted with the way the book is put together.

The book of Job begins with the familiar prose story of the testing of Job's righteousness by the adversary (the Satan).[1] The rather surprising fact that the satan is allowed into the presence of God raises the question of his identity. He is an intruder, and he comes as the adversary of the righteous man of God. He challenges the main assertion of the opening passage, namely that Job is a righteous man. But once this challenge is given effect in the attacks on Job's possessions and person the book has no more interest in the satan. If the book were primarily concerned with the problem of why righteous people suffer it would be a simple matter to say, 'Satan is getting at Job.' In fact, no such solution occurs to the writer and, surprisingly, the satan is irrelevant to the main discussion.

When Job is first stricken with tragedy and loss it is emphasized that he remains a righteous man (2:10). Then his three friends appear and, after a discreet period of

---

[1] The Hebrew word *satan* means the adversary or accuser. It cannot be assumed that it is here used for the personal name for the devil. In the New Testament the devil is called Satan because he is the adversary above all others. The adversary is seen also in Zechariah 3:1, Psalm 109:6, and in a number of narrative passages.

silence, begin their arguments. We enter now the section of the book which is written in poetry. Hebrew poetry does not work by the same rules as English poetry and this tends to make it difficult for the reader who is not used to it. To us it seems very wordy and repetitious. It uses the device of parallelism which we noted as characteristic of the proverbial wisdom sentences. Actually, parallelism can be of help to us when an obscure line is repeated in different and more familiar terms. However, the real difficulty lies not in the meaning of the individual lines but in the way the argument is pursued.

The book has a simple enough structure. Following the prose introduction the poetic sections begin with Job cursing the day he was born. This leads to the rounds of dialogue between Job and his three friends in turn: Job–Eliphaz, Job–Bildad, Job–Zophar (chapters 3–31). The sequence occurs three times except that in the third round Zophar does not appear. The last speech of Job in response to Bildad is exceptionally long (chapters 26–31), although the poem about wisdom in chapter 28 may be a later insertion into the book. A fourth friend, Elihu, arrives on the scene, but seems to add little to the arguments of the other three (32–37). Then the silence of God is broken as he speaks to Job in a magnificent poetic climax (38:1–42:6). Finally a brief prose epilogue has Job restored in wealth, family and health.

Many regard Job as a composite book. For example, it is frequently asserted that the original book consisted of the prose sections alone (1:1–2:13 and 42:7–17). These were then brought together with the dialogue and, probably later, the wisdom poem and the Elihu speeches added.[2]

---

2 The composition of the book is discussed in F. I. Anderson, *Job*, Tyndale Old Testament Commentaries (Leicester: Inter-Varsity Press, 1976), pp. 41–55.

For our purposes it is the finished book in its present form which is of interest, for it is this which has come down to us as holy Scripture and which stands as one of the literary classics of all time.

It can hardly be denied that a central theme of the book is the suffering of a righteous man. That is not necessarily to say that the purpose of the book is to give an answer to the problem of the righteous suffering. The very length and form of the book seem to increase the sense of oppressive mystery surrounding Job's suffering. From one point of view the problem does not exist for we know from the opening narrative that God approves of Job and confidently allows the genuineness of his faith to be tested. But this dialogue between God and the Satan is something that we know but that Job does not. This ignorance on Job's part of the true situation gives continuity between the prose story and the great poetic dialogues with the friends. Scripture supports the idea that God allows suffering among his people in order to chastise and correct them.[3] Also, Job's righteousness did not mean that he was without sin, and therefore without need of correction. Nevertheless, the book makes it clear that Job's suffering is not directly connected with any sin on his part.

Those who say that the prose sections originally formed the story of Job, and that the poetry was inserted into it at a later date, have a point. The story alone makes quite good sense. Job is righteous and his faith is tested. His righteousness is proved as the test fails to move him from his trust in God. Thus he is vindicated and everything is restored to him. This kind of vindication is consistent with the stage of biblical revelation which preceded the revealing of life after death as the sphere of judgment and redress of wrongs. But the

---

3 See Hebrews 12:3–11 which quotes Proverbs 3:11–12.

complete Book of Job is not interested in a doctrine which reduces the suffering of the righteous to testing of their faith. Nor does it suggest that suffering is something that we accept without questioning. We cannot suppose that the entire middle section of the book containing Job's search for understanding is put there so that it can be ruled out of order. Here is a piece of true wisdom in which the search for an understanding of God's ways refuses all trite answers which suggest either that we know it all or that we can know nothing.

Another way of stating the purpose of Job is that it is a striving for a theodicy. Theodicy means to justify the ways of God. In other words, the problem of the righteous sufferer seems to put God in a poor light. Someone will ask: 'How can God be a God of love if he lets such terrible things happen to innocent people?' Most of us will have worked out some kind of answer to this, and in so doing we have entered the realm of theodicy. In the New Testament one aspect of the answer lies in the future appearance of the kingdom of God and of his judgments.[4] This perspective of a future heavenly solution is not really open to the Old Testament. Furthermore, the future solution of the New Testament does not render the message of Job meaningless to Christians.

The variety of opinions about the purpose of Job indicates something of the complexity of its concern. Whether we see it as dealing with the righteous sufferer, with the meaning of faith, with the believer's sense of fellowship with God, or with the justification of the ways of a sovereign God, the book is still manifestly a wisdom book. To

---

[4] The suffering of Christians in relation to the coming kingdom is dealt with in my book *The Gospel in Revelation* (Exeter: Paternoster Press, 1984), ch. 2.

these other suggestions, all of which have something to contribute to our understanding of Job, we must add the overarching concern of the wisdom literature. Job is a book which asks, 'What is wisdom, and how can it be found?'

The Crisis of Wisdom

In the book of Proverbs we saw that the perception of order in the universe is a central concern of wisdom. Each observation based on experience invites us to try to understand it as fitting into a whole series of relationships with other events or experiences. Behind the order lies the creative activity of God, and the true understanding of all events must take account of God's revelation of himself. But even Proverbs recognizes that the orderliness of God's universe is sometimes very complex and hard to discern.

From the outset we can see that the arguments of the three friends of Job do not really apply to him. Their perception of order is very rigid and unable to handle exceptions to the 'normal.' We know Job is innocent. And Job, although he is unaware of God's approval as expressed in the prologue, nevertheless is sure that he has done nothing to merit such crushing misfortune. The friends argue the simple and, to them, obvious case that anyone who is on the receiving end of these calamities must indeed be a very great sinner.

Eliphaz is sure of his position because of a strange spiritual experience he claims to have had and which brought him out in goose-pimples (4:12–17). He poses the problem thus: either Job is unrighteous and deserves to suffer, or God is unrighteous for making him suffer. Since the latter is unthinkable, Job must be in the wrong:

> Can a mortal be more righteous than God?
> Can a man be more pure than his Maker?
>
> (Job 4:17)

Then comes Bildad whose appeal is not to spiritual experience but to tradition (8:8–10). He could have been a great teacher of wisdom if it were not for one thing. The truths he drew from the repository of past wisdom did not fit this particular case, and thus Bildad showed a fatal weakness in his understanding of wisdom. He had no better advice for Job than did Eliphaz, for he saw the solution only in Job's repentance:

> If you are pure and upright,
> even now he will rouse himself on your behalf
> and restore you to your rightful place.
>
> (Job 8:6)

Finally we have Zophar. He has been aptly described as a 'simple gospel' man.[5] It is all so clear, so black and white to this rigid and dogmatic man. He even suggests that God is being lenient with Job by overlooking some of his sins (11:6). Nevertheless he poses a real question that must be considered as part of the understanding of wisdom that the book is developing:

> Can you fathom the mysteries of God?
> Can you probe the limits of the Almighty?
>
> (Job 11:7)

Zophar clearly holds out little hope for Job's reformation and is quite scathing about it:

---

[5] H.L. Ellison, *From Tragedy to Triumph* (Exeter: Paternoster Press, 1958), p. 49.

> But a witless man can no more become wise
> than a wild donkey's colt can be born a man.
>
> (Job 11:12)

Thus each in his own way rebukes Job for his sin and urges him to repent and so find favour once more with God. The repetitions of this cycle of argument add little except more and more heat to the discussion. Job, on the other hand, continues to protest his innocence while paying little attention to the friends' arguments. With great skill the poet has our hero sparring with his opponents as if they were in different rooms or on the opposite bank of a river. There is never a head-on clash of ideas which leaves one or other the clear winner. We may suggest that this clever arrangement underlines the fact that the friends are never wholly wrong. In this lies some of the appeal of the book. It is an exercise in making contact between two aspects of wisdom. The one stresses the observable patterns of cause and effect, while the other stresses the mysteries of life's experiences.

So what does it mean to speak of the crisis of wisdom?[6] The crisis occurred when a particular view of wisdom hardened into a rigid interpretation of reality as a whole so that it sometimes clashed with experience. It is fairly obvious that Proverbs tends to emphasize the idea that there is a close relationship between what we do and what happens as a result. This is valid not only in the area of immediate cause and effect, but also in the broader effects of ethical behaviour. Many proverbs speak of the good that comes from righteous or wise actions. This is not simply due to the fact that the Old Testament has not arrived at a

---

[6] This term is used by H.H. Schmid, *Wesen und Geschichte der Weisheit* (Berlin: Alfred Töpelmann, 1966). See also H.D. Preuss, 'Erwägungen zum theologischer Ort alttestamentlicher Weisheitsliteratur,' *Evangelische Theologie*, Nr. 8. 1970.

view of life after death where all the scores can be settled. It really is a fact of experience that good begets good and that wisdom makes for life and its preservation. This deed-outcome relationship is what we sometimes refer to as natural retribution. We can observe it in our own experience so that we are reassured that there is an order which prevails.

Natural retribution is something most people can understand. We know that there are laws of life which it is wise for us to observe. There is little wisdom in living on a diet of junk foods or in heavy smoking. On the broader level, people are becoming more and more alarmed at the way we are making our planet uninhabitable. The cultural mandate given to man by God has been distorted into the dogma of economic growth at any cost. The nuclear arms race and the threat of the extinction of all life on earth is the starkest reminder that we have of natural retribution. This kind of wisdom is characteristic of the book of Proverbs. But Proverbs does not try to reconcile the contradictions of experience, nor does it theorize about what lies behind them.

The crisis of wisdom is best illustrated in the book of Job. The three friends have a simple doctrine of retribution. But it is not as though they represent the wisdom of Proverbs in collision with Job's experience. Rather they represent the wisdom of Proverbs fossilized so that the time-relatedness of the proverbs is forgotten. It seems that they have made fixed general rules out of proverbial wisdom and are incapable of dealing with the apparent contradictions that experience throws up. Thus their arguments amount to this: many experiences show a direct relationship between righteousness and prosperity, between folly and evil; therefore all experiences of evil must be the direct result of unrighteousness.

The friends of Job are God-fearing men and it would be inconceivable that they had nothing at all to say that is valid. We may not dismiss them as irrelevant, for their words are essentially true. It is just that they do not apply to Job's situation. Job will appear as a challenge to Proverbs only if we follow the example of the friends and turn the proverbial statements into general rules. Job's experience was not new in Israel. The suffering of righteous people is to be found at all times, and the problem is summed up in the lamentation of the godly man oppressed by evil:

> How long, O Lord? Will you forget me for ever?
> How long will you hide your face from me?
>
> (Psalm 13:1)

Job's friends have not succeeded in handling the contradictions of their own proverbial style of wisdom. For example, the logic which they applied to Job could be extended to the poor of the world. There are a number of places in Proverbs which connect poverty with laziness or folly.[7] It would be easy to generalize this either by saying that laziness always begets poverty, or (worse) that poverty is always the result of laziness. The wise men clearly do not see it this way since they often show compassion for the poor and praise those that help them.[8] A poor man may even be the show piece of integrity (Proverbs 19:1).

---

[7] Proverbs 6:6–11; 10:4,5; 12:11,24; 21:17,21,25.

[8] Proverbs 14:21,31; 19:17; 21:13. This example from Hartmut Gese, *Lehre und Wirklichkeit in der alten Weisheit* (Tübingen: J.C.B. Mohr, 1958), p. 38.

The Hiddenness of Order

We may now return to the subject of faith and trust. It is recognized that the wise men of Israel were not humanists but, on the contrary, saw wisdom in the light of trust in God.[9] In our discussion of the fear of the Lord we saw something of the centrality to wisdom of faith in the God who is known by revelation. Many passages speak of trust in a way that goes beyond a response to the saving acts of God which are the pivot of Israel's covenant faith. In wisdom it is because the Lord has established order in the universe that our perception of this order in daily experience also invites trust in the Lord. The extraordinary claim of Proverbs 2:1–15 is that the search for knowledge leads to an understanding of the fear of the Lord and to the knowledge of God. This underlines the point that the fear of the Lord is both our starting point and our goal. It is not that an objective examination of the universe by the open-minded unbeliever will lead him to acknowledge and trust God. Such a natural theology or perception of God is impossible. Rather it is the believer who accepts that God is the Creator, who then finds the whole universe reinforces this faith and trust.

Related to this idea of an orderly creation is the deed outcome relationship of natural retribution. But what happens when experience contradicts this as in the case of Job? Wisdom had to come to terms with the fact that even wisdom as a gift of God did not imply that God teaches us to think as he does with exhaustive or total knowledge of the universe. As von Rad puts it, some experiences put our trust under attack. [10] When this

---

[9] G. von Rad, *Wisdom in Israel*, see especially Chapter 12.
[10] Ibid.

happens to us we may lose faith in the sense that we see the contradiction as removing all grounds for our previous trust. On the other hand, we could try a wiser path. We could take the contradiction as a reminder that we cannot see the whole picture. Only he who truly believes in the one creator God could accept this view. It is faith in the infinite, personal and caring God which distinguishes true wisdom from the intellectual conceit of humanism. The wise man is always aware that his search for knowledge is strictly limited by that infinite greatness which distinguishes God from man. In this he agrees with the prophetic word from God:

> As the heavens are higher than the earth,
> so are my ways higher than your ways
> and my thoughts than your thoughts.
>
> (Isaiah 55:9)

Wisdom is aware of its limitations and it is ready to admit that there is much of God's order that is hidden from us. When faced with such mysteries it may be possible to see some reason in them. Wisdom acknowledges the function of suffering as training (Proverbs 3:11–12). But this is different from retribution only in degree, for correction implies some fault or imperfection that needs correction. This is certainly not the solution to the book of Job. The mystery is much deeper, and Job is left without even the assurance that a loving father is reproving him. His deepest suffering, surpassing that of his personal losses, is the silence of God.

Whatever we conclude about the originality of Job 28, this poem about wisdom is not irrelevant. From the frustrating failure of Job's friends to bring a solution to light we are taken to the heart of the problem:

> But where can wisdom be found?
> Where does understanding dwell?
> Man does not comprehend its worth;
> it cannot be found in the land of the living.
>
> Where then does wisdom come from?
> Where does understanding dwell?
> It is hidden from the eyes of every living thing,
> concealed even from the birds of the air.
>
> God understands the way to it
> and he alone knows where it dwells,
> for he views the ends of the earth
> and sees everything under the heavens.
>
> (Job 28:12–13, 20–21, 23–24)

If God has created all things in order, then he alone has all wisdom. For man to pursue wisdom without this essential qualification is the height of folly. The human mind must accept that there is mystery which it cannot penetrate, an order which God maintains but which is hidden beyond our ability to find it. Even when wisdom is regenerated and linked with faith in the revealed word of the Lord, the wise man will view all the marvels of the creation which are before him and confess with Job:

> And these are but the outer fringe of his works;
> how faint the whisper we hear of him!
> Who then can understand the thunder of his power?
>
> (Job 26:14)

Before we consider God's answer to Job we should note one other theme. There is a deep consciousness in Job of the separation between man and God. That which Israel's religion depicted in so many vivid ways was forced upon him in an intensely personal manner. The ministry of the tabernacle with its fence and its veil before the most holy place, was a reminder that sin made a separation between man and God. The priest and all his blood sacrifices showed that only by a mediator could people approach God. What the prophetic word said to Israel was Job's deepest experience. He was cut off from God and he did not know how he could seek God's face again. Here it is not so much his sinfulness as his creatureliness which separates them. But the solution is the same; he needs a mediator:

> He is not a man like me that I might answer him,
> that we might confront each other in court.
> If only there were someone to arbitrate between us,
> to lay his hand upon us both,
> someone to remove God's rod from me,
> so that his terror would frighten me no more.
> Then I would speak up without fear of him,
> but as it now stands with me, I cannot.
>
> (Job 9:32–35)

Somewhere there must be such a one:

> Even now my witness is in heaven;
> my advocate is on high.
>
> (Job 16:19)

Then finally a passage which, despite its difficulty of translation from the Hebrew, expresses a confidence that death cannot mean a final separation from his God.

> I know that my Redeemer lives,
> and that in the end he will stand upon the earth.
> And after my skin has been destroyed,
> yet in my flesh I will see God.
>
> (Job 19:25–26)

This is not a full understanding of resurrection but rather a working through of what it means for God to be righteous. Undoubtedly it forms one part of the revelation which brings us towards the New Testament doctrine of resurrection. Its relationship to Job's desire for a mediator is important. Somehow his vindicator or redeemer will enable him to see God. He will not then need an explanation for to see God will be enough for him.

God's Word on the Matter

It is not until we are almost to the end of the book that for the first time God speaks to Job (38:1–41:34). The reply to Job's questionings is powerful, overwhelming, but not destructive. It is baffling in that it seems to avoid all the questions that Job and the friends have thrown up. The difficulty in pin-pointing the significance of this mighty oracle can be seen in the variety of scholarly conclusions that have been reached concerning it. Perhaps we can say two things about that: first, there is no answer to Job's questions and, second, to say there is no answer is to give an answer that is open ended in the way we perceive its applications. Another way of saying this is that God gives no direct answers to Job's questions about his suffering, but rather points to certain inevitable truths which lead Job on wisdom's path to a satisfactory conclusion of the matter.

God's words are not without rebuke:

> Who is this that darkens my counsel
> with words without knowledge?

(Job 38:2)

Since in 42:7 God says that Job has spoken what is right about God, this verse cannot mean the opposite. Rather it indicates that Job is ignorant because he is without counsel on the matter.[11] So also:

> Will the one who contends with the Almighty correct him?
> Let him who accuses God answer him!
>
> (Job 40:2)

Job's answer (40:3–5) shows that the rebuke humbles him. But he has not yet reached the point to which God will bring him in the end. What, then, may we learn from this answer of God?

First, we may learn of God. The relentless questions put to Job confront him with the reality of the creation. This world in which Job lives is constant evidence of the order that embraces all things. The great poetic dialogues of the book show us the danger of thinking that by perceiving order in our limited experience, we thereby understand it all. It is a short step from seeing God as the creator and sustainer of order to thinking of God as himself bound to our simplistic notions of order. When we begin to give independent status to things like order, justice, goodness and truth, it is not long before we also begin to insist that God should conform to them. We then build up a picture of a just and good God on the basis of the supposedly self-evident ideas of justice and goodness. The biblical picture is the opposite. God reveals what he is like and in so doing shows us what justice and goodness are. So with order; the revelation of God must define it for us. God is not a creature subject to a higher independent principle called order. Order is what it is because God is what he is, and because he made it so.

---

[11] So Andersen, *Job*, p. 273f.

Job, then, learns of God as the God who is above the order which is perceptible to man.[12] This means that it is possible, indeed probable, that we all have experiences in which the deed-outcome relationship is really beyond our ability to perceive. The questions that God asks demand no answer, but rather invite Job once again to consider the greatness of the creation which bears witness to the kind of God that made it. What we sometimes refer to as the sovereignty of God, his absolute rule over all things, means that he is free. God is free, not to deny himself or capriciously to transform himself into a devil, but free nevertheless to do all things according to his will. That God reveals himself and makes himself knowable to us is a free act. The knowability of God must never be stretched so as to eliminate the mystery of God's unknowability. In other words, our knowledge of God is limited by what God chooses to reveal and by our ability to understand it. We must always allow that God is infinitely greater than our understanding can grasp both in his being and in his ways. Even the simple person can grasp that. On one occasion I asked a group of ghetto children in a New York childrens' shelter (where I worked as chaplain) what it would mean if we could understand everything about God. Without hesitation a diminutive seven-year-old showed wisdom beyond his years by answering, 'We'd be God!'

The silence of God has sat like an impenetrable mist on Job's world. While he was thus isolated from the one voice that could give meaning to his experience, the arguments of the friends became to him as creature noises in his swamp of suffering. His misery, like a fog, blotted out all points of reference by which he could get his bearings and know himself in relation to some meaningful reality. The

---

[12] Gese, *Lehre und Wirklichkeit*, p. 77.

triumph of Job's faith lay in his perseverance of purpose to find meaning in God. Job's vindication lies in the fact that God speaks to him, not a word of final judgment, but a word which reconnects him with reality. God speaks with majesty, but it is the majesty that God was to reveal in Israel as a caring shepherd-like kingship.[13] God lovingly leads his son beyond the horizons of his own world of suffering. By God's word the healing is effected in a way that reveals God's wisdom as transcending the wisdom of men.

Learning Wisdom from Job

Job's faith and trust penetrated the wall of silence more than he at first realized. He was as tenacious as a bull-dog in holding on to one thing: there must be an answer from God. Because his problem was wider than his suffering, Job speaks to those who suffer today and to a much wider audience. His problem lay in the fact that he lost the sense that anything had meaning. To compound the matter, God was silent. Everything that had made up his ordered existence was torn from him, but if God had only reassured him or told him of the arrangement with the satan things would have seemed different. Then there would have been suffering but not the same problem. It was as if all the living assurances that God, the shepherd of Israel, had given to his people were removed from Job's understanding. His was the suffering of a wordless pit that would bring him to understand the sufficiency of God's word to man.

---

[13] Compare with Isaiah 40:10–31. The Lord God who comes to rule Israel will feed his flock like a shepherd. It is remarkable that this description is followed by an oracle of creation which has much in common with the speech of God in Job

The kind of suffering to which Job speaks is not only the literal horror of bereavement, destitution and social isolation that the story depicts. It speaks to our alienation from others and from the world. To the unbeliever who drowns his sense of meaninglessness and worthlessness in narcotic stupors, Job points to meaning as a gift from God to all who will trust him. His cry for a mediator reached out, in a way that he could not have understood, towards the Word of God who was to come in the flesh so that we, in our flesh, might see God.

For some the epilogue of Job is trivial and an anticlimax. Perhaps it does represent an editorial attempt that is less than perfect from a literary point of view. But from the point of view of the message of the book the epilogue confirms the significance of the oracle of God. Even though Job repents in dust and ashes we know this is not for the sin of which the friends accused him. Rather it means that Job has been lifted out of his desire for a straight answer from God. Lovingly God has brought him to see that the solution to his problem is not to become as God but rather to cast himself as the trusting creature upon the care of his Creator. The epilogue expresses in the only way possible for the people of the Old Testament the fact that Job was vindicated and restored to fellowship with God and man.

So Job does not contradict the wisdom of Proverbs. It goes beyond Proverbs by developing for us the meaning of the fear of the Lord and of the greatness of God. It reminds us that such fear of God is truly a reverent awe of one whose infinite greatness, wisdom and care reach far beyond anything we can comprehend. Job anticipates Paul's assurance that 'in all things God works for the good of those who love him, who have been called according to his purpose' (Romans 8:28). He reduces us to size so that we may be delivered from our conceit in thinking that our pursuit of wisdom will lead us to know all the answers. In

Job's company we can be humbled by God only so that he might raise us up to a renewed trust in his goodness.

Questions for study

1. Summarize the structure of the book of Job by identifying its various parts.
2. Read Job 2–3 and in the light of these chapters describe the emerging clash of wisdom ideas expressed by Eliphaz in Job 4.
3. What concept of order in the universe underlies the book of Job?
4. What do you consider to be the main lesson of Job?

Chapter Eight

Ecclesiastes and the Confusion of Order

Summary

Qohelet is a further expression of rebellion against a rigid form of Israelite wisdom. Again we are reminded that the search for order does not mean that everything is open to man's view. Thus there are times when certain approaches to wisdom seem to yield no results. This does not prove that there is no order, but only that it can be mysterious. Furthermore, human sin has confused both the order and our ability to know it. The wise response to the apparent darkness is to acknowledge the reality of God, to go on trusting him and to receive life as his gift.

The Problem of Qohelet

The book of Proverbs, though cautious, is nevertheless optimistic in its view of the possibility for man to master the business of living as long as life is known to be the gift of God within an ordered universe. The book of Job makes a timely protest against the hardening of general patterns of retribution into a rigid dogma of cause and effect. Job warns us against the wrong interpretation of the wisdom of Proverbs which robs it of its relationship to time and history, that is, to the actual experiences of people. Another protest was raised against this generalizing of experience into strict rules, a protest which seems to lead its author to a position of hopelessness. 'All is vanity' says the preacher (or Qohelet).[1] This refrain 'everything is meaningless' (NIV) occurs time and time again through the book and casts over it a mood of gloom and pessimism.

It is not difficult to understand why some critics have proposed that Ecclesiastes should be replaced by the more optimistic and more self-consciously Israelite wisdom of the book of Ecclesiasticus or, as it is also known, the Wisdom of Jesus ben Sirach.[2] However, the fact is that both Church and Synagogue accepted Qohelet and not ben Sirach as canonical Scripture. This presents us with the problem of how the theme of meaninglessness in Qohelet can be squared with the overall view of the Bible that a rational and personal God reveals himself and his purposes for his creation.[3]

Despite the difficulties in the apparent negativeness of the author, we have to say that he is no atheist and no stranger to the faith of Israel. Who was he? Tradition often identifies him as Solomon and it is sometimes suggested that this identification is the reason that the book was accepted into the canon of Scripture. Qohelet describes

---

[1] *Qohelet* is the Hebrew word translated as preacher (RSV) or teacher (NIV). The root of the word signifies an assembly, the equivalent of the Greek *ekklesia*, and hence the name Ecclesiastes.

[2] One of the wisdom books in the apocrypha.

[3] The recurring Hebrew word is *hebel* which means vapour, vanity or that which has no substance. It is used over thirty times in Qohelet, sometimes in the intense form (vanity of vanities) and sometimes linked with a similar phrase 'a chasing after wind.'

himself as the son of David (1:1), and also says that he *has* been king in Jerusalem (1:12). The omission of his name and the past tense (I was king) would both be inappropriate for a reigning monarch. As we shall see, the internal evidence of the book points to a later development in the wisdom tradition, and thus to a date later than Solomon. The term 'son of David' could refer to any descendant of David, but in this case it is probably a back-handed reference to Solomon, not to claim identity, but to indicate continuity with the wisdom traditions of Israel of which Solomon was regarded as being the fountain-head.

Apart from the recurring themes there is no obvious development in Qohelet. The apparent disconnectedness of the various literary units of the book has led many to suggest that it is composite, embracing more than one point of view. But in spite of the seeming randomness of the arrangement of the material we find the constant theme inescapable: all is meaningless. Ironically it is the placement of this theme which rescues Qohelet from being for us a totally meaningless book. It is not possible to confuse Qohelet's mood of meaninglessness with the modern philosophy of nihilism. Nihilism is the logical outworking of an atheistic view of the universe. Once a personal and purposeful God is removed from the scene, everything becomes the result of pure chance and thus without meaning. Such a philosophy lies behind the modem theatre of the absurd, Dadaism and random composition music.[4] Atheistic nihilism is an impossible philosophy because it sets forth as meaningful the proposition that nothing has meaning. Qohelet's cry of utter meaninglessness is not of the same order. To begin with, he is convinced of the reality of God and of meaning which is known to God. That there is a personal, creator God makes

---

[4] See James W. Sire, *The Universe Next Door*, pp. 76–97.

it possible for us mortals to grasp life as his gift, and that alone gives reality meaning.

Of the various interpretations of this book there is one that appeals more than most to evangelical Christians with their high view of the inspiration of Scripture. It is proposed that the author actually went through a period of searching for the truth by means of various worldly ideas and pursuits, or that he undertook a more objective investigation of these godless approaches in order to test their validity. Either way the result is the same. The secular approaches are shown to be futile and only the fear of God is left as a viable alternative.[5] On this view the contest in Qohelet is between orthodoxy and worldliness, between faith in God and practical atheism. Qohelet is an apologetic work, that is, an argument for a particular view of reality which seeks to establish its superiority over all other views. An interesting variation on this general understanding of Qohelet is the suggestion that it was written to oppose the evil influences of Solomon after his apostasy.[6] This supposes that Qohelet (Solomon) looks upon his own life as vanity and without meaning. The author of the book, having presented Solomon's view, rejects it and argues against it from the orthodox position of the fear of the Lord and the joy of serving him.

In my view these particular conservative positions do not really come to grips with the real nature of Qohelet. They appeal to us principally because they provide a fairly straightforward solution to the apparent contradictions and the difficulties of the book. We must beware of

---

[5] So O.S. Hendry, 'Ecclesiastes' in (ed.) F. Davidson, *The New Bible Commentary* (London: Inter-Varsity Fellowship, 1953), also Derek Kidner, *A Time to Mourn and a Time to Dance* (Leicester: Inter-Varsity Press, 1976).

[6] Jack B. Scott, *God's Plan Unfolded*, revised edition (Wheaton: Tyndale House, 1978).

the tendency to rescue difficult parts of the Bible when they seem to strike a discordant note. What then are the other options open to us for an understanding of Qohelet? The view that it is a late work heavily influenced by Greek philosophy is not generally favoured by commentators any longer. Another approach is to see it as a notebook of the wise man's personal pilgrimage, thus accounting for the lack of form and the disarming honesty of the book. Others have suggested that the lack of form is explained if we suppose that it was originally a codex (a book with pages) rather than the usual scroll, and that the pages were put together in the wrong order. Still another view proposes that the book consists of an original composition of scepticism which was rescued for orthodoxy by the insertion of pieces of traditional wisdom. Most of these positions thus far mentioned have in common the idea that Qohelet is openly critical of some other approach to life. But to what does he really object? Is it to secularism, to Greek philosophical influences, to a scepticism that borders on atheism? If we can answer this we will be in a better position to understand the book as a whole.

The Content and Message of Qohelet

It would be difficult to show any developing theme running through the book, and the form of the finished work is part of its problem. There is no question posed and answered. However, there are some broad themes to be found. The prevailing theme of meaninglessness is found throughout from beginning (1:2) to end (12:8). Even in sections which seem to depart momentarily from the prevailing gloom we find this pessimistic word (2:26; 7:15; 8:10; 11:8; 12:8). Nevertheless, Qohelet does stand in the wisdom tradition as he asks questions about man's place in the total scheme of things. Constantly he raises the matter of our portion or lot (3:22; 5:18; 9:6,9), and our gain or benefit in life (e.g. 1:3; 2:11; 3:9; 5:16). Initially man's lot is seen as toil and vanity. But is there no relief from this unpromising situation?

What is wisdom's answer? Qohelet appears to be against wisdom at this point as he sets his mind to know how it can help us (1:13, 16–18; 2:3,12). Wisdom, at best, is very limited in its advantages (2:3,14; 4:13; 8:16–17). In fact wisdom sometimes seems to be of no advantage at all, and even to leave the wise man on an equal footing with the fool (1:16–17; 2:14–17; 6:8; 9:11). Occasionally wisdom is given some positive value (7:11–12,19; 8:1; 9:1; 13–18; 10:2, 10,12). This mixture of attitudes to wisdom is baffling on first sight but if we bear in mind some of the characteristics of wisdom itself we can make progress. Let us remember first of all what we learned from Proverbs about the specific nature of wisdom observations which allows contradictory assertions to be placed side by side. At the level of day by day experience there are many contradictions in life. Here Qohelet does with the subject of the pursuit of wisdom what Proverbs does with the general experiences of life. He considers the gains of wisdom in concrete situations, not from a general point of view or as a whole. Here wisdom shows its positive gains, but there it is qualified, and there again it seems to yield no advantage at all. Somehow the search for order is confused and the wise man finds himself standing with a feeling of nakedness and with nowhere to go. God, it appears, has set wisdom within very strict limits which prevent us from seeing a large enough picture of the reality into which we must somehow fit.

In Proverbs we looked at the prevailing optimism of wisdom in its perception of order in reality. Job was a revolt against the assumption that there are no mysteries in life. Now Qohelet looks at what appears to be a confusion of perceptible order. This confusion is more than the hiddenness to which the book of Job points. God is incomprehensible, but there is also the confusion injected by the human element of wickedness and oppression (3:16; 4:1–3; 5:8–9). This anticipates Paul's recognition that the creation has become subjected to futility because of sin and thus awaits its liberation along with the redeemed people of God (Romans 8:19–23).

Through all this comes the burning conviction of the unknowable nature of God. He is active in the world, but so much of what he does is unexplained and beyond finding out. Qohelet's scepticism is never in danger of becoming atheism for he knows that God is behind all this. Predestination is a fact of existence and everything has its appointed time (3:1–9), yet it is beyond our ability to penetrate it (3:10–11). There is nothing left for us to do but to live life a day at a time and fear God (3: 12–15).

Despite his pessimism Qohelet can affirm life in God's world. It may not always be happy (1:13) but it is under God's control. Justice and judgment are real expressions of God's care (2:26; 3:17; 9:1; 11:9; 12:14). Thus, within the mystery and the confusion we can live knowing that life is God's gift and that there is some gain in being happy in our work (2:24; 3:10–15,22; 5: 18–20; 9:7–10). Perhaps this is the most remarkable characteristic of Qohelet, that he refuses to give way to empty despair and so to say with the fool, 'There is no God.'

Learning Wisdom from Qohelet

In questioning the traditional and conservative interpretation of Qohelet I would not say that it is totally wrong. Qohelet is not directly concerned with secularism, but indirectly he shows that it is not the answer to life's problems. He does this by affirming that the world is God's and that nothing happens by chance. But his main attack is directed at a form of Israelite wisdom that found a few simple answers to the question of our existence in the world. The friends of Job gave one expression of this dogmatic wisdom, which operated on a perceptible rule of retribution. This meant that the principal factor in world order is the immediate link of events to the deeds of men. The book of Job establishes the need for an intellectual revolt against such a view, yet without in any way conflicting with the wisdom of Proverbs. Qohelet goes further than Job in his revolt and shows the impossibility of a point of view which reduces God's action in the world to the wholly predictable.

It seems to be an unavoidable conclusion from both Job and Qohelet that Israelite wisdom had developed in a way that threatened its own validity. Perhaps it was the very perspective of wisdom which put it in jeopardy. By placing the history of Israel's salvation into the background, wisdom was always in danger of trying to construct a comprehensive view of the world of experience without reference to God's revealing acts. One consequence was the development of the dogmatic wisdom of Job's friends. Its attractiveness lay in its sense of perceptible order which was available to man. Its strict notions of retribution in life provided a firm basis for ethical judgement, and spoke of a justice in the universe which affected us at the level of daily existence. The warning for us here is that we should avoid the mistake of using proverbial wisdom as timeless general rules, as primarily ethical implications of the moral law of God.

The other development, due to wisdom's lack of specific concern for the history of God's saving acts in Israel, is a concentration on the fact of God as Creator. This is a perfectly valid perspective but carries with it certain dangers. The obvious pitfall is that the God-as-Creator notion may become virtually the whole of one's idea of God. God, when he is distanced from his saving acts, easily becomes an impersonal abstraction. The creation event is beyond our reach as an historical event, and we begin to think of God as some kind of non-personal force behind the universe.

In Qohelet the idea of a totally predictable God clashes with the reality of his mystery. This provides us with a creative tension which points us to towards a comprehensive wisdom which does not lose sight of God's revelation in history. In a sense the epilogue of the book shows that real life will always be lived in tension, at least in this world. Whether we see this as an orthodox postscript to Qohelet's sceptical clash with dogmatic wisdom, or whether we see it as Qohelet's own resolution of the conflict, the result is the same for us. We see the sage as a man of integrity who refuses to toe the line of the orthodoxy of his day for the sake of being known as doctrinally sound.

If we detect a note of despair in Qohelet, we should not write him off for his failure to be a victorious Christian. Great reformers are usually tormented men, and the road to reform is seldom easy. Those who would light a candle in the dark must first wrestle with the darkness and even risk being tainted by it before they can point the way through it. Qohelet is a rebuke to the false optimism which comes from a simplistic view of wisdom's goal. If he had managed to convey a sense of resolving the tensions he would have failed in his task. He sets God's sovereign will and purpose over against the apparent vanity of all things. But he will not give in to despair. He warns us against slick solutions of life's mysteries, so that we must always be open to having the lessons of our experience contradicted by further experience. He also warns us against something more subtle than blatant secular atheism, and that is trite religiosity.

It is futile to ask why Qohelet did not resolve the tensions by reference to the prophetic view of history and the future. It is wisdom's distinctive role to look at life more in terms of the present than of the past or future. It is thus that it avoids obscuring the tensions of human experience. We must affirm the soundness of the decision to recognize Qohelet as canonical Scripture rather than ben Sirach. The latter brought wisdom and the law of Moses together so that they were almost completely merged. This was no solution to any of the apparent problems of wisdom for in ben Sirach's time the law was fast being divorced from God's saving grace.

So we are rebuked by Qohelet for our tendency to take wisdom's remarkable sense of universal order and to turn it into a world-view which lacks depth, and which has no answer, other than condemnation, for the person whose experience contradicts it. From the New Testament perspective it is true to say that we can know with certainty that confusion and futility are banished by Christ. But until he comes again and all things are renewed, faith in the grace of God must sustain us through many incomprehensible tensions in our experience. The peculiar tension for the Christian is that we know our final goal with its resolution of all ills, but we do not know what tomorrow brings. Slick views on how to get guidance and to know God's will in daily things must go under the hammer of the crisis of wisdom in Job and Qohelet. This sceptical sage has an important lesson for us as he bids us take life a day at a time and enjoy it with its toil as a gift from God. He who truly fears God will stand in awe of the mystery of his ways among men.

Questions for study

1. What are the features of the book of Ecclesiastes which at first sight seem to contradict the prevailing view of God and man in the Old Testament?
2. What interpretations of Ecclesiastes have been proposed in order to account for its contents?
3. What are some of the wisdom themes found in this book?
4. What view of the order of the universe is found in Ecclesiastes?

Chapter Nine

Wisdom in all Manner of Places

Summary

Many attempts to identify wisdom influences in non-wisdom parts of the Old Testament seem to involve the assumption that the wisdom movement was quite separate from the rest of Israelite religious thought. There is no evidence for this. Rather we see wisdom and salvation history as two perspectives on the one reality. Both contributed to the Israelite understanding of reality. Nevertheless it is legitimate to try to identify the distinctive characteristics of wisdom and to look for possible wisdom influences in the mainstream of Old Testament salvation history and worship. The difficulty of doing this is increased by the resistance of the main wisdom writers to any extensive combination of wisdom and salvation history. The two converge and interact within two main areas of theology: in the doctrine of creation and in the royal theology of the wise king who rules within the context of God's saving acts.

The Influence of the Wise Men

Since the wisdom literature contributes to our understanding of the world in which we live, it would be no surprise to discover that the wise men influenced the thinking of other Israelites. We have not found any evidence that they were rebels against Israelite religious thought or society. Were they, then, members of an identifiable group who were recognizable because they talked and wrote wisdom? Or were they less conspicuous members of the main-stream of Israelite society? The few biblical references to individual wise men and women, or to wise men as a recognizable group, do not establish that the wisdom movement was a clearly defined thing promoted by those who were known as the wise men of Israel.[1]

If the men responsible for the wisdom literature of the Bible were part of the community of the faithful it would be strange if the distinctive ideas of wisdom did not show up from time to time in other parts of the Old Testament. There is good reason to believe that such influences do occur in many writings of the prophets, in narratives and in a number of psalms. It is harder to explain why the wise men apparently resisted the influences in the opposite direction. By avoiding almost all reference to prophetic faith, to salvation history and law, the wisdom writers left us few clues to how they saw themselves in relation to these mainstream ideas of Israel's faith.

Unless we can stand close to the history of these things, deciding what is an outside influence on someone and by whom is not always easy. Fortunately we are able to observe very clear characteristics of thought and language shared by Proverbs, Job and Ecclesiastes. We can link these three books as wisdom without suggesting a clearly defined wisdom movement. We can observe also how these wisdom books differ from the

---

[1] e.g.: Exodus 36:4; Deuteronomy 1:13; 2 Samuel 14:2; Jeremiah 18:18; 50:35; 51:57.

perspectives of the narrative and prophetic writings. But if we are to suppose that significant wisdom influences have occurred, we must be able to show that it is the distinctly wisdom view of things that is impressing itself upon the non-wisdom writing. This is easier said than done. If wisdom was not a totally separate movement, it is conceivable that some narrative historians or prophets were also wise men. Then it would not be a matter of influences at all, but rather one of different ways of looking at things. It is important that we clearly understand these different perspectives within the Old Testament and their combined message for us.

The covenant theologians and the writers of salvation history emphasized the nature of God's revelation through prophetic word and saving act. They recognized that God's word was the only true source of knowledge about the whole of reality. It would have been clear to them that God's word does not tell us everything about our existence, but it does provide us with the necessary framework within which we can seek to know life and the world about us. On the other hand, the wise men, assuming that which is revealed in God's word, set about the God-given task of understanding the complexities of human experience that are not directly the subject of revelation. If there were experts in both perspectives, we do not need to see that as presenting the ordinary Israelite with an either-or choice. Revelation, which leads to the fear of the Lord, has priority over human experience because without revelation sinful man is not able to discern ultimate truth from his experience. But at the same time we see that revelation tells us of our task of learning wisdom from experience.

Wisdom in Non-wisdom Books

Once it had been suggested that the wise men influenced non-wisdom writers, there followed a steady stream of scholarly proposals as to where the evidence for such influences may be found.[2] A few examples will do for the moment. It was claimed that the Joseph story in Genesis 37–50 showed all the signs of being a wisdom novel.[3] The reasons given are such things as advanced literary technique, enlightened cultural tone, and emphasis on human factors. The story is said to highlight wise counsel and administration, while Joseph overcomes adversity by prudence and the fear of the Lord. The arguments are rather less than convincing, although we have to agree that the story does contain themes and ideas that occur in the wisdom literature. Some criteria given, such as interest in things outside of Israel's cult, are explicable by the fact that the events took place outside of Israel.

Another study places Amos the prophet in a wisdom context.[4] To be sure, Amos uses the numerical saying form that we observed in Proverbs (see Amos 1–2), but he does so in a manner which is different from that of Proverbs. Some have taken a more cautious approach and said that some prophets show that they were acquainted with wisdom and appreciated it.[5] Other parts of the Old Testament that have been nominated as showing the influence of

---

[2] A useful survey is given by Donn F. Morgan, *Wisdom in the Old Testament Traditions* (Atlanta: John Knox Press, 1981).

[3] G. von Rad, 'The Joseph Narrative and Ancient Wisdom', in *The Problem of the Hexateuch and Other Essays* (New York: McGraw Hill, 1966).

[4] H. W. Wolff, *Amos the Prophet* (Philadelphia: Fortress Press, 1973, German edition 1964).

[5] J. Lindblom, 'Wisdom in the Old Testament Prophets', *Supplements to Vetus Testamentum*, III, 1955.

wisdom include the books of Deuteronomy and Esther, the so-called succession narrative in 2 Samuel 9–20 and 1 Kings 1–2, and certain of the Psalms.

Most of the identifications of wisdom seem to assume that there were at least two distinct streams of thought in Israel which occasionally interacted. They highlight the problem of identifying wisdom as an entity, and of deciding what criteria can be used to identify its influences in non-wisdom literature. Many of the criteria proposed in these studies of alleged wisdom influences can be explained by the common background of history, experience and covenant faith.[6] It is, I believe, more satisfactory to refuse to segregate the wise men, and to see a plurality of perspectives dictated by the variety of concerns. What began with early folk wisdom in the home and market place would have developed within the overall perspective of the revealed faith of Israel. The interaction between the various perspectives is found rather by looking for the emphases of the various books, both wisdom and non-wisdom, and by trying to understand the relationships between these different literary expressions. Here we are concerned with how the perspectives of Proverbs, Job and Ecclesiastes relate to the more prominent Old Testament themes of covenant and salvation.

The wisdom psalms

A number of psalms are of special interest to us because they stand very close to the wisdom points of view. With a certain amount of confidence we can classify some of

---

[6] A stringent critique of many identifications of wisdom in non-wisdom books has been made by J. Crenshaw, *Journal of Biblical Literature*, 88, 1969, 129–142.

them as wisdom poems because they share the same distinctive emphases found in our major wisdom books. Other psalms invite our attention because they seem to join distinctively wisdom ideas with those of covenant and salvation history. There is a fair amount of scholarly agreement that the psalms which can be regarded as wisdom poems include Psalms 1, 37, 49, 73, 112, 127, 128 and 133, although there are some weighty protests against these opinions. Psalms 25, 34, 78, 111, 119 and 139 are considered to have been influenced to some degree by wisdom thought. Some psalms appear to place wisdom into a close relationship with the Israelite concept of salvation, and we may find them informative as to how the two perspectives interacted.

Psalm 78

The psalms illustrate in many places one of the basic principles of worship in Israel. Worship is ascribing worth to God which means responding to the way God has revealed himself to his people. The peculiar relationship of Israel to God focuses upon what God has done in saving his people. Thus all the words which describe God are given their definition in the acts of God as they are interpreted by his prophetic word. To worship God was, for Israel, to recall what God has done in the history of his saving acts.[7] It is this recital of salvation history that is not even hinted at in the main wisdom books.

Psalm 78 provides us with an unusual mixing of wisdom and salvation history. Although it is almost entirely

---

[7] See Psalms 68, 98, 105, 106, 114 and 136 for examples of salvation history recitals. Many other psalms refer to the marvellous works of God or look at specific events which have saving significance.

given over to the events of Israel's past, it begins with a section that has a distinctly wisdom sound to it:

O my people, hear my teaching;
listen to the words of my mouth.
I will open my mouth in parables,
I will utter things hidden from of old.

The call to hear, though not unique to wisdom, is suggestive of a teaching situation similar to that from which the instructions came. The word for *teaching* (Hebrew: *torah*) is also the word for God's law. Its root meaning is instruction and it always refers to God's instruction except here and in three wisdom passages (Proverbs 3:1; 4:2; 7:2) where it is the instruction given by a wisdom teacher. It is therefore probable that it is expressive of wisdom in this psalm.

The most significant wisdom indicators in Psalm 78 are the references to parables and hidden things in verse 2. The Hebrew word for parable is *mashal* which is used for proverb in the wisdom literature. This word has a diverse usage in the Old Testament but it appears to be rooted in popular wisdom. The hidden things translate the Hebrew *hidah* which is the word used for Samson's riddle (Judges 14), the queen of Sheba's hard questions (1 Kings 10) and Ezekiel's parable (Ezekiel 17). The overall impression of Psalm 78:1–3 is that of a wisdom teacher calling his pupils for instruction.

The problem of the psalm is that the instruction given is quite unlike any of the instructions given in the wisdom books. It is possible that it is a reworking of some older material which in this case consisted of a traditional salvation history recital. This is in keeping with verse 4:

> We will not hide them from their children;
> we will tell the next generation
> the praiseworthy deeds of the Lord,
> his power, and the wonders he has done.

But there are some significant differences from the usual salvation history recital.[8] The emphasis is more on the refusal of Israel to keep covenant with the Lord. The mighty deeds of God were intended to bind this people to himself, and so the word of God was given that they might not forget his saving acts (vv. 5–8). But Israel did not remember these things, either during the events or after. The miracle signs that God did in Egypt before the Exodus are seen as the prelude to Israel's disobedience in the wilderness. This faithlessness was the worse for being displayed in the midst of God's saving acts:

> In spite of this, they kept on sinning;
> in spite of his wonders, they did not believe. (v. 32)

> Their hearts were not loyal to him,
> they were not faithful to his covenant. (v. 37)

Once again the psalmist turns to the saving acts of God:

> They did not remember his power—
> the day he redeemed them from the oppressor,
> the day he displayed his miraculous signs in Egypt.
> (vv. 42–43)

Following this recital of salvation history (vv. 43–55) the theme of rebellion is again introduced (vv. 56–57), and this leads to the judgment on the temple in Shiloh (v. 60).

---

[8] Other salvation history recitals are found in Exodus 15; Deuteronomy 26:5–9; Joshua 24; and Nehemiah 9.

Finally, God stirs himself to reject the northern tribe of Ephraim, and to establish his rule through David in Zion of the tribe of Judah. This latter section is unique to Psalm 78 out of all the salvation history recitals in the Old Testament.

This psalm takes the position of the book of Chronicles in emphasizing that God's purposes are removed from the northern tribes centred on Ephraim, and established in David. By recapitulating the miracles in Egypt the psalm links the great redemptive event in the Exodus with the climax of saving history in David's rule. We have noted already that David and Solomon are central to the development of the wisdom tradition in Israel, and that Solomon was remembered not only for wise rule, but also for the wisdom of ordinary human experience. Royal wisdom has its roots in this empirical wisdom, and it is by such wisdom that kings reign, as Proverbs 8:12–16 reminds us. It is not surprising that these ideals which were associated with David and Solomon are taken up as characteristics of the messiah-prince of the house of David which the prophets expected. Observe the similarities in the relevant sections of Isaiah 11 and Proverbs 8 (RSV).

ISAIAH 11	PROVERBS 8
And the spirit of the Lord shall be upon him, the spirit of wisdom (*hokhmah*), and understanding (*binah*) . . . of counsel (*'etzah*) and might (*geburah*) . . . of knowledge and the fear of the Lord (v. 2) And his delight shall be in the fear of the Lord. (v. 3)	I, wisdom (*hokhmah*) . . . (v. 12) I have counsel (*'etzah*) and sound wisdom (*tushiah*) I have insight (*binah*) I have strength (*geburah*) (v. 14) The fear of the Lord is hatred of evil. (v. 13). By me kings reign. (v. 15)

This link between wisdom and the prophetic view of the messiah is relevant because the concluding section of Psalm 78 is suggestive of the messianic reign as the final outcome of God's redemptive acts:

And David shepherded them with integrity of heart;
with skilful hands he led them. (v. 72)

The final phrase is odd to say the least. But we note that the word translated *skilful* has a decidedly wisdom flavour.[9] The reference to his hand is a metaphor of David's kingly power.[10] The shepherd is also a commonly used image of rulership. In this context we may propose the translation of the last phrase as:

And he guided them with the wisdom of his rule.

What conclusions may we reach? We see in Psalm 78 a reshaping of the salvation history recital to make it the subject of a wisdom lesson. Here is the riddle of Israel's disobedience in the face of the astonishing grace of God shown in the redemption of Israel from Egypt in the Exodus. The solution to this problem of disobedience is found in the coming of the ideal rule of a kingship which is ordered according to true wisdom. The structure of the

---

[9] It is a noun in construct to *hands*, that is, it is the Hebrew way of saying the *skill of his hands*. The word *tebunah* is derived from the same root as *binah* noted above in Proverbs 8 and Isaiah 11. Of forty-one occurrences, five, possibly six, refer to a craftsman's skill, eight refer to God, and of these five concern creation (both are concerns of wisdom). Twenty-seven instances refer to human wisdom and twenty of these are in the wisdom books.

[10] See Judges 6:13, 1 Samuel 4:3. The Hebrew *kaph* (palm of hand) is used with the same force as *yad* (hand) in 2 Samuel 8:3, Psalm 78:42 (NIV:power), Exodus 14:31.

psalm emphasizes the rebellion of Israel against redeeming love. Then, by repeating the salvation history and extending it to David, it shows that the same events against which Israel rebelled are the solution to that rebellion. Salvation history is presented because it contains a riddle. It is joined to wisdom at the place where the two have long since met, in the royal wisdom.

Normally we would have expected salvation history to be outside the range of empirical wisdom. But something has happened in Psalm 78 to enable the totality of events from the Exodus to David's rule to be linked as one event to wisdom. The structure of the psalm is suggestive of a deliberate contrast of folly (Israel's rebellion) and wisdom (the wise rule of David). The events of salvation history, perhaps because of the passage of time, are able to be viewed by the psalmist as objective facts of Israel's experience. The retribution idea of Proverbs is at work: folly brings disaster, the wisdom of David saves the day and brings good. Thus, what would normally be a declaration of prophetic revelation is seen here through the eyes of the empirical observer. Even the pagans should have been able to see the wisdom of the nation through the effects of its covenant-keeping life. Instead, the stern warning of Deuteronomy has come true for a faithless nation:

> Observe them carefully, for this will show your wisdom and understanding to the nations, who will hear about all these decrees and say, 'Surely this great nation is a wise and understanding people.'
>
> (Deuteronomy 4:6)

> However, if you do not obey the Lord your God . . . You will become a thing of horror and an object of scorn (Hebrew: *mashal* = proverb) and ridicule to all the nations.
>
> (Deuteronomy 28:15,37)

But then wisdom triumphs in the glorious reign of David. The divinely placed order of the universe is established as the order of Israel's existence under the ideal messiah-king. He is the good shepherd whose royal wisdom restores his people.

Psalm 73

This psalm is also widely accepted as a wisdom poem, although it is not clearly grounded in the older folk wisdom of Israel. It can be regarded as a didactic composition, that is, one that is intended to instruct others. It raises the matter of theodicy which, though dealt with in wisdom, is by no means unique to it. The specific form of the problem is the arrogance of the prosperous evildoers who interpret their ability to gain through their unrighteousness as a proof that God is without knowledge (v. 11). The psalmist feels that his own righteousness has been in vain for he has no benefit from it.

In a sense this psalm ploughs the same ground as Job and Qohelet. But its answer is wholly different, and herein lies its special interest for us. The deed-outcome relationship, so prominent in Proverbs, is under attack. The evil man prospers and the good man suffers adversity. The solution is that the psalmist enters the sanctuary and comes near to God. We must not forget how important the actual place of the temple was for the Israelite even though he knew that God was not confined to the temple precincts. It was through the services and sacrifices held in that special place that the faithful drew near to God.

The significance of Psalm 73 is that it is a wisdom poem written from within the context of the temple cult. It thus provides us with a rare glimpse of how wisdom may have been merged with the prophetic faith of Israel. There are at least two possibilities here. The first is that wisdom is being adapted to the framework of Israel's law and temple worship. What God has done in his saving acts in history is given as the basis of confidence in the face of the apparent attack on the order of things. The second is that the wisdom perspective with its very individualistic standpoint is brought to bear on the ritual practices of the cult in order to focus on the inward reality to which the cult points, but which has always been in danger of mere outward observance.[11] It is the circumcision of the heart (Deuteronomy 30:6) rather than outward ritual that was needed.

This drawing together of wisdom and temple worship is no surprise. What is perhaps surprising, given the relationship of Solomon the temple builder to wisdom, is that there was not much more exploration of this relationship in the wisdom writings and elsewhere. It seems that most of the wisdom writers were content to presuppose the fear of the Lord, a concept born out of salvation history. Wisdom comes from God, and the wisdom of God is expressed in his revealed truth including the specific details of law given to Israel. While most of the wisdom writers pursued the matters of personal experience and of our humanity within this world, occasionally the question of Israel's covenant faith intruded into distinctly wisdom concerns.

Torah and Wisdom

If the fear of the Lord means, among other things, covenant faithfulness and observance of the law (torah), what

---

[11] Hans-Jürgen Hermisson, *Sprache und Ritus im alttestamentlichen Kult* (Neukirchen-Vluyn; Neukirchener Verlag, 1965), p. 146f.

connection was the law seen to have with wisdom? Many scholars have considered the apparent wisdom influences in the book of Deuteronomy.[12] Deuteronomy brings a concern for salvation history and the law into view with a number of themes and emphases that are shared with the wisdom books. But how far this means that wisdom influences are at work is difficult to say. One writer suggests the following wisdom traits in Deuteronomy: the idea of direct retribution coupled with the theme of 'life', education of children, and the spiritualizing of the faith away from mere ritual observance.[13] These catagories are too broad in that they are found also in areas where no wisdom distinctives are present. They can be no more than merely suggestive of wisdom influences here.

As a body of literature the Apocrypha is important to us in that it reveals a great deal about the religious and literary developments that took place between the Old and New Testaments. There are some significant wisdom works in this literature which were never included in the canon of Scripture. The most important is the Wisdom of Jesus ben Sirach, or Ecclesiasticus (not to be confused with the biblical Ecclesiastes). It was written by a wise man of Jerusalem in the early second century BC. Its main interest for us is its clear dependence on the traditions of Solomonic wisdom and its inclusion of law and salvation history. The style of ben Sirach is much more reflective than Proverbs, and it seems that he was facing the question of how the wisdom and salvation history perspectives may be drawn together. As in Proverbs wisdom is

---

[12] E.g.: M. Weinfeld, 'Deuteronomy—the present state of the enquiry', *Journal of Biblical Literature*, LXXXVI (1967), 249–262, and Joseph Blenkinsop, *Wisdom and Law in the Old Testament* (New York: Oxford University Press, 1983).

[13] Weinfeld, op. cit.

the achievement of men as well as a gift of God who is its source. Ben Sirach points to the law as a principal way in which the wisdom of God comes to reside in Israel: (here wisdom is speaking)

> Then the Creator of the universe laid a command upon me;
> my Creator decreed where I should dwell.
> He said, 'Make your home in Jacob;
> find your heritage in Israel.'
> Before time began he created me,
> and I shall remain forever.
> In the sacred tent I ministered in his presence,
> and so I came to be established in Zion.
>
> (Ecclesiasticus 24:8–10, NEB)

The last part of ben Sirach is a kind of salvation history recital from beginning to end. But it is not the usual recounting of the mighty acts of God. Rather the emphasis is on the people involved and their virtues:

> Let us now sing the praises of famous men,
> the heroes of our nation's history,
> through whom the Lord established his renown,
> and revealed his majesty in each succeeding age.
>
> (Ecclesiasticus 44:1–2, NEB)

Ben Sirach does not include wisdom under law, but rather turns law and salvation history to become expressions of the wisdom of God among his people Israel.[14] He presents a particular development of Old Testament perspectives on the wisdom of God. This tendency towards a full iden-tification of wisdom and law ignores the fact that wisdom functioned as a loosening of the absolute tutelage of the

---

[14] So von Rad, *Wisdom in Israel*, chapter 13.

law. The direction that ben Sirach takes would, I suggest, lead us towards something other than fulfilment in the gospel. The disqualification of this book from the canon of Scripture is soundly based.

Conclusion

The question of wisdom influences in non-wisdom books must remain open. At best, it seems we can detect the merging of certain perspectives which are characteristic of wisdom on the one hand and of salvation history on the other. There is no good reason for separating the origins of these strands into totally unrelated areas. We have noted that wisdom from human experience is characteristic of every culture, it is a part of being human. Likewise, every culture wrestles with the relationship of experience to the religious ideas which are held, particularly insofar as these ideas are thought of as having a distinct source in an authoritative revelation.

Because Israel's prophetic faith resisted all tendencies to pantheism which blurs the distinction between God, man and the world, the relation of human thought and action to the divine thought and action always retained an element of mystery. Wisdom acknowledged that the wisdom of God was somehow there behind all true wisdom in men. It did not try to analyse this relationship but placed the two elements side by side. The specific form of the problem for wisdom is how the task of the human quest for knowledge relates to the gift of the grace of God in saving act and revelation. Since wisdom is concerned with the whole created order, and since Israel's salvation history was never divorced from this created order, it is only to be expected that the relationship of salvation history to created order would in time force the wisdom and covenant perspectives into converging paths.[15] Wisdom and law both point to human responsibility before the One God whose wisdom is the source of both. It would, be strange if wisdom did not find itself included in the perspectives of law and prophecy.

These tensions in Old Testament thought must be set with all other aspects of Old Testament thought which raise the question of what it means to be human in God's world. Only in the place where God and man most perfectly relate will we find the last word on the matter. Here we will discover that to be human is not to solve the mystery nor to resolve the tension. The wisdom of God will be found to be the perfect union in the God-man Jesus Christ. Insofar as he preserves the mystery by being both God and man, he reminds us that somehow human wisdom is gift and task. It always remains distinct, though not separate, from its source – the wisdom of God.

Questions for study

1. Suggest some of the characteristics of form or thought which might indicate wisdom influences in material which would not be regarded as wisdom literature.
2. On what grounds could it be argued that Psalms 1, 37 and 111 are either wisdom poems or are influenced by wisdom?
3. What contacts between wisdom and salvation history do we find in the Old Testament?

---

[15] Donn F. Morgan, *op. cit.*, p. 53.

Chapter Ten

Wisdom in Old Testament Theology

Summary

The theology of wisdom makes contact with covenant theology in a number of ways. The God of the covenant was perceived to be the God of all creation and human existence. The wise men operated within the covenant as they explored God's creation. Creation itself implied the covenant. It spoke not only of what was once perfect but is now imperfect because of sin, but also of what will again be perfected through redemption. Wisdom explored a concept of righteousness that embraced the whole world order. Wisdom is not natural revelation but a way of interpreting nature and experience within the reality that is revealed in God's word. Thus wisdom has no independent theology. It depends upon, and is closely integrated with, the progressive revelation of God's kingdom. There is a special point at which wisdom theology converges on covenant in the wisdom of Solomon and in the subsequent prophetic idea of the wise messianic prince. This points finally to the New Testament perspective on Christ as the fulfilment of all the Old Testament expectations, including those of the perfecting of wisdom.

Wisdom and the Kingdom of God

It is now time to try to draw together some of the threads. Elsewhere I have proposed that one way of looking at the overall message of salvation is as the re-establishment of God's kingdom.[1] We can reduce the New Testament idea of the kingdom of God to some basic elements which are recognizable throughout the whole biblical story from creation to new creation. They are: God, mankind and the created universe all relating in the way God intended. Not only are these the essential ingredients of what the Bible is on about, they also include everything that exists. Thus we can say that reality (everything that exists) is God, man and creation. The kingdom of God is God, man and creation properly related to one another. What we have referred to as salvation history involves the whole process within history by which God saves, which means that he renews the relationships which were dislocated through human sin. But wisdom gives us another perspective on God, man and creation. The problem is how this perspective relates to that of salvation history.[2]

All religions and philosophies deal with the relationships between God (or gods), man and the world, even if they begin by asserting, or assuming that there is no God. So we haven't really got very far by saying that both wisdom and salvation history in the Old Testament are

---

[1] See my book *Gospel and Kingdom.*

[2] I have made some preliminary study of this relationship at a theoretical level in: 'The problem of the accommodation of wisdom literature in the writing of Old Testament theologies', (unpublished Th.M. dissertation, Union Theological Seminary in Virginia, 1970). I have also investigated a specific area of the problem in: 'Empirical wisdom in relation to salvation history in the Psalms', (unpublished Th.D. thesis, Union Theological Seminary in Virginia, 1973).

concerned about these three aspects of reality. But do their respective views or perspectives actually make contact? So far we have seen that there are many reasons for saying that they do. In looking at the history of wisdom in Israel and at the main wisdom books, we have seen many points of contact and overlap with the larger body of Old Testament literature dealing with the saving acts of God and their accompanying elements of covenant, law, cultic worship and prophecy.

Worldly Wisdom or Wisdom of the World?

There was a time when wisdom sayings which contained no reference to God, or no explicit concern with Israel's covenant thinking, were regarded as non-theological or secular. We now recognize the inadequacy of this judgment. And in this regard we should not misunderstand Paul's contrast between worldly wisdom and true wisdom. True wisdom includes a way of looking at the world. It is worldly in the proper sense of providing the basis for life in the world. It should not be confused with an atheistic world view because it proceeds from the fact of God as both Creator and Redeemer of the world.

The biblical wisdom that is without 'God-talk' is now recognised as being empirical in the sense of being based on human experience. But it does not fit the evidence to say that there is no thought of God behind it. The problem has been to understand precisely in what way empirical wisdom relates to the knowledge of God and man which is revealed in the inspired prophetic word. Even if those responsible for the propagation of folk wisdom and empirical wisdom in general never thought about this relationship, there came a time when both strands were seen to be expressions of a unified truth. We must take seriously the canonization of Scripture which was the recognition of the whole of it as God's word to his people.

Thus, what may at first seem to be a placing side by side of two quite irreconcilable views of reality, may in fact be the meeting of two different but valid perspectives of the same reality. The empirical wisdom of the Old Testament is not a godless or pagan assessment of reality. It is the work of Israelites who, precisely because of their heritage in the covenant and the history of God's saving acts, are driven to find a unitary view of the world. The implications of the salvation of Noah, of the covenant with Abraham, of the Exodus from Egypt, of Sinai and the theocratic state of Israel, are that the Lord God of Israel reigns in heaven above and in the earth beneath. Furthermore, the Israelites, though plagued by many forms of idolatry that came beating at their door, were as yet unaffected by the Greek thinking which rejected the world and everything material. If God was saving Israel it was into an earthly kingdom in the land of Canaan. Some people despise the apparently crude materialism of the Old Testament view of the kingdom of God, and flee to what they think are purer notions of spirit and the immortality of the soul. On both counts they betray a paganism as bad as anything that the Israelites toyed with. Spirituality in the Old Testament was never a world-hating retreat from materialism. Rather it was established on the covenant of God to man which restored man to right relationships with God and with the created order. It is ironic that the worldly wisdom which Paul shuns in 1 Corinthians is one which adopts a phoney spirituality without the world of matter, while true spirituality involves a wisdom that learns to understand the world in relation to God.

Wisdom and creation

The broad study of wisdom seems to show two things. First, the wisdom writers were Israelites through and through, and they acknowledged the prophetically revealed word of God. They did not reject the covenant but rather operated within this framework of the fear of the Lord. Secondly, despite this orthodox Israelite mind-set, the wisdom writers found that their subject matter and method of approach did not involve them in specific concerns of the covenant and the saving acts of God. Rather they looked at man in the world at large. Because of this, it has been suggested that wisdom is a working through of a theology of creation. If this is an accurate assessment, a warning must be sounded. Creation and salvation do not involve two totally different world-views in the Old Testament. Indeed, Israel's view of creation cannot really be understood apart from the doctrines of redemption. Nevertheless, we can concentrate our attention on one or the other without ignoring their close relationship.

A modern example may help us to see the issues which faced the wise men of Israel. In our twentieth-century western culture we can see at least two models of comprehensive Christian education in day schools. A more traditional model emerged when church and state were much more closely aligned than they are today. The curriculum mirrored the view of reality held by a society which was largely thought of as Christian. With the gradual secularizing of society and the breakdown of Christian values, the educational curriculum of many institutions simply followed the same process of secularization. A school chaplain and weekly religious instruction were all that marked the school out as Christian. The chaplain did his bit according to his convictions to try to inject a bit of

Christianity into the pupils' thinking. Meanwhile, a largely secular staff taught subjects from the same humanist perspectives as those which came to be established in state run schools. The traditional church-linked schools of today frequently exhibit this pattern. Such schools are often Christian in name only and in their being to some degree controlled by denominational synods or assemblies. There is no overall Christian view of reality underpinning their educational processes.

A relatively new phenomenon is the independent Christian school often organized on the 'parent-controlled' principle. This is a deliberate move by Christians to break the stranglehold on education of a secular humanist state.[3] Two distinct issues are involved. One is the right of Christian parents to control the education of their children. The other is the importance of a distinctly Christian view of reality. Some Christian schools have successfully established a measure of parental control within the limits of a state imposed standard, but find the development of a curriculum which embraces the whole of education within a Christian framework a much more difficult matter. Christian educators are being forced to ask whether being Christian affects in any marked way the approach we should adopt to teaching science, language, the humanities and mathematics. It is recognized that making Bible knowledge a full compulsory subject, teaching creation as an alternative model of origins to evolution, and using the Bible as a reading text, does not necessarily make the curriculum Christian. But what, after all, is a Christian approach to mathematics, or to the study of Japanese or Indonesian? The task is not so much to make these subjects somehow religious in themselves, as

---

[3] R. J. Rushdoony, *Intellectual Schizophrenia* (Phillipsburg: Presbyterian and Reformed Publishing Company, 1978).

to find their relationship to an integrated Christian interpretation of the world and of our place in it. I suggest that
the wisdom literature of the Bible has something to teach
us here.

In order to understand the relationship of wisdom to a
theology of creation we need to look at the possibilities of
such a theology. Creation may be taken into account with
an accent on origins. In the ongoing debate about creation
and evolution, creation may be proposed as an alternative
explanation of origins. Proponents of special creation
point to the philosophical and scientific inadequacies of
evolutionary dogma in its attempt to explain how we
came to be here. It is doubtful, however, that the biblical
doctrine of creation arose primarily out of a concern about
origins. Without entirely discarding the question of origins, we may propose that the biblical view of creation has
its emphasis on relationships. Of course origins and relationships are inseparable, but we need to understand the
perspective in which they come to us in the Bible. To do
that we will have to go back behind the creation-evolution
debate to something more basic: how do God, man and
the universe relate? In a real sense the doctrine of creation
is an implication of what the Bible says about God's character as a just and redeeming God.[4]

The place of creation in Old Testament theology is open
to debate. There is little doubt, however, that the Old Testament writers saw creation more for its present implications than for its solution to the question of how we began.
In this they are in full accord with Paul's extraordinary
statement in Colossians 1:15–20 where creation's blue-
print is the person and saving work of Christ. If Paul sees
the gospel here as God's forethought to creation, the Old

---

[4] J. L. Crenshaw, *Studies in Ancient Israelite Wisdom Literature*
(New York:KTAV, 1976), pp. 1–45.

Testament prophets and historians see creation as the prelude to salvation history. Indeed, the whole biblical understanding of regeneration (re-creation) as the kernel of salvation, stems from the Old Testament view of creation and recreation. In all this the matter of relationships is central. Genesis 1–2 stress the personal element in that the infinite, personal Creator brings things to be by the most distinctly inter-personal trait: the spoken word. If the Israelite asked the question, 'Where did I come from?' there is no doubt that the answer would be creation. But the prophetic view of redemption – a restoration and a buying back – implies that the constant emphasis on the new world order to come is a re-establishing of the original world order. Both old and new creations are the work of the one Creator. The emphasis is far more on where we are now and where we are going, than on where we came from.

Thus, without denying the question of origins, we see creation in the Old Testament as a way of giving meaning to the present and the future. If we are in need of redemption then we have fallen. If we have fallen then we have fallen from something. That something was a realm of relationships ordered by God, and that can be only if God is the one who created all things freely and sovereignly. We can understand, then, why some Old Testament scholars maintain that the real heart of the Old Testament is not salvation history but the creation of an orderly universe.[5] Creation becomes for us the rule of order. The prophetic view of the future, that order is being restored through

---

[5] J. L. Crenshaw, *Studies in Ancient Israelite Wisdom Literature*, pp. 26–35. H. H. Schmid, *'Schöpfung, Gerechtigkeit und Heil'* in *Altorientalische Welt in der Alttestamentlichen Theologie* (Zurich: Theologischer Verlag Zurich, 1974). Hans-Jürgen Hermisson, 'Observations on the creation theology in wisdom' in (ed.) J. Gammie, *Israelite Wisdom* (Missoula: Scholars Press, 1978).

redemption, reminds us that order still exists, though it is obscured to some degree by the forces of chaos.

Righteousness

Creation also provides a basis for understanding the biblical terms *righteousness* and *justice*. These two words are prominent in the Old Testament, especially in the prophets. They are constantly linked with God's judging and saving roles. Because they are usually connected with legal and moral ideas in the non-religious realm, we tend to think of their biblical use as likewise legal and moral. Such an assumption is being seriously questioned on the basis of the biblical evidence. One leading scholar, having examined the usage of righteousness in the Old Testament, argues that its meaning has to do with the created order in the universe.[6] This means that righteousness, while including human responsibility, embraces the whole of creation. Legal and moral ideas are derivative of this.

The creation-related idea of righteousness points to the harmonious principle underlying the order established by God at creation, and which is an aspect of the character of God imprinted on the creation. The restoration of the creation, as an integral part of salvation, is a restoration of justice and righteousness.[7] So Isaiah looks forward to the time when:

---

[6] H. H. Schmid, *Gerechtigkeit als Weltordnung* (Tübingen: J. C. B. Mohr, 1968). Schmid maintains that we can see six distinct areas in which righteousness is used: juristic, wisdom, nature, salvation, cult and sacrifice, kingship.

[7] Justice (Hebrew, *mishpat*) and righteousness (Hebrew, *tzedeq*) are frequently linked and may be regarded as virtually synonymous terms.

> ... the Spirit is poured upon us from on high,
> and the desert becomes a fertile field,
> and the fertile field seems like a forest.
> Justice will dwell in the desert
> and righteousness live in the fertile field.
> The fruit of righteousness will be peace;
> the effect of righteousness will be quietness
> and confidence forever.
> My people will live in peaceful dwelling-places,
> in secure homes,
> in undisturbed places of rest.   (Isaiah 32:15–18)

Here justice and righteousness mean that nature and man are restored to harmony as a result of the saving acts of God. Thus, while it is impossible to fit all the uses of righteousness into a legal-moral framework, it is possible to fit them, including the legal-moral, into a framework of universal order.

While the wisdom literature is lacking in the salvation perspectives, it uses the word righteousness frequently. It is likely, in the light of the considerations of order that we have observed in the wisdom books, that we have here an emphasis on the wider concept of righteousness as universal order. More recent studies have reminded us that it used to be accepted that wisdom was utilitarian and eudaemonistic in outlook.[8] Utilitarianism is a view of life that assesses things and actions by their usefulness. Eudaemonism assesses them according to the happiness they produce. Such a view of wisdom is no longer held. Rather, as H. H. Schmid suggests, the chief question of Israel's wisdom thinking is: how does one recognize the order of the world which is established and guaranteed by God?[9]

---

[8] H. H. Schmid, *Gerchtigkeit als Weltordnung*, pp. 96–98.
[9] *Ibid.*

To this end, the prologue of Proverbs indicates that the purpose of wisdom is instruction in righteousness (*tzedeq*), justice (*mishpat*) and equity (Proverbs 1:3). References to righteousness and the righteous person abound in the proverbial sentences. In most cases there is a contrast between the righteous and the wicked which reminds us that the moral sense is there. But it is wider than that. The contrasts of righteous and wicked are constantly posed in terms of the successful life of the former and the confusion of the latter. The religious context of covenant (the fear of the Lord), among other things, demanded that the perceptible relationships between one's manner of life and its outcome be assessed more accurately than as an expression of eudaemonism. The challenges to the perceptible order posed by Job and Ecclesiastes, do not in any way rule out the deed-outcome relationship of Proverbs. The proverbial literature is saying that despite the exceptions and the mysteries, there is a discernible relationship between lifestyle and outcome. The principle of order includes everything that God has specifically revealed in his law, and thus includes the legal-ethical idea of righteousness. But it goes beyond this to embrace the whole range of human existence in the world. The fact that God is the Creator of the world means that even those areas of human action which appear to be ethically neutral or which do not come within the scope of the revealed law of God or of the law of society, are within the scope of righteousness. In so saying, wisdom points to the truth that there are no neutral actions, no neutral thoughts.

Revelation

A consideration which follows from the nature of wisdom is that of natural revelation and natural law. If the scope of wisdom is beyond that of the specific word-revelation of God, does that mean that there is truth to be discerned from the world quite apart from God's prophetic revelation? Natural revelation means that truth about God is imprinted upon the creation. Natural theology assumes that this truth can be discerned from nature by means of our human senses without the aid of Scripture or the Holy Spirit. Natural law refers to a specific aspect of natural theology, namely, that part of such discernible revelation is a range of self-evident ethical principles. There are significant theological disagreements over this question. But we must consider the matter because it might appear to some that the implication of what we are saying is that there are two distinct sources of ultimate truth: revelation through God's word, and observation of experience in the world. Human behaviour would then be governed by God's words and by discernible rules of nature. Knowledge of God would come to us by the word of God and by our observation of the universe which bears the stamp of God's character.

We must first dispense with the idea that wisdom is Israelite humanism in the sense that man is the centre of things and is capable of interpreting the universe on his own. Wisdom is truly humanitarian in its concern for people and their well-being, but it is not humanistic. Humanism as a philosophical system rejects the possibility of God as the ultimate reality. If there is a God he is subject to the same laws of being as the rest of the universe. This is not the God of the Bible. Wisdom, even in its most sceptical moments (Ecclesiastes), never contemplated anything but a universe which is creature, and therefore subject to the laws of a personal, eternal and sovereign Creator.

Next, we must rule out the idea that real truth is discernible from both revelation and nature independently. Order was perceived by ancient religions and pagan wisdom, and it goes on being perceived in modern philosophy and experimental science. But it was, and is, a warped perception because it does not start from the facts given by revelation of an eternal, personal God who is the ultimate source of all things and their order. But there are Christians who adopt the position that creation is able to reveal to us truth about the existence of God the Creator, and thus natural theology is possible.[10] This means that without considering the truths that come only by special revelation, we can understand truly, even if only partially, the meaning of the universe. It is claimed that Romans 1:20–32 establishes this position. But what Paul in fact says is that God has revealed himself in creation, but that it is the nature of human sin to repress that revelation. Men knew God through the creation but did not acknowledge him. Rather, 'their thinking became futile and their foolish hearts were darkened' (v. 21). 'They exchanged the truth of God for a lie, and worshipped and served created things rather than the Creator' (v. 25). 'Since they did not think it worth while to retain the knowledge of God, he gave them over to a depraved mind, to do what ought not to be done' (v. 28). The problem with natural theology is that it does not recognize the naked rebellion of sin with the depravity of mind that it produces.

Wisdom is clearly not engaged in natural theology. It does not assume any neutral ground of knowledge open

---

[10] Thomas Aquinas (died 1274) proposed that revelation came through nature plus grace (special revelation). His thought was the basis of the position known as Scholasticism. This maintained that man is capable of establishing a valid natural philosophy, that is, a concept of truth through nature apart from the special revelation of the Bible as it is applied to us by the Holy Spirit. This has far reaching consequences for the interpretation of the Bible, for the self-evident truths of natural philosophy are adopted as the framework within which special revelation is understood and interpreted.

to all men alike. Its indisputable presupposition is God the Creator. But from where did this starting point come? The answer is special revelation. Israel's prophetic revelation of YHVH (or Jehovah) making covenant and acting to save his people undergirds true wisdom. It is the fear of the Lord which enabled the wise men to know what is the meaning of all life's experiences. Without a knowledge of the God of salvation history, there could be no true wisdom, no real knowledge of the world.

The contacts between Israel's wisdom and that of Egypt or Mesopotamia may suggest real common ground. But this is a superficial assessment. It was not that they all truly knew something of the ultimate meaning of the universe, and that Israel's wisdom was given a special boost by the addition of revealed knowledge. If the fear of the Lord is the beginning of wisdom, it can in no sense be merely a supplementary boost to common wisdom. Israel's wisdom says that only through the fear of the Lord can we know anything truly. Wisdom can never give ultimate meaning to the world of our experience except in terms of the Lord's creative and saving acts. Whenever Israel's wisdom seemed to coincide with Egypt's, or Solomon's with the queen of Sheba's, it was because they were operating at the level of immediate meaning, not ultimate meaning. An Israelite and an Egyptian might learn and state similar things from similar experiences. But the Israelite would explain the reality in the light of the revelation of the creator God of Israel as he reveals himself by his word. The Egyptian, on the other hand, would appeal to Ma'at, a no-god conceived in the minds of sinful men who have exchanged the truth of God for a lie. It is not possible rightly to interpret reality on the basis of a lie. Modern atheistic humanism sees ultimate meaning from the perspective of man as the final interpreter. In its relation to modern thought, Israel's wisdom shows a very contemporary concern for all life in this world, but refuses to understand it apart from the meaning given to it by God who created the universe.

Wisdom as part of Old Testament theology

We have come to the conclusion that wisdom does not have a completely independent theology in the Old Testament. It is not a self-contained and alternative way of looking at God and reality. Rather, it complements the perspective of salvation history. Indeed, we should go further than that and say that wisdom is a theology of the redeemed man living in the world under God's rule. It is thus as much an aspect of kingdom theology as salvation history is. In the kingdom of God all relationships between God, man and the created order are

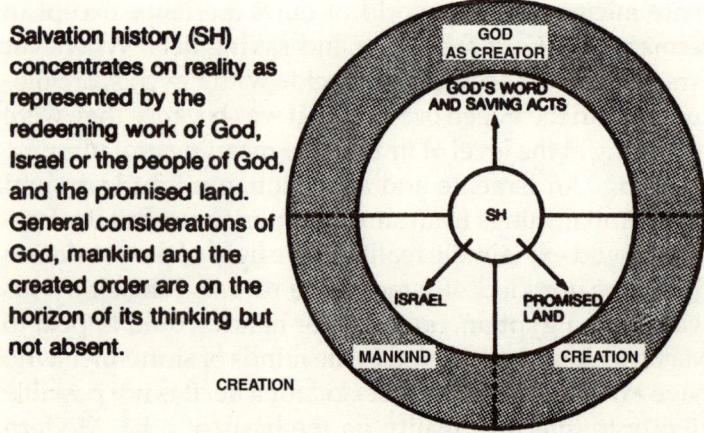

Salvation history (SH) concentrates on reality as represented by the redeeming work of God, Israel or the people of God, and the promised land. General considerations of God, mankind and the created order are on the horizon of its thinking but not absent.

Figure 4. The Perspective of Salvation History

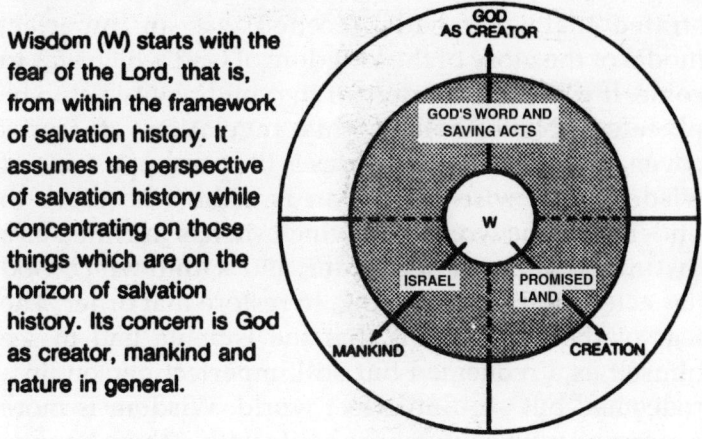

Wisdom (W) starts with the fear of the Lord, that is, from within the framework of salvation history. It assumes the perspective of salvation history while concentrating on those things which are on the horizon of salvation history. Its concern is God as creator, mankind and nature in general.

GOD AS CREATOR

GOD'S WORD AND SAVING ACTS

W

ISRAEL

PROMISED LAND

MANKIND

CREATION

Figure 5. The Perspective of Wisdom

perfectly restored. That is the final and completed expression of the kingdom in hope of which we still live. Wisdom in the Old Testament must be placed within the same structure of progressive revelation that exists for the saving acts of God. Broadly speaking, wisdom, along with every other dimension in the Bible, is revealed in three major stages:

a. Israel's history,
b. the prophetic view of the future kingdom, and
c. the fulfilment of these in Christ.

Wisdom was a part of Israel's life during the first of these stages, although it did not really flourish until the end of this period. It came into its own when the structures of the kingdom of God and of salvation had been revealed in the historical experience of Israel from

Abraham to David and Solomon. The decline of the kingdom of Israel after the death of Solomon demonstrated that what had preceded was an imperfect model of the glory of the kingdom of God which was to come. It was but a shadow of the solid reality yet to be revealed. Nevertheless, this revelation of God's covenant and saving purposes is the presupposition of wisdom. The wise man is an Israelite who seeks to understand the world into which sin has intruded as a disruption of the perfect order, and within which God has acted, and is now acting, to restore that order. The fear of the Lord means that the Israelite had to see himself as a redeemed but still imperfect person, in a redeemed but still imperfect world. Wisdom is more concerned with contemporary life within these bounds than with the possibilities of a wider future salvation.

As the prophets spoke of Israel's failure, they spoke also of the covenant faithfulness of God. This meant that a future restoration of the order was inevitable. From time to time the prophets saw the significance of this for wisdom in that a world made perfect would be a world fully displaying wisdom both in the new creation and in man's relationships to all things and to God. Thus part of the prophetic view of the coming kingdom is that it is characterized by wisdom:

> The Lord is exalted, for he dwells on high;
> he will fill Zion with justice and righteousness.
> He will be the sure foundation for your times,
> a rich store of salvation and wisdom and knowledge;
> the fear of the Lord is the key to this treasure.
>
> (Isaiah 33:5–6)

This is the reversal of the terrible judgment pronounced over the faithless Israel of the prophet's time:

Their worship of me
is made up only of rules taught by men.
Therefore once more I will astound these people
with wonder upon wonder;
the wisdom of the wise will perish,
the intelligence of the intelligent will vanish.

(Isaiah 29:13b–14)[11]

There is also a significant concentration on the royal wisdom of the future kingdom which recalls the place of David and Solomon as fountainheads of wisdom. In the new order the benign rule of God will be mediated by a messianic prince who will be the paragon of wise men. It is David's descendant who is to be the 'wonderful counsellor', and who will establish and uphold God's kingdom with justice and righteousness (Isaiah 9:6–7). When this Davidic shoot sprouts from the stump of Jesse –

The Spirit of the Lord will rest on him –
the Spirit of wisdom and of understanding,
the Spirit of counsel and of power,
the Spirit of knowledge and of the fear of the Lord.

(Isaiah 11:2)

The prophet goes on to describe this wise rule as both one of terrible judgment on the wicked who disrupt order, and one of restoration of universal harmony between man and beast. It is the time when the wolf lies down with the lamb, and when children can play amongst snakes without harm (vv. 6–9).

After these two Old Testament stages – wisdom in Israel's history, and wisdom in the prophetic kingdom of

---

[11] See also Isaiah 47:10 where Babylon's wisdom is shown to be folly, and Jeremiah 8:9; 9:23–24 (compare 1 Corinthians 1:31); 10:11–12.

God – we come to the fulfilment of wisdom in Christ. Jesus brings to a climax the wisdom of Solomon and of all the wise men of Israel. He fulfils all that was foretold by the prophets of the wise rule of the messianic prince. He comes as the God-man in whom is all the wisdom of God perfectly relating to the wisdom of man. All things are reconciled to God through him and the harmony of creation is restored (Colossians 1:19–20). Thus God makes him to be wisdom for us (1 Corinthians 1:30).

In all three stages of revelation we see on the one hand a focal point in one person who mediates God's rule and wisdom, and on the other hand the people who engage in the task of learning wisdom in the framework of God's revealed wisdom. In the Old Testament the wisdom of God is not so clearly identified with salvation as in the New Testament where its greatest expression is in the gospel. Christ expresses for us both the wisdom of God mediated to us as gift, and the wisdom of man in its perfect expression of a life totally in harmony with its Creator. In bringing wisdom so totally within the ambit of salvation history in Christ, the New testament does not lose sight of the Old Testament's emphasis on wisdom which turns more to creation than salvation. God reveals to us with all wisdom and understanding the mystery of his will, which is his plan to unite all things in Christ (Ephesians 1:9–10). The gospel, God's wisdom, is the means by which God restores the order of all things.

Wisdom, then, presents a theology of creation as God's perfectly decreed order. It places man within a special relationship to that order; as the unique creature of God whose task is to take up God's command to have dominion. He is to engage the world in his doing and his thinking. He is to investigate, analyse, reason, invent and be creative within the bounds of his creatureliness. To be able to do this he must understand the meaning of the universe as it is revealed in God's prophetic word and saving action. Wisdom highlights the fact that man, the sinner living in a world of distorted relationships, is nevertheless responsible to live before God. His task is to understand life within the dynamic order which moves toward the consummation of God's redemptive plan. When man entered his social, cultural and intellectual infancy, he had before him the wisdom of God's word to light the way and to guide in the search for knowledge. And today, he looks down and into the creation, to the microcosmic realm of molecules, atoms and sub-atomic particles. He goes out to the moon, and reaches into the solar system with his space craft. He uses new forms of telescope to open windows into the heavens where distances are measured by the speed of light. He exercises dominion, albeit corruptly. But only those who fear the Lord and hear the wisdom of God will understand the ultimate significance of these things.

Wisdom is a theology of covenant adulthood, both corporate and individual. It recognizes that an important aspect of man's relationship to God is his responsibility to think and act in a world that is not, and was never meant to be, an open book nor a static, passive blob of matter. Within an ever changing world a wonderful and finely tuned balance exists between living things and the inanimate. Tiny ecosystems within larger ones, spread out until the entire planet appears as a self-contained life-support system that also interacts with the wider universe. If, from the scientific point of view, the meaning of the universe can only be guessed at, the fear of the Lord provides the answer. It is the Father's creation. As he made all things good, so he is re-creating all things according to a purpose known to us only through Christ.

Questions for study

1. How does Old Testament wisdom that makes no direct reference to God differ from the worldly wisdom that Paul condemns in 1 Corinthians 1–2?
2. How does the Old Testament theology of creation provide a bridge between wisdom and salvation history?
3. How would you explain the meaning of the biblical word *righteousness*, and how does wisdom relate to it?
4. What is the difference between natural revelation and natural theology, and how does wisdom relate to each?

Chapter Eleven

Christ and the Perfection of Order

Summary

Wisdom is an important aspect of the person and work of Christ. Jesus embodied the true wisdom of both God and man. In his ministry he encountered the misconceptions which had thrown the Old Testament wisdom into crisis. Much of his teaching, including many of the parables, involves a confrontation with the false wisdom of the Jews of his day. The fact that Jesus fulfils wisdom means that the gospel presents a way of looking at the world. Thus we can identify an intellectual content of the gospel. Through the gospel God not only restores all relationships, but also reveals the nature of reality. Order and relationships that were the concern of wisdom are given their fullest and most perfect expression in Christ. Christ's being as God and man, and the perfect relationships he formed with all things, point to the unity and diversity of reality. The universe bears the stamp of its Creator who is 'one and many': trinity.

Return to the Starting Point

Now that we have considered wisdom in the context of Old Testament theology, we can move on to the point from which we started: Christ is our wisdom! I indicated at the beginning of this study that what the New Testament says about Christ as wisdom needs to be understood against the Old Testament teaching on the subject. This is consistent with the method of biblical theology which begins with Christ as the fullest revelation of God to man and the one through whom we are turned from darkness to light. Thus Christ himself directs us to the Old Testament as that which speaks of him and which he fulfils. A Christian understanding of the Old Testament means that we read it in the light of its relationship to Christ.

The three stages of revelation dealt with in the previous chapter give a bird's-eye view of the biblical message from the salvation history perspective. But what of the wisdom perspective? Wisdom, as we have seen, stands firmly on the same foundation of creation as does salvation history. Furthermore, it presupposes God's self-revelation in salvation history, the true response to which is described as the fear of the Lord. True wisdom develops within the framework of salvation history and is unintelligible apart from it. Although wisdom does not deal with them in the same way as salvation history does, it acknowledges the creation of all things in orderly relationships, and the dislocation of these relationships through human sin. In being built on the fear of the Lord, it recognizes that disorder and chaos are not the norms for life but are the characteristics of the less than human existence which has resulted from our rebellion against God.

In Proverbs, Job and Ecclesiastes, along with the other wisdom works of the Old Testament, we can catch many glimpses of how the Israelite learned to cope with life during the period in which God was revealing the nature of his kingdom through Israel's historical experience and through the prophets. I have referred to the fact that the wisdom literature did not really flourish until the end of the era of God's revelation in Israel's history, that is, until

Israel came of age under David and Solomon. During the period of historical decline when Israel as a nation came to mirror the reality of the kingdom of God less and less, wisdom had an important role in the daily life of the faithful. It was in that period that the major thrust of prophecy took on both a judgmental and promissory role. The prophetic view of the future which was expressed from Amos onwards projected the hope that the past glory would be restored along with the increase of glory in a nation made truly the people of God. There would also be a new glory in a restored world of right relationships. Thus, while the wise men of Israel were seeking to understand life in a world of confused order, the prophets were at the same time announcing a future day when true wisdom would characterize the nation. This prophetic view helps us to see how wisdom could be thought of within the processes of God's saving acts. A significant aspect of this prophetic view was the wisdom of the royal messianic rule.

Salvation history finds its goal and fulfilment in Christ. So too does wisdom. Three aspects of wisdom confront us in the New Testament. First, the Gospel narratives portray Jesus as the wise man who, in the form and content of many of his sayings, follows in the traditions of Israel's wisdom teachers. Secondly, Jesus goes beyond this actually to claim to be the wisdom of God. Thirdly, certain New Testament writers, notably Paul, understand the meaning of Christ's person and work in the light of certain wisdom ideas. Thus wisdom is seen as an important strand of Christology. We recognize also that to say that Jesus fulfils the Old Testament, including wisdom, means far more than that he is the end of a process and gains his meaning from what has preceded him. We should be clear about this point. The relationship of the two Testaments is such that while the New Testament presupposes the Old, the Old finds its real meaning in the New. As to the New presupposing the Old, we come to the New with the knowledge of the Old in order to understand much of its terminology and thought forms. But as to the New fulfilling the Old, we know what the Old is ultimately on about only as we see its goal in Jesus Christ.

We started with the gospel, with the testimony to Jesus of Nazareth, and found that it drove us back to the Old Testament in order to understand its presuppositions. But to go back to the Old Testament is like jumping into a swiftly flowing stream which carries us forward again to our starting point. There we see that all the various strands, images and perspectives of the Old Testament are drawn together in the person of Jesus.

The New Crisis of Wisdom

All four Gospels agree that the ministry of Jesus occasioned a rising tide of hostility towards him on the part of the Pharisees and Jewish religious leaders. We may describe this as a new crisis of wisdom. The first crisis arose because the old wisdom of Israel became fossilized and distorted in the thinking of many people so that it could not cope with new and contradictory experiences. Both Job and Qohelet rebelled against a simplistic notion of order which distorted the intention of Proverbs and prevented new insights from being added to those of the optimistic sages. The new crisis arose because of a fossilizing and distorting of the mainstream of Jewish thought so that a form of legalism became firmly established. Not only had the law gradually assumed an independence of grace, but the understanding of the future kingdom was bound by a particular and rather literalistic interpretation of the prophets.

The Scribes and the Pharisees displayed the same rigidity and dogmatism with their understanding of the wisdom of God as did the friends of Job. Thus they were incapable of accommodating the radical claims of Jesus. The old crisis was not a clash of empirical wisdom with speculative wisdom, but a clash of a distorted and shrivelled form of wisdom with something that did not fit its neat formulas. The new crisis was not a clash of the Old Testament with Jesus Christ, but a clash of a distorted form of Israel's faith with the unexpected and utterly surprising form of Old Testament fulfilment that Jesus announced in himself. The Old Testament prophetic faith should have led the Jews to a perception of the suffering messiah-prince. But Pharisaic Judaism had exalted law over grace, and thus lost sight of the need for a mediator. It submerged the great themes of the suffering servant under those of the glories of the restored land and people of Israel.

The constant use of wisdom forms by Jesus would seem to highlight this new crisis of wisdom. It is not only that the Gospels portray Jesus as the wise man above all wise men, but that he is presented as the teacher who uses and develops wisdom forms in a distinctive way. The actual sayings of Jesus involve wisdom forms more than any other type, so that we have much more to go on than the statements which explicitly link Jesus with wisdom. The Gospel narratives are full of sayings which have affinities with older wisdom even though they may betray a process of development beyond the major wisdom forms of the Old Testament.

The most characteristic form of saying that Jesus used was the parable. While recognizing that there is considerable diversity in the form of the parables, we can identify about seventy such sayings in the four Gospels.[1] It is

---

[1] This includes certain sayings recorded in John who never refers to them as parables.

sometimes said that parables are earthly stories with a heavenly meaning, thus suggesting that Jesus chose this medium in order to make plain to all the reality of the spiritual realm and of God's kingdom. In one sense this is true, but it is also very misleading. There are several pointers to the fact that the parables were a deliberate means of precipitating the new crisis of wisdom by confronting the false wisdom of the Pharisees. Thus we have the celebrated saying in Matthew 13:10–16 which follows the parable of the sower.[2] Jesus concluded the parable with the provocative statement: 'He who has ears, let him hear.' The disciples obviously felt that this constant use of parables was a problem and asked him: 'Why do you speak to the people in parables?' Jesus replied:

> 'The knowledge of the secrets of the kingdom of heaven has been given to you, but not to them. Whoever has will be given more, and he will have an abundance. Whoever does not have, even what he has will be taken from him. This is why I speak to them in parables. Though seeing, they do not see; though hearing, they do not hear or understand.'

Although not drawn from the wisdom literature, this passage shows one of the enigmas shared by wisdom and prophecy. Isaiah's call was first to bring hardening to the people who refused to turn to God. Jesus sees his parabolic messages fulfilling the same role at a critical point in the history of salvation. Contrary to the popular idea about parables, Jesus says that he uses them because they create a division between those who are wise in their own eyes and the humble children of the kingdom. Of the latter, his disciples, he says, 'Blessed are your eyes, for they see, and your ears, for they hear' (v. 16).

---

[2] Paralleled in Mark 4:10–12 and Luke 8:9–10.

In general, the nature of the parables was such that they were open to various interpretations. Only those whose understanding was enlightened by grace could perceive their application to the kingdom of God as it came with Jesus. Those who perceived this intended relationship were thus led to a greater understanding of Jesus. But for those, then or now, who see in the parables only illustrations of general religious truth, it is a matter of ears that hear not and eyes that see not.

This function of the parables, even though they now stand close to the redemptive history of the Bible, betrays their roots in the wisdom traditions. There are good reasons for maintaining that parables constitute a refinement of the Old Testament *mashal*. The fact that the Greek translation of the Old Testament (the Septuagint) uses *parabole* to translate *mashal* is suggestive. But the function of the parable to make comparisons after the fashion of proverbs is significant.[3] As with proverbial wisdom, the wisdom which comes in parabolic form is deceptive in that the uninitiated mistake parables for generalizations. Wisdom must penetrate to the meaning so that its specific application is perceptible. The parables can be understood only by those who recognize in Jesus the Messiah who now brings in the Kingdom of God.[4]

The ability of the new wise men, the disciples, to understand what Jesus was saying was strictly limited. But they had put themselves at the feet of *the* wise man and would learn from his instruction. At times they found his use of parables and metaphors difficult to grasp. Not only were they subject to their own humanness and the confusion of their sinfulness, but the truth was still in the process of

---

[3] Amos Wilder, *Early Christian Rhetoric* (Cambridge: Harvard University Press, 1971), Ch. 5.

[4] E. Hoskyns and N. Davey, *The Riddle of the New Testament* (London: Faber and Faber, 1958), p. 133.

being unveiled. Not until the gospel event was completed would they be able to see and understand the whole picture. John reminds us on a couple of occasions that it was after the event that the disciples understood certain matters in Jesus' life (John 2:22; 12:16). The disciples needed reminding that more was to come:

> I have much more to say to you, more than you can now bear. But when he, the Spirit of truth, comes, he will guide you into all truth. (John 16:12–13)

At one stage the disciples expressed relief that Jesus had stopped using figurative language and spoke plainly. Unhappily, though they had made progress, they did not really understand things as well as they thought (John 16:25, 29–32). To them the fear of the Lord was real, for in varying degrees they had perceived that Jesus was the one sent from God. A turning point came when Peter confessed, 'You are the Christ' (Mark 8:29). But it was only at Pentecost that the full significance of Jesus' person and work burst upon them.

The parables, though diverse in form, are relatively simple to identify in the Gospels. Less obvious are the proverbial forms of speech which occur frequently in the sayings of Jesus. It has been pointed out that some of the parables of Jesus actually illustrate Old Testament proverbs:[5]

> Do not exalt yourself in the king's presence,
> and do not claim a place among great men;
> it is better for him to say to you, 'Come up here,'
> than for him to humiliate you before a nobleman.
>
> (Proverbs 25:6–7)

---

[5] William A. Beardslee, 'Uses of the Proverb in the Synoptic Gospels', *Interpretation* XXIV, January 1970, 61–73.

But when you are invited, take the lowest place, so that when your host comes, he will say to you, 'Friend, move up to a better place.' Then you will be honoured in the presence of all your fellow guests.

(Luke 14:10)

And if you look for it as for silver
and search for it as for hidden treasure,
then you will understand the fear of the Lord
and find the knowledge of God.   (Proverbs 2:4–5)

The kingdom of heaven is like treasure hidden in a field. When a man found it, he hid it again, and then in his joy went and sold all he had and bought that field.

(Matthew 13:44)

Jesus also uttered proverbial sayings that have their counterpart in the book of Proverbs:

If your enemy is hungry, give him food to eat;
if he is thirsty, give him water to drink.

(Proverbs 25:21)

But I tell you, love your enemies and pray for those who persecute you.   (Matthew 5:44)

A man's pride brings him low,
but a man of lowly spirit gains honour.

(Proverbs 29:23)

For whoever exalts himself will be humbled, and whoever humbles himself will be exalted.   (Matthew 23:12)

Many other sayings of Jesus have a proverbial ring:

Ask and it will be given to you; seek and you will find; knock
and the door will opened to you. (Matthew 7:7)

You are the salt of the earth. But if the salt loses its saltiness,
how can it be made salty again? You are the light of the world.
A city on a hill cannot be hidden.

(Matthew 5:13–14)

The Sabbath was made for man, not man for the Sabbath.

(Mark 2:27)

It has long been considered by some scholars that the
blessings and woes of the Bible have roots in wisdom.[6] In
my opinion the case is not proven, especially as the word
woe does not appear in the wisdom literature except in
Proverbs 23:29, and (a different Hebrew word) in Job
10:15. Nevertheless, it is difficult to bypass the blessings
and woes of Jesus in our consideration of wisdom. Many
of them show the same concerns as the proverbial wisdom
of the Old Testament. For example, the woes recorded in
Luke 11:37–54 involve a series of contrasts between true
righteousness and the feigned righteousness of the Pharisees. The whole episode is brought on by the failure of
Jesus, before a meal, to fulfil the ritual expectations of a
certain Pharisee. This new, unexpected behaviour contra-
vened the Pharisees' rigid view of law which prevented
them from seeing the offensive things that Jesus did as
signs that the kingdom had come. They were so preoccu-
pied with the shadows of the kingdom that they failed to
see the reality when it was before their eyes. This event is

---

[6] E. Gerstenberger, 'The woe oracles of the prophets', *Journal of
Biblical Literature*, 81, 1962, 249–263. See also Waldemar Janzen,
'ASRE in the Old Testament', *Harvard Theological Review*, 58,
1965, 215–226, and W. J. Whedbee, *Isaiah and Wisdom* (Nashville:
Abingdon Press, 1971), p. 87–88.

another example of the crisis of wisdom. So serious is this failure to see the truth that it calls forth from Jesus the strongest expression of disapproval; the woe.

First there is a wisdom-like metaphor describing the Pharisees:

> Now then, you Pharisees clean the outside of the cup and dish, but inside you are full of greed and wickedness.
>
> (Luke 11:39)

Because they confuse ritual conformity with actual righteousness they are rejecting the very wisdom that Israel's laws were intended to express:

> You foolish people! Did not the one who made the outside make the inside also? But give what is inside to the poor, and everything will be clean for you. (vv. 40–41).

Then follow six woes, some of which make an explicit contrast of the folly of ritual legalism or pride, with the wisdom of inner righteousness. Thus they tithe even the herbs of the garden while neglecting justice and love of God, or they desire the praise of men rather than the praise of God (compare Proverbs 25:6–7). These false teachers have repudiated the wisdom of God by killing the prophets. Now note the biting irony of the last woe:

> Woe to you experts in the law, because you have taken away the key to knowledge. You yourselves have not entered, and you have hindered those who were entering. (v. 52)

The opposite to the woe is the blessing. Jesus pronounced many blessings which, like the Woes, occur in wisdom-like sayings. The most notable group, the Beatitudes, form the opening to the Sermon on the Mount. This, as we saw in Chapter 1, also ends with a wisdom comparison of the wise man and the fool,[7] and it contains many proverbial statements within it. The whole of the Sermon may thus be seen as a type of wisdom instruction which, if addressed to the multitude at large, throws the false path of the Pharisees into conflict with the wisdom of Jesus.

Enough has been said to indicate that Jesus deliberately chose the role of the wise man to complement his roles as prophet, priest and king. As the prophet he came not only to speak God's word of revelation, but to be the very Word incarnate by which alone we can know the truth. As the priest Jesus came to be the mediator between God and man, and to offer himself as the one true sacrifice for sin. As the king he came to bring in the glorious rule of God's kingdom. As the wise man he came as the very wisdom of God challenging the folly of a humanity that has turned its back on the word of God. He came to challenge the folly of every age, and to impart wisdom to those whom he would call to himself. He challenged the folly of the Judaism of his day and especially that of the Pharisees. He did this by showing up the assumptions of Torah-centred religion that had steadily lost sight of the dynamic nature of Israel's faith which propelled it towards the new age. The Jews continued to expect a new age, or at least a life after death, except for the Sadducees who seem to have lost faith in any vital new ordering of existence yet to come. In general, the expectations of the Jews left no room for a messiah like Jesus who did not move towards the kingdom as a present political reality. All four Gospels stress the growing tension between Jesus and the Jewish religious authorities. Some of the latter were nervous about.

---

[7] There are overtones here of Proverbs 10:25, 'When the storm has swept by, the wicked are gone, but the righteous stand firm for ever.' See Beardslee, *op. cit.*, p. 65.

Jesus because of a possible Roman reaction to any messianic movement which threatened the peace of the province. But the hostility of the Jews seems to have been due mainly to his teaching. He is shown to be constantly saying and doing things which excite the anger of the Jews. He challenges their claims to know the truth and to be its guardians. By appearing to flout the ritual laws so beloved by the Pharisees, Jesus was to them a blasphemer and an apostate. But, as the Gospels make clear, these very actions of Jesus point to the coming of the kingdom and the fulfilling of the Old Testament hopes. Not only did this occasion the hardening of the Jews, but for those that did believe it was still a matter of considerable surprise and wonderment.

The Intellectual Content of the Gospel

On our journey through the wisdom of the Old Testament we have seen that it belongs to the young and simple (as well as to the experienced and the complicated). The prerequisite for wisdom is not a high I.Q. but the fear of the Lord. Now that we have returned to the New Testament we find the same perspective on wisdom; it is the fear of the Lord, or faith in Christ, rather than intellectual wizardry that is at the heart of it. Faith in Christ is accompanied by a new view of reality which Paul speaks of as the renewing of our minds (Romans 12:2). This is a normal part of being Christian. Thus, from the biblical point of view, the youngster who is intellectually 'slow' but who has a simple trust in Jesus as his Saviour, is wiser than the brilliant philosopher who, despite his intellectual powers, refuses the knowledge of God in his word.

In accommodating those who are decidedly not what we would call intellectuals, through lack of ability or opportunity, we nevertheless must not neglect the importance of the mind.[8] This is one of the lessons of wisdom. Unfortunately, there is a tendency among Christians, particularly those oriented towards the inner spiritual experience, to neglect the relationship of the gospel to the way we think. It is almost as if careful thought and reasoning play no part in being Christian. This is seen not only in peculiar views of guidance, but also in a distrust of theology and of any attempt to achieve precision in the exegesis and interpretation of the Bible. This kind of Christianity rarely challenges the non-Christian mind-set in any meaningful way.[9] Such challenges belong not only to places of higher learning, but also in the context of the ordinary man's work place. The unskilled worker and the shop-assistant also have an intellectual interpretation of reality to which the gospel must be addressed.

The intellectual content of the gospel signifies that the life, death and resurrection of Jesus as God's way of saving sinners is closely related to the meaning of the whole of reality. Furthermore, the gospel is God's way of revealing to us what this ultimate meaning is. Thus, Christians must accept the responsibility of developing a world-view which is meaningful in contemporary terms and which is consistent with the gospel. Obviously a universe which came into being from eternally existing matter, a universe not created but rather the result of chance plus time, and a humanity which is not responsible before God, are all ideas which clash violently with the fact that Jesus died for our sins. Unless the universe is the creation of a personal and eternal God, the gospel has no meaning at all.

---

[8] See John Stott, *Your Mind Matters* (Leicester: Inter-Varsity Press, 1972).

[9] This is discussed in C. Van Til, *The intellectual Challenge of the Gospel* (London: Tyndale Press, 1950).

In Old Testament wisdom there are two complementary ideas: God endows his people with wisdom as a gift, and this gift demands the responsive task of learning wisdom. Solomon's prayer for understanding was granted but, having been equipped with the divine gift, he engaged in the continuing task of learning, discovering, classifying, reasoning and making decisions. The gift should not be seen as a purely private and supernatural energizing of Solomon's thinking powers. Gift and task go hand in hand. That Solomon recognized the fear of the Lord, even though he later let this reference point slip out of focus, shows that his faith and the object of that faith were inseparable from his wisdom. In other words, Solomon's wisdom cannot be understood apart from all of his perceptions of the covenant and God's saving acts. What God has done for him under the covenant was the prior gift from which the gift of wisdom stemmed. In the same way that the gift of redemption demanded the task prescribed by the law, so the gift of wisdom demanded the task of learning and applying wisdom.

Jesus fulfilled the role of Solomon as the wise king of Israel. Solomon's wisdom was imperfect, but Jesus' wisdom was perfect. Solomon's perceptions of his relationship with the Father were marred by sin and ignorance, but Jesus had a perfect perception of all relationships. By being the perfectly wise man for us, Jesus is qualified to redeem us from sinful ignorance and its effects. Included in this redemptive process is the instruction of our minds. By what he was and did, Jesus shows us how things are in reality. Thus he patterns the reality of our relation to God, to others and to the world. We do not ignore his uniqueness as the God-man and Saviour of the world. We cannot imitate these attributes, but we can learn from the nature of the relationships that are actually restored to perfection in the person of Christ.

What, then, is the intellectual framework of the gospel? The Christian faith proclaims that the universe was created by God who is Trinity. The knowledge of God as Trinity comes to us as a result of the gospel. Once it was recognized that somehow Jesus was God come in human flesh, it was inevitable that a distinction would have to be made between him and the Father in heaven. The same distinction was also indicated by the reality of the Holy Spirit as divine person. God, it would seem is a community of being, three persons *and* one God. In the same way Jesus came to be perceived as communal in that he was two natures *and* one person. But this kind of relationship had been recognized as a reality in human and other relationships from earliest times in Israel. It was just that it had not been clearly understood with respect to the being of God.

The way God relates within himself as Father, Son and Holy Spirit is reflected in the relationships of the universe which he created. This is the question of order that exercised the wisdom writers. A particular form of the question is the relationship of the one and the many, the individual to all other individuals, and the one group (or class) to the many individuals. All the questions of human relationships that concern us are variations of the problem of the one and the many. All the questions raised in the wisdom literature are expressions of this concern. This is the problem behind the relationship of males to females in general, of husband to wife in particular, of parents to children, of believer to unbeliever, of worker to employer, of humans to animals, of humans to inanimate creation, and so on. The list is endless. But above all we seek to know the relationship of God to man.

In order to highlight the importance of a truly Christian approach to these matters let us first consider a couple of examples of where non-Christian thinking takes us. A humanist who rejects the possibility of God is left with only the results of blind chance in the shaping of the universe. If humanity is the outcome of natural selection, fortuitous mutation, or survival of the fittest, then all human relationships are cast in that mould. If the humanist is going to be consistent with his own premises he has no real basis for establishing right or wrong in human relationships. In our western society it would be true to say that humanists and non-Christians in general have actually used an ethical base which is borrowed from Christianity. Unhappily that is changing and ethics more consistent with humanism are becoming more and more prevalent. For example, abortion on demand expresses a survival of the fittest ethic which is totally at variance with the Christian view of human life and of man created in God's image. The modern sexual revolution shows a confusion which arises when the proper basis for ethics and human relationships is removed.

Another non-Christian view of reality is that of the Pharisaic Judaism that Jesus encountered. This is not a God denying position in the sense of being atheistic. Furthermore, it shares its beginnings with Christianity in the same Scriptures of the Old Testament. Yet when Jesus, claiming to be the one to which the Old Testament points, made claims to oneness with God, the Jews were provoked to anger (e.g. see John 5:17–18). It may be that their convictions concerning the oneness of God made it difficult for them to accept the implication that God could have come in human flesh while still being the one who dwells above the heavens. But this was not because such a concept is inconceivable in the light of the Old Testament. The enduring statement of faith, still central to Judaism today, was the *Shema'* from Deuteronomy 6:4–5:

> Hear, O Israel: the Lord our God, the Lord is one. Love the
> Lord your God with all your heart and with all your soul and
> with all your strength.

Here, as we find it consistently throughout the Old Testament, God is proclaimed as one (Hebrew: *'echad*). The nature of God's oneness must be understood from the revelation of the whole Bible, but this word *one* does not rule out a complexity or plurality within the oneness. Thus, the same word is used of husband and wife becoming one flesh (Genesis 2:24), of Pharaoh's two dreams being one (Genesis 41:25), and of a nation gathering as one man (Judges 20:1).[10]

The problem of one-and-many is illustrated in the confusion people experience over the use of collective nouns in English. It used to be taught that proper English usage demanded a singular verb with a collective noun: the committee *is* agreed, the team *is* playing well, the flock *is* following the shepherd. Test cricket commentators seem to have changed the rules in that they usually report that England (or Australia) *are* all out for a score of . . . The problem is that the idea of team is both singular (one team)

---

[10] Gordon Jessup, *No Strange God* (London: Olive Press, 1976), p. 105. Jessup comments: 'It has been suggested, by at least one notable Jewish scholar and professor, that there was a time when Judaism could have accepted a Trinitarian doctrine of God. By the time of Maimonides, Christian anti-Jewish behaviour had made this emotionally impossible. From his time onwards it has also been intellectually impossible (except by the grace of God) for an Orthodox Jew to believe in a God whose Unity is so complex that it can also be called Trinity.' The reference to Maimonides is to a twelfth century AD Jewish philosopher who, in speaking of God, introduced the use of the Hebrew word *yachid*, which is related to *'echad* but which emphasizes the solitary nature of oneness.

and plural (many members). Logically it is the aspect we wish to stress that determines whether we think of it as singular or plural. But if we are to do justice to the reality of team-ness we somehow have to handle both the one-ness and the many-ness together.

We can press this same illustration further. The reference to England or Australia being in to bat is accepted without question. But England and Australia are never in, that is, neither a land nor a nation can play as a cricket team. England here means a team of eleven players who represent the nation. And while fifty thousand spectators in the stands must be clearly distinguished from the team that represents them (or else there would be chaos on the ground), yet such is the unity between spectators and team that, after it is all over, every one of those spectators will have in his mind, 'we won' or 'we lost'.

To return to the *Shema'*, the illustrations above help us to understand why Israel's conviction that God is one does not rule out the possibility that he is something greater than undifferentiated, solitary oneness. In fact, if God has indeed imprinted his character on the universe then at least it would be possible that somehow God is one and many, for that is what we see all around us. Every aspect of our experience makes sense only if we understand ourselves and all relations as expressing both unity and distinction. According to the New Testament, God as the source of this fact of reality is like that himself.

This doctrine of God's tri-unity begins with Jesus as the God-man. The incarnation is the supreme expression of this truth within our world of space and time. There are two distinct aspects to this. First, Jesus is both God and man. If someone, seeing Jesus walking along the road, had said, 'There's God', his statement would have been correct but inadequate. Likewise, if he had said, 'There's a man', this statement also would have been correct but inadequate. Until the two aspects are put together so that we say, 'There's the God-man', the truth is not only inadequate, it is actually distorted by being left out of its relationship to the other part of the truth.

This points us to the question of the kind of relationship existing between the two truths. If we say that because Jesus is both God and man, he must be two persons, then we are in error. He is, as theologians say, two natures in one person; he is uni-plural. At the fifth-century council of Chalcedon, after much controversy, the Christian church devised a manner of speaking which made it clear that we could not solve the mystery of uniplurality by simple logic (or any other kind of logic). Rather, to be true to the facts we must come to terms with the existence of the mystery. So, if Jesus is properly described as being both truly God and truly man, we recognize the unity of the two natures without confusing them, or, to put it the other way, we recognize the distinction of the two natures without separating them.

The second aspect of the incarnation is that it points us to God as Trinity. The numbers may differ, but the same kind of relationship exists here as in the person of Jesus. What Chalcedon said about the person of Jesus could be adapted to help us speak more accurately about the nature of God as Trinity.[11] We must always maintain the unity of God, so that whatever he does, he does as Trinity; Father,

---

[11] The so-called Creed of Saint Athanasius expresses the uni-plurality of the Godhead and of Jesus Christ. The creed is thought to pre-date the formula of Chalcedon (451 AD) as it presents a somewhat cumbersome expression of the doctrines. That it was thought suitable for the ordinary Christian's consumption is seen in the fact that the English Prayer Book directed that it be said on certain days at Morning Prayer in place of the Apostles' Creed. The wordiness of this creed illustrates the impossibility of giving adequate expression to uni-plurality. It can be

Son and Holy Spirit. On the other hand the distinctions must be maintained so that we do not simply interchange the three persons in their distinctive roles.

One other point should be mentioned. Jesus expressed the same uni-plural relationship between himself and the Father.[12] This is similar to the relationship between his two natures. Again it is a matter of both the oneness and the plurality, the unity and the distinction. Jesus stressed the distinction when he addressed the Father as 'Thou', or when he spoke of the Father as 'greater than I'. But he also made frequent assertions of unity such as 'I and the Father are one', or 'He who has seen me has seen the Father'. Both sides must be grasped if we are not to reach a false view of Christ.

All relationships express some kind of uni-plurality through unity and distinction. We have seen that the prime concern of wisdom is that of relationships and the order of things in the universe. Christ fulfils for us the function of wisdom by being the fullest expression of wisdom. Thus the gospel event becomes for us wisdom in the sense that the nature of order is revealed in Christ. His uni-plurality points to that of the Godhead and thus to that of the universe which bears the stamp of his nature. The wisdom literature constantly examines the unity and distinctions of relationships which characterize the order within the universe. It is the function of wisdom to perceive in any situation how to maintain the appropriate relationship of unity and distinction. For example, in Proverbs 6:6

Footnote 11 (continued)   found in the 1662 *Book of Common Prayer* under the heading 'At Morning Prayer' (immediately after Evening Prayer) and in *An Australian Prayer Book* (1978) on p. 625.

[12] John 14–16, Jesus' discourse about the giving of the Spirit, contains frequent references to both unity and distinction of Father, Son and Holy Spirit which compel us to recognize the tri-unity of God.

the industry of the ant, by being an example to the lazy man, shows the kind of unity that exists between the man and the insect:

> Go to the ant, you sluggard;
> consider its ways and be wise!

But another saying, Proverbs 26:14 warns that the lazy man is in danger of taking unity to the point where there is no distinction between him and a certain inanimate object:

> As a door turns on its hinges,
> so a sluggard turns on his bed.

The gospel presses home this unity and distinction perspective by showing that this is the way the universe is because this is the way God is.

From this gospel-based perspective, the New Testament letters take up all kinds of human relationships in this light. In a practical way they show that the gospel provides the proper framework, the fear of the Lord, within which we pursue wisdom. An example of this is seen in Paul's discussion of the husband-wife relationship in Ephesians 5:21–33. This relationship is a reflection of the relationship between Christ and the Church, which in turn echoes the relationship between God and his people. It is significant that in this discourse Paul recalls Genesis 2:24 and its perspective of uni-plurality: 'the two will become one flesh.' We should note that unity-distinction is only one aspect of the relationship. We still have to take into account the characteristics of those persons or things that are relating. While unity-distinction characterizes all relationships, God and man can relate only *as* God and man. That will be very different from the relationship between husband and wife, which is different again from the relationship of brother and sister. That is why we stress that in the incarnation it is God relating to man. It is the nature of God, among other things, to be absolutely sovereign, while it is the nature of man to be absolutely responsible. They remain thus while relating perfectly in the one person Jesus Christ. Likewise, for a husband and wife to become one flesh does not mean that they lose their maleness or femaleness.

The fact that we cannot understand how there can be a uni-plurality in God or in Christ is only expressive of the real distinction between us, with our finite minds, and the infinite God. But that it *is* so is something we grasp because the Bible shows us that it is so. The examples given will suffice to show that there is a structure to all relationships that stems from the 'structure' of relationships within the communal oneness of God. The fear of the Lord as the beginning of wisdom points to the intellectual content of the gospel where we see Jesus Christ as the pattern of all truth.

The Gospel of Restored Relationships

I want now to touch on another aspect of how wisdom relates to the person of Christ. It is sometimes suggested that Proverbs 8 involves a personification of wisdom which is intimately related to God's creative activity. It is also suggested that Paul points to this in some of his statements about Christ as wisdom (e.g., 1 Corinthians 1:24,30). But it is not at all clear that Proverbs 8 is a real personification, that is, wisdom credited with a personal, independent existence alongside of God. It seems more likely that it is a poetic way of speaking about God's wisdom which is expressed in the creation of the world.[13]

How, then, can we speak of Christ as the wisdom of God? This is a complex question, and we shall focus on one aspect of it. We have seen that wisdom in the Old Testament sits very close to the doctrine of creation. We have also seen that both wisdom and creation are closely related to salvation history in their own characteristic ways. If we reduce these three areas, wisdom, creation and salvation history, to their bare skeletons, we find they all have the same underlying structure. Creation is God bringing all things to be so that there is God, mankind and the rest of creation, all relating properly as God determines. Sin is seen to disrupt these relationships in such a radical way that the only relationships not dislocated are those within the Godhead. Salvation is God's way of restoring all things to their proper order, so that once again there will be God, man and the rest of creation in proper relationships. Wisdom proceeds from the basis of God's revelation of what these relationships once were, and how God is restoring them to what they will be again. Then it strives for knowledge and understanding of where we are now, with the aim of knowing how to relate properly to a world in flux. Thus wisdom is concerned with the present relationships of God, mankind and the world, not as a static reality, but as a reality which is moving towards the restoration of all things. Creation, salvation history and wisdom thus contain the same type of skeleton, namely God, mankind and the world which together are presented as a peculiarly biblical understanding of the nature of reality, and of the relationships of everything in it.

---

[13] See James D. G. Dunn, *Christology in the Making* (London: SCM Press, 1980), Ch. 5.

The Bible thus presents us with at least two distinct, though related, perspectives of reality. These appear to diverge for a while, but are then brought back together in the person of Jesus Christ. Both perspectives deal with the same biblical raw material of reality and stand on the same base line of creation. Salvation history, as one perspective, embraces the whole history of a specific family of humanity which includes Israel. When we follow the sacred genealogy by way of Adam, Seth, Noah, Shem, Abraham, and Jacob, we are caught up in the manner of God's dealing with this family. God's acts are structured by covenant and redemption, promise of salvation and fulfilment. The sequence of events can also be reduced to basics:

a) Creation is God bringing all things into existence and into proper and harmonious relationship.
b) The fall of mankind through Adam's sin results in all relationships being dislocated and confused.
c) Salvation is God's action to bring all things back to proper relationships.
d) Jesus Christ is God and man in right relationship in that he is the only sinless man since the fall. Jesus' human nature means that he also participates in the physical creation. Thus we can say that the person of Jesus was, for the first time since the fall, a true expression of God, man and created order in right relationships.[14]

Salvation history culminates in the gospel, but at the same time embraces the subsequent history of mankind until

---

[14] See *Gospel and Kingdom* where salvation history is worked out in some detail as God's people in God's place under God's rule. This summary of the components of the kingdom of God is simply another way of expressing God, man and created order in right relationships. The kingdom concept is a model of the right relationships that God intends.

Christ returns. We are bound to express the whole New Testament perspective in relation to Jesus Christ and to the Old Testament. Furthermore, we are justified in using the concept of *order* to signify the ordered reality of God, man and world. Thus we can restate the progression of salvation history which is summarized above in the following way:

a) Creation: *order*.
b) Fall: dislocation of *order*.
c) Covenant: promise of restored *order*.
d) Exodus: a redemptive pattern of *order* being restored.
e) Kingdom of David and Solomon: a pattern of the *order* to come.
f) Jesus Christ: the reality of *order* representatively established.[15]
g) Christ's kingdom revealed at his return: *order*.

The perspective of wisdom takes its departure from the same starting point as salvation history, that is, creation. It presupposes the revealed significance of salvation history while focusing more on the creation than on redemption. It comes to its culmination in Jesus of Nazareth. In our study of wisdom we have seen that the question of the order of relationships is paramount. Again, using the concept of *order* to signify God, man and world in right relationships, we can summarize wisdom's perspective:

a) Creation: *order*.
b) Sin and folly: dislocation of *order*.

---

[15] When Jesus brought in the kingdom at his coming it was he who was the kingdom. It is important to understand that God restored all things in him as the means of restoring all things in themselves. Jesus came as our representative as well as our substitute. All the right relationships of reality actually existed in Jesus of Nazareth; he was the one who stood for the many.

c) Wisdom is understanding the present confused *order*, and the future restored *order*, so that one can live according to what is real.

d) Jesus Christ is made wisdom, that is, *order* for us.

We can see that wisdom and salvation history are two sides to the one reality. This is not a static reality, but dynamic, moving from original perfection, to disruption, through restoration to ultimate consummation and perfection. Salvation history has a strong eschatological emphasis in that it continually envisages the end or goal of the process. Wisdom is not eschatologically oriented for the most part. Its concentration is on the life we live in the present, and the relationships that we must pursue in a fallen and confused world. Its eschatology is implicit for its goal is life, and life ultimately is lived in perfect relationship to God, fellow man and the universe. In the framework of salvation history the concern of wisdom is for an understanding of where the one who fears the Lord is now, and what his relationship should be to a world under judgment but also under promise.

To conclude this discussion we may sum up the meaning of Christ as the wisdom of God. First, Christ as eternally God was present at the creation and active in the expression of God's wisdom. Secondly, the wisdom of God was such that Jesus Christ in the gospel event was the eternally devised plan of God upon which creation was based. Thirdly, the redemptive work of God, for the benefit of a sin-laden creation, was achieved not only by an atoning death, but by the new creation in Christ's person where God, man and the created order perfectly related. Fourthly, the disruption of sin was of such a nature that it brought all human thought about ultimate reality into opposition to the actual truth. Fifthly, God gives true wisdom to his people as a gift when he sends

Christ into the world. Christ justifies our confused wisdom by having perfect human wisdom for us. He sanctifies our confused wisdom by patterning the truth and by giving his Holy Spirit to lead us in the paths of that truth. Finally, he will glorify our wisdom when we are renewed through our resurrection and are made to reflect his character perfectly.

Questions for Study

1. In what way were the parables of Jesus the new wisdom sayings, and in what way did this wisdom clash with that of the Jews of Jesus' day?
2. How does the gospel – the life, death and resurrection of Jesus – provide Christians with the only valid foundation for wisdom and an understanding of the universe?
3. How does the gospel bring together the two Old Testament perspectives of wisdom of salvation history?

Chapter Twelve

Christians and the Transformation to Order

Summary

Since wisdom has been fulfilled in the person and work of Jesus, Christians must read the Old Testament wisdom literature in the light of this fulfilment. Wisdom always functions within the framework of God's saving acts and word. Christ not only died to save us, but was also the perfectly wise man of God living the absolutely responsible life. He lived this life in our place that we might be accounted wise before God. His life was also the example of true wisdom so that we might learn wisdom from him. The overview of wisdom in the Bible provides us with a base for our decision making. Guidance is primarily directed at the responsibility of Christians to make decisions which conform to reality as it is revealed in the gospel.

Interpreting Old Testament Wisdom

Given the distinctive perspective of wisdom in the Old Testament, does it require a special approach to its interpretation? In the previous chapter I pointed to the manner in which the real meaning of wisdom is linked to the person and work of Jesus Christ. This means that he cannot be bypassed when we are seeking to interpret Old Testament wisdom texts. The interpretation of any text of the Bible begins with its exegesis. Exegesis aims at finding out what the text meant in its original biblical context. Then, if we are to understand how the text relates to us as Christians, we must first understand how it relates to the gospel. Hermeneutics, or interpretation, means asking what the text means when seen in its proper relationship to the gospel.

Wisdom is tied to the same two reference points as is salvation history, namely, creation and the new creation in Christ. Furthermore, it is practised on the presuppositions of revelation in salvation history. Thus we would expect the interpretation of wisdom to proceed on much the same basis as the interpretation of salvation history texts. Essentially, our method of interpretation is our response to the nature of the Bible as a whole, taking into account both the unity of the Bible and the diversity of expression within that unity. Without some attention to the theological unity of the Bible it is not possible to appreciate the important relationships between the various stages of biblical revelation.

Our brief excursion into the wisdom sources of the Old Testament has concentrated on understanding how wisdom was to be pursued. Of necessity we had to forgo the detailed exegesis of the texts. The Christian Bible student can approach such exegesis with confidence that it will yield many insights into authentic Christian existence. To arm ourselves with these insights can only be beneficial, provided that we understand how the wise men meant them to function in the learning of wisdom. The other qualification is that we always recognize the incomplete nature of the Old Testament without the New.

In order to understand what a particular text meant in its original context, we need to consider both its historical and theological context. We must think our way into the situation of the original hearers or readers, and how they would have been expected to understand the text against their contemporary situation. The process of moving from the text to Jesus Christ depends upon where the text stands in the historical progression of God's revelation.

Wisdom expresses the existence of God's people at the climax of the period from Abraham to Solomon during which the kingdom of God is given expression in the historical experience of Israel. Wisdom continues as a significant area of Israelite thought after the historical decline of the kingdom and right up to the era of the New Testament. In chapter 4 we saw that wisdom flourished from Solomon's time as an expression of the nation's coming to maturity. Wisdom texts express the responsible humanity of the people within the framework of God's revelation of his kingdom. Wisdom thus reflected the human task of the cultural mandate which had been given to Adam, but which now operated within the political and earthly reality of the kingdom in an unredeemed world. The fact that the people of God lived then, and continue to do so now, in an unredeemed world, raised all kinds of questions about the kind of responses the redeemed should make to that which is redeemed and that which is not redeemed.

God created human beings to function by the integrating of two sources of truth. These are not equal sources which operate side by side, but they are complementary. The first is revelation through word from God. As a rational thinking being, man is nevertheless incapable of knowing of himself what is necessary to be known in order to interpret the world around him. A rational and personal God has made man in his image, including his rational-personal nature, to respond to word revelation from God. Through this revelation man receives the reference points he needs for an understanding of relationships. In short, God reveals to man something of the nature of the order in the universe. The second source of truth is the combined operation of senses and reason. Reason is not in itself a source of truth but a way of programming information. The reason must first be compliant with the truth of revelation if it is to process correctly the information of our senses. That is why geniuses can in biblical terms be fools. The way our reasoning operates is not primarily a function of how clever we are, nor of how much information we have managed to cram into our minds. Rather it is a moral choice either to be independent of God or to be subject to him in our thinking as well as our doing. The moral choice to be independent of God was made in what we refer to as the fall of man. Only the regenerative power of gospel and Holy Spirit can enable us to make the second and correct choice to submit to God.

Revelation is thus pre-eminent. God must address us and define our humanity in relation to his being and to the world. Knowing God and knowing ourselves in this relationship are the prerequisites for the pursuit of understanding of the details of human experience. In Eden God addressed Adam and defined his cultural task and the bounds of his freedom. The very fact that God so spoke to his creature also defined the proper relationship between God and man. In the fallen world in which salvation history operates, God addressed his people by covenants of promise and law, both of which were linked to the acts of redemption in Israel's history. Israel's cultural task, of which wisdom is a principal expression, needed the revelation of God if it was to be understood and pursued. Now Christ has come as the fullest and most perfect word of God to man. By Christ God is interpreting the meaning of the universe, of our world and of the whole history of the human race. Christ interprets you and me so that we do not have to flounder in the ambiguity of our existence. He reveals to us what we need to know in order to get on with the business of living as responsible Christians.

In applying these broad principles to the book of Proverbs we begin by asking how it functioned in its original context. How did it function, that is, in instructing the people of God about their relationship to God, each other and the world? This is a theological question because *all* relationships involve our relationship to God. Proverbs highlights the practical side of learning how to relate to everything. It stresses the responsible task of the life of faith. Its theological function is to provide us with insights into how we translate our relationship to God into right relationships to man and the world. But because it emerged from the pre-Christian context of the Old Testament, its perception of relationships is limited by the incomplete nature of the revelation of God in the Old Testament.

The Old Testament prophets reveal a future kingdom in which the people of God will live in perfect relationships to each other and the world. Central to this perfection of wisdom among the people is the fact that the messianic king will be the living example of all true wisdom. But the reality of the kingdom does not mean that there will be no task in wisdom. Ignorance and imperfection in the knowledge of God, along with sinful hardness of heart towards God's revelation, will be removed. The people of God will be perfectly conformed to God's will through a renewal of their nature (Jeremiah 31:31–34; Ezekiel 36:25–28). The responsible task of wisdom is demanded not because we are sinful, but because we are finite creatures of God. The cultural mandate was given to Adam in his innocence and not subsequent to the fall.

The responsible task of Proverbs is given its full and perfect expression by Jesus. This fulfils the prophetic expectation of the perfectly wise messianic king. As tempting as it is to rush from the texts of Proverbs to an application in our Christian life, we must discipline ourselves to relate our texts first of all to their fulfilment in Christ. Jesus in every way fulfils God's requirements for Israel. He was the perfectly wise man of God living the absolutely responsible life before his heavenly Father. In his perfectly human existence he lived according to his true perception of reality, making right decisions in the right place and at the right time. In all this he constantly lived as the one who perfectly feared the Lord. Thus, in our application to ourselves of the individual textual units of Proverbs, we need to be aware of the meaning of the gospel for our human existence. We cannot simply apply proverbial wisdom out of the Old Testament to ourselves as if we had never heard of Jesus Christ. Wisdom points to righteousness, but we know that Jesus' life was lived for us in order to provide a perfect righteousness for us that counts for our acceptance with God. Jesus justifies our feeble attempts to live wisely by being what we should be but cannot. Thus, God regards all believers as having the very wisdom of Christ. In other words, Christ has been made wisdom for us (1 Corinthians 1:30).

Moving a text via the gospel to ourselves has a transforming effect on the significance of that text. The fear of the Lord is given its specific and definitive meaning in terms of faith in the person and work of Jesus Christ as our Saviour. The intellectual content of the gospel illuminates the nature of the order within the universe with a clarity that did not belong to Old Testament revelation. It is here that the New Testament teaching of the Holy Spirit's work should be understood. Spirit and gospel go hand in hand, for it is the Spirit's principal work to apply the gospel of

Jesus to the hearts and minds of God's people. The New Testament never suggests that the Spirit takes over our humanity. This would be a total negation of the nature of the gospel which is to restore our true humanity, not to remove it. The doctrine of creation establishes that there is a real distinction between God and man that must be maintained in the order of things. When it is suggested in any way that our humanity is absorbed by the Spirit of God this order is destroyed. Furthermore, the reason for Christ's coming in the flesh as true man is dissolved if God's purpose is to absorb us into his being. Salvation means the humanizing of man not his deification (or divinizing). Our unity with God lies in our being created in his image and reflecting his character. Our distinction from God lies in the fact that our destiny is to remain God's greatest creation and to live in response to his revelation of himself to us. All the wisdom literature is eloquent of these facts and explores their implications in life.

The differences between Proverbs, Job and Ecclesiastes are found mainly in their distinct emphases. Proverbs emphasizes the practicalities relating to observable order. This order is not self-interpreting; it needs God's revelation to interpret it. Job and Ecclesiastes emphasize the infinite greatness of God and of his wisdom. Consequently man is cut down to size and thereby discovers that his real humanity is not diminished by the recognition that he relates to God on an unequal footing. The mystery of order points to the comforting fact that God is infinitely greater than our minds can comprehend. Both Job and Qohelet invite an openness to the sovereignty of God and thus urge trust in him. Again we see that the wisdom of these books is given its purest expression in the person of Christ. All the tribulations of the Son of man were an assault upon the orderliness of his God-man relationship. But even the tribulation of the cross did not destroy his trust in the

Father. Finally the resurrection demonstrated that the God-man relationship cannot be destroyed even by the intrusion of the ultimate disorder: death.

The gospel thus transforms all the wisdom of the Old Testament by showing its place in the ultimate destiny of God's people. The gospel does not thereby render the Old Testament material superfluous for it constantly presupposes it. The New Testament does not go over old ground but shows how the old ground is to be understood and applied. Because Christ is the perfect expression of every facet of human wisdom in the Old Testament, he is able to be the grounds of our acceptance with God. Then he shows us the goal of our continual growth towards conformity to his character. Because he has become our wisdom we of necessity must study the Old Testament wisdom in the light of his fulfilment. The wisdom literature in its own distinctive way steers us towards responsible Christian living which applies the reality of Christ to every level of human existence. On the one hand it gives

The Christian understands himself and all creation in the light of the revelation of God in the person and work of Jesus Christ.

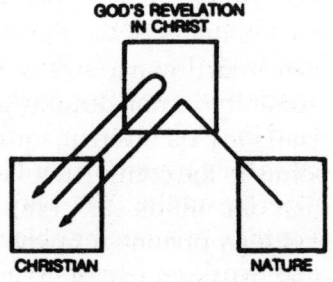

Figure 6. Christian Wisdom

us the perception to make sense of our world, and on the other hand it strengthens our trust in God in the face of things we cannot make sense of. As we pursue wisdom in this gospel-centred way, we discover more and more how Christ is both the starting point and the goal.

The Gift of Wisdom

What does the gift of wisdom entail for the Christian? In the Old Testament wisdom as gift appears to be available to all, yet there is clearly a special gifting of certain people for specific tasks. The same distinction appears in the New Testament. In the gospel every Christian has wisdom, but there is also that gift of wisdom which is a special manifestation of the Spirit (1 Corinthians 12:8). The specific gift must be examined in the light of the general gift given to all Christians.

The objective gift

I have indicated my understanding of the gift of wisdom to Solomon as something wider than the subjective enabling or mental power to perceive and know in a special way. The subjective aspect went hand in hand with wisdom as an objective gift. This lay in the revelation of God in the 'out there' events of salvation history. I would class the prophetic word which interprets these events as objective in the same way that the Bible is objective for us. For the Christian the objective gift of wisdom is the person and work of Christ. We cannot separate this from the whole biblical testimony of saving history because the entire Bible finds its ultimate meaning in the gospel. There are a number of New Testament references that make wisdom the equivalent of gospel so that he who possesses the gospel, truly believing it, possesses wisdom. For example, Stephen's wisdom in disputing with the Hellenists is reasonably inferred to be his ability to proclaim the gospel (Acts 6:10). It is an instance of that which Jesus promised in Luke 21:12–45, namely, the wisdom to bear testimony. Such testimony in the New Testament usually means testifying to the saving acts of God in Christ.

Essentially, the objective gift of wisdom is the self-revelation of God by which the people of God gain their bearings. Christians do well when they acknowledge that the Bible is wisdom for us. They do even better when they understand that the whole Bible finds its fulfilment in the gospel event. Thus, objective wisdom is the wisdom of God being shared with us through the revelation in the Bible of God's saving purposes in Christ. So, says Paul, the riches of God's grace, the benefits of the gospel, are lavished upon us with all wisdom and understanding (Ephesians 1:8). The saving activity of God, as it is proclaimed to the world, becomes an objective demonstration of the wisdom of God to the whole universe (Ephesians 3:8–10). It is an objective wisdom when the brethren teach and admonish one another according to the word of Christ in the gospel (Colossians 3:16). Likewise, it is an objective wisdom that we have already considered as the intellectual content of the gospel.

The subjective gift

The gospel as the wisdom of God ought to be our guide. The gospel is objective in that it is 'out there'. The finished work of Christ was effected entirely without our participation. But this 'out there' gospel must be applied to the sinner. It must become a part of his perceived world as something that applies to him and demands his involvement through faith and repentance. This subjective awareness that Jesus' life and death is 'for me' is a self-conscious going out from one's self to relate to the objective. The subjective perception of the gospel is never something that is wholly within me. It is always a response of what is in me to that which is out there. The gospel is always the same: it is Jesus Christ, the same yesterday, today and for ever (Hebrews 13:8). Our subjective perceptions of the gospel will vary from person to person. Many factors are involved such as how clearly and meaningfully the gospel is communicated, as well as our own background, training, and temperament. None of these has a predictable bearing on the response since it is the sovereign work of God through the power of the gospel to subdue whom he will. The grace of God in the gospel is the sovereign working of God by which the objective facts of the gospel become the subjective reality for the believer without ever losing their objective nature. Grace is gift as the gospel exemplifies it. The response to the gospel is the life of faith, the life of practical Christian wisdom. This is task. Gift and task can never be separated, for this is how God relates to his people.

I have risked labouring this matter because of its importance. The pattern of wisdom in the Old Testament conforms to the New Testament pattern of the responsible life of faith: gift and task. There are, however, some passages relating to the gift of wisdom that seem to emphasize the gift more than the task. Joseph is a case in point. In rejecting von Rad's contention that the Joseph narrative in Genesis 37–45 is a piece of wisdom literature (see chapter 9), we cannot overlook the references to wisdom within it.[1]

---

[1] The fact that Joseph acts as a wise man does not make the narrative a wisdom story as von Rad suggests, any more than the references to Solomon's wisdom in I Kings 3–10 make that narrative the work of a wise man. These are narratives and not specially contrived compositions for imparting wisdom.

Although Joseph is not referred to as receiving the gift of wisdom, he does what the wise men of Egypt could not do, that is, interpret the dreams of Pharaoh. It is Stephen (Acts 7:10) who recalls Joseph as being given wisdom by God so that he became Pharaoh's right-hand man. While this wisdom would probably have included interpretation of dreams, it is described more as a general ability than as direct supernatural knowledge. Joshua's wisdom was of a similar kind, although it came as a result of the laying on of hands (Deuteronomy 34:9). It was a charismatic gift for leadership in much the same way that Solomon's was. In all, the gift and the task went hand in hand, but with Joseph there was a gift of direct knowledge through a supernatural revelation from God.[2]

The other major passages in which wisdom involves the supernatural gift of knowledge relate to Daniel. The narrative of Daniel 2 contains many close parallels to the Joseph story. In both, the Israelites are captives among foreigners. Both involve the dreams of foreign kings which their own wise men fail to interpret. The dreams are from God and only he can interpret them through his own wise men. When the dreams are interpreted, the outcome has saving significance for the people of God, a point which is of utmost importance for the understanding of these events. I stress that because all events of saving significance in the Old Testament point towards Jesus Christ in the gospel event. Their fulfilment is in what Jesus did for us rather than in similar events in our own experience. The revelation of dreams to Joseph and Daniel are more in the stream of salvation history than of wisdom as practical

---

[2] All modern psychological theories of dream interpretation work from some concept of cause and effect. What a person dreams is somehow related to factors in his past, including how he has come to think about the future. There would be no question of the prediction of future events such as we see in Joseph.

living. Such saving revelation reaches its fulness in Jesus Christ. Without saying that God would not or could not make such direct revelations to Christians today, we must assert that any such revelation in the present would be of a different order from that of the Old Testament revelations, since we now have God's final word in Christ.

I conclude from all this that there is little in the Old Testament, either in the narratives about the wise men, or in the wisdom literature itself, to support the idea that a gift of wisdom in the New Testament would consist of some fresh supernatural revelation from God. To this we must add also that there is no hint of such an idea in the extensive treatment of wisdom in 1 Corinthians 1–2, which surely must be definitive for the understanding of the significance of 1 Corinthians 12:8. Taking all the evidence of the nature of wisdom in both Old and New Testaments, it is more realistic to conclude that Paul is speaking of a God-given ability to apply the meaning of the gospel in specific real life situations. It presumably is to be distinguished from the wisdom that belongs to all Christians, but probably only in degree. The normal Christian experience would be that of steady growth towards maturity through a willing involvement in the task of learning wisdom. The special gift of which Paul speaks may well be demonstrated in a maturity that is far beyond a person's years of Christian experience.

One problem of Paul's list of gifts in 1 Corinthians 12:4–11 is that it appears to distinguish the message of wisdom from the message of knowledge. In most Old Testament contexts wisdom and knowledge are almost synonymous, or at least overlap to a greater or lesser degree. Even the skill of the craftsman, which accounts for the uses of the word *wisdom* in Exodus, has *knowledge* as a synonym.[3]

---

[3] Exodus 31:3; 35:31.

If Paul intends a distinction he has not explained what it is. It is important in this discussion that we recognize what the gifts of wisdom and knowledge almost certainly are not. Whatever they are, they will not usurp the supreme place of Jesus Christ, or that of the canon of Scripture which testifies to him, in making known to us all that we need to know in order to make sense of ourselves and the world around us. Nor will they displace our task of using our brains and sanctified common sense. This does not rule out the possibility of such gifts being displayed as a manifestly supernatural ability to penetrate to the reality of any given situation.

Wisdom in James

The Epistle of James has long been considered as a work that is heavily influenced by Israelite wisdom. In some respects, James fulfils a role in the New Testament similar to that of Proverbs in the Old Testament. There are some obvious parallels in the way James exhorts the Christian to gain true wisdom. There are some problems with James, as is commonly recognized, not least of which is the lack of reference to the gospel. It would be difficult to reconstruct the nature of the gospel from this epistle beyond the fact that Jesus Christ is the Lord of glory and will return to judge the world. (Though James is far more explicit in his references to salvation history than 3 John where Jesus is not even mentioned.) Few would accept the view that James deliberately contradicts Paul in his treatment of faith and works (James 2:14–26), and what he says is consistent with the wisdom view of gift and task. So, to begin with, we note that James, like the wisdom literature of the Old Testament, makes few explicit references to God's saving acts but clearly presupposes them.

A second characteristic of this epistle is its lack of any theme or development. There are a number of practically oriented sections dealing with a variety of subjects relating to daily life. But it would be as erroneous to conclude of James that it is not theological as it would be of Proverbs. James writes as a Christian whose faith in the Lord of glory presupposes the life, death and resurrection of Jesus. The wisdom characteristics of James are not confined to the discourses on the subject (i.e. 1:5–8; 3:13–18). He everywhere displays the concerns of old wisdom as they would exist for first-century Christians.

The contrast in James between earthly wisdom and wisdom from above is intensely practical. Every good gift is from above, that is, comes from God (1:17). Wisdom is one such gift and shows itself in the good life (3:13). It is pure, peace-loving, considerate, submissive, merciful, bearing good fruit (3:17). It is not unreasonable to suppose that what follows in James 4 and 5 (and perhaps what precedes) is the detailing of such wisdom in certain areas of life. James speaks of wisdom as gift and task which are based on the fear of the Lord, that is in his terms, faith in Jesus Christ the Lord of glory. There is no hint of a special charismatic gift of wisdom. Wisdom belongs to all and, indeed, it manifests itself in good works which witness to the reality of faith.

Decisions

As I stated in chapter 1, this book is not primarily about guidance and decision making. If we wanted a comprehensive treatment of the subject of guidance we would have to range far wider than the wisdom literature. Wisdom, however, is an important dimension in the matter. Many of the hang-ups people have about making decisions could be avoided by means of the perspective given by the subject of wisdom.

If we are to understand the biblical view of guidance, we need to look at it in the context of the progressive nature of revelation. The truth of God's revelation comes by stages until it reaches the full intensity of the light of the knowledge of God in Christ. There are two things to be said about guidance in this biblical framework. First, guidance of individuals by direct means of dreams, visions and prophetic word decreases as the repository of God's revealed will grows. This does not mean that such direct and supernatural guidance necessarily ceases once the canon of Scripture is completed, but it does mean that the likelihood of God adding to his final word in Christ recorded in the New Testament is very remote indeed. Secondly, I believe it is accurate to say that every case of special guidance given to individuals in the Bible has to do with that person's place in the outworking of God's saving purposes. To put it another way, there are no instances in the Bible in which God gives special and specific guidance to the ordinary believing Israelite or Christian in the details of their personal existence.

It was, in fact, in Israel come of age that we saw wisdom flourish as the practice of prudence in decision making among other things. Thus, we may justifiably say that a very important aspect of God's guidance in the Bible is that he refuses to guide us in every detail of existence beyond giving us the framework of his general will and purpose. The wisdom literature contributes very greatly to the overall impact of the Bible in establishing that God has given his children the freedom to make real choices between real options. None of this negates God's sovereignty, but it does highlight our redeemed humanity. It ought to be very clear by now that any notion that God removes the responsibility of decision making from us by some kind of perceptible inner (or even external) guidance simply does not accord with what is being said in the wisdom literature. It is also a denial of the biblical teaching of our humanity restored in Christ.

The Bible shows us the overall sovereign will of God in that all things will be brought to praise him. Within this will there is much that we cannot comprehend or which is not revealed to us. Job and Ecclesiastes point us to such mysteries as evil and suffering. Yet we know that these too will be made to praise God. The clearest example of this is seen in the crucifixion, the ultimate assault upon God by devil and man. Yet it was ordained by God as the means of saving God's people and of restoring universal order (Acts 2:23; 4:27–28).

Within this all-embracing sovereign will is the specific will of God revealed in the gospel. This is the will of God to save a people for himself and to bring them to glory in a regenerated universe. God has revealed to us his purpose in Jesus Christ. We know his will for us, namely, to conform us to Christ's image (Romans 8:29). This primarily is where guidance in the Bible is directed. It is impossible for God's people to miss out on this will of God for them because Christ will lose none of those given to him by the Father, and he will raise them up on the last day (John 6:35–40). We cannot miss out on God's best since we are possessed by Christ and will be like him.

But how does God bring us to this goal? Paul sums it up in terms of the Christian's growth in holiness: 'It is God's will that you should be holy' (1 Thessalonians 4:3). We know that we will be brought to the goal, but none of us can predict the path along which we will go. There are two possible ways of conceiving of this progress from conversion to glorification. The first is the special guidance approach which assumes that God has not only mapped out all the details of our lives but that we must discover them through special guidance. Thus we must seek God's guidance for every specific instance if we are not to miss out on his purpose for us. The Bible knows nothing of this, and in any case, it cannot work. It is tailor-made to produce a lot of anxiety-ridden Christians who are unsure about God's guidance with regard to which foot to put first.

The second approach to guidance is the wisdom way. That is, God has given us the framework within which to make our decisions for life. In the gospel lie all the principles needed for us to make wise and responsible decisions. In being urged to use our God-given brains to make decisions which are consistent with the gospel, we recognize that many situations, even those of great importance, present us with two or more options to choose from, none of which needs to be more acceptable than the others.

In the course of his daily decision making, the Christian can rest assured that he will not miss out on God's best. Through momentary insanity or stupidity he may choose a course of action that results in a lot of trouble, even tragedy. But even that cannot permanently remove him from the ultimate purpose of God. We all have much to repent of daily, and wiser (more gospel-directed) decisions would keep us from causing ourselves and others much hurt. Proverbs is largely directed to that end. The perspective of wisdom as gift and task is seen in Paul's saying which, for aptness of translation, I quote from J. B. Phillips's version:

> So then, my dearest friends, as you have always followed my advice – and that not only when I was present to give it – so now that I am far away be keener than ever to work out the

salvation that God has given you with a proper sense of awe and responsibility. For it is God who is at work within you, giving you the will and the power to achieve his purpose.

(Philippians 2: 12–13)[4]

Paul is saying here that the Christians at Philippi must stop depending on him to make their decisions for them. They themselves must work out the implications of their salvation into daily living. This is the task every Christian has in response to the love of God shown to us in Christ. Notice Paul's reassurance. God is working in us in a way that affects both our willing and doing. God does not make our decisions for us, but as we struggle to understand the world in the light of revelation, God is at work in the decision-making of all his people, working through our thinking and willing in order to bring about our sanctification.

Christian Wisdom in the Technological Age

I would like to conclude this discussion with a comment on wisdom and technology. A simple definition of technology is man's ability to make things. This is the very thing that the word *wisdom* is applied to in the book of Exodus. Another way of looking at technology is as the practical application of scientific knowledge. Technology may be said to be one of the first implications of the cultural mandate as man became a tool-maker. There have been many significant technological break-throughs which radically altered the course of human history. However, until this century the rate at which technological advances have been made was relatively slow. The full

---

[4] *Letters to Young Churches* (London: Geoffrey Bles, 1947).

significance of the invention of the wheel, for example, would hardly have occurred to those who first used it. The linking of the use of the lever with that of the wheel had extraordinary results over a very long period. When these were together linked with the invention of the steam engine and, later, the internal combustion engine, the results came thick and fast. But generally speaking, prior to the industrial revolution, man had time to adapt to the ramifications of such technological developments. He had more opportunity than we have today to think through the ethical implications of such advances.

But now changes occur so fast that adapting to them is more than man can handle. Now we find that we already have the technology to do many things before we have given enough thought to the ethical implications of doing them. Even though we are more than forty years on from the first harnessing of nuclear energy, the bombing of Hiroshima remains a graphic illustration of the moral dilemmas posed by technology. The debate continues because the implications of Hiroshima are becoming better understood by more and more people. The arms race demonstrates that understanding the issues does not provide the means of controlling the monster that has been created.

The ethical problems created by technology are also clearly seen in the fields of medicine and biology. It is not only Christians who are alarmed by the possible applications of present achievements in in-vitro fertilization, organ transplants and genetic engineering. Many people are saying that research in these areas should be slowed to give us time to think through the issues. Thus, on the one hand it is seen as a race against time to develop new ways of controlling our bodies and our environment in order to achieve some perceived good (babies for the childless, new lease of life for the dying and the abolition of genetic defects such as Down's syndrome). On the other hand there is very great unease about technology for its own sake, about things created for good purposes but with the potential for horrendous harm to society. We are concerned about the depersonalization of the individual and the restriction of certain freedoms. There is little comfort in the secular civil liberties groups, for these often seem to espouse a libertarianism that undermines the Christian concept of well-ordered society. The secular mind that kicks against the idolizing of technology invites the Christian to join in a common cause. But secular groups for nuclear disarmament, alternative life-style, conservation and civil liberties, seldom provide a rationale for action that is really satisfying to the Christian mind.

One of the distinctive problems of modern technology is something that would hardly have presented itself in biblical times. The explosion of knowledge means that more and more people become specialists concentrating on ever narrower fields of knowledge. The specialist is hardly even aware of the vast array of other specializations, let alone of how his field fits in with others. In the light of the biblical view of wisdom and knowledge we see that specialization makes the development of a total world view less probable. The psalmist said:

Teach us to number our days aright,
  that we may gain a heart of wisdom:

(Psalm 90:12)

For him, this was a matter of life-span as a gift of God. Wisdom, then, reckons on our mortality as something which is bound up with the total order of things as they are now. It is not technology which can teach us the ultimate meaning of our life, for technology was meant to be ruled by what God revealed about this meaning. But specialist technology has all but taken over in matters of birth and death. The ultimate questions have become how to control both the rate and the quality of births, and how long life can and should be prolonged by means of all the technology at our disposal. The individual no longer numbers his days but passes that responsibility over to the technocrats to do it for him.

There must be a multitude of specific considerations for the Christian assessing various aspects of technology. But can we see a broad biblical framework to shape our thinking so that our response is neither mindless conformity nor insecure reaction? I believe we can, and I have no doubt that the biblical concept of wisdom provides the necessary framework. Furthermore, I suspect that the biblical framework may demand some radical re-evaluations of our use of technology. The framework may be relatively simple, but its application to life has the appearance of an ever increasing complexity.

Because science and technology are expressions of the cultural mandate they must be affirmed and welcomed by Christians. Indeed, the Christian view of man and creation provides the scientist and technologist with a perspective of their pursuits which not only made them possible, but which should have prevented them from creating the monster. When the cultural mandate is accepted on the basis of revelation, the proper distinctions between God, man (scientists) and the world can be maintained. But when it ceases to be seen as mandate, that is, as task authorized by a superior, it comes to be regarded as the natural extension of the autonomous man. Removed from its benign relationship to the order of the universe, it is adopted as the power base for all kinds of domination. The dominion of man was intended to reflect the gracious shepherd-rule of God, but it became corrupted into self-seeking power play. Wisdom urges us to go on struggling to translate the fear of the Lord as the beginning of knowledge into the means of living by faith in the world. Its base in the doctrine of creation, and its emphasis on the practicalities of life here and now, provide a check against the wrongful use of an orientation towards the future life to escape our responsibilities in the present. Wisdom reminds us that the resurrection life will be reached by means of our pilgrimage through this life in this world.

If wisdom, which is perfected in the gospel, is to have any impact in the world, it must be seen as the implication of that gospel. Far from removing the wisdom literature of the Old Testament from the concern of Christians, the gospel completes and interprets it. With the total perspective of Old and New Testaments we have the basis for understanding the fear of the Lord and how it brings us to a comprehensive view of reality. The nature of the unity of all things and the proper distinction between them are obscured once we have rejected the ultimate points of reference. The Christian mind begins with the being of God as Trinity. It is not just vaguely theistic in some unspecified way. To say, 'I believe in God' is not good enough unless it is the God of the Bible we are referring to. The secular mind has rejected this most significant reference point and has consequently cast a cloud of ignorance and folly over every area of its knowledge. Humanism defeats its own goal of the good of man. It cannot know what is the ultimate good of man since it has rejected the possibility of the God of the Bible existing. New gods have taken the place of the true God, and technology has been turned into a particularly tenacious twentieth-century idol, It is a very powerful god since it is the diversion of something that was at the centre of God's purposes for good.

The Israelite was called upon to pursue the good order of the kingdom of God insofar as this was possible in this sinful world. This would have been a meaningless pursuit without the perspective of the future kingdom which God himself would establish by means of the transformation of all things to the perfect order. This was to be the long awaited day of the Lord. According to the New Testament the day of the Lord has come in Jesus Christ, but the old age continues for a time until Christ appears again in glory. Within this overlap of the two ages, between the two comings of Christ, the books of Proverbs, Job and Ecclesiastes are words of God calling us to pursue the order of the kingdom as it applies to this ambiguous age. That order is attained not only through personal conversion and sanctification, but in the communal sanctification of the body of Christ, and through the proclamation of the gospel throughout the world. The gospel judges the disorder that is within us and around us.

The perspective which leads back from Jesus Christ to Old Testament wisdom and then to the creation, reminds us that the transformation to order that we so earnestly desire in ourselves will not happen without the transformation of the whole person, body, mind and spirit, and of the universe around us. It is impossible for us to imagine what the complete absence of disorder will mean in the new earth. The anticipation of that experience is one of the joys of holding to the certainty of our resurrection on the last day. But it is never solely anticipation, for the process of transforming us to that order has already begun from the moment Christ takes hold of us through his gospel. The wisdom literature of the Old Testament plays a vital part in structuring for us the inevitable effect of the gospel in our lives as we are transformed by the renewing of our minds (Romans 12:2).

In an age when technology and the race to possess it have replaced the ancient tribal rivalries, the wise men of Israel remind us that the word *wisdom* was, at least for a while, a synonym for technology as it then existed. These sages are worthy companions as we press on towards the cosmic regeneration. In unexpected ways they teach us trust and the fear of the Lord. In doing so, they compel us to the source of true wisdom in the person and work of Christ. He who is the way, the truth and the life, remains the beginning and the goal of every man's search for order and meaning in the universe. The men of Israel may surprise and even offend us with their earthiness and home-spun wisdom. At times we may find it difficult to recognize God's voice speaking to us through them. But God's highest wisdom was himself to become one with them and us as the God-man. Thus he made the world our classroom. Whether we consider the ways of Solomon's ant, ponder Job's leviathan, or marvel with Qohelet at life's deepest mysteries, Christ alone will transform all the distortions and ambiguities of our myopic view. He is our Wisdom, and thus turns the words of the ancient Hebrew wise men into the urgent proclamation of the gospel which summons us to trust him for everything that is in life;

> Blessed is the man who listens to me,
> watching daily at my doors,
> waiting at my doorway.
> For whoever finds me finds life
> and receives favour from the Lord.
>
> (Proverbs 8:34–35)

Questions for Study

1. Why must all Old Testament texts be understood in the light of the gospel?
2. On what biblical evidence may we build our understanding of what Paul referred to as the gift of wisdom in 1 Corinthians 12:8?
3. How does the biblical concept of wisdom help us understand the nature of guidance and decision-making?
4. How does biblical wisdom help us address the gospel to this technological age?

Volume Indexes

Gospel and Kingdom

Subjects Index

Index of Subjects and Names

Scripture Index

Gospel and Wisdom

Index of Subjects and Names

Scripture and Apocrypha Index